World Military Guide
Australia

Compiled by
Edith Cothran

Scribbles

Year of Publication 2018

ISBN : 9789352979097

Book Published by

Scribbles

(An Imprint of Alpha Editions)

email - alphaedis@gmail.com

Produced by: PediaPress GmbH
Limburg an der Lahn
Germany
http://pediapress.com/

The content within this book was generated collaboratively by volunteers. Please be advised that nothing found here has necessarily been reviewed by people with the expertise required to provide you with complete, accurate or reliable information. Some information in this book may be misleading or simply wrong. Alpha Editions and PediaPress does not guarantee the validity of the information found here. If you need specific advice (for example, medical, legal, financial, or risk management) please seek a professional who is licensed or knowledgeable in that area.

Sources, licenses and contributors of the articles and images are listed in the section entitled "References". Parts of the books may be licensed under the GNU Free Documentation License. A copy of this license is included in the section entitled "GNU Free Documentation License"

The views and characters expressed in the book are those of the contributors and his/her imagination and do not represent the views of the Publisher.

Contents

Articles   1

Introduction   1
    Australian Defence Force 1

History   43
    Military history of Australia 43

Army   109
    History of the Australian Army 109
    Australian Army 130
    List of equipment of the Australian Army 146

Navy   161
    History of the Royal Australian Navy 161
    Royal Australian Navy 211
    List of active Royal Australian Navy ships 229

Air Force   251
    History of the Royal Australian Air Force 251
    Royal Australian Air Force 260

Women in Military   285
    Women in the Australian military 285

Sexual Orientation in Military   **293**
    Sexual orientation and gender identity in the Australian military . . 293

Defence Industry   **299**
    Defence industry of Australia 299

Military Bases   **303**
    List of Australian military bases 303

Appendix   309
    References 309
    Article Sources and Contributors 326
    Image Sources, Licenses and Contributors 328

Article Licenses   335

Index   337

Introduction

Australian Defence Force

<indicator name="featured-star"> ★ </indicator>

Australian Defence Force	
The ADF Tri-Service Flag	
Founded	1901
Current form	9 February 1976 (ADF established)
Service branches	Royal Australian Navy Australian Army Royal Australian Air Force
Headquarters	Part of the Australian Defence Organisation
Leadership	
Commander-in-Chief	Governor-General Sir Peter Cosgrove
Minister for Defence	Marise Payne
Chief of the Defence Force	General Angus Campbell
Manpower	
Military age	16.5 years for selection process, 17 years to serve, 18 years to deploy on operations
Active personnel	58,206 (June 2017)
Reserve personnel	21,694 (June 2017)
Deployed personnel	2,350 (December 2017)
Expenditures	
Budget	A$34.6 billion (2017–2018)
Percent of GDP	1.9 percent
Industry	

Domestic suppliers	Defence industry of Australia
Annual exports	Around A$2 billion (2018)
Related articles	
History	Military history of Australia
Ranks	Australian Defence Force ranks and insignia

The **Australian Defence Force** (**ADF**) is the military organisation responsible for the defence of Australia. It consists of the Royal Australian Navy (RAN), Australian Army, Royal Australian Air Force (RAAF) and a number of 'tri-service' units. The ADF has a strength of just under 80,000 full-time personnel and active reservists, and is supported by the Department of Defence and several other civilian agencies.

During the first decades of the 20th century, the Australian Government established the armed services as separate organisations. Each service had an independent chain of command. In 1976, the government made a strategic change and established the ADF to place the services under a single headquarters. Over time, the degree of integration has increased and tri-service headquarters, logistics and training institutions have supplanted many single-service establishments.

The ADF is technologically sophisticated but relatively small. Although the ADF's 58,206 full-time active-duty personnel and 21,694 active reservists make it the largest military in Oceania, it is smaller than most Asian military forces. Nonetheless, the ADF is supported by a significant budget by worldwide standards and is able to deploy forces in multiple locations outside Australia.

Role

The ADF's legal standing draws on the executive government sections of the Australian Constitution. Section 51 (vi) gives the Commonwealth Government the power to make laws regarding Australia's defence and defence forces. Section 114 of the Constitution prevents the States from raising armed forces without the permission of the Commonwealth and Section 119 gives the Commonwealth responsibility for defending Australia from invasion and sets out the conditions under which the government can deploy the defence force domestically.[1]

Section 68 of the Constitution sets out the ADF's command arrangements. The Section states that "the command in chief of the naval and military forces of the Commonwealth is vested in the Governor-General as the Queen's representative". In practice, the Governor-General does not play an active part in the ADF's command structure, and the elected government controls the ADF. The Minister for Defence and several subordinate ministers exercise this control. The Minister acts on most matters alone, though the National Security Committee of Cabinet considers important matters. The Minister then advises the Governor-General who acts as advised in the normal form of executive government.[1] The Commonwealth Government has never been required by the Constitution or legislation to seek parliamentary approval for decisions to deploy military forces overseas or go to war.[2]

The ADF's current priorities are set out in the *2016 Defence White Paper*, which identifies three main areas of focus. The first of these is to defend Australia from direct attack or coercion. The second priority is to contribute to the security of South East Asia and the South Pacific. The third priority is to contribute to stability across the Indo-Pacific region and a "rules-based global order which supports our interests".[3] The white paper states that the government will place equal weight on the three priorities when developing the ADF's capabilities.[4]

History

Formation

Australia has maintained military forces since federation as a nation in January 1901. Shortly after Federation, the Australian Government established the Australian Army and Commonwealth Naval Force by amalgamating the forces each of the states had maintained.[6] In 1911, the Government established the Royal Australian Navy, which absorbed the Commonwealth Naval Force.[7] The Army established the Australian Flying Corps in 1912 which was separated to form the Royal Australian Air Force in 1921.[8] The services were not linked by a single chain of command, as they each reported to their own separate Minister and had separate administrative arrangements. The three services saw action around the world during World War I and World War II, and took part in conflicts in Asia during the Cold War.[9]

The importance of 'joint' warfare was made clear to the Australian military during World War II when Australian naval, ground and air units frequently served as part of single commands. Following the war, several senior officers lobbied for the appointment of a commander in chief of the three services. The government rejected this proposal and the three services remained fully independent.[10] The absence of a central authority resulted in poor co-ordination between the services, with each service organising and operating on the basis of a different military doctrine.[11]

The need for an integrated command structure received more emphasis as a result of the inefficient arrangements which at times hindered the military's

Figure 1: *The retirement of the aircraft carrier HMAS Melbourne without replacement in 1982 marked a shift away from the policy of "forward defence".*[5]

efforts during the Vietnam War.[11] In 1973, the Secretary of the Department of Defence, Arthur Tange, submitted a report to the Government that recommended the unification of the separate departments supporting each service into a single Department of Defence and the creation of the post of Chief of the Defence Force Staff. The government accepted these recommendations and the Australian Defence Force was established on 9 February 1976.[12]

Defence of Australia era

Until the 1970s, Australia's military strategy centred on the concept of 'forward defence', in which the role of the Australian military was to co-operate with allied forces to counter threats in Australia's region. In 1969, when the United States began the Guam Doctrine and the British withdrew 'east of Suez', Australia developed a defence policy which emphasised self-reliance and the defence of the Australian continent. This was known as the Defence of Australia Policy. Under this policy, the focus of Australian defence planning was to protect Australia's northern maritime approaches (the "Air-Sea Gap") against enemy attack.[14] In line with this goal, the ADF was restructured to increase its ability to strike at enemy forces from Australian bases and to counter

Figure 2: *Australian soldiers lead a column of American troops during Exercise Kangaroo '89, which was held in northern Australia.*[13]

raids on continental Australia. The ADF achieved this by increasing the capabilities of the RAN and RAAF and relocating regular Army units to northern Australia.[15]

At this time, the ADF had no military units on operational deployment outside Australia. In 1987, the ADF made its first operational deployment as part of Operation Morris Dance, in which several warships and a rifle company deployed to the waters off Fiji in response to the 1987 Fijian coups d'état. While broadly successful, this deployment highlighted the need for the ADF to improve its capability to rapidly respond to unforeseen events.[16]

Since the late 1980s, the Government has increasingly called upon the ADF to contribute forces to peacekeeping missions around the world. While most of these deployments involved only small numbers of specialists, several led to the deployment of hundreds of personnel. Large peacekeeping deployments were made to Namibia in early 1989, Cambodia between 1992 and 1993, Somalia in 1993, Rwanda between 1994 and 1995 and Bougainville in 1994 and from 1997 onwards.[17]

The Australian contribution to the 1991 Gulf War was the first time Australian personnel were deployed to an active war zone since the establishment of the ADF. Although the warships and clearance diving team deployed to the Persian Gulf did not see combat, the deployment tested the ADF's capabilities and

Figure 3: *A RAAF C-130 Hercules being unloaded at Tallil Air Base, Iraq, during April 2003*

command structure. Following the war the Navy regularly deployed a frigate to the Persian Gulf or Red Sea to enforce the trade sanctions imposed on Iraq.[18]

East Timor and after

In 1996, John Howard led the Liberal Party's election campaign and became Prime Minister. Subsequently, there were significant reforms to the ADF's force structure and role. The new government's defence strategy placed less emphasis on defending Australia from direct attack and greater emphasis on working in co-operation with regional states and Australia's allies to manage potential security threats.[19] From 1997 the Government also implemented a series of changes to the ADF's force structure in an attempt to increase the proportion of combat units to support units and improve the ADF's combat effectiveness.[20]

The ADF's experiences during the deployment to East Timor in 1999 led to significant changes in Australia's defence policies and to an enhancement of the ADF's ability to conduct operations outside Australia. This successful deployment was the first time a large ADF force had operated outside of Australia since the Vietnam War, and revealed shortcomings in its ability to mount and sustain such operations.

In 2000, the Government released a new Defence White Paper, *Defence 2000 – Our Future Defence Force*, that placed a greater emphasis on preparing the ADF for overseas deployments. The Government committed to improve the ADF's capabilities by improving the readiness and equipment of ADF units, expanding the ADF and increasing real Defence expenditure by 3% per year;[21] in the event, expenditure increased by 2.3% per annum in real terms in the period to 2012–13.[22] In 2003 and 2005, the *Defence Updates* emphasised this focus on expeditionary operations and led to an expansion and modernisation of the ADF.[23]

Since 2000, the ADF's expanded force structure and deployment capabilities have been put to the test on several occasions. Following the 11 September 2001 terrorist attacks on the United States, Australia committed a special forces task group and an air-to-air refuelling aircraft to operations in Afghanistan, and naval warships to the Persian Gulf as Operation Slipper.[24] In 2003, approximately 2,000 ADF personnel, including a special forces task group, three warships and 14 F/A-18 Hornet aircraft, took part in the invasion of Iraq.[25]

The ADF was subsequently involved in the reconstruction of Iraq. From 2003 until 2005 this was mainly limited to a Security Detachment which protected the Australian embassy, the attachment of officers to multi-national headquarters, small numbers of transport and maritime patrol aircraft, and teams of air traffic controllers and medical personnel. From 2005 until 2008 a battalion-sized Australian Army battle group (initially designated the Al Muthanna Task Group, and later Overwatch Battle Group (West)) was stationed in southern Iraq. In addition, teams of ADF personnel were deployed to train Iraqi military units. In line with a 2007 election commitment, the Rudd Government withdrew combat-related forces from Iraq in mid-2008, and most of the remaining Australian units left the country the next year.

The ADF also undertook several operations in Australia's immediate region during the 2000s. In 2003, elements of all three services were dispatched to the Solomon Islands as part of the Regional Assistance Mission to the Solomon Islands. Regular deployments of Australian forces continued to the islands until 2017. Between December 2004 and March, 1,400 ADF personnel served in Indonesia as part of Operation Sumatra Assist, which formed part of Australia's response to the devastating 2004 Indian Ocean earthquake.[26] In May 2006, approximately 2,000 ADF personnel deployed to East Timor in Operation Astute following unrest between elements of the Timor Leste Defence Force.[27] This deployment concluded in March 2013.

From 2006 until 2013 a battalion-sized Australian Army task force operated in Urozgan Province, Afghanistan; this unit was primarily tasked with providing assistance for reconstruction efforts and training Afghan forces, but was frequently involved in combat. In addition, Special Forces Task Groups were

Figure 4: *Australian Army ASLAV armoured vehicles in Afghanistan during 2011*

deployed from 2005 to 2006 and 2007 until 2013. Other specialist elements of the ADF, including detachments of CH-47 Chinook helicopters and RAAF radar and air traffic control units, were also periodically deployed to the country. A total of 40 ADF personnel were killed in Afghanistan between 2002 and 2013, and 262 wounded. Following the withdrawal of the combat forces in 2013, ADF training teams have continued to be stationed in the country to train Afghan forces.

The Australian Labor Party (ALP) governments led by Prime Ministers Rudd and Julia Gillard between 2007 and 2013 commissioned two defence white papers, which were published in 2009 and 2013. The 2009 document, *Defending Australia in the Asia Pacific Century: Force 2030*, had a focus on responding to China's rapidly growing influence. It included commitments to expand the RAN, including acquiring twelve submarines, and increasing defence spending by three percent per year in real terms. This increase in spending did not occur, however.[28] The *Defence White Paper 2013* had similar strategic themes, but set out a more modest program of defence spending which reflected the government's constrained finances. As part of an election commitment, the Liberal–National Coalition Abbott Government commissioned a further defence white paper that was published in 2016.[29] This document also included a commitment to expand the ADF's size and capabilities.[30]

There has generally been bipartisan agreement between the ALP and the Liberal–National Coalition on the ADF's role since the mid-1970s. Both political groupings currently support the ADF's focus on expeditionary operations, and the broad funding target set out in the *2016 Defence White Paper*.[31] The ADF's broad force structure has also experienced little change since the 1980s. For instance, throughout this period the Army's main combat formations have

Figure 5: *An Australian soldier with Iraqi soldiers during a training exercise in November 2015*

been three brigades and the RAAF has been equipped with around 100 combat aircraft. Most of the equipment used by the services has been replaced or upgraded, however.[32]

Current operations

In December 2017, 2,350 ADF personnel were deployed on operations in Australian territory and overseas.

The ADF currently has several forces deployed to the Middle East. The ADF's contribution to the Military intervention against ISIL makes up the largest overseas commitment with 780 personnel deployed as part of Operation Okra. As of December 2017, six F/A-18F Super Hornets, one E-7A Wedgetail and one KC-30A tanker were deployed to strike Islamic State targets in Iraq and Syria. Approximately 300 personnel were deployed to Iraq as part of an international effort to provide training to the Iraqi security forces and a further 80 were in the country as part of a Special Operations Task Group. At this time the Super Hornets were scheduled to return to Australia without replacement during January 2018. Deployments in Afghanistan number 270 personnel in Operation Highroad, a non-combat training mission supporting the Afghan National Army. A frigate is also deployed to the Middle East in maritime security operations in and around the Gulf of Aden as part of the Combined Maritime

Figure 6: *The Australian Government intends to buy at least 72 F-35A Lightning II aircraft to re-equip the RAAF's air combat force*

Forces. Small parties of Australian personnel also form part of peacekeeping missions in Israel, Jordan, Egypt and Sudan. The ADF has a further 500 personnel based in the Middle East to support operations in the region.

The ADF continues to play a role in the United Nations Command in Korea via commanding the UNC-Rear logistics element in Japan.[33]

Australian military units are also deployed on operations in Australia's immediate region. As of December 2017, 500 personnel were deployed on Australia's northern approaches in maritime security operations, forming Operation Resolute. ADF units undertake periodic deployments in the South China Sea and South West Pacific. Since October 2017 over 80 Australian soldiers have been deployed to the Philippines to provide training for the Armed Forces of the Philippines. RAN patrol boats and RAAF maritime patrol aircraft have also been deployed to the Philippines. This deployment may involve the Australian Secret Intelligence Service, and form a continuation of secretive ADF counter-terrorism operations in the Middle East.

Future trends

Australia's changing security environment will lead to new demands being placed on the Australian Defence Force. Although it is not expected that Australia will face any threat of direct attack from another country, terrorist groups and tensions between nations in East Asia pose threats to Australian security. More broadly, the Australian Government believes that it needs to make a contribution to maintaining the rules-based order globally. There is also a risk that climate change, weak economic growth and social factors could cause instability in South Pacific countries.[34]

Australian demographic trends will put pressure on the ADF in the future.[35] Excluding other factors, the ageing of the Australian population will result in smaller numbers of potential recruits entering the Australian labour market each year. Some predictions are that population ageing will result in slower economic growth and increased government expenditure on pensions and health programs. As a result of these trends, the ageing of Australia's population may worsen the ADF's manpower situation and may force the Government to reallocate some of the Defence budget.[36] Few young Australians consider joining the military and the ADF has to compete for recruits against private sector firms which are able to offer higher salaries.[37]

The ADF has developed strategies to respond to Australia's changing strategic environment. The *2016 Defence White Paper* states that "the Government will ensure Australia maintains a regionally superior ADF with the highest levels of military capability and scientific and technological sophistication". To this end, the government intends to improve the ADF's combat power and expand the number of military personnel. This will include introducing new technologies and capabilities. The ADF is also seeking to improve its intelligence capabilities and co-operation between the services.[38]

Current structure

The Australian Defence Force and Department of Defence make up the Australian Defence Organisation (ADO), which is often referred to as "Defence". A diarchy of the Chief of the Defence Force (CDF) and the Secretary of the Department of Defence administers the ADO.[39] The Department of Defence is staffed by both civilian and military personnel, and includes agencies such as the Defence Intelligence Organisation (DIO) and Defence Science and Technology Group (DST Group).[40]

Command arrangements

The ADF's command arrangements are specified in the *Defence Act (1903)* and subordinate legislation.[41] This act states that the Minister of Defence "shall have the general control and administration of the Defence Force" and that the CDF, the Secretary of the Department of Defence and the chiefs of the three services must act "in accordance with any directions of the Minister". The leaders of the ADO are also responsible to the junior ministers who are

Figure 7: *The ADF headquarters and the main offices of the Department of Defence are located in the Russell Offices complex in Canberra*

appointed to manage specific elements of the defence portfolio.[41] Under the Second Turnbull Ministry two cabinet-level ministers have been responsible for the Defence portfolio since July 2016: the position of Minister for Defence is held by Senator Marise Payne, and Christopher Pyne is the Minister for Defence Industry. Michael McCormack is the Minister for Defence Personnel, a junior ministry.

The CDF is the most senior appointment in the ADF and commands the force.[41] The CDF is the only four-star officer in the ADF and is a general, admiral or air chief marshal. As well as having command responsibilities, the CDF is the Minister for Defence's principal military adviser.[42] General Angus Campbell is the current CDF, and assumed this position on 1 July 2018. Hugh White, a prominent academic and former Deputy Secretary in the Department of Defence, has criticised the ADF's current command structure. White argues that the Minister plays too large a role in military decision-making and does not provide the CDF and Secretary of Defence with necessary and sufficient authority to manage the ADO effectively.

Under the current ADF command structure the day-to-day management of the ADF is distinct from the command of military operations.[43] The services are administered through the ADO, with the head of each service (the Chief of

Figure 8: *Australian Army soldiers providing security for a RAN LHD Landing Craft during a joint exercise in 2018*

Navy, Chief of Army and Chief of Air Force) and the service headquarters being responsible for raising, training and sustaining combat forces. Each chief is also the CDF's principal adviser on matters concerning the responsibilities of their service. The CDF chairs the Chiefs of Service Committee which comprises the service chiefs, Vice Chief of the Defence Force and the Chief of Joint Operations (CJOPS).[44] The CDF and service chiefs are supported by an integrated ADF Headquarters, which replaced separate service headquarters on 1 July 2017.

While the individual members of each service ultimately report to their service's Chief, the Chiefs do not control military operations. Control of ADF operations is exercised through a formal command chain headed by the CJOPS, who reports directly to the CDF. The CJOPS commands the Headquarters Joint Operations Command (HQJOC) as well as temporary joint task forces. These joint task forces comprise units assigned from their service to participate in operations or training exercises.[45,46]

Joint combat forces

Operational command of the ADF is exercised by HQJOC, which is located at a purpose-built facility near Bungendore, New South Wales. This is a 'joint' headquarters comprising personnel from the three services and includes a continuously manned Joint Control Centre. HQJOC's main role is to "plan, monitor and control" ADF operations and exercises, and it is organised around groups of plans, operations and support staff. HQJOC also monitors the readiness of the ADF units which are not assigned to operations and contributes to developing Australia's military doctrine.[45]

As well as HQJOC, the ADF has permanent joint operational commands responsible to the CJOPS. Joint Operations Command (JOC) includes the two headquarters responsible for patrolling Australia's maritime borders on a day-to-day basis, Northern Command and Maritime Border Command. Other JOC units include the Joint Movements Group and the Air and Space Operations Centre. Individual ADF units and Joint Task Groups are assigned to JOC during operations, and HQJOC includes officers responsible for submarine and special operations forces.[47]

Royal Australian Navy

The Royal Australian Navy is the naval branch of the Australian Defence Force. The RAN operates just under 50 commissioned warships, including frigates, submarines, patrol boats and auxiliary ships, as well as a number of non-commissioned vessels. In addition, the RAN maintains a force of combat, logistics and training helicopters.

There are two parts to the RAN's structure. One is an operational command, Fleet Command, and the other is a support command, Navy Strategic Command.[48] The Navy's assets are administered by five 'forces' which report to the Commander Australian Fleet. These are the Fleet Air Arm, the Mine Warfare, Clearance Diving, Hydrographic, Meteorological and Patrol Force, Shore Force, Submarine Force and Surface Force.[49]

Australian Army

The Army is organised into three main elements which report to the Chief of Army; the Headquarters of the 1st Division, Special Operations Command and Forces Command. As of 2017, approximately 85% of Army personnel were in units assigned to Forces Command, which is responsible for preparing units and individuals for operations. Headquarters 1st Division is responsible for high-level training activities and is capable of being deployed to command large scale ground operations. Only a small number of units are permanently assigned to the 1st Division; these include the 2nd Battalion, Royal Australian Regiment which forms the pre-landing force for the Australian Amphibious Force, a signals regiment and three training and personnel support units.

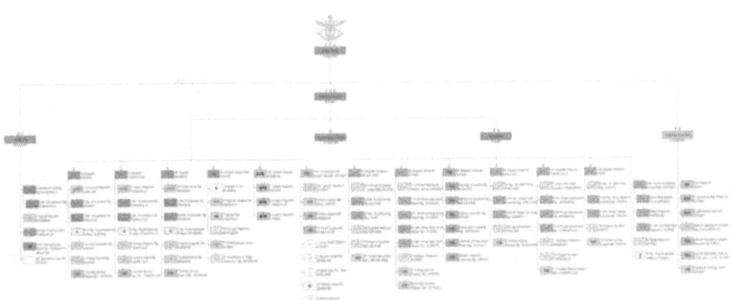

Figure 9: *The Australian Army's structure from 2018*

The Australian Army's main combat forces are grouped in brigades. Its main conventional forces are three regular combat brigades which are organised on a common structure; the 1st, 3rd and 7th Brigades.[50] Support for the units in these formations is provided by an aviation brigade (16th Aviation Brigade), a combat support and ISTAR brigade (6th Brigade) and a logistics brigade (the 17th Brigade).[51] In addition, there are six Army Reserve brigades; these brigades are administered by the 2nd Division and "paired" with the three regular combat brigades.[52] The Army's main tactical formations are combined arms battlegroups made up of elements drawn from different units.[53,54]

The Special Operations Command commands the Army's special forces units. It comprises the Special Air Service Regiment, the 2nd Commando Regiment, the reserve 1st Commando Regiment and the Special Operations Engineer Regiment as well as logistics and training units.[55] The Army's special forces units have been expanded since 2001 and are well equipped and capable of being deployed by sea, air or land.[56] As of 2014, Special Operations Command comprised approximately 2,200 personnel.[57]

Royal Australian Air Force

The Royal Australian Air Force (RAAF) is the air power branch of the ADF. The RAAF has modern combat and transport aircraft and a network of bases in strategic locations across Australia.[58]

The RAAF has a single operational command, Air Command.[59] Air Command is the operational arm of the RAAF and consists of Air Combat Group, Air Mobility Group, Surveillance and Response Group, Combat Support Group, Air Warfare Centre and Air Force Training Group.[60] Each group consists of several wings.[61]

Figure 10: *CHC Helicopters has been contracted to provide search and rescue and crash response services to all three branches of the ADF*

The RAAF has nineteen flying squadrons; four combat squadrons, two maritime patrol squadrons, six transport squadrons, six training squadrons (including three Operational Conversion Units and a forward air control training squadron) as well as one Airborne Early Warning & Control squadron and a Joint Terminal Attack Controller squadron. The ground units supporting these flying squadrons include three expeditionary combat support squadrons, three security force squadrons and a range of intelligence, air traffic control, communications, radar and medical units.[61,62]

Logistic support

The ADF's logistics are managed by the Department of Defence's Capability Acquisition and Sustainment Group (CASG). The CASG was established in 2015 from the previously semi-independent Defence Materiel Organisation. The CASG is responsible for purchasing all forms of equipment and services used by the ADF and maintaining this equipment throughout its life of type.

The CASG is not responsible for directly supplying deployed ADF units; this is the responsibility of the Joint Logistics Command (JLC) and the single service logistic units. These units include the Navy's Strategic Command and replenishment ships, the Army's 17th Combat Service Support Brigade and Combat Service Support Battalions, and the Combat Support Group RAAF.[63]

The ADF maintains stockpiles of ammunition, fuel and other supplies. Since the late 1990s, ammunition for the three services has been stored in a network of facilities managed by the JLC.⁶⁴ The ADF also holds several months' worth of fuel for the Navy's vessels and several weeks' worth for aircraft and vehicles. A number of defence analysts have raised concerns over the adequacy of the fuel stockpile, especially as Australia is largely dependent on imports which could be disrupted in the event of war.

The increasing role of the private sector forms an important trend in the ADF's logistics arrangements. During the 1990s many of the ADF's support functions were transferred to the private sector to improve the efficiency with which they were provided. Since these reforms most of the 'garrison' support services at military bases have been provided by private firms. The reforms also led to many of the ADF's logistics units being disbanded or reduced in size.⁶⁵ Since this time private firms have increasingly been contracted to provide critical support to ADF units deployed outside Australia. This support has included transporting equipment and personnel and constructing and supplying bases.⁶⁶

Military intelligence and surveillance

The Australian Defence Force's intelligence collection and analysis capabilities include each of the services' intelligence systems and units, two joint civilian-military intelligence gathering agencies and two strategic and operational-level intelligence analysis organisations.⁶⁷

Each of the three services has its own intelligence collection assets.⁶⁷ RAN doctrine stresses the importance of collecting a wide range of information, and combining it to inform decisions. It also notes that the *Collins*-class submarines are particularly effective sources of "acoustic, electromagnetic and environmental information".⁶⁸ The Army's intelligence and surveillance units include the 1st Intelligence Battalion, 7th Signal Regiment (Electronic Warfare), 20th Surveillance and Target Acquisition Regiment, three Regional Force Surveillance Units and the Special Air Service Regiment.⁶⁹ The RAAF monitors the airspace of Australia and neighbouring countries using the Vigilare system, which combines input from the service's Jindalee Operational Radar Network, other ADF air defence radars (including airborne and naval systems) and civilian air traffic control radars.⁷⁰ The RAAF's other intelligence assets include No. 87 Squadron and the AP-3C Orion aircraft operated by No. 92 Wing.⁷¹ A C band radar and a telescope located at Naval Communication Station Harold E. Holt provide a space situational awareness capability, which includes tracking space assets and debris.⁷² Australia also provides personnel to the US Joint Space Operations Center in Colorado Springs which tracks and identifies any man-made object in orbit.

Figure 11: *A Royal Australian Air Force AP-3C Orion aircraft. These aircraft are fitted with advanced signals intelligence and electronic signals intelligence equipment.*

The Defence Strategic Policy and Intelligence Group within the Department of Defence supports the services and co-operates with the civilian agencies within the Australian Intelligence Community. This Group consists of the Australian Geospatial-Intelligence Organisation (AGO), Australian Signals Directorate (ASD) and Defence Intelligence Organisation (DIO). The AGO is responsible for geospatial intelligence and producing maps for the ADF, the ASD is Australia's signals intelligence agency, and the DIO is responsible for the analysis of intelligence collected by the other intelligence agencies. The three agencies are headquartered in Canberra, though the AGO has staff in Bendigo and the ASD maintains several permanent signals collection facilities in other locations.[73]

The ASD also includes the Australian Cyber Security Centre (ACSC) which is responsible for protecting Defence and other Australian Government agencies against cyberwarfare attacks. The ACSC was established in January 2010 and is jointly staffed by the ASD and personnel from the Attorney-General's Department, Australian Security Intelligence Organisation, and Australian Federal Police. Unlike the United States military, the ADF does not class cyberwarfare as being a separate sphere of warfare. In July 2017 an Information Warfare Division was raised, tasked with both defensive and offensive cyber operations.

Figure 12: *Personnel from the Army's 16th Air Land Regiment with one of the unit's RBS 70 systems*

The Australian Secret Intelligence Service (ASIS) has been involved in ADF operations since the Vietnam War including East Timor, Iraq and Afghanistan. In 2012, the Director-General of ASIS stated that the service's agents had saved the lives of Australian soldiers, enabled special forces operations and that "it's difficult to see a situation in the future where the ADF would deploy without ASIS alongside". It has been reported that one of the Special Air Service Regiment's squadrons works with ASIS and has undertaken independent covert intelligence-collection operations outside Australia.

Personnel

The Australian military has been an all-volunteer force since the abolition of conscription in 1972. Both men and women can enlist in the ADF, with women being able to apply for all roles. Only Australian citizens and permanent residents who are eligible for Australian citizenship can enlist. Recruits must be aged at least 17, and meet health and educational standards. The ADF is one of the few areas of the Australian Government to continue to have compulsory retirement ages: permanent personnel must retire at 60 years of age and reservists at 65. Both permanent and reserve personnel can work through flexible arrangements, including part-time hours or remotely from their duty station, subject to approval.[74] Discipline of defence personnel is guided by the *Defence Force Discipline Act* (1982), ultimately overseen by the Judge Advocate General of the ADF.

Personnel numbers

As of 30 June 2017, the ADF comprised 58,206 permanent (full-time) and 21,694 active reserve (part-time) personnel.[75] There were 22,166 inactive members of the Standby Reserve as at June 2009. The Army is the largest service, followed by the RAAF and RAN. The ADO also employed 18,397 civilian Australian Public Service (APS) staff as at 30 June 2017.[75] During the 2016–17 financial year 5,462 people enlisted in the ADF on a permanent basis and 5,270 left, representing a net increase of 192 personnel.[75]

The distribution of ADF personnel between the services and categories of service on 30 June 2017 was as follows:[75]

Service	Permanent	Active Reserve	Total
Navy	13,657	2,823	16,480
Army	30,161	13,801	43,962
Air Force	14,388	5,070	19,458
Total	58,206	21,694	79,900

The number of ADF personnel has changed over the last 20 years. During the 1990s the strength of the ADF was reduced from around 70,000 to 50,000 permanent personnel as a result of budget cuts and the outsourcing of some military functions. The ADF began to grow from 2000 after the defence white paper released that year called for an expansion to the military's strength, though the size of the military decreased between the 2003–04 to 2005–06 financial years due to problems with attracting further recruits. By 2009–10 the ADF was above its budgeted size, leading to reductions until 2014–15. The size of the ADF grew between the 2014–15 and 2016–17 financial years.[77] The ADF has not met its recruitment targets over the period since the 1995–96 financial year.[78]

The ADF is small compared to many other national militaries. Both the number of personnel in the ADF and the share of the Australian population this represents is smaller than that in many countries in Australia's immediate region. Several NATO member countries, including France and the United States, also have a higher share of their population in the military.[79] This is a continuation of long-term trends, as outside of major wars Australia has always had a relatively small military. The size of the force is a result of Australia's relatively small population and the military being structured around a maritime strategy focused on the RAN and RAAF rather than a manpower-intensive army.[80,81]

Australian Defence Force

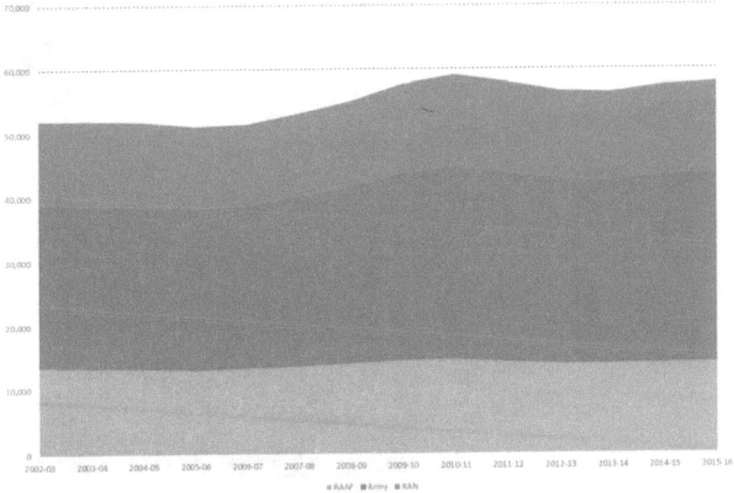

Figure 13: *The average permanent strengths of the services between the 2002–03 and 2015–16 financial years*[76]

Reserves

Each of the branches of the ADF has a reserve component. These forces are the Royal Australian Naval Reserve, Australian Army Reserve and Royal Australian Air Force Reserve.[82] The main role of the reserves is to supplement the permanent elements of the ADF during deployments and crises, including natural disasters. This can include attaching individual reservists to regular units or deploying units composed entirely of reserve personnel.[83] As reservists serve on a part-time basis, they are less costly to the government than permanent members of the ADF, but the nature of their service can mean that reservists have a lower level of readiness than regular personnel and require further training before they can be deployed.[84] It has historically proven difficult to set a level of training requirements which allows reservists to be rapidly deployable yet does not act as a disincentive to recruitment and continued participation.[85] Successive governments since the 1960s have also been reluctant to use the 'call out' powers to require reservists to undertake active service.

There are two main categories of reserve personnel; those in the active reserve and those in the standby reserve. Members of the active reserve have an annual minimum training obligation.[86] Reservists can volunteer to undertake more than the minimum periods of training and active service.[87] Members of the standby reserve are not required to undertake training, and would only be called

Figure 14: *Members of the Army Reserve 5th/6th Battalion, Royal Victoria Regiment marching through Melbourne on Anzac day 2006*

up in response to a national emergency or to fill a specialised position. Most standby reservists are former full-time members of the ADF.[88,89]

While Australian Naval Reserve personnel are assigned to permanent units, most members of the Army Reserve and Air Force Reserve are members of reserve units. Most of the RAAF's reserve units are not intended to be deployed, and reserve personnel are generally attached to regular air force units during their periods of active service.[90] The Army Reserve is organised into permanent combat and support units, though most are currently manned at levels well below their authorised strengths and are not capable of deploying as formed units.[91]

The ADF's increased activities since 1999 and shortfalls in recruiting permanent personnel has led to reservists being more frequently called to active service.[37] This has included large scale domestic deployments, which have included providing security for major events such as the 2000 Summer Olympics and responding to natural disasters. Large numbers of reserve personnel have also been deployed as part of ADF operations in Australia's region; this has included the deployment of Army Reserve rifle companies to East Timor and the Solomon Islands. Smaller numbers of reservists have taken part in operations in locations distant from Australia.[92] Notably, companies of the Army

Figure 15: *The Australian Defence Force Academy in Canberra*

Reserve 1st Commando Regiment were regularly deployed to Afghanistan as part of the Special Operations Task Group.

Training

Individual training of Australian servicemen and women is generally provided by the services in their own training institutions. Each service has its own training organisation to manage this individual training. Where possible, however, individual training is increasingly being provided through tri-service schools.[93]

Military academies include HMAS *Creswell* for the Navy, Royal Military College, Duntroon, for the Army, and the Officers' Training School for the Air Force. The Australian Defence Force Academy is a tri-service university for officer cadets of all services who wish to attain a university degree through the ADF. Navy recruit training is conducted at HMAS *Cerberus*, Army recruits are trained at the Army Recruit Training Centre and Air Force recruits at RAAF Base Wagga.[94]

Figure 16: *A RAAF pilot conducting pre-flight checks of a C-130J-30 Super Hercules deployed to the Middle East in 2009*

Women in the ADF

Women first served in the Australian military during World War II when each service established a separate female branch. The RAAF was the first service to fully integrate women into operational units, doing so in 1977, with the Army and RAN following in 1979 and 1985 respectively.[95] The ADF initially struggled to integrate women, with integration being driven by changing Australian social values and Government legislation rather than a change in attitudes within the male-dominated military.[96]

The number of positions available to women in the ADF has increased over time. Although servicewomen were initially barred from combat positions, these restrictions began to be lifted in 1990.[97] In September 2011 Minister for Defence Stephen Smith announced that the Cabinet had decided to remove all restrictions on women serving in combat positions, and that this change would come into effect within five years. This decision was supported by the CDF and the chiefs of the services. Women became able to apply for all positions other than special forces roles in the Army on 1 January 2013. This remaining restriction was removed during 2016.[98]

Despite the expansion in the number of positions available to women and other changes which aim to encourage increased female recruitment and retention, the growth in the proportion of female permanent defence personnel has been

Figure 17: *A RAAF airman assembling a bomb*

slow.[99] In the 1989–1990 financial year women made up 11.4% of the ADF personnel. In the 2008–2009 financial year women occupied 13.5% of ADF positions. During the same period the proportion of civilian positions filled by women in the Australian Defence Organisation increased from 30.8% to 42.8%.[100] As of 30 June 2017, women made up 16.7% of the ADF's permanent force and 17.1% of reservists. The proportion of women in the permanent force differs by service: 13.2% of members of the Army are female, compared to 20.4% of the RAN and 20.6% for the RAAF.[101] In 2015 the ADF adopted targets to increase the proportion of service personnel who are female by 2023: by this time it is planned that women will make up 25% of the RAN, 15% of the Army and 25% of the RAAF.[102]

There continue to be concerns over the incidence of sexual abuse and gender-based discrimination in the ADF. In 2014 the Defence Abuse Response Taskforce estimated that around 1,100 currently-serving ADF personnel had abused other members of the military, and recommended that a royal commission be conducted to investigate long-running allegations of sexual abuse and assault of servicewomen at the Australian Defence Force Academy. In 2013 Chief of Army General David Morrison publicly released a video in which he warned against gender-based discrimination, and stated that he would dismiss members of the Army who engaged in such conduct.

Ethnic and religious composition

A high percentage of ADF personnel are drawn from the Anglo-Celtic portion of Australia's population. In 2011 the proportion of ADF personnel born in Australia and the other predominately Anglo-Celtic countries was higher than this population group's share of both the Australian workforce and overall population.[103] As a result, analyst Mark Thomson has argued that the ADF is unrepresentative of Australia's society in this regard and that recruiting more personnel from other ethnic backgrounds would improve the ADF's language skills and cultural empathy.[104] As of 2017, the ADF's recruiting efforts included a campaign aimed at attracting more volunteers from culturally and linguistically diverse backgrounds.[105]

The ADO is seeking to expand the number of Indigenous Australians it recruits and improve their retention rate.[106] Restrictions on Indigenous Australians' ability to enlist in the military existed until the 1970s, though hundreds of Indigenous men and women had joined the military when restrictions were reduced during the world wars. By 1992 the representation of Indigenous Australians in the ADF was equivalent to their proportion of the Australian population, though they continue to be under-represented among the officer corps. Two of the Army's three Regional Force Surveillance Units (NORFORCE and the 51st Battalion, Far North Queensland Regiment) are manned mostly by Indigenous Australian reservists.[107] In 2015 Indigenous Australians made up around 2% of ADF personnel, which was smaller than the Indigenous share of the total Australian population.[108]

In line with trends across the broader Australian population, the proportion of ADF personnel who are not religious has increased considerably over recent years. The proportion of ADF personnel who reported that their religion was Christianity in service censuses and human relations databases decreased from around 66% in 2003 to just over 52% in 2015. Over this period, the proportion who stated that they do not have a religious affiliation increased from 31% to 47%. Only 1% of ADF members reported having a non-Christian religious affiliation in 2015.[109]

Sexuality

Australia allows gay men and lesbians to serve openly. Openly gay and lesbian personnel were banned from the ADF until November 1992 when the Australian Government decided to remove this prohibition. The heads of the services and most military personnel opposed this change at the time, and it caused considerable public debate.[110,111] Opponents of lifting the ban on gay and lesbian personnel argued that doing so would greatly harm the ADF's cohesiveness and cause large numbers of resignations. This did not eventuate,

Figure 18: *Soldiers marching in the 2013 Sydney Mardi Gras*

and the reform caused few problems.[112] A 2000 study found that lifting the ban on gay service did not have any negative effects on the ADF's morale, effectiveness or recruitment and retention, and may have led to increased productivity and improved working environments.[113]

Since 1 January 2009 same-sex couples have had the same access to military retirement pensions and superannuation as opposite-sex couples. Transgender personnel are also permitted to serve in the ADF, and are provided with support when necessary. The ADF has permitted a contingent of gay and lesbian personnel to march together in the Sydney Mardi Gras since 2008, and since 2013 these personnel have been authorised to wear their uniforms during the parade. Despite the removal of restrictions on gay and lesbian personnel, harassment and discrimination still occurs; for instance a 2013 survey found that 10% of gay soldiers had experienced discrimination and more than 30% hid their sexuality.

Defence expenditure and procurement

Current expenditure

The Australian Government allocated A$34.7 billion to the Australian Defence Organisation in the 2017–18 financial year. This level of expenditure is equivalent to approximately 1.9% of Australian Gross Domestic Product (GDP) and 7.28% of total Australian Government expenditure. This was an increase in nominal terms from the A$32 billion allocated in the 2016–17 financial year which represented approximately 1.83% of GDP.[114] In broad terms the Defence budget is divided into expenditure on personnel, operating costs and capital investment; in 2016–17 37% of expenditure was on personnel, 36% on operational costs and 27% on capital investments.[115]

Australia's defence expenditure is much larger in dollar terms to that of most countries in Australia's immediate region.[116] The share of GDP Australia spends on defence is also larger than that in most developed economies and major South-East Asian countries. China allocates approximately the same proportion of GDP to Defence as Australia does, and has been rapidly increasing its nominal expenditure.[117] The Stockholm International Peace Research Institute has estimated that Australia's defence spending in 2015 was the 13th highest of any country in real terms. As a proportion of GDP Australia's defence spending ranks as 49th of the countries for which data is available.

Long term procurement projects

The 2016–17 budget forecasts that defence expenditure will increase to $42 billion in 2020–21, which is estimated to represent 2.03% of GDP.[114] This reflects a bipartisan commitment to increase defence expenditure to 2% of GDP.[31] The *2016 Defence White Paper* included a commitment to further increases in spending beyond this time, with nominal expenditure being projected to be around $58.8 billion in 2020–25; the Australian Strategic Policy Institute has estimated that this would represent about 2.16% of GDP.[118]

The *Integrated Investment Program* that was released alongside the *2016 Defence White Paper* sets out the ADF's long term capital programs.[119] This document is the successor to the *Defence Capability Plans* which were regularly produced from 2000.[120] The total value of the projects in the Integrated Investment Program over the period to 2025–26 is $162 billion.[119]

Current equipment

The ADF seeks to be a high-technology force.[121] Although most of the ADF's weapons are only used by single service, there is an increasing emphasis on commonality. The three services use the same small arms and the FN Herstal 35 is the ADF's standard hand gun, the F88 Austeyr the standard rifle, the F89 Minimi the standard light support weapon, the FN Herstal MAG-58 the standard light machine gun and the Browning M2HB the standard heavy machine gun.[122]

The ADF is equipped with conventional weapons only. Australia does not possess weapons of mass destruction and has ratified the Biological Weapons Convention, Chemical Weapons Convention and Nuclear Non-Proliferation

Figure 19: *Canberra-class landing helicopter dock HMAS Canberra*

Treaty.[123] Australia is also a party to international agreements which prohibit land mines and cluster munitions.

As of September 2017, the Royal Australian Navy operates 48 commissioned ships and submarines, and 2 non-commissioned vessels. The Navy's main surface combatants are three *Adelaide*-class frigates, eight *Anzac*-class frigates and one *Hobart*-class destroyer (with two more to be completed). The RAN's submarine force has six *Collins*-class submarines. There are 13 *Armidale*-class patrol boats for border security and fisheries patrol duties in Australia's northern waters. The RAN's amphibious force comprises the two *Canberra*-class landing helicopter docks and the dock landing ship HMAS *Choules*. The Navy's minesweeping force is equipped with six *Huon*-class minehunters, of which two are in reserve. Two replenishment vessels (*Sirius* and *Success*) and six survey vessels (the *Leeuwin* and *Paluma* classes) support these combatants. Non-commissioned ships operated by the RAN include the sail training ship *Young Endeavour* and two Cape-class patrol boats leased to the RAN from the Australian Border Force. As of October 2017, the Fleet Air Arm's helicopter force comprised 24 MH-60R Seahawk and 3 S-70 Seahawk anti-submarine helicopters, 7 MRH 90 transport helicopters and a training force equipped with 15 EC 135T2+, 4 Bell 429s and 6 Squirrels.[124] The S-70 and Squirrel helicopters were retired in December 2017.

The Australian Army is equipped with a wide range of equipment in order to be able to employ combined arms approaches in combat.[125] As of 2016[126],

Figure 20: *Three of the RAAF's F/A-18A Hornets in flight*

the Army's armoured fighting vehicle holdings included 59 M1A1 Abrams main battle tanks, 1,426 M113 armoured personnel carriers (of which 431 had been upgraded, with many of the remainder being placed in reserve), and 253 ASLAV armoured reconnaissance vehicles. A total of 995 Bushmaster Protected Mobility Vehicles were in service with more on order. The Army's artillery holdings consisted of 54 155 mm towed M777 howitzers, 188 81 mm mortars, RBS-70 surface-to-air missiles and FGM-148 Javelin anti-tank missiles.[127] As of October 2017, Australian Army Aviation operated over 100 helicopters. These included including 23 Kiowa reconnaissance and training helicopters and 22 Eurocopter Tiger armed reconnaissance helicopters, as well as 33 S-70A-9 Blackhawk, 10 CH-47F Chinook and 40 MRH 90 transport helicopters.[128] The Army also operated 10 RQ-7B Shadow 2000 unmanned aerial vehicles in 2016. The Army's fleet of watercraft at this time included 13 LCM-8 landing craft.[127]

The Royal Australian Air Force operates combat, maritime patrol, transport and training aircraft. As at October 2017 the combat aircraft force comprised 71 F/A-18A and B Hornets, 24 F/A-18F Super Hornets, 12 EA-18G Growlers and 2 F-35A Lightning IIs with another 70 on order. The Intelligence, surveillance and reconnaissance force was equipped with 13 AP-3C Orion and 4 P-8 Poseidon maritime patrol aircraft as well as 6 E-7A Wedgetail AEW&C aircraft. The air transport force operated 12 C-130J-30 Super Hercules, 8 C-17 Globemaster IIIs and 7 C-27J Spartans with 3 on order. A further 16 Super

Figure 21: *Adelaide class frigates HMAS Newcastle and HMAS Melbourne moored at Fleet Base East*

King Air 350s were used in both the transport and training roles. The RAAF also operates 3 Challenger and 2 Boeing 737 aircraft as VIP transports. A total of six KC-30 Multi-Role Tanker Transports were in service with another on order. The RAAF's training units were equipped with 62 PC-9s, 10 PC-21s (with another 39 on order) and 33 Hawk 127s.[62]

Current bases

The Australian Defence Force maintains 60 major bases and many other facilities across all the states and territories of Australia. These bases occupy millions of hectares of land, giving the ADO Australia's largest real estate portfolio. Defence Housing Australia manages around 19,000 residences occupied by members of the ADF. While most of the Army's permanent force units are based in northern Australia, the majority of Navy and Air Force units are based near Sydney, Brisbane and Perth. Few ADF bases are currently shared by different services.[129] Small Army and RAAF units are also located at Royal Malaysian Air Force Base Butterworth.[130] The administrative headquarters of the ADF and the three services is located in Canberra alongside the main offices of the Department of Defence.

The Royal Australian Navy has two main bases; Fleet Base East (HMAS *Kuttabul*) in Sydney and Fleet Base West (HMAS *Stirling*) near Perth. The Navy's operational headquarters, Fleet Headquarters, is located adjacent to Fleet Base East. The majority of the Navy's patrol boats are based at HMAS *Coonawarra* in Darwin, Northern Territory, with the remaining patrol boats and the hydrographic fleet located at HMAS *Cairns* in Cairns. The Fleet Air Arm is based at HMAS *Albatross* near Nowra, New South Wales.[131]

The Australian Army's regular units are concentrated in a few bases, most of which are located in Australia's northern states. The Army's operational headquarters, Forces Command, is located at Victoria Barracks in Sydney. Most elements of the Army's three regular brigades are based at Robertson Barracks near Darwin, Lavarack Barracks in Townsville, Queensland, and Gallipoli Barracks in Brisbane. The 1st Division's Headquarters is also located at Gallipoli Barracks. Other important Army bases include the Army Aviation Centre near Oakey, Queensland, Holsworthy Barracks near Sydney, Woodside Barracks near Adelaide, South Australia, and Campbell Barracks in Perth. Dozens of Army Reserve depots are located across Australia.[132]

The Royal Australian Air Force maintains several air bases, including three which are only occasionally activated. The RAAF's operational headquarters, Air Command, is located at RAAF Base Glenbrook near Sydney. The Air Force's combat aircraft are based at RAAF Base Amberley near Ipswich, Queensland, RAAF Base Tindal near Katherine, Northern Territory, and RAAF Base Williamtown near Newcastle, New South Wales. The RAAF's maritime patrol aircraft are based at RAAF Base Edinburgh near Adelaide and most of its transport aircraft are based at RAAF Base Richmond in Sydney. RAAF Base Edinburgh is also home to the control centre for the Jindalee Operational Radar Network. Most of the RAAF's training aircraft are based at RAAF Base Pearce near Perth with the remaining aircraft located at RAAF Base East Sale near Sale, Victoria, and RAAF Base Williamtown. The RAAF also maintains a network of bases in northern Australia to support operations to Australia's north. These bases include RAAF Base Darwin and RAAF Base Townsville and three 'bare bases' in Queensland and Western Australia.[133] Of the RAAF's operational bases, only Tindal is located near an area in which the service's aircraft might feasibly see combat. While this protects the majority of the RAAF's assets from air attack, most air bases are poorly defended and aircraft are generally hangared in un-hardened shelters.[134]

Domestic responsibilities

In addition to its military role, the ADF contributes to domestic security as well as disaster relief efforts in Australia and overseas. These functions are primarily the responsibility of civilian agencies, and the ADF's role in them requires specific justification and authorisation.[135]

Figure 22: *The Navy's Armidale class patrol boats (HMAS Albany pictured) are mainly used for border and fisheries patrol tasks*

Elements of the ADF are frequently "called out" to contribute to relief efforts following natural disasters in Australia or overseas. The ADF's role in these efforts is set out in Australia's emergency management plans. The ADF typically contributes specialist capabilities, such as engineers or transport, to support the civil authorities.[136] For major disasters, this can involve a large-scale deployment of personnel and assets. While the ADF has a commitment to assist relief efforts, several defence white papers have specified that this is a secondary responsibility to the force's focus on maintaining combat capabilities. As a result, requests for assistance have to be balanced against military priorities.[137] No elements of the ADF are specifically tasked with or equipped for disaster relief efforts.[138]

The ADF can also be tasked with providing aid to civil authorities outside of natural disasters; for instance in response to industrial action or to assist civilian police maintain law and order. This rarely occurs, however, and most Australians consider the use of military personnel to break strikes or undertake law enforcement to be inappropriate.[139] Due to the political sensitivities associated with strike breaking, the ADF conducts little planning or other preparations for this role and the *Defence Act* explicitly states that reservists may not be called out or deployed in response to industrial action.[140]

The ADF makes a significant contribution to Australia's domestic maritime security. ADF ships, aircraft and Regional Force Surveillance Units conduct patrols of northern Australia in conjunction with the Australian Border Force (ABF). This operation, which is code-named Operation Resolute, is commanded by the Maritime Border Command which is jointly manned by members of the ADF and ABF. This operation involves a considerable proportion of the ADF's assets, with the forces assigned typically including two major naval vessels, multiple patrol boats, Regional Force Surveillance Unit patrols and AP-3 Orion aircraft. The ADF also often contributes to search and rescue efforts coordinated by the Australian Maritime Safety Authority and other civilian agencies.[135]

While the ADF does not have a significant nation-building role, it provides assistance to remote Indigenous Australian communities through the Army Aboriginal Community Assistance Program. Under this program, which has been conducted since 1997, an engineer squadron works with one community for several months each year to upgrade local infrastructure and provide training. The ADF also took part in the intervention in remote Northern Territory Indigenous communities between June 2007 and October 2008. During this operation more than 600 ADF personnel provided logistical support to the Northern Territory Emergency Response Task Force and helped conduct child health checks.

The ADF shares responsibility for counter-terrorism with civilian law enforcement agencies. Under *Australia's Counter-Terrorism Strategy*, the state and territory police and emergency services have the primary responsibility for responding to any terrorist incidents on Australian territory. If a terrorist threat or the consequences of an incident are beyond the capacity of civilian authorities to resolve, the ADF may be called out to provide support following a request from the relevant state or territory government. The Commonwealth Government has responsibility for responding to offshore terrorist incidents.[141] ADF liaison officers are posted to civilian law enforcement agencies, and the military offers specialised training to police counter-terrorism teams. To meet its counter-terrorism responsibilities the ADF maintains two elite Tactical Assault Groups, the Special Operations Engineer Regiment as well as a company-sized high readiness group in each Army Reserve brigade and the 1st Commando Regiment. ADF intelligence assets also work with other Australian Government and police agencies to counter foreign terrorist threats.[142,143] While these forces provide a substantial counter-terrorism capability, the ADF does not regard domestic security as being part of its 'core business'.[144]

Figure 23: *Australian, British and United States C-17 Globemasters and aircrew in Britain during 2007*

Foreign defence relations

The Australian Defence Force cooperates with militaries around the world. Australia's formal military agreements include the ANZUS Alliance with the United States, the Closer Defence Program with New Zealand, the Five Power Defence Arrangements with Malaysia, Singapore, New Zealand and the United Kingdom, and the ABCA Armies Standardisation Program with the United States, the United Kingdom, Canada and New Zealand.[145,146] Australia has also established a partnership with NATO. ADF activities under these agreements include participating in joint planning, intelligence sharing, personnel exchanges, equipment standardisation programs and joint exercises.[147] Australia is also a member of the UKUSA signals intelligence gathering agreement.[148] Members of the ADF are posted to Australian diplomatic missions around the world as defence attachés; in 2016 the role of these officers was expanded to include promoting export sales for the Australian defence industry. The *2016 Defence White Paper* stated that the Government will seek to further expand the ADF's international engagement.[149]

New Zealand, Singapore and the United States maintain military units in Australia. The New Zealand and Singaporean forces are limited to small training units at ADF bases, with the New Zealand contingent comprising nine personnel involved in air navigation training.[130] Two Republic of Singapore Air Force pilot training squadrons with a total of 230 personnel are based in Australia; 126 Squadron at the Oakey Army Aviation Centre and 130 Squadron at

Figure 24: *An Australian commando (at left) training with a Filipino soldier in 2017*

RAAF Base Pearce.¹³⁰ The Singapore Armed Forces also uses the Shoalwater Bay Military Training Area in Queensland for large-scale exercises; under the terms of a bilateral agreement, these run for up to 18 weeks each year and involve as many as 14,000 Singaporean personnel.

The United States maintains intelligence facilities in Australia, and regularly rotates military forces to the country for training purposes. The intelligence facilities comprise the Pine Gap satellite tracking station near Alice Springs and Naval Communication Station Harold E. Holt near Exmouth, Western Australia. Pine Gap is jointly operated by Australian and United States personnel and Naval Communication Station Harold E. Holt has been an exclusively Australian-operated facility since 1999.¹⁵⁰ In early 2007 the Australian Government approved the construction of a new US communications installation at the Defence Signals Directorate Australian Defence Satellite Communications Station facility near Geraldton, Western Australia, to provide a ground station for the US-led Wideband Global System which Australia is partly funding. The United States Military also frequently uses Australian exercise areas and these facilities have been upgraded to support joint Australian-United States training. As well as these facilities, between 200 and 300 US Military personnel are posted to Australia to liaise with the ADF. In November 2011 the Australian and American Governments announced plans to rotate United States Marine Corps and United States Air Force (USAF) units through bases in the Northern Territory for training purposes. As part of this agreement, the Marine Rotational Force – Darwin has been deployed to Australia for six months each year since 2012. It is planned for this force to eventually comprise around 2,500 personnel with supporting aircraft and equipment.[151] The expanded rotations of USAF units to Australia began in early 2017.

The ADF provides assistance to militaries in Australia's region through the Defence Cooperation Program. Under this program the ADF provides assistance with training, infrastructure, equipment and logistics and participates in joint exercises with countries in South East Asia and Oceania. The Pacific Patrol Boat Program is the largest Defence Cooperation Program activity and supports 22 Pacific class patrol boats operated by twelve South Pacific countries. Other important activities include supporting the development of the Timor Leste Defence Force and Papua New Guinea Defence Force and supplying watercraft to the Armed Forces of the Philippines.[152] Australia also directly contributes to the defence of Pacific countries by periodically deploying warships and aircraft to patrol their territorial waters; this includes an annual deployment of RAAF AP-3 Orions to the region as part of a multi-national maritime surveillance operation. Under an informal agreement Australia is responsible for the defence of Nauru.

References

Works consulted

<templatestyles src="Template:Refbegin/styles.css" />

- Air Power Development Centre (2015). *Air Force – Serving Australia's Interests*[153]. Canberra: Royal Australian Air Force.
- Air Power Development Centre (2016). *Air Force Capability Guidebook*[154]. Canberra: Air Power Development Centre. OCLC 950573401[155].
- Australian Army (2014). "The Australian Army: An Aide-Memoire"[156] (PDF). Canberra: Australian Army.
- Australian Government (2014). *Defence Issues Paper*[157] (PDF). Canberra: Department of Defence. ISBN 978-0-9925662-0-3.
- Australian Government (2016). *2016 Defence White Paper*[158]. Canberra: Department of Defence. ISBN 9780994168054.
- Australian National Audit Office (2001). *Australian Defence Force Reserves*[159]. Canberra: Australian National Audit Office. ISBN 0-642-44257-6.
- Australian National Audit Office (2014). *Emergency Defence Assistance to the Civil Community*[160] (PDF). Canberra: Australian National Audit Office. ISBN 0642814376.

- Ball, Desmond; Robinson, Bill; Tranter, Richard (2016). "Australia's participation in the Pine Gap enterprise"[161] (PDF). Nautilus Institute for Security and Sustainability.
- Australian Parliamentary Library (22 December 2000). "Women in the Armed Forces: The Role of Women in the Australian Defence Force"[162]. Parliament of Australia. Archived from the original[163] on 7 February 2012. Retrieved 16 December 2006.
- Beaumont, Joan (2001). *Australian Defence Sources and Statistics*. Melbourne: Oxford University Press. ISBN 0-19-554118-9.
- Belkin, Aaron; McNichol, Jason (2000). "The Effects of Including Gay and Lesbian Soldiers in the Australian Defence Forces: Appraising the Evidence"[164] (PDF). Palm Center. Retrieved 14 January 2018.
- Blaxland, John (2014). *The Australian Army from Whitlam to Howard*. Port Melbourne, Victoria: Cambridge University Press. ISBN 9781107043657.
- Bullard, Steven (2017). *In their Time of Need: Australia's Overseas Emergency Relief Operations 1918-2006*. Official History of Australian Peacekeeping, Humanitarian and Post-Cold War Operations. Cambridge: Cambridge University Press. ISBN 978-1-107-02634-6.
- Chief of Navy (2017). *Australian Maritime Operations*[165] (PDF). Canberra: Sea Power Centre — Australia. ISBN 9780992500412.
- Council of Australian Governments (2015). *Australia's Counter-Terrorism Strategy*[166] (PDF). Canberra: Attorney-General's Department. ISBN 978-1-925237-70-2.
- Davies, Andrew (2010). "Army capability review 2010"[167]. Australian Strategic Policy Institute.
- Davies, Andrew; Jennings, Peter; Schreer, Benjamin (April 2014). *A Versatile Force: The Future of Australia's Special Operations Capability*[168]. Canberra: Australian Strategic Policy Institute. ISBN 978-1-921302-97-8.
- Defence People Group (2017). "ADF Total Workforce Model Frequently Asked Questions"[169] (PDF). Department of Defence.
- Dennis, Peter; et al., eds. (2008). *The Oxford Companion to Australian Military History* (2nd ed.). South Melbourne: Oxford University Press. ISBN 9780195517842.
- Department of Defence (2009). *Defending Australia in the Asia Pacific Century: Force 2030*[170]. Department of Defence. ISBN 978-0-642-29702-0.
- Department of Defence (2016). "Women in the ADF Report 2015–16"[171] (PDF). Canberra: Department of Defence.
- Department of Defence (2017). "Explosive Ordnance Logistics Reform Program Project : Statement of Evidence to the Parliamentary Standing Committee on Public Works"[172]. Parliament of Australia.

- Department of Defence (2017a). *2016-17 Defence Annual Report*[173]. Canberra: Department of Defence. ISSN 1323-5036[174].
- Edwards, Peter (2016). *Defence White Papers at 40*[175]. Canberra: Australian Strategic Policy Institute. ISBN 9781925229271.
- Foreign Affairs, Defence and Trade Group (2000). "Women in the armed forces: the role of women in the Australian Defence Force"[176]. *Parliamentary Library*. Parliament of Australia. Retrieved 8 January 2018.
- Grey, Jeffrey (2008). *A Military History of Australia* (Third ed.). Port Melbourne: Cambridge University Press. ISBN 978-0-521-69791-0.
- Henry, Ken (2005). "Australia's Defence to 2045: The Macro-economic Outlook". *Defender* (Spring 2005): 19–24.
- Hoglin, Phillip (2016). "Religious Diversity and Secularism in the ADF"[177] (PDF). *Australian Defence Journal* (199): 20–27.
- Horner, David (2001). *Making the Australian Defence Force*. The Australian Centenary History of Defence Volume IV. Melbourne: Oxford University Press. ISBN 0-19-554117-0.
- Horner, David (2007). "The Higher Command Structure for Joint ADF Operations". In Huisken, Ron; Thatcher, Meredith. *History as Policy: Framing the debate on the future of Australia's defence policy*[178]. Canberra: ANU E Press. pp. 143–161. ISBN 9781921313561.
- International Institute for Strategic Studies (2016). *The Military Balance 2016*. Abingdon, United Kingdom: Routledge. ISBN 9781857438352.
- Jennings, Peter (2016). "The Politics and Practicalities of Designing Australia's Force Structure". In Ball, Desmond; Lee, Sheryn. *Geography, Power, Strategy and Defence Policy: Essays in Honour of Paul Dibb*[179]. Canberra: ANU Press. ISBN 9781760460143.
- Joint Standing Committee on Treaties (2014). "Report 145: Treaties tabled on 26 August and 2 September 2014"[180]. Parliament of Australia. ISBN 978-1-74366-240-3.
- Khosa, Raspal (2010). *Australian Defence Almanac 2010–2011*[181]. Canberra: Australian Strategic Policy Institute. ISSN 1449-9355[182].
- Khosa, Raspal (2011). *Australian Defence Almanac 2011–2012*[183]. Canberra: Australian Strategic Policy Institute.
- McKeown, Deirdre; Jordan, Roy (22 March 2010). "Parliamentary involvement in declaring war and deploying forces overseas"[184] (PDF). *Background note*. Department of Parliamentary Services. Retrieved 16 June 2014.
- Peacock, Lindsay; von Rosenbach, Alexander (2011). *Jane's World Air Forces, Issue Thirty Four*. Coulsdon, UK: IHS Jane's. ISSN 1748-2526[185].
- Pittaway, Nigel (February 2014). "Small, but deadly : Australia's Forces". *Air Forces Monthly*. No. 311. pp. 74–84.

- Smith, Andrew; Bergin, Anthony (2006). "Strategic Insights 31 - Australian domestic security: The role of Defence"[186]. Australian Strategic Policy Institute.
- Smith, Mark (2014). "Focusing the Army Reserve: force structuring as an operational rather than strategic reserve"[187] (PDF). *Australian Defence Force Journal* (193): 40–55.
- Sutton, John (2017). "The increasing convergence of the role and function of the ADF and civil police"[188] (PDF). *Australian Defence Force Journal* (202): 38–43.
- Tewes, Alex; Rayner, Laura; Kavanaugh, Kelly (2004). "Research Brief no. 4 2004–05"[189] (PDF). *Australia's Maritime Strategy in the 21st century*. Australian Parliamentary Library.
- Thomson, Mark (2005). "Punching above our weight? Australia as a middle power"[190] (PDF[191]). Canberra: Australian Strategic Policy Institute.
- Thomson, Mark (2005a). "War and Profit: Doing business on the battlefield"[192] (PDF[193]). Canberra: Australian Strategic Policy Institute.
- Thomson, Mark (2006). "Defence Budget 2006/07: 'Planning on Hope or Pessimism'". *Defender*.
- Thomson, Mark (2009). *The Cost of Defence: ASPI Defence Budget Brief 2009–2010*[194]. Canberra: Australian Strategic Policy Institute. ISSN 2200-6613[195].
- Thomson, Mark (2012). *The Cost of Defence: ASPI Defence Budget Brief 2012–2013*[196]. Canberra: Australian Strategic Policy Institute. ISSN 2200-6613[195].
- Thomson, Mark (2016). *The Cost of Defence : ASPI Defence Budget Brief 2016-17*[197]. Canberra: Australian Strategic Policy Institute. ISSN 2200-6613[195].
- Thomson, Mark (2017). "The Cost of Defence: ASPI Defence Budget Brief 2017-2018"[198]. Canberra: Australian Strategic Policy Institute. ISSN 2200-6613[195].
- Wilson, Stewart; Pittaway, Nigel (2017). "Airpower Australia". *Aero Australia special edition*. ISSN 1448-8086[199].

External links

 Wikimedia Commons has media related to *Military of Australia*.

- Australian Defence Organisation website[200]

History

Military history of Australia

<indicator name="good-star"> ⊕ </indicator>

Part of a series on the
History of Australia
Chronological
• Prehistory • European exploration (sea) • European exploration (land) • 1788–1850 • 1851–1900 • 1901–1945 • 1945–present • Timeline
By topic
• Constitution • Diplomacy • Economy • Federation • Immigration • Indigenous people • Military • Monarchy • Rail transport
By region

State/Territory	Capital
ACT	Canberra
New South Wales	Sydney
Northern Territory	Darwin
Queensland	Brisbane
South Australia	Adelaide
Tasmania	Hobart
Victoria	Melbourne
Western Australia	Perth

Australia portal

- v
- t
- e[201]

The **military history of Australia** spans the nation's 230-year modern history, from the early Australian frontier wars between Aboriginals and Europeans to the ongoing conflicts in Iraq and Afghanistan in the early 21st century. Although this history is short when compared to that of many other nations, Australia has been involved in numerous conflicts and wars, and war and military service have been significant influences on Australian society and national identity, including the Anzac spirit. The relationship between war and Australian society has also been shaped by the enduring themes of Australian strategic culture and its unique security dilemma.

As British offshoots, the Australian colonies participated in Britain's small wars of the 19th century, while later as a federated dominion, and then an independent nation, Australia fought in the First World War and Second World War, as well as in the wars in Korea, Malaya, Borneo and Vietnam during the Cold War. In the Post-Vietnam era Australian forces have been involved in numerous international peacekeeping missions, through the United Nations and other agencies, including in the Sinai, Persian Gulf, Rwanda, Somalia, East Timor and the Solomon Islands, as well as many overseas humanitarian relief operations, while more recently they have also fought as part of multi-lateral forces in Iraq and Afghanistan. In total, nearly 103,000 Australians died during the course of these conflicts.[202]

War and Australian society

For most of the last century military service has been one of the single greatest shared experiences of white Australian males, and although this is now changing due to the professionalisation of the military and the absence of major wars during the second half of the 20th century, it continues to influence Australian society to this day. War and military service have been defining influences in

Figure 25: *The interior courtyard of the Australian War Memorial in Canberra. Almost 877,000 people visited the Australian War Memorial during 2009–10 and another 204,000 visited its travelling exhibitions.*[203]

Australian history, while a major part of the national identity has been built on an idealised conception of the Australian experience of war and of soldiering, known as the Anzac spirit. These ideals include notions of endurance, courage, ingenuity, humour, larrikinism, egalitarianism and mateship; traits which, according to popular thought, defined the behaviour of Australian soldiers fighting at Gallipoli during the First World War. The Gallipoli campaign was one of the first international events that saw Australians taking part as Australians and has been seen as a key event in forging a sense of national identity.

The relationship between war and Australian society has been shaped by two of the more enduring themes of Australian strategic culture: bandwagoning with a powerful ally and expeditionary warfare.[204] Indeed, Australian defence policy was closely linked to Britain until the Japanese crisis of 1942, while since then an alliance with the United States has underwritten its security. Arguably, this pattern of bandwagoning—both for cultural reasons such as shared values and beliefs, as well as for more pragmatic security concerns—has ensured that Australian strategic policy has often been defined by relations with its allies. Regardless, a tendency towards strategic complacency has also been evident, with Australians often reluctant to think about defence issues or to allocate resources until a crisis arises; a trait which has historically resulted in unpreparedness for major military challenges.[205]

Reflecting both the realist and liberal paradigms of international relations and the conception of national interests, a number of other important themes in Australian strategic culture are also obvious. Such themes include: an acceptance of the state as the key actor in international politics, the centrality of notions of Westphalian sovereignty, a belief in the enduring relevance and legitimacy of armed force as a guarantor of security, and the proposition that the status quo in international affairs should only be changed peacefully.[206] Likewise, multilateralism, collective security and defence self-reliance have also been important themes.[207] Change has been more evolutionary than revolutionary and these strategic behaviours have persisted throughout its history, being the product of Australian society's democratic political tradition and Judaeo-Christian Anglo-European heritage, as well its associated values, beliefs and economic, political and religious ideology.[208] These behaviours are also reflective of its unique security dilemma as a largely European island on the edge of the Asia-Pacific, and the geopolitical circumstances of a middle power physically removed from the centres of world power. To be sure, during threats to the core Australia has often found itself defending the periphery and perhaps as a result, it has frequently become involved in foreign wars. Throughout these conflicts Australian soldiers—known colloquially as Diggers—have often been noted, somewhat paradoxically, for both their fighting abilities and their humanitarian qualities.[209]

Colonial era

British Forces in Australia, 1788–1870

From 1788 until 1870 the defence of the Australian colonies was mostly provided by British Army regular forces. Originally Marines protected the early settlements at Sydney Cove and Norfolk Island, however they were relieved of these duties in 1790 by a British Army unit specifically recruited for colonial service, known as the New South Wales Corps. The New South Wales Corps subsequently was involved in putting down a rebellion of Irish convicts at Castle Hill in 1804. Soon however shortcomings in the corps convinced the War Office of the need for a more reliable garrison in New South Wales and Van Diemen's Land. Chief of these shortcomings was the Rum Rebellion, a coup mounted by its officers in 1808. As a result, in January 1810 the 73rd (Perthshire) Regiment of Foot arrived in Australia. By 1870, 25 British infantry regiments had served in Australia, as had a small number of artillery and engineer units.[210]

Although the primary role of the British Army was to protect the colonies against external attack, no actual threat ever materialised.[211] The British Army

Figure 26: *A painting depicting the Castle Hill convict rebellion in 1804.*

was instead used in policing, guarding convicts at penal institutions, combating bushranging, putting down convict rebellions—as occurred at Bathurst in 1830—and to suppress Aboriginal resistance to the extension of European settlement. Notably British soldiers were involved in the battle at the Eureka Stockade in 1854 on the Victorian goldfields. Members of British regiments stationed in Australia also saw action in India, Afghanistan, New Zealand and the Sudan.[212]

During the early years of settlement the naval defence of Australia was provided by detached Royal Navy units of the East Indies Station, based in Sydney. However, in 1859 Australia was established as a separate squadron under the command of a commodore, marking the first occasion that Royal Navy ships had been permanently stationed in Australia. The Royal Navy remained the primary naval force in Australian waters until 1913, when the Australia Station ceased and responsibility handed over to the Royal Australian Navy; the Royal Navy's depots, dockyards and structures were given to the Australian people.[213]

Figure 27: *Poster issued in Van Diemen's Land during the Black War implying a policy of friendship and equal justice for white settlers and Indigenous Australians. Such a policy did not actually exist at the time.*

Frontier warfare, 1788–1934

The reactions of the native Aboriginal inhabitants to the sudden arrival of British settlers in Australia were varied, but were inevitably hostile when the settlers' presence led to competition over resources, and to the occupation of the indigenous inhabitants' lands. European diseases decimated Aboriginal populations, and the occupation or destruction of lands and food resources sometimes led to starvation.[214] By and large neither the British nor the Aborigines approached the conflict in an organised sense and conflict occurred between groups of settlers and individual tribes rather than systematic warfare. At times, however, the frontier wars did see the involvement of British soldiers and later mounted police units. Not all Aboriginal groups resisted white encroachment on their lands, while many Aborigines served in mounted police units and were involved in attacks on other tribes.

Fighting between Aborigines and Europeans was localised as the Aborigines did not form confederations capable of sustained resistance. As a result, there was not a single war, but rather a series of violent engagements and massacres across the continent.[215] Organised or disorganised however, a pattern of frontier warfare emerged with Aboriginal resistance beginning in the 18th century and continuing into the early 20th century. This warfare contradicts the popular and at times academic "myth" of peaceful settlement in Australia. Faced with Aboriginal resistance settlers often reacted with violence, resulting in a number of indiscriminate massacres. Among the most famous is the Battle of Pinjarra in Western Australia in 1834. Such incidents were not officially sanctioned however, and after the Myall Creek massacre in New South Wales in 1838 seven Europeans were hanged for their part in the killings.[216] However, in Tasmania the so-called Black War was fought between 1828 and 1832, and aimed at driving most of the island's native inhabitants onto a number of isolated peninsulas. Although it began in failure for the British, it ultimately resulted in considerable casualties amongst the native population.[217,218]

It may be inaccurate though to depict the conflict as one sided and mainly perpetrated by Europeans on Aborigines. Although many more Aborigines died than British, this may have had more to do with the technological and logistic advantages enjoyed by the Europeans.[219] Aboriginal tactics varied, but were mainly based on pre-existing hunting and fighting practices—using spears, clubs and other primitive weapons. Unlike the indigenous peoples of New Zealand and North America, on the main Aborigines failed to adapt to meet the challenge of the Europeans. Although there were some instances of individuals and groups acquiring and using firearms, this was not widespread.[220] The Aborigines were never a serious military threat to European settlers, regardless of how much the settlers may have feared them.[221] On occasions large groups of Aborigines attacked the settlers in open terrain and a conventional battle ensued, during which the Aborigines would attempt to use superior numbers to their advantage. This could sometimes be effective, with reports of them advancing in crescent formation in an attempt to outflank and surround their opponents, waiting out the first volley of shots and then hurling their spears while the settlers reloaded. However, such open warfare usually proved more costly for the Aborigines than the Europeans.[222]

Central to the success of the Europeans was the use of firearms. However, the advantages afforded by firearms have often been overstated. Prior to the late 19th century, firearms were often cumbersome muzzle-loading, smooth-bore, single shot muskets with flint-lock mechanisms. Such weapons produced a low rate of fire, while suffering from a high rate of failure and were only accurate within 50 metres (160 ft). These deficiencies may have initially given the Aborigines an advantage, allowing them to move in close and engage with spears or clubs. Yet by 1850 significant advances in firearms gave the Europeans a distinct advantage, with the six-shot Colt revolver, the Snider single shot breech-loading rifle and later the Martini-Henry rifle, as well as rapid-fire rifles such as the Winchester rifle, becoming available. These weapons, when used on open ground and combined with the superior mobility provided by

Figure 28: *Mounted police engaging Indigenous Australians during the Waterloo Creek massacre of 1838.*

horses to surround and engage groups of Aborigines, often proved successful. The Europeans also had to adapt their tactics to fight their fast-moving, often hidden enemies. Tactics employed included night-time surprise attacks, and positioning forces to drive the natives off cliffs or force them to retreat into rivers while attacking from both banks.[223]

The conflict lasted for over 150 years and followed the pattern of British settlement in Australia.[224] Beginning in New South Wales with the arrival of the first Europeans in May 1788, it continued in Sydney and its surrounds until the 1820s. As the frontier moved west so did the conflict, pushing into outback New South Wales in the 1840s. In Tasmania, fighting can be traced from 1804 to the 1830s, while in Victoria and the southern parts of South Australia, the majority of the violence occurred during the 1830s and 1840s. The southwest of Western Australia experienced warfare from 1829 to 1850. The war in Queensland began in the area around Brisbane in the 1840s and continued until 1860, moving to central Queensland in the 1850s and 1860s, and then to northern Queensland from the 1860s to 1900. In Western Australia, the violence moved north with European settlement, reaching the Kimberley region by 1880, with violent clashes continuing until the 1920s. In the Northern Territory conflict lasted even later still, especially in central Australia, continuing from the 1880s to the 1930s. One estimate of casualties places European deaths at 2,500, while at least 20,000 Aborigines are believed to have perished. Far more devastating though was the effect of disease which significantly reduced the Aboriginal population by the beginning of the 20th century; a fact

Figure 29: *HMCSS Victoria in 1867. In 1861, Victoria was dispatched to assist the New Zealand colonial government during the First Taranaki War.*

which may also have limited their ability to resist.[225]

New Zealand Wars, 1861–64

Taranaki War

In 1861, the Victorian ship HMCSS *Victoria* was dispatched to help the New Zealand colonial government in its war against Māori in Taranaki. *Victoria* was subsequently used for patrol duties and logistic support, although a number of personnel were involved in actions against Māori fortifications. One sailor died from an accidental gunshot wound during the deployment.[226]

Invasion of the Waikato

In late 1863, the New Zealand government requested troops to assist in the invasion of the Waikato province against the Māori. Promised settlement on confiscated land, more than 2,500 Australians (over half of whom were from Victoria) were recruited to form four Waikato Regiments. Other Australians became scouts in the Company of Forest Rangers. Despite experiencing arduous conditions the Australians were not heavily involved in battle, and were primarily used for patrolling and garrison duties. Australians were involved in actions at Matarikoriko, Pukekohe East, Titi Hill, Ōrākau and Te Ranga. Fewer than 20 were believed to have been killed in action.[227] The conflict was

Figure 30: *Members of the Hobart Town Volunteer Artillery in August 1869.*

over by 1864, and the Waikato Regiments disbanded in 1867. However, many of the soldiers who had chosen to claim farmland at the cessation of hostilities had drifted to the towns and cities by the end of the decade, while many others had returned to Australia.[228]

Colonial military forces, 1870–1901

From 1870 until 1901, each of the six colonial governments was responsible for their own defence. The colonies had gained responsible government between 1855 and 1890, and while the Colonial Office in London retained control of some affairs, the Governor of the each colony was required to raise their own colonial militia. To do this, they were granted the authority from the British crown to raise military and naval forces. Initially these were militias in support of British regulars, but when military support for the colonies ended in 1870, the colonies assumed their own defence responsibilities. The colonial military forces included unpaid volunteer militia, paid citizen soldiers, and a small permanent component. They were mainly infantry, cavalry and mounted infantry, and were neither housed in barracks nor subject to full military discipline. Even after significant reforms in the 1870s—including the expansion of the permanent forces to include engineer and artillery units—they remained too small and unbalanced to be considered armies in the modern sense. By 1885, the forces numbered 21,000 men. Although they could not

Figure 31: *The torpedo boat Avernus of the New South Wales Naval Brigade, c. 1890s.*

be compelled to serve overseas many volunteers subsequently did see action in a number conflicts of the British Empire during the 19th century, with the colonies raising contingents to serve in Sudan, South Africa and China.[229]

Despite a reputation of colonial inferiority, many of the locally raised units were highly organised, disciplined, professional, and well trained. During this period, defences in Australia mainly revolved around static defence by combined infantry and artillery, based on garrisoned coastal forts. However, by the 1890s, improved railway communications between the mainland eastern colonies led Major General James Edwards—who had recently completed a survey of colonial military forces—to the belief that the colonies could be defended by the rapid mobilisation of brigades of infantry. As a consequence he called for a restructure of defences, and defensive agreements to be made between the colonies. Edwards argued for the colonial forces to be federated and for professional units—obliged to serve anywhere in the South Pacific—to replace the volunteer forces. These views found support in the influential New South Wales Commandant, Major General Edward Hutton, however suspicions held by the smaller colonies towards New South Wales and Victoria stifled the proposal. These reforms remaining unresolved however, and defence issues were generally given little attention in the debate on the political federation of the colonies.[230,231]

With the exception of Western Australia, the colonies also operated their own navies. In 1856, Victoria received its own naval vessel, HMCSS *Victoria*, and its deployment to New Zealand in 1860 during the First Taranaki War marked the first occasion that an Australian warship had been deployed overseas.[232] The colonial navies were expanded greatly in the mid-1880s and consisted of a number of gunboats and torpedo-boats for the defence of harbours and rivers, as well as naval brigades to man vessels and forts. Victoria became the

Figure 32: *Departure of the New South Wales contingent from Sydney for the Suakin Expedition in Sudan, 1885.*

most powerful of all the colonial navies, with the ironclad HMVS *Cerberus* in service from 1870, as well as the steam-sail warship HMS *Nelson* on loan from the Royal Navy, three small gunboats and five torpedo-boats. New South Wales formed a Naval Brigade in 1863 and by the start of the 20th century had two small torpedo-boats and a corvette. The Queensland Maritime Defence Force was established in 1885, while South Australia operated a single ship, HMCS *Protector*. Tasmania had also a small Torpedo Corps, while Western Australia's only naval defences included the Fremantle Naval Artillery. Naval personnel from New South Wales and Victoria took part in the suppression of the Boxer Rebellion in China in 1900, while HMCS *Protector* was sent by South Australia but saw no action.[233] The separate colonies maintained control over their military and naval forces until Federation in 1901, when they were amalgamated and placed under the control of the new Commonwealth of Australia.[234]

Sudan, 1885

During the early years of the 1880s, an Egyptian regime in the Sudan, backed by the British, came under threat from rebellion under the leadership of native Muhammad Ahmad (or Ahmed), known as Mahdi to his followers. In 1883, as part of the Mahdist War, the Egyptians sent an army to deal with the revolt, but they were defeated and faced a difficult campaign of extracting their forces. The British instructed the Egyptians to abandon the Sudan, and sent General Charles Gordon to co-ordinate the evacuation, but he was killed in January 1885. When news of his death arrived in New South Wales in February 1885, the government offered to send forces and meet the contingent's expenses.[235] The New South Wales Contingent consisted of an infantry battalion of 522 men and 24 officers, and an artillery battery of 212 men and sailed from Sydney on 3 March 1885.[236]

The contingent arrived in Suakin on 29 March and were attached to a brigade that consisted of Scots, Grenadier and Coldstream Guards. They subsequently marched for Tamai in a large "square" formation made up of 10,000 men. Reaching the village, they burned huts and returned to Suakin: three Australians were wounded in minor fighting. Most of the contingent was then sent to work on a railway line that was being laid across the desert towards Berber, on the Nile. The Australians were then assigned to guard duties, but soon a camel corps was raised and 50 men volunteered. They rode on a reconnaissance to Takdul on 6 May and were heavily involved in a skirmish during which more than 100 Arabs were killed or captured.[237] On 15 May, they made one last sortie to bury the dead from the fighting of the previous March. Meanwhile, the artillery were posted at Handoub and drilled for a month, but they soon rejoined the camp at Suakin.

Eventually the British government decided that the campaign in Sudan was not worth the effort required and left a garrison in Suakin. The New South Wales Contingent sailed for home on 17 May, arriving in Sydney on 19 June 1885. Approximately 770 Australians served in Sudan; nine subsequently died of disease during the return journey while three had been wounded during the campaign.

Second Boer War, 1899–1902

British encroachment into areas of South Africa already settled by the Afrikaner Boers and the competition for resources and land that developed between them as a result, led to the Second Boer War in 1899. Pre-empting the deployment of British forces, the Afrikaner Republics of the Orange Free State and the Transvaal Republic under President Paul Kruger declared war on 11 October 1899, striking deep into the British territories of Natal and the Cape Colony.[238] After the outbreak of war, plans for the dispatch of a combined Australian force were subsequently set aside by the British War Office and each of the six colonial governments sent separate contingents to serve with British formations, with two squadrons each of 125 men from New South Wales and Victoria, and one each from the other colonies.[239] The first troops arrived three weeks later, with the New South Wales Lancers—who had been

Figure 33: *Depiction of Australians and New Zealanders at Klerksdorp, 24 March 1901 by Charles Hammond.*

training in England before the war, hurriedly diverted to South Africa. On 22 November, the Lancers came under fire for the first time near Belmont, and they subsequently forced their attackers to withdraw after inflicting significant casualties on them.[240]

Following a series of minor victories, the British suffered a major setback during Black Week between 10–17 December 1899, although no Australian units were involved. The first contingents of infantry from Victoria, South Australia, Western Australia, and Tasmania arrived in Cape Town on 26 November and were designated the *Australian Regiment* under the command of Colonel John Charles Hoad. With a need for increased mobility, they were soon converted into mounted infantry. Further units from Queensland and New South Wales arrived in December and were soon committed to the front.[241] The first casualties occurred soon after at Sunnyside on 1 January 1900, after 250 Queensland Mounted Infantry and a column of Canadians, British and artillery attacked a Boer laager at Belmont. Troopers David McLeod and Victor Jones were killed when their patrol clashed with the Boer forward sentries. Regardless, the Boers were surprised and during two hours of heavy fighting, more than 50 were killed and another 40 taken prisoner. Five hundred Queenslanders and the New South Wales Lancers subsequently took part in the Siege of Kimberley in February 1900.[242]

Despite serious set-backs at Colenso, Stormberg, Magersfontein, and Spion Kop in January—and with Ladysmith still under siege—the British mounted a five division counter-invasion of the Orange Free State in February. The

Figure 34: *Troops of the 1st Battalion, Australian Commonwealth Horse in the Transvaal, 1902.*

attacking force included a division of cavalry commanded by Lieutenant General John French with the New South Wales Lancers, Queensland Mounted Infantry and New South Wales Army Medical Corps attached.[243] First, Kimberley was relieved following the battles of Modder River and Magersfontein, and the retreating Boers defeated at Paardeberg, with the New South Wales Mounted Rifles locating the Boer general, Piet Cronjé. The British entered Bloemfontein on 13 March 1900, while Ladysmith was relieved. Disease began to take its toll and scores of men died. Still the advance continued, with the drive to Pretoria in May including more than 3,000 Australians. Johannesburg fell on 30 May, and the Boers withdrew from Pretoria on 3 June. The New South Wales Mounted Rifles and Western Australians saw action again at Diamond Hill on 12 June. Mafeking was relieved on 17 May.[244]

Following the defeat of the Afrikaner republics still the Boers held out, forming small commando units and conducting a campaign of guerrilla warfare to disrupt British troop movements and lines of supply. This new phase of resistance led to further recruiting in the Australian colonies and the raising of the Bushmen's Contingents, with these soldiers usually being volunteers with horse-riding and shooting skills, but little military experience. After Federation in 1901, eight Australian Commonwealth Horse battalions of the newly created Australian Army were also sent to South Africa, although they saw little fighting before the war ended. Some Australians later joined local South African irregular units, instead of returning home after discharge. These soldiers were part of the British Army, and were subject to British military discipline. Such units included the Bushveldt Carbineers which gained notoriety as the unit in which Harry "Breaker" Morant and Peter Handcock served in before their court martial and execution for war crimes.[245]

With the guerrillas requiring supplies, Koos de la Rey lead a force of 3,000 Boers against Brakfontein, on the Elands River in Western Transvaal. The post held a large quantity of stores and was defended by 300 Australians and 200 Rhodesians. The attack began on 4 August 1900 with heavy shelling causing 32 casualties. During the night the defenders dug in, enduring shelling and rifle fire. A relief force was stopped by the Boers, while a second column turned back believing that the post had already been relieved. The siege lasted 11 days, during which more than 1,800 shells were fired into the post. After calls to surrender were ignored by the defenders, and not prepared to risk a frontal attack, the Boers eventually retired. The Siege of Elands River was one of the major achievements of the Australians during the war, with the post finally relieved on 16 August.[246]

In response the British adopted counter-insurgency tactics, including a scorched earth policy involving the burning of houses and crops, the establishment of concentration camps for Boer women and children, and a system of blockhouses and field obstacles to limit Boer mobility and to protect railway communications. Such measures required considerable expenditure, and caused much bitterness towards the British, however they soon yielded results.[247] By mid-1901, the bulk of the fighting was over, and British mounted units would ride at night to attack Boer farmhouses or encampments, overwhelming them with superior numbers. Indicative of warfare in last months of 1901, the New South Wales Mounted Rifles travelled 1,814 miles (2,919 km) and were involved in 13 skirmishes, killing 27 Boers, wounding 15, and capturing 196 for the loss of five dead and 19 wounded. Other notable Australian actions included Slingersfontein, Pink Hill, Rhenosterkop and Haartebeestefontein.[248]

Australians were not always successful however, suffering a number of heavy losses late in the war. On 12 June 1901, the 5th Victorian Mounted Rifles lost 19 killed and 42 wounded at Wilmansrust, near Middleburg after poor security allowed a force of 150 Boers to surprise them.[249] On 30 October 1901, Victorians of the Scottish Horse Regiment also suffered heavy casualties at Gun Hill, although 60 Boers were also killed in the engagement. Meanwhile, at Onverwacht on 4 January 1902, the 5th Queensland Imperial Bushmen lost 13 killed and 17 wounded. Ultimately the Boers were defeated, and the war ended on 31 May 1902. In all 16,175 Australians served in South Africa, and perhaps another 10,000 enlisted as individuals in Imperial units; casualties included 251 killed in action, 267 died of disease and 43 missing in action,

Figure 35: *The crew of HMCS Protector in 1900. In the same year, the gunboat was sent to China by the South Australian government.*

while a further 735 were wounded.[250,251] Six Australians were awarded the Victoria Cross.

Boxer Rebellion, 1900–01

The Boxer Rebellion in China began in 1900, and a number of western nations—including many European powers, the United States, and Japan—soon sent forces as part of the China Field Force to protect their interests. In June, the British government sought permission from the Australian colonies to dispatch ships from the Australian Squadron to China. The colonies also offered to assist further, but as most of their troops were still engaged in South Africa, they had to rely on naval forces for manpower. The force dispatched was a modest one, with Britain accepting 200 men from Victoria, 260 from New South Wales and the South Australian ship HMCS *Protector*, under the command of Captain William Creswell.[252] Most of these forces were made up of naval brigade reservists, who had been trained in both ship handling and soldiering to fulfil their coastal defence role. Amongst the naval contingent from New South Wales were 200 naval officers and sailors and 50 permanent soldiers headquartered at Victoria Barracks, Sydney who originally enlisted for the Second Boer War. The soldiers were keen to go to China but refused to be enlisted as sailors, while the New South Wales Naval Brigade objected to having soldiers in their ranks. The Army and Navy compromised and titled the contingent the NSW Marine Light Infantry.[253]

The contingents from New South Wales and Victoria sailed for China on 8 August 1900. Arriving in Tientsin, the Australians provided 300 men to an 8,000-strong multinational force tasked with capturing the Chinese forts at Pei Tang, which dominated a key railway. They arrived too late to take part in the battle, but were involved in the attack on the fortress at Pao-ting Fu, where the Chinese government was believed to have found asylum after Peking was captured by western forces. The Victorians joined a force of 7,500 men on a ten-day march to the fort, once again only to find that it had already surrendered. The Victorians then garrisoned Tientsin and the New South Wales contingent undertook garrison duties in Peking. HMCS *Protector* was mostly used for survey, transport, and courier duties in the Gulf of Chihli, before departing in November. The naval brigades remained during the winter, unhappily performing policing and guard duties, as well as working as railwaymen and fire-fighters. They left China in March 1901, having played only a minor role in a few offensives and punitive expeditions and in the restoration of civil order. Six Australians died from sickness and injury, but none were killed as a result of enemy action.

Australian military forces at Federation, 1901

The Commonwealth of Australia came into existence on 1 January 1901 as a result of the federation of the Australian colonies. Under the Constitution of Australia, defence responsibility was now vested in the new federal government. The co-ordination of Australia-wide defensive efforts in the face of Imperial German interest in the Pacific Ocean was one of driving forces behind federalism, and the Department of Defence immediately came into being as a result, while the Commonwealth Military Forces (early forerunner of the Australian Army) and Commonwealth Naval Force were also soon established.[254,255]

The Australian Commonwealth Military Forces came into being on 1 March 1901 and all the colonial forces—including those still in South Africa—became part of the new force.[256] 28,923 colonial soldiers, including 1,457 professional soldiers, 18,603 paid militia and 8,863 unpaid volunteers, were subsequently transferred. The individual units continued to be administered under the various colonial Acts until the *Defence Act 1903* brought all the units under one piece of legislation. This Act also prevented the raising of standing infantry units and specified that militia forces could not be used in industrial disputes or serve outside Australia. However, the majority of soldiers remained

Figure 36: *The battlecruiser HMAS Australia enter Sydney Harbour for the first time in 1913. The light cruisers HMAS Sydney and HMAS Melbourne are in the background.*

in militia units, known as the Citizen Military Forces (CMF). Major General Sir Edward Hutton—a former commander of the New South Wales Military Forces—subsequently became the first commander of the Commonwealth Military Forces on 26 December and set to work devising an integrated structure for the new army. In 1911, following a report by Lord Kitchener the Royal Military College, Duntroon was established, as was a system of universal National Service.

Prior to federation each self-governing colony had operated its own naval force. These navies were small and lacked blue water capabilities, forcing the separate colonies to subsidise the cost of a British naval squadron in their waters for decades. The colonies maintained control over their respective navies until 1 March 1901, when the Commonwealth Naval Force was created. This new force also lacked blue water capable ships, and ultimately did not lead to a change in Australian naval policy. In 1907 Prime Minister Alfred Deakin and Creswell, while attending the Imperial Conference in London, sought the British Government's agreement to end the subsidy system and develop an Australian navy. The Admiralty rejected and resented the challenge, but suggested diplomatically that a small fleet of destroyers and submarines would be sufficient. Deakin was unimpressed, and in 1908 invited the American Great White Fleet to visit Australia. This visit fired public enthusiasm for a modern

Figure 37: *An Australian recruitment poster used during World War I.*

navy and in part led to the order of two 700-ton River-class destroyers.[257] The surge in German naval construction prompted the Admiralty to change their position however and the Royal Australian Navy was subsequently formed in 1911, absorbing the Commonwealth Naval Force.[258] On 4 October 1913, the new fleet steamed through Sydney Heads, consisting of the battlecruiser HMAS *Australia*, three light cruisers, and three destroyers, while several other ships were still under construction. And as a consequence the navy entered the First World War as a formidable force.

The Australian Flying Corps (AFC) was established as part of the Commonwealth Military Forces in 1912, prior to the formation of the Australian Military Forces in 1916 and was later separated in 1921 to form the Royal Australian Air Force, making it the second oldest air force in the world.[259] Regardless, the service branches were not linked by a single chain of command however, and each reported to their own minister and had separate administrative arrangements and government departments.[260]

First World War, 1914–18

Outbreak of hostilities

When Britain declared war on Germany at the start of the First World War, the Australian government rapidly followed suit, with Prime Minister Joseph Cook declaring on 5 August 1914 that "...when the Empire is at war, so also is Australia"[261] and reflecting the sentiment of many Australians that any declaration of war by Britain automatically included Australia. This was itself in part due to the large number of British-born citizens and first generation Anglo-Australians that made up the Australian population at the time. Indeed, by the end of the war almost 20% of those who served in the Australian forces had been born in Britain.[262]

As the existing militia forces were unable to serve overseas under the provisions of the *Defence Act 1903*, an all-volunteer expeditionary force known as the Australian Imperial Force (AIF) was formed and recruitment began on 10 August 1914. The government pledged 20,000 men, organised as one infantry division and one light horse brigade plus supporting units. Enlistment and organisation was primarily regionally based and was undertaken under mobilisation plans drawn up in 1912.[263] The first commander was Major General William Bridges, who also assumed command of the 1st Division.[264] Throughout the course of the conflict Australian efforts were predominantly focused upon the ground war, although small air and naval forces were also committed.[265]

Occupation of German New Guinea

Following the outbreak of war Australian forces moved quickly to reduce the threat to shipping posed by the proximity of Germany's Pacific colonies. The Australian Naval and Military Expeditionary Force (AN&MEF), a 2000-man volunteer force—separate from the AIF—and consisting of an infantry battalion plus 500 naval reservists and ex-sailors, was rapidly formed under the command of William Holmes. The objectives of the force were the wireless stations on Nauru, and those at Yap in the Caroline Islands, and at Rabaul in German New Guinea. The force reached Rabaul on 11 September 1914 and occupied it the next day, encountering only brief resistance from the German and native defenders during fighting at Bita Paka and Toma. German New Guinea surrendered on 17 September 1914. Australian losses were light, including six killed during the fighting, but were compounded by the mysterious loss offshore of the submarine AE1 with all 35 men aboard.[266]

Figure 38: *Australian troops landing at Gallipoli, 1915.*

Gallipoli

The AIF departed by ship in a single convoy from Albany on 1 November 1914. During the journey one of the convoy's naval escorts—HMAS *Sydney*—engaged and destroyed the German cruiser SMS *Emden* at the Battle of Cocos on 8 November, in the first ship-to-ship action involving the Royal Australian Navy.[267] Although originally bound for England to undergo further training and then for employment on the Western Front, the Australians were instead sent to British-controlled Egypt to pre-empt any Turkish attack against the strategically important Suez Canal, and with a view to opening another front against the Central Powers.[268,269]

Aiming to knock Turkey out of the war the British then decided to stage an amphibious lodgement at Gallipoli and following a period of training and re-organisation the Australians were included amongst the British, Indian and French forces committed to the campaign. The combined Australian and New Zealand Army Corps (ANZAC)—commanded by British general William Birdwood—subsequently landed at Anzac Cove on the Gallipoli peninsula on 25 April 1915. Although promising to transform the war if successful, the Gallipoli Campaign was ill-conceived and ultimately lasted eight months of bloody stalemate, without achieving its objectives.[270] Australian casualties totalled 26,111, including 8,141 killed.[271]

For Australians and New Zealanders the Gallipoli campaign came to symbolise an important milestone in the emergence of both nations as independent

Figure 39: *Charge of the 4th Light Horse Brigade, 1917.*

actors on the world stage and the development of a sense of national identity.[272] Today, the date of the initial landings, 25 April, is known as Anzac Day in Australia and New Zealand and every year thousands of people gather at memorials in both nations, as well as Turkey, to honour the bravery and sacrifice of the original Anzacs, and of all those who have subsequently lost their lives in war.

Egypt and Palestine

After the withdrawal from Gallipoli the Australians returned to Egypt and the AIF underwent a major expansion. In 1916 the infantry began to move to France while the cavalry units remained in the Middle East to fight the Turks. Australian troops of the Anzac Mounted Division and the Australian Mounted Division saw action in all the major battles of the Sinai and Palestine Campaign, playing a pivotal role in fighting the Turkish troops that were threatening British control of Egypt.[273] The Australian's first saw combat during the Senussi uprising in the Libyan Desert and the Nile Valley, during which the combined British forces successfully put down the primitive pro-Turkish Islamic sect with heavy casualties.[274] The Anzac Mounted Division subsequently saw considerable action in the Battle of Romani against the Turkish between 3–5 August 1916, with the Turks eventually pushed back.[275] Following this victory the British forces went on the offensive in the Sinai, although the pace of the advance was governed by the speed by which the railway and water pipeline could be constructed from the Suez Canal. Rafa was captured on 9 January 1917, while the last of the small Turkish garrisons in the Sinai were eliminated in February.[276]

The advance entered Palestine and an initial, unsuccessful attempt was made to capture Gaza on 26 March 1917, while a second and equally unsuccessful attempt was launched on 19 April. A third assault occurred between 31 October and 7 November and this time both the Anzac Mounted Division and the Australian Mounted Division took part. The battle was a complete success for the British, over-running the Gaza-Beersheba line and capturing 12,000 Turkish soldiers. The critical moment was the capture of Beersheba on the first day, after the Australian 4th Light Horse Brigade charged more than 4 miles (6.4 km). The Turkish trenches were overrun, with the Australians capturing the wells at Beersheeba and securing the valuable water they contained along with over 700 prisoners for the loss of 31 killed and 36 wounded.[277] Later, Australian troops assisted in pushing the Turkish forces out of Palestine and took part in actions at Mughar Ridge, Jerusalem and the Megiddo. The Turkish government surrendered on 30 October 1918.[278] Units of the Light Horse were subsequently used to help put down a nationalist revolt in Egypt in 1919 and did so with efficiency and brutality, although they suffered a number of fatalities in the process.

Meanwhile, the AFC had undergone remarkable development, and its independence as a separate national force was unique among the Dominions. Deploying just a single aircraft to German New Guinea in 1914, the first operational flight did not occur until 27 May 1915 however, when the Mesopotamian Half Flight was called upon to assist in protecting British oil interests in Iraq. The AFC was soon expanded and four squadrons later saw action in Egypt, Palestine and on the Western Front, where they performed well.[279]

Western Front

Five infantry divisions of the AIF saw action in France and Belgium, leaving Egypt in March 1916.[280] I Anzac Corps subsequently took up positions in a quiet sector south of Armentières on 7 April 1916 and for the next two and a half years the AIF participated in most of the major battles on the Western Front, earning a formidable reputation. Although spared from the disastrous first day of the Battle of the Somme, within weeks four Australian divisions had been committed.[281] The 5th Division, positioned on the left flank, was the first in action during the Battle of Fromelles on 19 July 1916, suffering 5,533 casualties in a single day. The 1st Division entered the line on 23 July, assaulting Pozieres, and by the time that they were relieved by the 2nd Division on 27 July, they had suffered 5,286 casualties.[282] Mouquet Farm was attacked in August, with casualties totalling 6,300 men.[283] By the time the AIF was withdrawn from the Somme to re-organise, they had suffered 23,000 casualties in just 45 days.

Figure 40: *Soldiers of an 4th Division field artillery brigade on a duckboard track passing through Chateau Wood, near Hooge in the Ypres Salient, 1917.*

In March 1917, the 2nd and 5th Divisions pursued the Germans back to the Hindenburg Line, capturing the town of Bapaume. On 11 April, the 4th Division assaulted the Hindenburg Line in the disastrous First Battle of Bullecourt, losing over 3,000 casualties and 1,170 captured.[284] On 15 April, the 1st and 2nd Divisions were counter-attacked near Lagnicourt and were forced to abandon the town, before recapturing it again.[285] The 2nd Division then took part in the Second Battle of Bullecourt, beginning on 3 May, and succeeded in taking sections of the Hindenburg Line and holding them until relieved by the 1st Division. Finally, on 7 May the 5th Division relieved the 1st, remaining in the line until the battle ended in mid-May. Combined these efforts cost 7,482 Australian casualties.[286]

On 7 June 1917, the II Anzac Corps—along with two British corps—launched an operation in Flanders to eliminate a salient south of Ypres.[287] The attack commenced with the detonation of a million pounds (454,545 kg) of explosives that had been placed underneath the Messines ridge, destroying the German trenches.[288] The advance was virtually unopposed, and despite strong German counterattacks the next day, it succeeded. Australian casualties during the Battle of Messines included nearly 6,800 men.[289] I Anzac Corps then took part in the Third Battle of Ypres in Belgium as part of the campaign to capture the Gheluvelt Plateau, between September and November 1917. Individual

Figure 41: *Members of the 45th Battalion at the Battle of St. Quentin Canal in September 1918.*

actions took place at Menin Road, Polygon Wood, Broodseinde, Poelcappelle and Passchendaele and over the course of eight weeks fighting the Australians suffered 38,000 casualties.[290]

On 21 March 1918 the German Army launched its Spring Offensive in a last-ditched effort to win the war, unleashing sixty-three divisions over a 70 miles (110 km) front.[291] As the Allies fell back the 3rd and 4th Divisions were rushed south to Amiens on the Somme.[292] The offensive lasted for the next five months and all five AIF divisions in France were engaged in the attempt to stem the tide. By late May the Germans had pushed to within 50 miles (80 km) of Paris.[293] During this time the Australians fought at Dernancourt, Morlancourt, Villers-Bretonneux, Hangard Wood, Hazebrouck, and Hamel.[294] At Hamel the commander of the Australian Corps, Lieutenant General John Monash, successfully used combined arms—including aircraft, artillery and armour—in an attack for the first time.[295]

The German offensive ground to a halt in mid-July and a brief lull followed, during which the Australians undertook a series of raids, known as Peaceful Penetrations.[296] The Allies soon launched their own offensive—the Hundred Days Offensive—ultimately ending the war. Beginning on 8 August 1918 the offensive included four Australian divisions striking at Amiens.[297] Using the combined arms techniques developed earlier at Hamel, significant gains were made on what became known as the "Black Day" of the German Army.[298] The offensive continued for four months, and during Second Battle of the Somme the Australian Corps fought actions at Lihons, Etinehem, Proyart, Chuignes, and Mont St Quentin, before their final engagement of the war on 5 October 1918 at Montbrehain.[299] The AIF was subsequently out of the line when the armistice was declared on 11 November 1918.[300]

In all 416,806 Australians enlisted in the AIF during the war and 333,000 served overseas. 61,508 were killed and another 155,000 were wounded (a total casualty rate of 65%). The financial cost to the Australian government was calculated at £376,993,052.[301] Two referendums on conscription for overseas service had been defeated during the war, preserving the volunteer status of the Australian force, but stretching the reserves of manpower available, particularly towards the end of the fighting. Consequently, Australia remained one of only two armies on either side not to resort to conscription during the war.[302]

The war had a profound effect on Australian society in other ways also. Indeed, for many Australians the nation's involvement is seen as a symbol of its emergence as an international actor, while many of the notions of Australian character and nationhood that exist today have their origins in the war. 64 Australians were awarded the Victoria Cross during the First World War.

Inter-war years

Russian Civil War, 1918–19

The Russian Civil War began after the Russian provisional government collapsed and the Bolshevik party assumed power in October 1917. Following the end of the First World War, the western powers—including Britain—intervened, giving half-hearted support to the pro-tsarist, anti-Bolshevik White Russian forces. Although the Australian government refused to commit forces, many Australians serving with the British Army became involved in the fighting. A small number served as advisors to White Russian units with the North Russian Expeditionary Force (NREF). Awaiting repatriation in England, about 150 Australians subsequently enlisted in the British North Russia Relief Force (NRRF), where they were involved in a number of sharp battles and several were killed.[303]

The Royal Australian Navy destroyer HMAS *Swan* was also briefly engaged, carrying out an intelligence gathering mission in the Black Sea in late 1918. Other Australians served as advisers with the British Military Mission to the White Russian General, Anton Denikin in South Russia, while several more advised Admiral Aleksandr Kolchak in Siberia.[304] Later, they also served in Mesopotamia as part of Dunsterforce and the Malleson Mission, although these

Figure 42: *Australian soldiers of the North Russia Relief Force during the Allied intervention in the Russian Civil War, 1919.*

missions were aimed at preventing Turkish access to the Middle East and India, and did little fighting.[305]

Although the motivations of those Australian's that volunteered to fight in Russia can only be guessed at, it seems unlikely to have been political. Regardless, they confirmed a reputation for audacity and courage, winning the only two Victoria Crosses of the land campaign, despite their small numbers. Yet Australian involvement was barely noticed at home at the time and made little difference to the outcome of the war.[306] Total casualties included 10 killed and 40 wounded, with most deaths being from disease during operations in Mesopotamia.[307]

Malaita, 1927

In October 1927, HMAS *Adelaide* was called to the British Solomon Islands Protectorate as part of a punitive expedition in response to the killing of a district officer and sixteen others by Kwaio natives at Sinalagu on the island of Malaita on 3 October, known as the Malaita massacre. Arriving at Tulagi on 14 October, the ship proceeded to Malaita to protect the landing of three platoons of troops, then remained in the area to provide personnel support for the soldiers as they searched for the killers. The ship's personnel took no part in operations ashore, providing only logistic and communications support. *Adelaide* returned to Australia on 23 November.[308,309]

Spanish Civil War, 1936–39

A small number of Australian volunteers fought on both sides of the Spanish Civil War, although they predominantly supported the Spanish Republic through the International Brigades. The Australians were subsequently allocated to the battalions of other nationalities, such as the British Battalion and the Lincoln Battalion, rather than forming their own units. Most were radicals motivated by ideological reasons, while a number were Spanish-born migrants who returned to fight in their country of origin. At least 66 Australians volunteered, with only one—Nugent Bull, a conservative catholic who was later killed serving in the RAF during the Second World War—known to have fought for General Francisco Franco's Nationalist forces.[310]

While a celebrated cause for the Australian left—particularly the Communist Party of Australia and the trade union movement—the war failed to spark particular public interest and the government maintained its neutrality.[311] Australian opposition to the Republican cause was marshalled by B.A. Santamaria on an anti-communist basis, rather than a pro-Nationalist basis. Equally, although individual right wing Australians may have served with the Nationalist rebels, they received no public support. Service in a foreign armed force was illegal at the time, however as the government received no reports of Australians travelling to Spain to enlist, no action was taken.[312] Consequently, returned veterans were neither recognised by the government or the Returned and Services League of Australia (RSL). Although the number of Australian volunteers was relatively small compared to those from other countries, at least 14 were killed.[313]

Second World War, 1939–45

Europe and the Middle East

Australia entered the Second World War on 3 September 1939. At the time of the declaration of war against Germany the Australian military was small and unready for war.[314] Recruiting for a Second Australian Imperial Force (2nd AIF) began in mid-September. While there was no rush of volunteers like the First World War, a high proportion of Australian men of military age had enlisted by mid-1940. Four infantry divisions were formed during 1939 and 1940, three of which were dispatched to the Middle East.[315] The RAAF's resources were initially mainly devoted to training airmen for service with the Commonwealth air forces through the Empire Air Training Scheme (EATS), through which almost 28,000 Australians were trained during the war.[316]

The Australian military's first major engagements of the war were against Italian forces in the Mediterranean and North Africa. During 1940 the light cruiser

Figure 43: *The light cruiser HMAS Sydney in 1940.*

HMAS *Sydney* and five elderly destroyers (dubbed the "Scrap Iron Flotilla" by Nazi Propaganda Minister Joseph Goebbels—a title proudly accepted by the ships) took part in a series of operations as part of the British Mediterranean Fleet, and sank several Italian warships.[317] The Army first saw action in January 1941, when the 6th Division formed part of the Commonwealth forces during Operation Compass. The division assaulted and captured Bardia on 5 January and Tobruk on 22 January, with tens of thousands of Italian troops surrendering at both towns.[318] The 6th Division took part in the pursuit of the Italian Army and captured Benghazi on 4 February. In late February it was withdrawn for service in Greece, and was replaced by the 9th Division.[319]

The Australian forces in the Mediterranean endured a number of campaigns during 1941. During April, the 6th Division, other elements of I Corps and several Australian warships formed part of the Allied force which unsuccessfully attempted to defend Greece from German invasion during the Battle of Greece. At the end of this campaign, the 6th Division was evacuated to Egypt and Crete.[320] The force at Crete subsequently fought in the Battle of Crete during May, which also ended in defeat for the Allies. Over 5,000 Australians were captured in these campaigns, and the 6th Division required a long period of rebuilding before it was again ready for combat.[321] The Germans and Italians also went on the offensive in North Africa at the end of March and drove the Commonwealth force there back to near the border with Egypt. The 9th Division and a brigade of the 7th Division were besieged at Tobruk; successfully defending the key port town until they were replaced by British units

Figure 44: *Australian soldiers during the Siege of Tobruk, 1941.*

in October.[322] During June, the main body of the 7th Division, a brigade of the 6th Division and the I Corps headquarters took part in the Syria-Lebanon Campaign against the Vichy French. Resistance was stronger than expected; Australians were involved in most of the fighting and sustained most of the casualties before the French capitulated in early July.[323]

The majority of Australian units in the Mediterranean returned to Australia in early 1942, after the outbreak of the Pacific War. The 9th Division was the largest unit to remain in the Middle East, and played a key role in the First Battle of El Alamein during June and the Second Battle of El Alamein in October.[324] The division returned to Australia in early 1943, but several RAAF squadrons and RAN warships took part in the subsequent Tunisia Campaign and the Italian Campaign from 1943 until the end of the war.[325]

The RAAF's role in the strategic air offensive in Europe formed Australia's main contribution to the defeat of Germany. Approximately 13,000 Australian airmen served in dozens of British and five Australian squadrons in RAF Bomber Command between 1940 and the end of the war.[326] Australians took part in all of Bomber Command's major offensives and suffered heavy losses during raids on German cities and targets in France.[327] Australian aircrew in Bomber Command had one of the highest casualty rates of any part of the Australian military during the Second World War and sustained almost

Figure 45: *Members of No. 460 Squadron RAAF and the Lancaster bomber G for George in August 1943.*

Figure 46: *The Bombing of Darwin in 1942 was the largest single attack ever mounted by a foreign power on Australia.*

20 percent of all Australian deaths in combat; 3,486 were killed and hundreds more were taken prisoner.[328] Australian airmen in light bomber and fighter squadrons also participated in the liberation of Western Europe during 1944 and 1945[329] and two RAAF maritime patrol squadrons served in the Battle of the Atlantic.[330]

Asia and the Pacific

From the 1920s Australia's defence thinking was dominated by British Imperial defence policy, which was embodied by the "Singapore strategy". This strategy involved the construction and defence of a major naval base at Singapore from which a large British fleet would respond to Japanese aggression in the region. To this end, a high proportion of Australian forces in Asia were concentrated in Malaya during 1940 and 1941 as the threat from Japan increased.[331] However, as a result of the emphasis on co-operation with Britain, relatively few Australian military units had been retained in Australia and the Asia-Pacific region. Measures were taken to improve Australia's defences as war with Japan loomed in 1941, but these proved inadequate. In December 1941, the Australian Army in the Pacific comprised the 8th Division, most of which was stationed in Malaya, and eight partially trained and equipped divisions in Australia. The RAAF was equipped with 373 aircraft, most of which were obsolete trainers, and the RAN had three cruisers and two destroyers in Australian waters.[332]

The Australian military suffered a series of defeats during the early months of the Pacific War. The 8th Division and RAAF squadrons in Malaya formed a part of the British Commonwealth forces which were unable to stop a smaller Japanese invasion force which landed on 7 December. The British Commonwealth force withdrew to Singapore at the end of January, but was forced to surrender on 15 February after the Japanese captured much of the island.[333] Smaller Australian forces were also overwhelmed and defeated during early 1942 at Rabaul, and in Ambon, Timor, and Java.[334] The Australian town of Darwin was heavily bombed by the Japanese on 19 February, to prevent it from being used as an Allied base.[335] Over 22,000 Australians were taken prisoner in early 1942 and endured harsh conditions in Japanese captivity. The prisoners were subjected to malnutrition, denied medical treatment and frequently beaten and killed by their guards. As a result, 8,296 Australian prisoners died in captivity.[336]

The rapid Allied defeat in the Pacific caused many Australians to fear that the Japanese would invade the Australian mainland. While elements of the Imperial Japanese Navy proposed this in early 1942, it was judged to be impossible by the Japanese Imperial General Headquarters, which instead adopted a strategy of isolating Australia from the United States by capturing New Guinea, the Solomon Islands, Fiji, Samoa, and New Caledonia.[337] This fact was not known by the Allies at the time, and the Australian military was greatly expanded to meet the threat of invasion. Large numbers of United States Army and Army Air Forces units arrived in Australia in early 1942, and the Australian military was placed under the overall command of General Douglas MacArthur in March.[338]

Australians played a central role in the New Guinea campaign during 1942 and 1943. After an attempt to land troops at Port Moresby was defeated in the Battle of the Coral Sea, the Japanese attempted to capture the strategically

Figure 47: *Australian infantry and tanks during the final assault on Buna, 1943.*

important town by advancing overland across the Owen Stanley Ranges and Milne Bay. Australian Army units defeated these offensives in the Kokoda Track campaign and Battle of Milne Bay with the support of the RAAF and USAAF.[339] Australian and US Army units subsequently assaulted and captured the Japanese bases on the north coast of Papua in the hard-fought Battle of Buna-Gona.[340] The Australian Army also defeated a Japanese attempt to capture the town of Wau in January 1943 and went onto the offensive in the Salamaua-Lae campaign in April. In late 1943, the 7th and 9th Divisions played an important role in Operation Cartwheel, when they landed to the east and west of Lae and secured the Huon Peninsula during the Huon Peninsula campaign and Finisterre Range campaign.[341]

The Australian mainland came under attack during 1942 and 1943. Japanese submarines operated off Australia from May to August 1942 and January to June 1943. These attacks sought to cut the Allied supply lines between Australia and the US and Australia and New Guinea, but were unsuccessful. On 14 May 1943 the hospital ship AHS *Centaur* was sunk by a Japanese submarine off Brisbane with the loss of 268 lives.[342] Japanese aircraft also conducted air raids against Allied bases in northern Australia which were being used to mount the North Western Area Campaign against Japanese positions in the Netherlands East Indies (NEI).[343]

Figure 48: *Australian-designed CAC Boomerang aircraft at Bougainville in early 1945.*

Australia's role in the Pacific War declined from 1944. The increasing size of the US forces in the Pacific rendered the Australian military superfluous and labour shortages forced the Government to reduce the size of the armed forces to boost war production.[344] Nevertheless, the Government wanted the Australian military to remain active, and agreed to MacArthur's proposals that it be used in relatively unimportant campaigns. In late 1944, Australian troops and RAAF squadrons replaced US garrisons in eastern New Guinea, New Britain, and Bougainville, and launched offensives aimed at destroying or containing the remaining Japanese forces there. In May 1945, I Corps, the Australian First Tactical Air Force and USAAF and USN units began the Borneo Campaign, which continued until the end of the war. These campaigns contributed little to Japan's defeat and remain controversial.[345]

Following Japan's surrender on 15 August 1945 Australia assumed responsibility for occupying much of Borneo and the eastern Netherlands East Indies until British and Dutch colonial rule was restored. Australian authorities also conducted a number of war crimes trials of Japanese personnel. 993,000 Australians enlisted during the war, while 557,000 served overseas. Casualties included 39,767 killed and another 66,553 were wounded.[346] 20 Victoria Crosses were awarded to Australians.

Figure 49: *Australian Guard of Honour, at the British Commonwealth Occupation Force headquarters, 1946.*

Post-war period

Demobilisation and peace-time defence arrangements

The demobilisation of the Australian military following the end of the Second World War was completed in 1947. Plans for post-war defence arrangements were predicated on maintaining a relatively strong peacetime force. It was envisioned the Royal Australian Navy would maintain a fleet that would include two light fleet carriers, two cruisers, six destroyers, 16 others ships in commission and another 52 in reserve. The Royal Australian Air Force would have a strength of 16 squadrons, including four manned by the Citizen Air Force. Meanwhile, in a significant departure from past Australian defence policy which had previously relied on citizen forces, the Australian Army would include a permanent field force of 19,000 regulars organised into a brigade of three infantry battalions with armoured support, serving alongside a part-time force of 50,000 men in the Citizen Military Forces.[347] The Australian Regular Army was subsequently formed on 30 September 1947, while the CMF was re-raised on 1 July 1948.[348]

Occupation of Japan, 1946–52

In the immediate post-war period Australia contributed significant forces to the Allied occupation of Japan as part of the British Commonwealth Occupation Force (BCOF), which included forces from Australia, Britain, India and

New Zealand.³⁴⁹ At its height in 1946 the Australian component consisted of an infantry brigade, four warships and three fighter squadrons, totalling 13,500 personnel.³⁵⁰ The Australian Army component initially consisted of the 34th Brigade which arrived in Japan in February 1946 and was based in Hiroshima Prefecture.³⁵¹,³⁵² The three infantry battalions raised for occupation duties were designated the 1st, 2nd and 3rd battalions of the Royal Australian Regiment in 1949, and the 34th Brigade became the 1st Brigade when it returned to Australia in December 1948, forming the basis of the post-war Regular Army. From that time the Australian Army contribution to the occupation of Japan was reduced to a single under-strength battalion. Australian forces remained until September 1951 when the BCOF ceased operations, although by that time the majority of units had been committed to the fighting on the Korean peninsula following the outbreak of the Korean War in 1950.³⁵³ The RAAF component consisted of Nos. 76, 77 and 82 Squadrons as part of No. 81 Wing RAAF flying P-51 Mustangs, initially based at Bofu from March 1946, before transferring to Iwakuni in 1948. However, by 1950 only No. 77 Squadron remained in Japan.³⁵⁴ A total of ten RAN warships served in Japan during this period, including HMA Ships *Australia*, *Hobart*, *Shropshire*, *Arunta*, *Bataan*, *Culgoa*, *Murchison*, *Shoalhaven*, *Quadrant* and *Quiberon*, while HMAS Ships *Manoora*, *Westralia* and *Kanimbla* also provided support.³⁵⁵

Cold War

Early planning and commitments

During the early years of the Cold War, Australian defence planning assumed that in the event of the outbreak of a global war between the Western world and Eastern bloc countries it would need to contribute forces under collective security arrangements as part of the United Nations, or a coalition led by either the United States or Britain. The Middle East was considered the most likely area of operations for Australian forces, where they were expected to operate with British forces.³⁵⁶ Early commitments included the involvement of RAAF aircrew during the Berlin Airlift in 1948–49 and the deployment of No. 78 Wing RAAF to Malta in the Mediterranean from 1952 to 1954.³⁵⁷ Meanwhile, defence preparedness initiatives included the introduction of a National Service Scheme in 1951 to provide manpower for the citizen forces of the Army, RAAF and RAN.³⁵⁸,³⁵⁹

Figure 50: *Members of 3rd Battalion, Royal Australian Regiment move forward in 1951.*

Korean War, 1950–53

On 25 June 1950, the North Korean Army (KPA) crossed the border into South Korea and advanced for the capital Seoul, which fell in less than a week. North Korean forces continued toward the port of Pusan and two days later the United States offered its assistance to South Korea. In response the United Nations Security Council requested members to assist in repelling the North Korean attack. Australia initially contributed P-51 Mustang fighter-bomber aircraft from No. 77 Squadron RAAF and infantry from the 3rd Battalion, Royal Australian Regiment (3 RAR), both of which were stationed in Japan as part of the BCOF. In addition, it provided the majority of supply and support personnel to the British Commonwealth Forces Korea. The RAN frigate HMAS *Shoalhaven*, and the destroyer HMAS *Bataan*, were also committed. Later, an aircraft carrier strike group aboard HMAS *Sydney* was added to the force.[360]

By the time 3 RAR arrived in Pusan on 28 September, the North Koreans were in retreat following the Inchon landings. As a part of the invasion force under the UN Supreme Commander, General Douglas MacArthur, the battalion moved north and was involved in its first major action at Battle of Yongju near Pyongyang on 22 October, before advancing towards the Yalu River.[361] Further successful actions followed at Kujin on 25–26 October 1950 and at Chongju on 29 October 1950.[362] North Korean casualties were heavy,

Figure 51: *Firefly aircraft on board HMAS Sydney off Korea.*

while Australian losses included their commanding officer, Lieutenant Colonel Charles Green, who was wounded in the stomach by artillery fire after the battle and succumbed to his wounds and died two days later on 1 November.[363] Meanwhile, during the last weeks of October the Chinese had moved 18 divisions of the People's Volunteer Army across the Yalu River to reinforce the remnants of the KPA. Undetected by US and South Korean intelligence, the 13th Army Group crossed the border on 16 October and penetrated up to 100 kilometres (62 mi) into North Korea, and were reinforced in early November by 12 divisions from the 9th Army Group; in total 30 divisions composed of 380,000 men.[364] 3 RAR fought its first action against the Chinese at Pakchon on 5 November.[365] The fighting cost the battalion heavily and despite halting a Chinese division the new battalion commander was dismissed in the wake.[366] Following the Chinese intervention, the UN forces were defeated in successive battles and 3 RAR was forced to withdraw to the 38th parallel.

A series of battles followed at Uijeongbu on 1–4 January 1951, as the British and Australians occupied defensive positions in an attempt to secure the northern approaches to the South Korean capital. Further fighting occurred at Chuam-ni on 14–17 February 1951 following another Chinese advance, and later at Maehwa-San between 7–12 March 1951 as the UN resumed the offensive.[367] Australian troops subsequently participated in two more major battles in 1951, with the first taking place during fighting which later became known as the Battle of Kapyong. On 22 April, Chinese forces attacked the Kapyong valley and forced the South Korean defenders to withdraw. Australian and Canadian troops were ordered to halt this Chinese advance. After a night of fighting the Australians recaptured their positions, at the cost of 32 men killed and 59 wounded.[368] In July 1951, the Australian battalion became part of the combined Canadian, British, Australian, New Zealand, and Indian 1st Commonwealth Division. The second major battle took place during Operation Commando and occurred after the Chinese attacked a salient in a bend of the Imjin River. The 1st Commonwealth Division counter-attacked on 3 October, capturing a number of objectives including Hill 355 and Hill 317 during the Battle of Maryang San; after five days the Chinese retreated. Australian casualties included 20 dead and 104 wounded.[369]

The belligerents then became locked in static trench warfare akin to the First World War, in which men lived in tunnels, redoubts, and sandbagged forts behind barbed wire defences. From 1951 until the end of the war, 3 RAR held trenches on the eastern side of the division's positions in the hills northeast of the Imjin River. Across from them were heavily fortified Chinese positions. In March 1952, Australia increased its ground commitment to two battalions, sending 1 RAR. This battalion remained in Korea for 12 months, before being replaced by 2 RAR in April 1953.[370] The Australians fought their last battle during 24–26 July 1953, with 2 RAR holding off a concerted Chinese attack along the Samichon River and inflicting significant casualties for the loss of five killed and 24 wounded.[371] Hostilities were suspended on 27 July 1953. 17,808 Australians served during the war, with 341 killed, 1,216 wounded and 30 captured.[372]

Malayan Emergency, 1950–60

The Malayan Emergency was declared on 18 June 1948, after three estate managers were murdered by members of the Malayan Communist Party (MCP).[373] Australian involvement began in June 1950, when in response to a British request, six Lincolns from No. 1 Squadron and a flight of Dakotas from No. 38 Squadron arrived in Singapore to form part of the British Commonwealth Far East Air Force (FEAF). The Dakotas were subsequently used on cargo runs, troop movement, as well as paratroop and leaflet drops, while the Lincoln bombers carried out bombing raids against the Communist Terrorist (CT) jungle bases.[374] The RAAF were particularly successful, and in one such mission known as Operation Termite, five Lincoln bombers destroyed 181 communist camps, killed 13 communists and forced one into surrender, in a joint operation with the RAF and ground troops. The Lincolns were withdrawn in 1958, and were replaced by Canberra bombers from No. 2 Squadron and CAC

Figure 52: *A Lincoln from No. 1 Squadron RAAF bombing communist targets during the Malayan Emergency, c. 1950.*

Sabres from No. 78 Wing. Based at RAAF Base Butterworth they also carried out a number ground attack missions against the guerrillas.[375]

Australian ground forces were deployed to Malaya in October 1955 as part of the Far East Strategic Reserve. In January 1956, the first Australian ground forces were deployed on Malaysian peninsula, consisting of the 2nd Battalion, Royal Australian Regiment (2 RAR). 2 RAR mainly participated in "mopping up" operations over the next 20 months, conducting extensive patrolling in and near the CT jungle bases, as part of 28th British Commonwealth Brigade. Contact with the enemy was infrequent and results small, achieving relatively few kills. 2 RAR left Malaysia October 1957 to be replaced by 3 RAR. 3 RAR underwent six weeks of jungle training and began driving MCP insurgents back into the jungle of Perak and Kedah. The new battalion extensively patrolled and was involved in food denial operations and ambushes. Again contact was limited, although 3 RAR had more success than its predecessor. By late 1959, operations against the MCP were in their final phase, and most communists had been pushed back and across the Thailand border. 3 RAR left Malaysia October 1959 and was replaced by 1 RAR. Though patrolling the border 1 RAR did not make contact with the insurgents, and in October 1960 it was replaced by 2 RAR, which stayed in Malaysia until August 1963. The Malayan Emergency officially ended on 31 July 1960.

Figure 53: *HMAS Perth* firing on North Vietnamese targets in 1968. Perth joined the fleet in 1965 as part of the RAN's naval expansion program.

Australia also provided artillery and engineer support, along with an air-field construction squadron. The Royal Australian Navy also served in Malayan waters, firing on suspected communist positions between 1956 and 1957. The Emergency was the longest continued commitment in Australian military history; 7,000 Australians served and 51 died in Malaya—although only 15 were on operations—and another 27 were wounded.

Military and Naval growth during the 1960s

At the start of the 1960s, Prime Minister Robert Menzies greatly expanded the Australian military so that it could carry out the Government's policy of "Forward Defence" in South East Asia. In 1964, Menzies announced a large increase in defence spending. The strength of the Australian Army would be increased by 50% over three years from 22,000 to 33,000; providing a full three-brigade division with nine battalions. The RAAF and RAN would also both be increased by 25%. In 1964, conscription or National Service was re-introduced under the *National Service Act*, for selected 20-year-olds based on date of birth, for a period of two years' continuous full-time service (the previous scheme having been suspended in 1959).[376]

In 1961, three *Charles F. Adams*-class destroyers were purchased from the United States to replace the ageing Q-class destroyers. Traditionally, the RAN

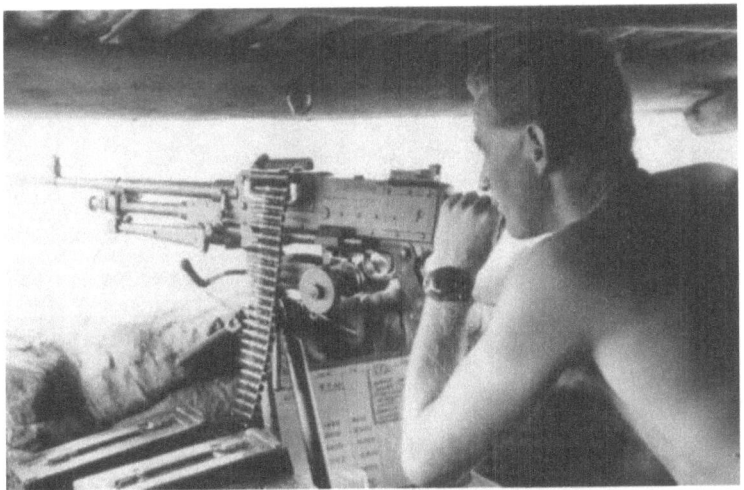

Figure 54: *An Australian soldier manning the machine gun while on guard duty in Borneo during 1965*

had purchased designs based on those of the Royal Navy and the purchase of American destroyers was significant. HMAS *Perth* and HMAS *Hobart* joined the fleet in 1965, followed by HMAS *Brisbane* in 1967. Other projects included the construction of six River-class frigates, the conversion of the aircraft carrier HMAS *Melbourne* to an anti-submarine role, the acquisition of ten Wessex helicopters, and the purchase of six *Oberon*-class submarines.[377]

The RAAF took delivery of their first Mirage fighters in 1967, equipping No. 3, No. 75 and No. 77 Squadrons with them. The service also received American F-111 strike aircraft, C-130 Hercules transports, P-3 Orion maritime reconnaissance aircraft and Italian Macchi trainers.[378]

Indonesia-Malaysia Confrontation, 1962–66

The Indonesia-Malaysia confrontation was fought from 1962 to 1966 between the British Commonwealth and Indonesia over the creation of the Federation of Malaysia, with the Commonwealth attempting to safeguard the security of the new state. The war remained limited, and was fought primarily on the island of Borneo, although a number of Indonesian seaborne and airborne incursions onto the Malay Peninsula did occur.[379] As part of Australia's continuing military commitment to the security of Malaysia, army, naval and airforce units were based there as part of the Far East Strategic Reserve. Regardless the Australian government was wary of involvement in a war with Indonesia and initially limited its involvement to the defence of the Malayan peninsula

Figure 55: *A RAAF UH-1 Iroquois landing at Terendak Camp in 1964.*

only. On two occasions Australian troops from 3 RAR were used to help mop up infiltrators from seaborne and airborne incursions at Labis and Pontian, in September and October 1964.

Following these raids the government conceded to British and Malaysian requests to deploy an infantry battalion to Borneo. During the early phases, British and Malaysian troops had attempted only to control the Malaysian/Indonesian border, and to protect population centres. However, by the time the Australian battalion deployed the British had decided on more aggressive action, crossing the border into Kalimantan to obtain information and conduct ambushes to force the Indonesians to remain on the defensive, under the codename Operation Claret. The fighting took place in mountainous, jungle-clad terrain, and a debilitating climate, with operations characterised by the extensive use of company bases sited along the border, cross-border operations, the use of helicopters for troop movement and resupply, and the role of human and signals intelligence to determine enemy movements and intentions.[380]

3 RAR deployed to Borneo in March 1965, and served in Sarawak until the end of July, operating on both sides of the border. The battalion had four major contacts with Indonesian forces and several smaller ones—including at Sungei Koemba, Kindau and Babang during which they inflicted heavy casualties on the Indonesians—as well as suffering casualties in two mine incidents. 4 RAR served a less-eventful tour between April and August 1966, and also operated over the border, successfully clashing with the Indonesians on a number of

Figure 56: *An iconic image of Australian soldiers from 7 RAR waiting to be picked up by UH-1 Iroquois helicopters following a routine cordon and search operation.*

occasions. A squadron of the Special Air Service Regiment (SASR) was also deployed in 1965 and again in 1966, taking part in cross-border operations and inflicting significant casualties on the Indonesians, even though they were often tasked with covert reconnaissance.[381] Other units included artillery and engineers, while a number of RAN ships were involved in shelling Indonesian positions in Borneo and in repelling infiltrators in the Singapore Strait. The RAAF played a relatively minor role, although it would have been used far more extensively had the war escalated.[382,383]

Operations in Borneo were extremely sensitive and they received little press coverage in Australia, while official acknowledgement of involvement in cross-border missions only occurred in 1996. Following a military coup in Indonesia in early 1966 which brought General Suharto to power, a peace treaty was signed in August 1966 which ended the conflict. 3,500 Australians served during Confrontation; casualties included 16 dead, with seven killed in action and eight wounded.

Vietnam War, 1962–73

Australia's involvement in the Vietnam War was driven largely by the rise of communism in Southeast Asia after the Second World War, and the fear of its spread which developed in Australia during the 1950s and early 1960s.[384] As a consequence, Australia supported South Vietnam throughout the early 1960s. In 1961 and 1962, the leader of the South Vietnamese government, Ngo Dinh Diem, asked for assistance from the US and its allies in response to a growing insurgency supported by communist North Vietnam. Australia offered 30 military advisors from the Australian Army Training Team Vietnam, which became known simply as "The Team". They arrived in July and August 1962, beginning Australia's involvement in the war. Later in August 1964, the RAAF sent a flight of Caribou transport aircraft to the port city of Vung Tau.[385]

However, with the security situation in South Vietnam continuing to deteriorate, the US increased its involvement to 200,000 combat troops by early 1965. Australia also committed ground forces, dispatching the 1 RAR to serve with the US 173rd Airborne Brigade in Bien Hoa province in June 1965 and it subsequently fought a number of significant actions, including Gang Toi, Operation Crimp and Suoi Bong Trang. In March 1966, the Australian government announced the deployment of a brigade-sized unit—the 1st Australian Task Force (1 ATF)—to replace 1 RAR. Included were a large number of conscripts, under the increasingly controversial National Service Scheme. Consisting of two infantry battalions as well as armour, aviation, artillery and other support arms, the task force was assigned primary responsibility for its own area and was based at Nui Dat, in Phuoc Tuy Province. Included were the Iroquois helicopters of No. 9 Squadron RAAF. At the Battle of Long Tan on 18 August 1966, D Company, 6 RAR with considerable artillery support held off and defeated a Viet Cong force that was at least six times bigger than itself. 18 Australians were killed and 24 wounded, while 245 communist dead were later recovered from the battlefield.[386] The battle allowed the Australians to gain dominance over Phuoc Tuy Province and 1 ATF was not fundamentally challenged again.[387] Regardless, during February 1967 the Australians suffered their heaviest casualties in the war to that point, losing 16 men killed and 55 wounded in a single week, the bulk during Operation Bribie.[388]

Yet with the Phuoc Tuy province coming progressively under control throughout 1967, the Australians increasingly spent a significant period of time conducting operations further afield.[389] 1 ATF was subsequently deployed astride infiltration routes leading to Saigon to interdict communist movement against the capital as part of Operation Coburg during the 1968 Tet Offensive and later during the Battle of Coral–Balmoral in May and June 1968. At Fire Support Bases Coral and Balmoral the Australians had clashed with regular North Vietnamese Army and Viet Cong main force units operating in battalion and regimental strength for the first time in near conventional warfare, ultimately fighting their largest, most hazardous and most sustained battle of the war. During 26 days of fighting Australian casualties included 25 killed and 99 wounded,

Figure 57: *Personnel and aircraft of RAAF Transport Flight Vietnam arrive in South Vietnam in 1964.*

while communist casualties included 267 killed confirmed by body count, 60 possibly killed, 7 wounded and 11 captured.[390] Other significant Australian actions included Binh Ba in June 1969, Hat Dich in late-December 1968 and early 1969 and Long Khanh in June 1971. At the height of the Australian commitment, 1 ATF numbered 8,500 troops, including three infantry battalions, armour, artillery, engineers, logistics and aviation units in support. A third RAAF unit, No. 2 Squadron RAAF, flying Canberra bombers, was sent in 1967, and four RAN destroyers joined US patrols in the waters off North Vietnam.[391]

The Australian withdrawal effectively commenced in November 1970. As a consequence of the overall allied strategy of Vietnamization and with the Australian government keen to reduce its own commitment to the war, 8 RAR was not replaced at the end of its tour of duty. 1 ATF was again reduced to just two infantry battalions, albeit with significant armour, artillery and aviation support remaining.[392] Australian combat forces were further reduced during 1971 as part of a phased withdrawal, and 1 ATF ceased operations in October. Meanwhile, the advisors remained to train South Vietnamese troops until withdrawn on 18 December 1972 by the newly elected Labor government of Gough Whitlam. The last Australian forces were finally withdrawn in 1973.

Figure 58: *The Russell Offices complex in Canberra houses the Australian Defence Force administrative headquarters. The three military branches amalgamated into the ADF in 1976.*

The Vietnam War was Australia's longest and most controversial war and although initially enjoying broad support, as the nation's military involvement increased a vocal anti-war movement developed.[393] More than 50,000 Australians served in Vietnam; 519 were killed and 2,398 were wounded. Four were awarded the Victoria Cross.

Post-Vietnam era

Creation of the Australian Defence Force, 1976

Although the importance of 'joint' warfare had been highlighted during Second World War when Australian naval, ground and air units frequently served as part of single commands, the absence of a central authority continued to result in poor co-ordination between the services in the post-war era, with each organising and operating on the basis of a different military doctrine.[394] The need for an integrated command structure received more emphasis during the Australian military's experiences in the Vietnam War. In 1973, the Secretary of the Department of Defence, Arthur Tange, submitted a report to the Government that recommended the unification of the separate departments supporting each service into a single department and the creation of the post of Chief of the Defence Force Staff.[395]

The Whitlam Labor Government subsequently amalgamated the five defence ministries (Defence, Navy, Army, Air Force, and Supply) into a single Department of Defence in 1973, while conscription under the National Service scheme was abolished. On 1 January 1976, the three branches of the Australian military were brought together as a unified, all-volunteer, professional force known as the Australian Defence Force (ADF).[396] Today, the ADF is headquartered at Russell Offices in Canberra and is divided into Air, Land, Maritime and Special Operations Commands. In addition, Northern Command is based in Darwin, and is responsible for operations in Northern Australia.[397]

Defence of Australia, 1980s and 1990s

Until the 1970s, Australia's military strategy centred on the concept of *Forward Defence*, in which the role of Australian military and naval forces were to co-operate with Allied forces to counter threats in Australia's region. Following the adoption of the Guam Doctrine by the United States in 1969, and the British withdrawal 'east of Suez' in the early 1970s, Australia developed a defence policy emphasising self-reliance and the defence of the Australian continent. Known as the Defence of Australia Policy, it focused Australian defence planning on protecting the nation's northern maritime approaches (the 'air-sea gap') against possible attack.[398]

In line with this goal, the ADF was restructured to increase its ability to strike at enemy forces from Australian bases and to counter raids on continental Australia. This was achieved by increasing the capabilities of the RAN and RAAF, and relocating regular Army units to Northern Australia.[399] During this time the ADF had no military units on operational deployment outside Australia. However, in 1987 the ADF made its first operational deployment as part of Operation Morris Dance, in which several warships and a rifle company deployed to the waters off Fiji in response to the 1987 Fijian coups d'état. While broadly successful, this deployment highlighted the need for the ADF to improve its capability to rapidly respond to unforeseen events.[400]

During this period Australia continued to retain forces in Malaysia as part of the Five Power Defence Arrangements (FPDA) agreed in 1971 to defend it in the event of external attack, with this commitment initially including significant air, ground and naval forces. However, these forces were gradually reduced with the infantry battalion withdrawn from Singapore in 1973, and the two Mirage fighter squadrons in 1988. Since then a detachment of Orion maritime patrol aircraft, support personnel, and an infantry company known as Rifle Company

Figure 59: *HMAS Sydney in the Persian Gulf in 1991.*

Butterworth have been maintained, as well as occasional deployments of F/A-18 Hornet fighter aircraft.[401,402] Australian submarines reportedly undertook a number of clandestine surveillance missions throughout Asian waters in the last decades of the Cold War. Airforce and Navy units were also involved in tracking Soviet ship and submarine movements in the region. Since then the Orions have continued to participate in maritime security operations as part of Operation Gateway, conducting patrols over the Indian Ocean, Strait of Malacca and South China Sea. They have reportedly also been involved in freedom of navigation flights.

Gulf War, 1991

Australia was a member of the international coalition which contributed military forces to the 1991 Gulf War, deploying a naval task group of two warships, a support ship and a clearance diving team; in total about 750 personnel. The Australian contribution was the first time Australian personnel were deployed to an active war zone since the establishment of the ADF and the deployment tested its capabilities and command structure. However, the Australian force did not see combat, and instead playing a significant role in enforcing the sanctions put in place against Iraq following the invasion of Kuwait. Some ADF personnel serving on exchange with British and American units did see combat, and a few were later decorated for their actions.[403] Following the war, the Navy regularly deployed a frigate to the Persian Gulf or Red Sea to enforce the trade sanctions which continued to be applied to Iraq.[404] A number of Australian airmen and ground crew posted to or on exchange with US and British air forces subsequently participated in enforcing no-fly zones imposed over Iraq between 1991 and 2003.

Global security, late-1990s

Since the late 1980s, the Australian government had increasingly called upon the ADF to contribute forces to peacekeeping missions around the world. While most of these deployments involved only small numbers of specialists, several led to the deployment of hundreds of personnel. Large peacekeeping deployments were made to Namibia in early 1989, Cambodia between 1992 and 1993, Somalia in 1993, Rwanda between 1994 and 1995 and Bougainville in 1994 and from 1997 onwards.[405] The 1996 election of the Howard Liberal government resulted in significant reforms to the ADF's force structure and role, with the new government's defence strategy placed less singular emphasis on defending Australia from direct attack and greater emphasis on working in co-operation with regional states and Australia's allies to manage potential security threats in recognition of Australia's global security interests. In line with this new focus, the ADF's force structure changed in an attempt to increase the proportion of combat units to support units and to improve the ADF's combat effectiveness.[406]

New Millennium

East Timor, 1999–2013

The former-Portuguese colony of East Timor was invaded by Indonesia in 1975, however, following years of violent struggle the new Indonesian government of President B.J. Habibie subsequently agreed to allow the East Timorese to vote on autonomy in 1999. The United Nations Mission in East Timor (UNAMET) was established to organise and conduct the vote, which was held at the end of August 1999 and resulted with 78.5% of voters deciding in favour of independence. However, following the announcement of the results pro-Indonesian militias supported by elements of the Indonesian military, launched a campaign of violence, looting and arson and many East Timorese were killed, while perhaps more than 500,000 were displaced. Unable to control the violence, Indonesia subsequently agreed to the deployment of a multinational peacekeeping force. Australia, which had contributed police to UNAMET, organised and led an international military coalition, known as the International Force for East Timor (INTERFET), a non-UN force operating in accordance

Figure 60: *Australian members of International Force East Timor, 2000.*

with UN resolutions. The total size of the Australian force committed numbered 5,500 personnel, and included a significant ground force, supported by air and naval forces,[407] in the largest single deployment of Australian forces since 1945.[408]

Under the overall command of Australian Major General Peter Cosgrove, INTERFET began arriving on 12 September 1999 and was tasked with restoring peace and security, protecting and supporting UNAMET, and facilitating humanitarian assistance operations. With the withdrawal of the Indonesian armed forces, police and government officials from East Timor, UNAMET re-established its headquarters in Dili on 28 September. On 19 October 1999, Indonesia formally recognised the result of the referendum and shortly thereafter a UN peacekeeping force, the United Nations Transitional Administration in East Timor (UNTAET) was established, becoming fully responsible for the administration of East Timor during its transition to independence. The hand-over of command of military operations from INTERFET to UNTAET was completed on 28 February 2000. Australia continued to support the UN peacekeeping operation with between 1,500 and 2,000 personnel, as well as landing craft and Blackhawk helicopters and remained the largest contributor of personnel to the peacekeeping mission. During these operations Australian forces regularly clashed with pro-Indonesian militia and on a number of occasions Indonesian forces as well, especially along the border with West Timor. Significant actions occurred in Suai, Mota'ain and at Aidabasalala in October

1999. However, with the security situation stabilised the bulk of the Australian and UN forces were withdrawn by 2005. Two Australians died from non-battle related causes, while a number were wounded in action.

The unexpected deployment to East Timor in 1999 led to significant changes in Australian defence policy and to an enhancement of the ADF's ability to conduct operations outside Australia. This successful deployment was the first time a large Australian military force had operated outside of Australia since the Vietnam War and revealed shortcomings in the ADF's ability to mount and sustain such operations. In response, the 2000 Defence White Paper placed a greater emphasis on preparing the ADF for overseas deployments. The Australian government committed to improve the ADF's capabilities by improving the readiness and equipment of ADF units, expanding the ADF to 57,000 full-time personnel and increasing real Defence expenditure by 3% per year.[409]

In May 2006, 2,000 ADF personnel were again deployed to East Timor as part of Operation Astute, following unrest between elements of the Timor Leste Defence Force. Australian forces were involved in a number skirmishes during this time, including a heavy clash with rebels commanded by Alfredo Reinado at Same on 4 March 2007. However, by early-2010 the security situation had been stabilised and just 400 Australian personnel remained to train the local security forces as part of a small international force. Following a drawdown, the International Stabilisation Force commenced withdrawing from Timor-Leste in November 2012, a process which was completed in April 2013.

Afghanistan, 2001–present

Shortly after the Islamist inspired terrorist attacks in New York and Washington on 11 September 2001, Australian forces were committed to the American-led international coalition against terrorism. The ADF's most visible contribution—codenamed Operation Slipper—has been a special forces task group operating in Afghanistan from 2001 to 2002 and again from mid-2005 to fight against the Taliban. Over time the Australian commitment has grown, with the addition of further ground forces in the form of a Reconstruction Task Force from 2006 to provide security, reconstruction and to mentor and train the Afghan National Army. Australia has also contributed a frigate and two AP-3C Orion surveillance aircraft and three C-130 Hercules transport aircraft to international operations in the Persian Gulf and Indian Ocean since 2001, supporting both the operations in Afghanistan and those in Iraq under Operation Catalyst. A detachment of four F/A-18 Hornet fighter-bombers was based at Diego Garcia from late-2001 to mid-2002, while two Boeing 707 air-to-air refuelling aircraft were also based in Manas Air Base in Kyrgyzstan to provide support to coalition aircraft operating in Afghan airspace but were later

Figure 61: *Members of 3 RAR on a foot patrol in Tarinkot, 2008.*

withdrawn.[410] A Special Operations Task Group was deployed to support the Reconstruction Taskforce in April 2007. In addition to radar crews, logistics and intelligence officers, and security personnel, this brought the number of Australian personnel in Afghanistan to 950 by mid-2007, with further small increases to 1,000 in mid-2008, 1,100 in early 2009 and 1,550 in mid-2009.

A modest force remained in Afghanistan over this time and was involved in counter-insurgency operations in Uruzgan Province in conjunction United States and other coalition forces, including the Dutch prior to their withdrawal. The force consisted of motorised infantry, special forces, engineers, cavalry, artillery and aviation elements. By 2010 it included a combined arms battalion-sized battle group known as the Mentoring Task Force, and the Special Operations Task Group, both based at Forward Operation Base Ripley outside of Tarin Kowt, as well as the Rotary Wing Group flying CH-47D Chinooks, the Force Logistics Asset and an RAAF air surveillance radar unit based in Kandahar.[411,412] In addition, a further 800 Australian logistic personnel were also based in the Middle East in support, but are located outside of Afghanistan. Meanwhile, detachments of maritime patrol and transport aircraft continued to support operations in Iraq and Afghanistan, based out of Al Minhad Air Base in the United Arab Emirates. Also included is the deployment of one of the RAN's frigates to the Arabian Sea and Gulf of Aden on counter piracy and maritime interdiction duties.[413]

Figure 62: *An ASLAV providing security for ground troops in the Tangi Valley in 2010.*

Australian forces were at times involved in heavy fighting, and significant actions included Operation Anaconda in 2002 and Operation Perth in 2006, as well as actions in Chora in 2007, Kakarak in 2009, the Shah Wali Kot and Derapet in 2010, and Doan in 2011; although others have yet to be publicly acknowledged due to operational security requirements. Casualties include 41 killed and 256 wounded, while another Australian also died serving with the British Army. Four Australians have been awarded the Victoria Cross for Australia, the first such decorations in forty years. Following a drawdown in forces, the last combat troops were withdrawn on 15 December 2013; however, approximately 400 personnel remain in Afghanistan as trainers and advisers, and are stationed in Kandahar and Kabul. Over 26,000 Australian personnel have served in Afghanistan.

Iraq, 2003–11

Australian forces later joined British and American forces during the 2003 invasion of Iraq. The initial contribution was also a modest one, consisting of just 2,058 personnel—codenamed Operation Falconer. Major force elements included special forces, rotary and fixed wing aviation and naval units. Army units included elements from the SASR and 4th Battalion, Royal Australian Regiment (Commando), a CH-47 Chinook detachment and a number of other specialist units. RAN units included the amphibious ship HMAS *Kanimbla*

Figure 63: *An Australian cavalry scout in Iraq in October 2007.*

and the frigates HMAS *Darwin* and HMAS *Anzac*, while the RAAF deployed 14 F/A-18 Hornets from No. 75 Squadron, a number of AP-3C Orions and C-130 Hercules.[414] The Australian Special Forces Task Force was one of the first coalition units forces to cross the border into Iraq, while for a few days, the closest ground troops to Baghdad were from the SASR. During the invasion the RAAF also flew its first combat missions since the Vietnam War, with No. 75 Squadron flying a total of 350 sorties and dropping 122 laser-guided bombs.[415]

The Iraqi military quickly proved no match for coalition military power, and with their defeat the bulk of Australian forces were withdrawn. While Australia did not initially take part in the post-war occupation of Iraq, an Australian Army light armoured battlegroup—designated the Al Muthanna Task Group and including 40 ASLAV light armoured vehicles and infantry—was later deployed to Southern Iraq in April 2005 as part of Operation Catalyst. The role of this force was to protect the Japanese engineer contingent in the region and support the training of New Iraqi Army units. The AMTG later became the Overwatch Battle Group (West) (OBG(W)), following the hand back of Al Muthanna province to Iraqi control. Force levels peaked at 1,400 personnel in May 2007 including the OBG(W) in Southern Iraq, the Security Detachment in Baghdad and the Australian Army Training Team—Iraq. A RAN frigate was based in the North Persian Gulf, while RAAF assets included C-130H Hercules and AP-3C elements.[416] Following the election of a new Labor government

Figure 64: *An RAAF F/A-18 Hornet taking off for a mission over Iraq in 2017.*

under Prime Minister Kevin Rudd the bulk of these forces were withdrawn by mid-2009, while RAAF and RAN operations were redirected to other parts of the Middle East Area of Operations as part of Operation Slipper.

Low-level operations continued, however, with a small Australian force of 80 soldiers remaining in Iraq to protect the Australian Embassy in Baghdad as part of SECDET under Operation Kruger. SECDET was finally withdrawn in August 2011, and was replaced by a private military company which took over responsibility for providing security for Australia's diplomatic presence in Iraq. Although more than 17,000 personnel served during operations in Iraq, Australian casualties were relatively light, with two soldiers accidentally killed, while a third Australian died serving with the British Royal Air Force. A further 27 personnel were wounded. Two officers remained in Iraq attached to the United Nations Assistance Mission for Iraq as part of Operation Riverbank. This operation concluded in November 2013.

Military intervention against ISIL, 2014–present

In June 2014 a small number of SASR personnel were deployed to Iraq to protect the Australian embassy when the security of Baghdad was threatened by the 2014 Northern Iraq offensive. Later, in August and September a number of RAAF C-17 and C-130J transport aircraft based in the Middle East were used to conduct airdrops of humanitarian aid to trapped civilians and to airlift arms and munitions to forces in Kurdish-controlled northern Iraq. In late September

Figure 65: *Australian peacekeeping deployments since 1945.*

2014 an Air Task Group (ATG) and Special Operations Task Group (SOTG) were deployed to Al Minhad Air Base in the United Arab Emirates as part of the coalition to combat Islamic State forces in Iraq. Equipped with F/A-18F Super Hornet strike aircraft, a KC-30A Multi Role Tanker Transport, and an E-7A Wedgetail Airborne Early Warning & Control aircraft, the ATG began operations on 1 October. The SOTG is tasked with operations to advise and assist Iraqi Security Forces, and was deployed to Iraq after a legal framework covering their presence in the country was agreed between the Australian and Iraqi Governments. It began moving into Iraq in early November. In April 2015 a 300-strong unit known as Task Group Taji was deployed to Iraq to train the regular Iraqi Security Forces. In September 2015 airstrikes were extended to Syria. Strike missions concluded in December 2017.

Peacekeeping and humanitarian relief operations

Australia's involvement in international peacekeeping operations has been diverse, and included participation in both United Nations sponsored missions, as well as those as part of ad-hoc coalitions. Australians have been involved in more conflicts as peacekeepers than as belligerents; however "in comparative international terms, Australia has only been a moderately energetic peacekeeper."[417] Although Australia has had peacekeepers in the field continuously for 60 years—being among the first group of UN military observers in Indonesia in 1947—its commitments have generally been limited, consisting mostly of small numbers of high-level and technical support troops such as signallers, engineers, medics, observers, and police. One significant commitment has been Australia's ongoing involvement with the long running Multinational Force and Observers in the Sinai. The operational tempo started increasing in the mid-1990s, when Australia became involved in a series of high-profile operations, deploying significantly larger combat units in support of a number of missions including Cambodia, Rwanda, Somalia, East Timor, and the Solomon Islands. Australia has been involved in close to 100 separate missions, involving more than 30,000 personnel; 14 Australians have died during these operations. In addition, approximately 7,000 personnel have been involved in 66 different overseas humanitarian relief operations between 1918 and 2006. Ten personnel lost their lives during these missions.[418]

Military statistics

Conflict	Date	Number enlisted	Killed	Wounded	Prisoners of war	Notes
New Zealand	1860–61	Crew of HMVS Victoria 2,500 in Waikato Regiments	1 <20	Nil Unknown	Nil	
Sudan	1885	770 in NSW Contingent	9	3	Nil	
South Africa	1899–1902	16,463 in Colonial and Commonwealth contingents	589	538	100	
China	1900–01	560 in NSW, SA and VIC colonial naval contingents	6	Unknown	Nil	
First World War	1914–18	416,809 enlisted in AIF (includes AFC) 324,000 AIF members served overseas 9,000 in RAN Total: 425,809	61,511	155,000	4,044 (397 died in captivity)	
Russian Civil War	1918–19	100–150 in NREF and NRRF 48 in Dunsterforce Crew of HMAS Swan	10	40	Nil	
Second World War	1939–45	727,200 in 2nd AIF and Militia 48,900 in RAN 216,900 in RAAF Total: 993,000	39,761	66,553	8,184 (against Germany and Italy) 22,376 (against Japan) (8,031 died in captivity) Total: 30,560	

Conflict	Dates	Strength	Deaths	Wounded	POW
Post-war mine clearance (Northern Queensland coast and New Guinea)	1947–50		4		
Japan (British Commonwealth Occupation Force)	1947–1952	16,000	3		
Papua New Guinea	1947–1975		13		
Middle East (UNTSO)	1948–present		1		
Berlin Airlift	1948–1949		1		
Malayan Emergency	1948–60	7,000 in Army	39	20	Nil
Kashmir	1948–1985		1		
Korean War	1950–53	10,657 in Army 4,507 in RAN 2,000 in RAAF Total: 17,164	340	1,216	29 (1 died in captivity)
Malta	1952–1955		3		
Korea (Post-armistice)	1953–1957		16		
South-East Asia (SEATO)	1955–1975		6		
Indonesia-Malaysia Confrontation	1962–66	3,500 in Army	16	9	Nil
Malay Peninsula	1964–1966		2		
Vietnam War	1962–73	42,700 in Army 2,825 in RAN 4,443 in RAAF Total: 49,968	521	2,398	Nil
Thailand	1965–1968		2		
Irian Jaya (Operation Cenderawasih)	1976–1981		1		
Gulf War	1991	750	Nil	Nil	Nil
Western Sahara (MINURSO)	1991–1994		1		
Somalia	1992–94	1,480	1		Nil
Bougainville	1997–2003	3,500	1		
East Timor	1999–2013	> 40,000	4		Nil
Afghanistan	2001–present	> 26,000	41	256	Nil

Iraq	2003–11	17,000	3	27	Nil	
Solomon Islands	2003–2013	7,270	1			
Fiji	2006		2			
		Total	~ 102,930	~ 226,060	~ 34,733	

Note: In addition, approximately another 3,100 Australians died in various conflicts, serving in either British or other Commonwealth or Allied forces, or the Merchant Navy, or were civilians working with philanthropic organisations, official war correspondents, photographers, or artists.

Notes

Footnotes

Citations

References

<templatestyles src="Template:Refbegin/styles.css" />

- Australian War Memorial (2010). *Australian War Memorial Annual Report 2009–2010*[419] (PDF). Canberra: Australian War Memorial. ISSN 1441-4198[420].
- Australian Army (2008). *The Fundamentals of Land Warfare*[421] (PDF). Canberra: Australian Army. OCLC 223250226[422]. Archived from the original[423] (PDF) on 6 December 2008.
- Bean, Charles (1921). *The Story of Anzac: From the Outbreak of War to the End of the First Phase of the Gallipoli Campaign May 4, 1915*[424]. Official History of Australia in the War of 1914–1918. Volume One (1st ed.). Sydney: Angus and Robertson. OCLC 251999955[425].
- Bean, Charles (1946). *Anzac to Amiens*[426]. Canberra: Australian War Memorial. OCLC 220477286[427].
- Beaumont, Joan (1995). "Australia's War". In Beaumont, Joan. *Australia's War, 1914–1918*. Sydney: Allen & Unwin. pp. 1–34. ISBN 1863734619.
- Beaumont, Joan (1996a). "Australia's War: Europe and the Middle East". In Beaumont, Joan. *Australia's War, 1939–1945*. Sydney: Allen & Unwin. pp. 1–25. ISBN 1-86448-039-4.
- Beaumont, Joan (1996b). "Australia's War: Asia and the Pacific". In Beaumont, Joan. *Australia's War, 1939–1945*. Sydney: Allen & Unwin. pp. 26–53. ISBN 1-86448-039-4.

- Bullard, Steven (2017). *In Their Time of Need: Australia's Overseas Emergency Relief Operations, 1918–2006*. The Official History of Australian Peacekeeping, Humanitarian and Post-Cold War Operations. Volume VI. Port Melbourne, Victoria: Cambridge University Press. ISBN 9781107026346.
- Breen, Bob (1992). *The Battle of Kapyong: 3rd Battalion, the Royal Australian Regiment, Korea 23–24 April 1951*. Georges Heights, New South Wales: Headquarters Training Command. ISBN 0-642-18222-1.
- Cassells, Vic (2000). *The Capital Ships: Their Battles and Their Badges*. East Roseville, New South Wales: Simon & Schuster. ISBN 0-7318-0941-6. OCLC 48761594[428].
- Coates, John (2006). *An Atlas of Australia's Wars*. Melbourne: Oxford University Press. ISBN 0-19-555914-2.
- Connery, David; Cran, David; Evered, David (2012). *Conducting Counterinsurgency – Reconstruction Task Force 4 in Afghanistan*. Newport, New South Wales: Big Sky Publishing. ISBN 9781921941771.
- Coulthard-Clark, Chris (1998). *Where Australians Fought: The Encyclopaedia of Australia's Battles* (First ed.). St Leonards: Allen & Unwin. ISBN 1-86448-611-2. OCLC 39097011[429].
- Coulthard-Clark, Chris (2001). *The Encyclopaedia of Australia's Battles* (Second ed.). Sydney: Allen & Unwin. ISBN 1-86508-634-7. OCLC 48793439[430].
- Dennis, Peter; Grey, Jeffrey; Morris, Ewan; Prior, Robin (1995). *The Oxford Companion to Australian Military History*. Melbourne: Oxford University Press. ISBN 0-19-553227-9.
- Dennis, Peter; Grey, Jeffrey (1996). *Emergency and Confrontation: Australian Military Operations in Malaya and Borneo 1950–1966*. St Leonards: Allen & Unwin. ISBN 1-86373-302-7. OCLC 187450156[431].
- Dennis, Peter; Grey, Jeffrey; Morris, Ewan; Prior, Robin; Bou, Jean (2008). *The Oxford Companion to Australian Military History* (Second ed.). Melbourne: Oxford University Press. ISBN 978-0-19-551784-2.
- Eather, Steve (1996). *Odd Jobs: RAAF Operations in Japan, the Berlin Airlift, Korea, Malaya & Malta, 1946–1960*[432]. RAAF Williams, Victoria: RAAF Museum. ISBN 0-642-23482-5.
- Evans, Mark, ed. (2005). *The Tyranny of Dissonance: Australia's Strategic Culture and Way of War 1901–2005*. Study Paper No. 306. Canberra: Land Warfare Studies Centre. ISBN 0-642-29607-3.
- Frame, Tom (2004). *No Pleasure Cruise. The Story of the Royal Australian Navy*. Sydney: Allen & Unwin. ISBN 1-74114-233-4.
- Grey, Jeffrey (1999). *A Military History of Australia* (Second ed.). Port Melbourne: Cambridge University Press. ISBN 0-521-64483-6.

- Grey, Jeffrey (2008). *A Military History of Australia* (Third ed.). Port Melbourne: Cambridge University Press. ISBN 978-0-521-69791-0.
- Ham, Paul (2007). *Vietnam: The Australian War*. Sydney: Harper Collins. ISBN 978-0-7322-8237-0.
- Holmes, Tony (2006). "RAAF Hornets at War". *Australian Aviation*. Manly: Aerospace Publications (224): 38–39. ISSN 0813-0876[433].
- Horner, David (1989). *SAS: Phantoms of the Jungle: A History of the Australian Special Air Service*. St. Leonards: Allen & Unwin. ISBN 0-04-520006-8. OCLC 23828245[434].
- Horner, David (May 1993). "Defending Australia in 1942". *The Pacific War 1942*. War and Society. Canberra: Department of History, Australian Defence Force Academy. pp. 1–21. ISSN 0729-2473[435].
- Horner, David (2001). *Making the Australian Defence Force*. The Australian Centenary History of Defence. Volume IV. Melbourne: Oxford University Press. ISBN 0-19-554117-0.
- Horner, David; Bou, Jean, eds. (2008). *Duty First: A History of the Royal Australian Regiment* (2nd ed.). Crows Nest, New South Wales: Allen & Unwin. ISBN 978-1-74175-374-5.
- Kirkland, Frederick (1991). *Operation Damask: The Gulf War Iraq – Kuwait 1990–1991*. Cremorne: Plaza Historical Service. ISBN 0-9587491-1-6. OCLC 27614090[436].
- Kuring, Ian (2004). *Red Coats to Cams. A History of Australian Infantry 1788 to 2001*. Sydney: Australian Military History Publications. ISBN 1-876439-99-8.
- Londey, Peter (2004). *Other People's Wars: A History of Australian Peacekeeping*. Crows Nest: Allen & Unwin. ISBN 1-86508-651-7. OCLC 57212671[437].
- Long, Gavin (1963). *The Final Campaigns*[438]. Australia in the War of 1939–1945. Series 1 – Army. Volume 7. Canberra: Australian War Memorial. OCLC 1297619[439].
- Long, Gavin (1973). *The Six Years War: A Concise History of Australia in the 1939–1945 War*. Canberra: The Australian War Memorial and the Australian Government Printing Service. ISBN 0-642-99375-0.
- Macintyre, Stuart (1999). *A Concise History of Australia*. Cambridge Consise Histories (First ed.). Cambridge: Cambridge University Press. ISBN 0-521-62577-7.
- McIntyre, William David (1995). *Background to the Anzus Pact: Policy-making, Strategy and Diplomacy, 1945–55*. Basingstoke: Macmillan. ISBN 0-312-12439-2.
- Macdougall, Anthony (2001) [1991]. *Australians at War: A Pictorial History*. Noble Park: Five Mile Press. ISBN 1-86503-865-2.
- McNeill, Ian; Ekins, Ashley (2003). *On the Offensive: The Australian*

Army and the Vietnam War 1967–1968. The Official History of Australia's Involvement in Southeast Asian Conflicts 1948–1975. Volume Eight. St Leonards: Allen & Unwin. ISBN 1-86373-304-3.
- Millar, Thomas (1978). *Australia in Peace and War: Foreign Relations 1788–1977*. Canberra: Australian National University Press. ISBN 0-7081-1575-6.
- Murphy, John (1993). *Harvest of Fear: Australia's Vietnam War*. Sydney: Allen & Unwin. ISBN 1-86373-449-X. OCLC 260164058[440].
- Nicholls, Bob (1986). *Bluejackets & Boxers: Australia's Naval Expedition to the Boxer Uprising*. North Sydney: Allen & Unwin. ISBN 0-86861-799-7.
- Odgers, George (1994). *Diggers: The Australian Army, Navy and Air Force in Eleven Wars*. Volume 1. London: Lansdowne. ISBN 978-1-86302-385-6. OCLC 31743147[441].
- Odgers, George (1999). *100 Years of Australians at War*. Sydney: Lansdowne. ISBN 1-86302-669-X.
- Odgers, George (2000). *Remembering Korea: Australians in the War of 1950–53*. Sydney: Landsdowne Publishing. ISBN 1-86302-679-7. OCLC 50315481[442].
- Reeve, John; Stevens, David (2001). *Southern Trident: Strategy, History, and the Rise of Australian Naval Power*. Crows Nest: Allen & Unwin. ISBN 1-86508-462-X. OCLC 47367004[443].
- Reeve, John; Stevens, David (2003). *The Face of Naval Battle: The Human Experience of Modern War at Sea*. Crows Nest: Allen & Unwin. ISBN 1-86508-667-3. OCLC 52647129[444].
- Stephens, Alan (2001). *The Royal Australian Air Force*. The Australian Centenary History of Defence. Volume II. London: Oxford University Press. ISBN 0-19-554115-4.
- Stevens, David (2001). *The Royal Australian Navy*. The Australian Centenary History of Defence. Volume III. London: Oxford University Press. ISBN 0-19-554116-2.
- Tewes, Alex; Rayner, Laura; Kavanaugh, Kelly (2004). *Australia's Maritime Strategy in the 21st Century*[445]. Australian Parliamentary Library Research Brief. 4 2004–05. Canberra: Australian Parliament House. OCLC 224183782[446]. Archived from the original[447] on 30 September 2008.
- Thomson, Mark (2005). *Punching Above Our Weight? Australia as a Middle Power*[448]. Canberra: Australian Strategic Policy Institute. OCLC 224546956[449].
- Turner, Trevor (2014). "The Camel Corps: New South Wales Sudan contingent, 1885". *Sabretache*. Garran, Australian Capital Territory: Military Historical Society of Australia. **LV** (4, December): 40–53. ISSN

0048-8933[450].
- Walhert, Glenn (2008). *Exploring Gallipoli: An Australian Army Battlefield Guide*. Canberra: Army History Unit. ISBN 978-0-9804753-5-7.
- White, Hugh (2002). "Australian Defence Policy and the Possibility of War". *Australian Journal of International Affairs*. Canberra: The Institute. **56** (2): 253–264. doi: 10.1080/10357710220147451[451]. ISSN 1465-332X[452].

Further reading

<templatestyles src="Template:Refbegin/styles.css" />

- Dean, Peter J. (2018). *McArthur's Coalition: US and Australian operations in the Southwest Pacific Area, 1942–1945*. Lawrence: University Press of Kansas. ISBN 9780700626045.

External links

 Wikimedia Commons has media related to *Military history of Australia*.

- Australian War Memorial[453]

Army

History of the Australian Army

The **history of the Australian Army** dates back to colonial forces, prior to the Federation of Australia in 1901. Some of the colonial forces, which served the states of Australia at the time, were gradually united into federal units between 1899 and 1903; thus forming the beginning of the Australian Army. The colonial armies were officially united as the *Commonwealth Military Forces* in the Defence Act of 1903. Since then the Australian Army as an organization has changed to suit to needs of the nation; with particular changes occurring during, and following, the World Wars, Korean War, Vietnam War and Gulf War. In 1916 the title *Australian Military Forces* was adopted and remained its official name until 1980, after which it became known as the *Australian Army*.[454]

The Two Armies: Militia and Permanent forces 1870–1947

For more than 80 years after the first British settlement, the only professional soldiers in Australia were members of British Army garrisons. The first conflicts in which large numbers of Australian-born soldiers fought overseas were the Maori Wars, between 1863–1872, although almost all of these—about 2,500 men—served in New Zealand colonial units, or the British Army. By the time that the garrisons were withdrawn in 1870, the six separate self-governing colonies in Australia already had their own separate, part-time reserve units, known as militia or "volunteers". The colonial governments began to raise professional artillery units, to staff coastal batteries. From 1877 onwards, the British sent officers to advise the colonies on defence matters, and in the early 1880s, the first inter-colonial defence conferences were held.

Figure 66: *Australian and British officers in South Africa during the Second Boer War*

In 1885, the government of New South Wales sent an infantry battalion, with artillery and support units to the short-lived British campaign in Sudan. During the economic depression of the early 1890s, large-scale strikes in various colonies were met with governments mobilising and/or threatening to use militia against strikers. This was very unpopular and led to successful and historically-significant campaigns against the formation of standing, regular forces. The "two armies" system was established whereby the only infantry units would be militia, although permanent artillery and other support units remained. As Federation of the colonies approached, on 24 August 1899 the colonial artillery units were merged into the first Australian federal army unit.

Boer War 1899–1902

Before Federation of Australia and the forming of the national army, the six self-governing and independent Australian colonial governments sent contingents to South Africa to serve in the Second Boer War. The first offer of 250 mounted troops came from the new colony of Queensland in July 1899, some months before the declaration of war.

The first arrivals of Australian troops was the First New South Wales Contingent which arrived in November 1899, after departing London. A detachment, sent from Australia in October 1899, was known as The Australian Regiment and was an infantry unit, made up mainly of volunteers from the Colonies of Victoria, Tasmania, South Australia and Western Australia, who left on one ship for Cape Town. Due to the way the war developed, these troops were converted from infantry to mounted infantry.

Strong resistance from the Boer Afrikaner forces led to further recruiting in the Australian colonies. Known as Bushmen's Contingents, these soldiers were usually volunteers with horse-riding and shooting skills but no military experience. After Federation in 1901, eight Australian Commonwealth Horse battalions were sent.

Many of the Australian units had a short tour of duty and some were subject to restructuring. Later Australians transferred to, or enlisted into multinational units, such as the Bushveldt Carbineers, in which Harry "Breaker" Morant and Peter Hancock served, before their court martial and execution for alleged war crimes.

Australian units served at many notable actions, including the relief of Mafeking, Sunnyside, Slingersfontein, Pink Hill, the Relief of Kimberley, Paardeburg, Bloemfontein, the Siege of Eland's River, Rhenosterkop and Haartebeestefontein. Australians were there for the capture of Johannesburg and were first into Pretoria. Later they participated at Diamond Hill.

In all, 16,175 Australians, with 16,314 horses, served in the Boer War; 251 were killed in action, 267 died of other causes and 43 went missing in action. Six Victoria Crosses were awarded to Australians, five serving with Australian contingents and one serving with the South African Constabulary. Many Australians did more than one tour of duty and a number remained after the war and settled in-country; while others returned to Australia then returned to South Africa.

The Boxer Rebellion 1900

The Boxer Rebellion in China began in 1900, and a number of western nations—including many European powers, the United States, and Japan—soon sent forces as part of the China Field Force to protect their interests. In June, the British government sought permission from the Australian colonies to dispatch ships from the Australian Squadron to China with Naval Brigade reservists, who had been trained in both ship handling and soldiering to fulfil their coastal defence role. The colonies dispatched 200 men from Victoria, 260 from New South Wales and the South Australian ship HMCS Protector, under the command of Captain William Creswell. Amongst the naval contingent from New South Wales were 200 naval officers and sailors and 50 soldiers headquartered at Victoria Barracks, Sydney who originally enlisted for the Second Boer War. The soldiers were keen to go to China but refused to be enlisted as sailors. The NSW Naval Brigade objected to having soldiers in their ranks. The Army and Navy compromised and titled the contingent the NSW Marine Light Infantry.[455]

1901–1914

As the Boer War raged, the Commonwealth of Australia was founded on 1 January 1901. On 1 March, 28,923 colonial soldiers, being 1,457 professional soldiers, 18,603 paid militia and 8,863 unpaid volunteers, were transferred to the new Australian Army. However, the individual units continued to be administered under the various colonial Acts. Major General Sir Edward Hutton, a former commander of the New South Wales Military Forces, became the first commander of the Commonwealth Forces' on 26 December and set to work devising an integrated structure for the new army. The Defence Act of 1903 brought all of the units under one piece of legislation; more significantly, it prevented the raising of standing infantry units and specified that militia forces could not be used in industrial disputes, and *could not serve outside Australia*. The vast majority of soldiers remained in militia units, now known as the Citizen Military Forces (CMF). In 1911, two significant changes followed a report by Lord Kitchener: the Royal Military College, Duntroon was established and; a system of universal national service began: boys aged 12 to 18 became cadets, and men aged 18–26 had to serve in the CMF.

World War I

When the United Kingdom declared war on Germany at the start of World War I, the Australian government followed without hesitation. This was considered to be expected by the Australian public, because of the very large number of British-born citizens and first generation Anglo-Australians at the time. By the end of the war, almost 20% of those who served in the Australian forces had been born in the United Kingdom, even though nearly all enlistments had occurred in Australia.

Because existing militia forces were unable to serve overseas, an all-volunteer expeditionary force, the Australian Imperial Force (AIF) was formed from 15 August 1914. The Australian government had pledged to supply 20,000 men, organised as one infantry division and one light horse brigade plus supporting units. The first commander of the AIF was General William Bridges, who also assumed direct command of the infantry division.

However, the first target for Australian action was close to home, seizing German colonial outposts in the south-west Pacific and New Guinea. The 2000-man force assembled for this purpose, known as the Australian Naval and Military Expeditionary Force (AN&MEF), landed near Rabaul on 11 September

Figure 67: *Recruitment poster, 1914–1918.*

1914 and after some fighting, the German garrison surrendered on 21 September.

Departing from Western Australia on 1 November 1914, the AIF was sent initially to British-controlled Egypt, to pre-empt any attack by the Ottoman Empire, and with a view to opening another front against the Central Powers. The AIF had four infantry brigades with the first three making up the 1st Division. The 4th Brigade was joined with the sole New Zealand infantry brigade to form the New Zealand and Australian Division.

The combined Australian and New Zealand Army Corps (ANZAC), commanded by British general William Birdwood, went into action when Allied forces landed on the Gallipoli peninsula on 25 April 1915 (now commemorated as Anzac Day). The Gallipoli Campaign would last for eight months of bloody stalemate. By the end of the campaign, Australian casualties were 8,700 killed and 19,000 wounded or sick. The original AIF contingent had continued to grow with the arrival of the 2nd Division which was formed in Egypt and went to Gallipoli in August.

After the withdrawal from Gallipoli, the infantry underwent a major expansion with the first four brigades, the 1st Division and the 4th Brigade being split to create the 12th, 13th, 14th and 15th Brigades. The four new brigades together with the 4th and 8th Brigades formed two additional divisions (4th and 5th).

Figure 68: *Australian soldiers landing at ANZAC Cove*

The 3rd Division was formed in Australia and sailed directly to England for further training before moving to the Western Front, in November 1916. The light horse brigades had served dismounted at Gallipoli. In 1916, they were reunited with their horses and formed into the 1st Anzac Mounted Division in Egypt to campaign against Turkish forces in the Sinai and Palestine. Australia also supplied the majority of troops for the newly formed Imperial Camel Corps Brigade.

The first Australian division to mount a major attack on the Western Front was the 5th Division. The attack, the Battle of Fromelles, was a disaster with the division suffering 5,500 casualties for no gain. The 1st, 2nd and 4th Divisions, combined as I Anzac Corps, fought the Battle of Pozières and subsequent Battle of Mouquet Farm, part of the Battle of the Somme. In Egypt, the light horse had helped repulse the Turkish attempt to capture the Suez Canal in the Battle of Romani.

During 1917, the five divisions in France fought in three Allied offensives: the Battle of Bullecourt (part of the Battle of Arras), the Battle of Messines and the Third Battle of Ypres. Meanwhile, the light horse had entered southern Palestine. After two attempts to break through the Turkish defences at Gaza, the decisive victory was achieved in the Third Battle of Gaza in which the Australians captured the town of Beersheba in a dramatic cavalry charge. By the end of the year, British forces had captured Jerusalem.

The German Spring Offensive of early 1918 broke through British lines north and south of the Somme. The five Australian divisions which had been formed

Figure 69: *The 10th Reinforcements of the 5th Pioneers at Port Melbourne prior to embarkation, October 1917*

into the Australian Corps on 1 November 1917, were moved south to help halt the German advance. In May, Australian General John Monash was given command of the Australian Corps and the first operation he planned as a corps commander, the Battle of Hamel, is widely regarded as the finest set-piece strategy of the war on the Western Front. The final Allied offensive began with the Battle of Amiens on 8 August, and the Australian Corps, along with the Canadian Corps and the III British Corps, spearheaded the advance north and south of the Somme. By the end of September, the Australian divisions were severely depleted, with only the 3rd and the 5th fit for immediate action. On 5 October the Australian Corps was withdrawn to rest and saw no more fighting before the war ended.

In the Middle East, the light horse had endured summer in the Jordan Valley before leading the British offensive in the final Battle of Megiddo. The 10th Light Horse Regiment was the first Allied unit to reach Damascus.

A total of 331,814 Australians were sent overseas to serve as part of the AIF, which represented 13% of the Australian male population. About 2,100 women served with the 1st AIF, mainly as nurses. 18% (61,859) of those who served in the AIF were killed or died. The casualty rate (killed or wounded) was 64%, reportedly the highest of any country which took part in World War I. The AIF remained a volunteer force for the duration of the war—the only

British or Dominion force to do so. Two referendums on conscription had been defeated, preserving the volunteer status, but stretching the reserves towards the end of the war. The AIF also had a desertion rate larger than Britain, mainly because the death penalty was not in force.

1919–1939

After the end of the First World War, the Australian Army dramatically cut back on its standing forces. There was still a large pool of volunteers to choose from, and due to the Great Depression vacancies were quickly filled, as they were steady, relatively well paying jobs.

The contingent of soldiers sent to Britain for the coronation of King George VI and Queen Elizabeth in 1937 became the first Australian soldiers to mount the King's Guard in London.

In 1938 the first moves towards the establishment of a regular infantry force were undertaken with the establishment of the Darwin Mobile Force. Due to the provisions of the Defence Act 1903 this force was raised as part of the Royal Australian Artillery, even though it consisted of a large number of infantry.[456]

World War II

When the Second World War broke out between Britain and Germany in September 1939, the Second Australian Imperial Force (2nd AIF) was formed, to fight in France. The AIF's main strength would consist of four divisions raised in 1939–1940: the 6th, 7th, 8th and 9th. Major General Thomas Blamey was appointed commander of the 2nd AIF. Compulsory military service was introduced: all men over 21 had to complete three months training with the Militia. However, to ensure home defences, Militia members were barred from joining the AIF.

After the British Expeditionary Force (BEF) withdrew from France in the Dunkirk evacuation in the face of the German Blitzkrieg, the 6th, 7th and 9th Divisions, as I Corps, were sent to Egypt. From late 1940, the individual divisions faced Italian and German forces in the North African Campaign. The 6th Division then experienced many casualties in mainland Greece, and on Crete, and 3,000 of its personnel were taken prisoner in this campaign. The 7th Division formed the body of the successful Allied invasion of Vichy French-controlled Lebanon and Syria in 1941. The 9th Division and part of the 7th played a celebrated defensive role at the Siege of Tobruk.

In 1941, a start was made on raising the 1st Armoured Division, as part of the AIF. As fears of war with Japan mounted, most of the 8th Division was sent

Figure 70: *A patrol from the 2/13th Battalion at Tobruk (AWM 020779).*

to Singapore, to strengthen the British garrison; the remaining battalions were deployed in the islands to Australia's north, at Rabaul, Ambon and Timor. Following short but bloody campaigns in Malaya and the islands, virtually all of the 8th Division was lost when stronger Japanese forces swept through South East Asia, in early 1942. In the Battle of Singapore alone, more than 15,000 Australians were taken prisoner. The 6th and 7th Divisions were recalled to Australia, as the country faced the prospect of invasion. While Winston Churchill, the British Prime Minister, had requested that the two AIF divisions be sent to Burma, the Australian Prime Minister, John Curtin, turned down this request, though he did agree to land two brigades of the 6th Division in Ceylon where they formed part of the island's defences during the early months of 1942.

Blamey was appointed Commander-in-Chief (C-in-C) in March 1942; in April a major re-organisation took place: the name First Army —which previously referred to a Militia formation—was reassigned to I Corps, which was expanded to army size with the inclusion of Militia divisions. The First Army's initial area of responsibility was the defence of Queensland and northern New South Wales. The Second Army was responsible for south-eastern Australia; the other components of Australia's defences were III Corps (in Western Australia), the Northern Territory Force and New Guinea Force. Conscription was effectively introduced in mid-1942, when all men 18–35, and single men aged

Figure 71: *Australian soldiers display Japanese flags they captured at Kaiapit, New Guinea in 1943*

35–45, were required to join the CMF. In addition, the Army's armoured force was greatly expanded.

In February 1942, a change in regulations meant that if 65% of the official, establishment strength of a Militia unit, or 75 per cent of the actual personnel, volunteered for the AIF, the unit became an AIF unit. At the time, the CMF were often scorned as "chocolate-tin soldiers", or "chockos", because it was thought they would melt in the heat of battle. Nevertheless, Militia units distinguished themselves and suffered extremely high casualties during 1942, in New Guinea, which was then an Australian territory. The prime example was the 39th (Militia) Battalion, many of them very young, untrained and poorly equipped, who distinguished themselves and suffered heavy casualties, in the stubborn rearguard action on the Kokoda Trail.

By late 1942, the 7th Division was beginning to relieve the Militia in New Guinea. In August, as the Kokoda battles raged, Militia and 7th Division units formed the bulk of Australian forces at the Battle of Milne Bay, the first outright defeat inflicted on Japanese land forces. The 6th and 7th Divisions, with Militia units and elements of the 1st Armoured, formed a large part of Allied forces which destroyed the major Japanese beachhead in New Guinea, at the Battle of Buna-Gona. In 1943, the Defence Act was changed to allow Militia units to serve south of the Equator in South East Asia. The 9th Division

Figure 72: *Australian soldiers in New Britain in 1945 (AWM 092342).*

remained in North Africa and distinguished itself at the Second Battle of El Alamein, after which victory over Erwin Rommel was assured, and returned to Australia in 1943. Later that year it was pitched into battle against Japanese forces in New Guinea.

General Douglas MacArthur, the Supreme Allied Commander in the South West Pacific, was resented for his treatment of Australian forces. After the surrender of American forces in the Philippines, Australian ground forces constituted almost all of MacArthur's ground forces. As US forces re-built, however, he increasingly used Australian units for secondary assignments. The campaign on Bougainville after the departure of US forces is considered to be an example of this.

The 1st Army took responsibility for mopping-up and controlling areas which flanked US forces' "island-hopping" campaign towards Japan. Australian units were also responsible for the last phase of amphibious assaults during the Pacific War: the attacks on Japanese-occupied Borneo, including Tarakan, Brunei, British Borneo, Balikpapan and other targets in Sarawak. Meanwhile, Australian prisoners of the Japanese, were often held in inhumane conditions, such as Changi prison, or in Japan itself. Some were also subject to severe forced labour, including the Burma Railway, or forced long distance marches, such as on Sandakan. There was a very high death rate among Allied prisoners of the Japanese.

A planned invasion of the Japanese home island of Honshū in 1946, Operation Coronet, would probably have included a proposed 10th Division, formed from existing AIF personnel. The operation never proceeded as Japan surrendered prior. Compulsory military service ended in 1945, and most Australian personnel had been demobilised by the end of 1946. Out of more than 724,000 army personnel during World War II, almost 400,000 served outside Australia. More than 18,000 died; 22,000 were wounded and more than 20,000 became prisoners of war.

Occupation of Japan

The British Commonwealth Occupation Force (BCOF), was the name of the joint Australian, British, Indian and New Zealand military forces in occupied Japan, from 21 February 1946 until the end of occupation in 1952. Overall, Australians made up by far the biggest proportion of BCOF, and the army made up of most of the Australians. At its peak, BCOF comprised 40,000 personnel, equal to about 10% of the US military personnel in Japan. The army contingent was centred around Australia's first ever standing infantry unit, the 34th Infantry Brigade, which had been formed from 2nd AIF and Militia personnel on Morotai in late 1945. The three battalions in the Brigade were redesignated to form the Royal Australian Regiment in 1947. The position of GOC BCOF was always filled by an Australian Army officer.

While US forces were responsible for military government, BCOF was responsible for supervising demilitarisation and the disposal of Japan's war industries. BCOF was also responsible for occupation of the western prefectures of Shimane, Yamaguchi, Tottori, Okayama, Hiroshima and Shikoku Island. BCOF headquarters was at Kure. According to the AWM:

> Australian army .... personnel were involved in the location and securing of military stores and installations. The Intelligence Sections of the Australian battalions were given targets to investigate by BCOF Headquarters, in the form of grid references for dumps of Japanese military equipment. Warlike materials were destroyed and other equipment was kept for use by BCOF or returned to the Japanese. The destruction or conversion to civilian use of military equipment was carried out by Japanese civilians under Australian supervision. Regular patrols and road reconnaissances were initiated and carried out in the Australian area of responsibility as part of BCOF's general surveillance duties.

The Australian component of BCOF was responsible for over 20 million Japanese citizens, within a 57,000 square kilometre area. During 1947, the BCOF began to wind down its presence in Japan. However, BCOF bases provided staging posts for Australian and other Commonwealth forces deployed

Figure 73: *Soldiers from 3 RAR watch as a Korean village burns in late 1950*

to the Korean War, from 1949 onwards. BCOF was effectively wound-up in 1951, as control of Commonwealth forces in Japan was transferred to British Commonwealth Forces Korea.

The modern army, 1947–present

Plans for post-war defence arrangements were predicated on maintaining a relatively strong peacetime force. In a significant departure from past Australian defence policy which had previously relied on citizen forces, the Australian Army would include a permanent field force of 19,000 regulars organised into a brigade of three infantry battalions with armoured support, serving alongside a part-time force of 50,000 men in the Citizen Military Forces.[457] The Australian Regular Army was subsequently formed on 30 September 1947, while the CMF was re-raised on 1 July 1948.[458]

In 1953, a contingent of the army was again sent to the coronation, this time of Queen Elizabeth II. Again it mounted the Queen's Guard alongside the Canadian Army contingent.

Korean War

Malayan Emergency (1955–1963)

Although the Royal Australian Air Force had been conducting operations in Malaya since 1950, it was not until October 1955 that the first Army battalion, 2nd Battalion, Royal Australian Regiment (2RAR), was deployed to Penang. However, the battalion did not have approval from the government to conduct operations until January 1956, when it conducted a search and security mission in Kedah. The mission, code-named Operation Deuce, lasted until late April 1956 when 2RAR transferred responsibility of their area to the 1st Battalion, Royal Malay Regiment. In May, 2RAR conducted Operation Shark North in Perak. It was withdrawn from combat operations in August 1957 and left Malaya in October 1957. The battalion suffered 14 killed.

In September 1957, 2RAR was replaced by the 3rd battalion, Royal Australian Regiment (3RAR), which began patrols as part of Operation Shark North in December. In January 1958, 3RAR began Operation Ginger, a major operation designed to disrupt the food supply to the communist forces. Ginger continued until April 1959 when Perak was declared a safe area. The battalion was withdrawn from operations in September 1959, returning to Australia in October. It had four killed during its tour

In October 1959, 3RAR was replaced by 1RAR. Following a month spent climatising to the jungle, 1RAR participated in Operation Bamboo, a deep jungle search near the Thai-Malay border. This operation met with little success, as insurgents could cross over the border into Thailand, where they could not be followed. In April 1960, 1RAR began Operation Magnet, the first operation in which Australian forces were able to cross the border into Thailand. However, Magnet did not result in any engagements.

In July 1960, the Malayan Prime Minister declared the emergency over. Despite this, 1RAR continued operations until the end of its tour in October 1961. The battalion suffered two deaths during its tour.

From October 1961 to August 1963, 2RAR conducted its second tour of duty in Perlis and Kedah.

1960–1965

In 1960 the Army was restructured onto the Pentropic organisation in an attempt to improve its combat power and align it with the US Army. This organisation proved unsuccessful, however, and it reverted to its previous unit organisations in 1965.

Figure 74: *Australians arrive at Tan Son Nhut Airport, Saigon*

Vietnam War

Australian Army's commitment into Vietnam commenced with a contingent of a specialist group called the Australian Army Training Team Vietnam (AATTV) which commenced in 1962. Later Australian troops and their supports arrived and were assigned the Phuoc Tuy province. The 1st Australian Task Force was based in the province between 1966 and 1971 and consisted of infantry battalions, a Special Air Service Squadron, an artillery regiment and supporting engineer, armoured and armoured personnel carrier squadrons.

The Australian Army performed well in Vietnam and inflicted losses on the enemy. While the Army fought few major battles, Australian soldiers fought and destroyed large Vietnamese Communist forces during the Battle of Long Tan 1966 and the fighting around Firebase Coral and the heavy operations in the Long Hai hills (1970). The Australian Army was highly trained at jungle warfare as all infantry and combat units completed a gruelling jungle training course at Canungra in Queensland pre-posting into Vietnam. In all, some 50,000 Australians served in Vietnam of which 520 were killed in battles and many due to mines.

The Australians style of warfare differed to that used by the United States Army. The Australians were masters of stealth, patrolling, tracking, searching & ambushing and hitting the enemy's flanks. In 1970, the 1st Australian Task

Figure 75: *Australian engineers board the United States C-5 Galaxy aircraft which will transport them to Namibia*

Force in Phuoc Tuoy Province was "the most potent allied military force ... yet was frequently tied up with reconnaissance-in-force operations".[459]

1972–1990

In 1988, as part of the celebrations for Australia's bicentennial, a detachment of soldiers from the 1st Battalion, Royal Australian Regiment became the first Australian troops in a generation to mount the Queen's Guard at Buckingham Palace in London.

United Nations Transition Assistance Group (UNTAG) 1989–90

In 1979, the UN General Assembly passed Resolution 435 which called for a peace keeping force to be deployed into the then South West Africa to provide assistance with its transition to the independent nation of Namibia. The multinational force was to comprise approximately 8,000 military personnel and a large contingent of Civilian Police. However, due to significant difficulties within the UN and in having South African forces withdrawn, the UN force did not deploy until 1989.

Australia deployed a combat engineer force of approximately 310 all ranks as part of the military force. The Australian contingent provided engineering support to the UN Force throughout its deployment. Tasks included numerous major construction projects including road and airfield construction, buildings, barracks, schools and other infrastructure to support the UN. The Australians also provided a wide range of assistance to the Namibian people by constructing a variety of civil projects.

Of note was the task of battlefield clearance after twenty years of warfare. Much of Namibia was in conflict and resulted in millions of land mines being laid around civilian communities and areas along the northern land border. The removal of these land mines was left to the South African Army, however, tens of thousands remained when RSA forces finally withdrew in 1990. The task then fell to the Australians. Despite the significant danger of this task, a 98% success rate was achieved with many civil communities becoming safe for the first time in decades.

The Australia force rotated once after six months deployment and provided continuous engineer support to the UN and Namibia. The force achieved its mission without sustaining any fatalities, making it one of the few military units in UNTAG to do so. Australia's contribution to UNTAG was a success and, as the first deployment of troops to a war zone since the Vietnam War, paved the way for future deployments.

Gulf War

The Australian Army's contribution to the 1991 Gulf War was limited to a small detachment from the 16th Air Defence Regiment. This detachment provided point defence for the Royal Australian Navy ships HMAS *Success* and HMAS *Westralia*. A small number of Australian officers on exchange to the British and United States armies served as part of the units they had been posted to. While the Special Air Service Regiment was placed on heightened alert during the war, reports that elements of the SAS were deployed to the Gulf are incorrect.Wikipedia:Citation needed Following the end of the war an Australian Medical Unit of 75 personnel drawn mostly from the Army's 2nd Field Ambulance was briefly deployed to northern Iraq as Australian's contribution to Operation Provide Comfort (designated 'Operation Habitat' by the Australian Defence Force). The Australian Medical Unit operated in Northern Iraq between 16 May and 30 June 1991.

1991–present

In 2000, the Federation Guard was formed – this was a tri-service unit consisting of personnel from the army, RAN and RAAF to serve as ceremonial

Figure 76: *Australian soldiers in Somalia during Operation Solace*

guards during the celebrations of Australia's Centenary of Federation the following year. In July 2000, a detachment mounted the Queen's Guard in London for three weeks; this included four women, under the command of Captain Cynthia Anderson. These were the first women ever to serve as guards at Buckingham Palace.

In August 2009, an alleged plan to attack the Holsworthy Barracks was uncovered by the Australian Federal Police. The alleged terrorist plot was to storm Holsworthy Barracks, a training area and artillery range for the Australian Army located in the outer south-western Sydney suburb of Holsworthy, with automatic weapons; and shoot army personnel or others until they were killed or captured.[460,461]

Peacekeeping in East Timor

War in Afghanistan

Australia, as one of the many countries who sent troops to Afghanistan, provided specialist SAS teams for use against Taliban/Al Qaeda forces.

Figure 77: *Australian troops in East Timor in May 2002*

Iraq War

Australia was one of the countries to provide combat forces for the US-led invasion of Iraq. In Australia it was known as Operation Falconer. In all Australia contributed some 2,000 personnel. The Army contribution to this was 500 soldiers. Following the end of major combat operations, Australia announced a withdrawal of most of its forces in Iraq. It left behind approximately 950 troops in the theatre. These included naval forces, support troops (such as air traffic controllers) and a security detachment of about 75 soldiers in strength to defend key Australian interests. In February 2005, Prime Minister John Howard announced an increase in the Australian presence by about 450 to provide protection for Japanese troops and assist in training Iraqi troops. This force, designated the Al Muthanna Task Group, was deployed to Southern Iraq in May 2005. After Al Muthanna province gained provincial control in mid 2006, the Australian force transitioned into a new role and was retitled the Overwatch Battle Group. OBG(W) relocated its forward operating base from Camp Smitty (outskirts of As Samawah, Al Muthanna province) to Tallil Air Base (outskirts of Nasiriyah, Dhi Qar province) effectively co-locating with the Australian Army Training Team Iraq (AATTI). Australia's contribution to operations in Southern Iraq involved combat overwatch of both Al Muthanna and Dhi Qar province, conduct of CIMIC operations and provision of support and training to the Iraqi Security Forces. After the Labor Government gained power in late 2007, most Australian forces were withdrawn from Iraq in mid-2008.

References

<templatestyles src="Template:Refbegin/styles.css" />

- Dennis, Peter; Grey, Jeffrey; Morris, Ewan; Prior, Robin; Bou, Jean (2008). *The Oxford Companion to Australian Military History* (Second ed.). Melbourne: Oxford University Press. ISBN 978-0-19-551784-2.
- Grey, Jeffrey (1999). *A Military History of Australia* (Second ed.). Port Melbourne: Cambridge University Press. ISBN 0-521-64483-6.
- Grey, Jeffrey (2008). *A Military History of Australia* (3rd ed.). Melbourne: Cambridge University Press. ISBN 978-0-521-69791-0.
- Hall, Robert A. (2000). *Combat Battalion: The Eight Battalion in VietNam*. Crows Nest: Allen & Unwin.
- Kuring, Ian (2004). *Red Coats to Cams. A History of Australian Infantry 1788 to 2001*. Sydney: Australian Military History Publications. ISBN 1-876439-99-8.
- Nicholls, Bob (1986). *Bluejackets & Boxers: Australia's Naval Expedition to the Boxer Uprising*. North Sydney: Allen & Unwin. ISBN 0-86861-799-7.

Further reading

<templatestyles src="Template:Refbegin/styles.css" />

- Abbott, J.M. (1902). *Tommy Cornstalk*. London: Longmans. OCLC 500113513[462].
- Bou, Jean (2012). "Ambition and Adversity: Developing an Australian Military Force, 1901–1914"[463] (PDF). *Australian Army Journal*. Canberra, Australian Capital Territory: Land Warfare Studies Centre. **IX** (1): 71–86. ISSN 1448-2843[464].
- Grey, Jeffrey (2001). *The Australian Army*. The Australian Centenary History of Defence. Volume I. Melbourne, Victoria: Oxford University Press. ISBN 0195541146.
- Haken, John (2014). "The Formation of the Australian Army". *Sabretache*. Garran, Australian Capital Territory: Military Historical Society of Australia. Volume LV (No. 3, September): 51–52. ISSN 0048-8933[465].
- Morgan, Benjamin (2017). "The Structure of the Post-Federation Australian Army, 1901–1910". *Sabretache*. Garran, Australian Capital Territory: Military Historical Society of Australia. Volume LVIII (No. 3, September): 37–52. ISSN 0048-8933[465].

- Palazzo, Albert (2001). *The Australian Army: A History of its Organisation 1901–2001*. Melbourne, Victoria: Oxford University Press. ISBN 0195515072.
- Perry, Warren (1973). "Lieutenant-General Sir Edward Hutton: The Creator of the Post-Federation Army"[466] (PDF). *Australian Army Journal*. Melbourne: Directorate of Military Training (No. 291, August): 14–23. OCLC 30798241[467].
- Stockings, Craig (2007). *The Making and Breaking of the Post-Federation Australian Army, 1901–09*[468] (PDF). Study Paper No. 311. Duntroon, Australian Capital Territory: Land Warfare Studies Centre. ISBN 9780642296665. Archived from the original[469] (PDF) on 19 January 2015.
- Stockings, Craig (2015). *Britannia's Shield: Lieutenant-General Sir Edward Hutton and Late-Victorian Imperial Defence*. Port Melbourne, Victoria: Cambridge University Press. ISBN 9781107094826.
- Tyquin, Michael (1999). *Neville Howse: Australia's First Victoria Cross Winner*. Melbourne, Victoria: Oxford University Press. ISBN 0-19-551190-5.
- Vazenry, G.R. (February 1963). "Re-organization: The Australian Military Force 1800–1962"[470] (PDF). *Australian Army Journal*. Directorate of Military Training (No. 165): 32–43. OCLC 30798241[467].
- Wilcox, Craig (2002). *Australia's Boer War: The War in South Africa 1899–1902*. South Melbourne: Oxford University Press. ISBN 0-19-551637-0.

Australian Army

Australian Army	
Active	1 March 1901 – present
Country	Australia
Type	Army
Size	30,764 (Regular) 14,662 (Active Reserve)
Part of	Australian Defence Force
Engagements	• Second Boer War • World War I • World War II • Korean War • Malayan Emergency • Indonesian Confrontation • Vietnam War • War in Somalia • Rwanda • East Timor • Regional Assistance Mission to Solomon Islands • War in Afghanistan • Iraq War • 2006 East Timorese crisis • 2014 Military Intervention in Iraq
Website	www<wbr/>.army<wbr/>.gov<wbr/>.au[471]
Commanders	
Commander-in-chief	General Sir Peter Cosgrove As Governor-General of Australia
Chief of the Defence Force	General Angus Campbell
Chief of Army	Lieutenant General Richard Burr
Deputy Chief of Army	Major General Jake Ellwood
Commander Forces Command	Major General Gus McLachlan
Insignia	

Australian Army flag	
Roundel (aviation)	
Roundel (armoured vehicles)	

The **Australian Army** is Australia's military land force. It is part of the Australian Defence Force (ADF) along with the Royal Australian Navy and the Royal Australian Air Force. While the Chief of the Defence Force (CDF) commands the ADF, the Army is commanded by the Chief of Army (CA). The CA is therefore subordinate to the CDF, but is also directly responsible to the Minister for Defence. Although Australian soldiers have been involved in a number of minor and major conflicts throughout its history, only in World War II has Australian territory come under direct attack.

History

Formed in March 1901, with the amalgamation of the six separate colonial military forces, the history of the Australian Army can be divided into two periods:

- 1901–47, when limits were set on the size of the regular Army, the vast majority of peacetime soldiers were in reserve units of the Citizens Military Force (also known as the CMF or Militia), and expeditionary forces (the First and Second Australian Imperial Forces) were formed to serve overseas,[472,473] and
- Post-1947, when a standing peacetime regular infantry force was formed and the CMF (known as the Army Reserve after 1980) began to decline in importance.[474,473]

During its history the Australian Army has fought in a number of major wars, including: Second Boer War (1899–1902), First World War (1914–18), the Second World War (1939–45), Korea War (1950–53), Malayan Emergency (1950–60), Indonesia-Malaysia Confrontation (1962–66), Vietnam War (1962–73),[475] and more recently in Afghanistan (2001 – present) and Iraq (2003–09).[476] Since 1947 the Australian Army has also been involved in many peacekeeping operations, usually under the auspices of the United Nations, however the non-United Nations sponsored Multinational Force and Observers in the Sinai is a notable exception. Australia's largest peacekeeping deployment

Figure 78: *Soldiers of the Australian 39th Battalion in September 1942*

Figure 79: *Two Australian soldiers during the Shah Wali Kot Offensive in Afghanistan*

Figure 80: *Australian Cavalry Scout in Iraq, 2007*

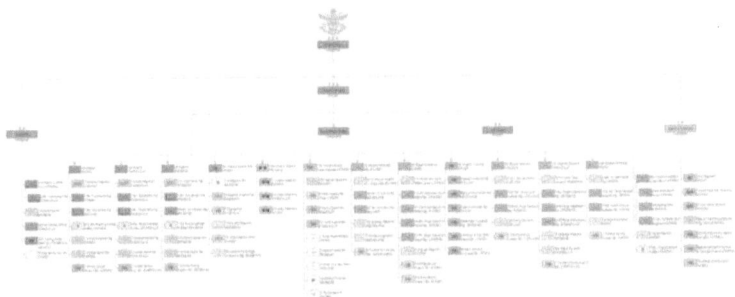

Figure 81:
The Australian Army's structure from 2018

began in 1999 in East Timor, while other ongoing operations include peacekeeping on Bougainville, in the Sinai, and in the Solomon Islands. Humanitarian relief after 2004 Indian Ocean earthquake in Aceh Province, Indonesia, Operation Sumatra Assist, ended on 24 March 2005.

Current organisation

The 1st Division comprises a deployable headquarters, while 2nd Division under the command of Forces Command is the main home-defence formation, containing Army Reserve units. 2nd Division's headquarters only performs

Figure 82: *1 RAR machine-gun team training in Hawaii during RIMPAC 2012*

administrative functions. The Australian Army has not deployed a divisional-sized formation since 1945 and does not expect to do so in the future.[477]

1st Division

1st Division carries out high-level training activities and deploys to command large-scale ground operations. It has few combat units permanently assigned to it, although it does currently command the 2nd Battalion, Royal Australian Regiment as part of Australia's amphibious task group.

Forces Command

Forces Command controls for administrative purposes all non-special-forces assets of the Australian Army. It is neither an operational nor a deployable command.

- **1 Brigade** – Multi-role Combat Brigade based in Darwin and Adelaide.
- **3 Brigade** – Multi-role Combat Brigade based in Townsville.
- **6 Brigade (CS&ISTAR)** – Mixed brigade based in Sydney.
- **7 Brigade** – Multi-role Combat Brigade based in Brisbane.
- **16 Aviation Brigade** – Army Aviation brigade based in Enoggera, Brisbane.
- **17 Combat Service Support Brigade** – Logistic brigade based in Sydney.

Figure 83: *A 1st Commando Regiment soldier jumping from a 16th Aviation Brigade, 171st Aviation Squadron Black Hawk helicopter*

- **2nd Division** administers the reserve forces from its headquarters located in Sydney.
  - **4 Brigade** – based in Victoria.
  - **5 Brigade** – based in New South Wales.
  - **8 Brigade** – training brigade with sub units around Australia
  - **9 Brigade** – based in South Australia and Tasmania.
  - **11 Brigade** – based in Queensland.
  - **13 Brigade** – based in Western Australia.

Additionally, Forces Command includes the following training establishments:

- Army Recruit Training Centre at Kapooka, NSW;
- Royal Military College, Duntroon in the ACT;
- Combined Arms Training Centre at Puckapunyal, Vic;
- Army Logistic Training Centre at Bonegilla, Vic and Bandiana, Vic; and
- Army Aviation Training Centre at Oakey, QLD.

Special Forces

Special Operations Command comprises a command formation of equal status to the other commands in the ADF. It includes all of Army's special forces assets.

Figure 84: *Australian special forces in Afghanistan, 2009*

Planned restructuring

Under a restructuring program known as Plan Beersheba announced in late 2011, the 1st, 3rd and 7th Brigades will be re-formed as combined-arms multi-role manoeuvre brigades with the 2nd Battalion, Royal Australian Regiment (part of the 3rd Brigade) forming the core of a future amphibious force. The force will be known as the Amphibious Ready Element and will be embarked on the Navy's new *Canberra*-class amphibious assault ships.

Colours, standards and guidons

Infantry, and some other combat units of the Australian Army carry flags called the Queen's Colour and the Regimental Colour, known as "the Colours".[478] Armoured units carry Standards and Guidons – flags smaller than Colours and traditionally carried by Cavalry, Lancer, Light Horse and Mounted Infantry units. The 1st Armoured Regiment is the only unit in the Australian Army to carry a Standard, in the tradition of heavy armoured units. Artillery units' guns are considered to be their Colours, and on parade are provided with the same respect.[479] Non-combat units (combat service support corps) do not have Colours, as Colours are battle flags and so are only available to combat units. As a substitute, many have Standards or Banners. Units awarded battle honours have them emblazoned on their Colours, Standards and Guidons. They are a link to the unit's past and a memorial to the fallen. Artillery do not have Battle Honours – their single Honour is "Ubique" which means "Everywhere" – although they can receive Honour Titles.[480]

The Army is the guardian of the National Flag and as such, unlike the Royal Australian Air Force, does not have a flag or Colours. The Army, instead, has a banner, known as the Army Banner. To commemorate the centenary of the Army, the Governor General Sir William Deane, presented the Army with a new Banner at a parade in front of the Australian War Memorial on 10 March 2001. The Banner was presented to the Regimental Sergeant Major of the Army (RSM-A), Warrant Officer Peter Rosemond.

The Army Banner bears the Australian Coat of Arms on the obverse, with the dates "1901–2001" in gold in the upper hoist. The reverse bears the "rising sun" badge of the Australian Army, flanked by seven campaign honours on small gold-edged scrolls: South Africa, World War I, World War II, Korea, Malaya-Borneo, South Vietnam, and Peacekeeping. The banner is trimmed with gold fringe, has gold and crimson cords and tassels, and is mounted on a pike with the usual British royal crest finial.

Personnel

Strength

In the 2014–15 financial year the Army had an average strength of 43,667 personnel: 29,366 permanent (regular) and 14,301 active reservists (part-time). In addition, there are another 12,496 members of the Standby Reserve. The regular Army is targeted to expand to 30,464 (regular) and 15,250 (part-time) personnel by 2015–16. Personnel numbers have trended upwards since a peak in 2010–11 with an actual strength of 29,366 full-time personnel. Army Reserve numbers are 14,301, which does not include Standby Reserves. This gives the Army a combined strength of 43,667 active personnel for the year 2014–15.

Rank and insignia

The ranks of the Australian Army are based on the ranks of the British Army, and carry mostly the same actual insignia. For officers the ranks are identical except for the shoulder title "Australia". The Non-Commissioned Officer insignia are the same up until Warrant Officer, where they are stylised for Australia (for example, using the Australian, rather than the British coat of arms). The ranks of the Australian Army are as follows:

1. Private (PTE) – OR-2

2. Private Proficient (PTE(P)) Also used within the Private equivalent ranks – OR-3
3. Lance Corporal or Lance Bombardier (LCPL or LBDR) – OR-4
4. Corporal or Bombardier (CPL or BDR) – OR-5
5. Sergeant (SGT) – OR-6
6. Staff Sergeant (SSGT) – OR-7 (SSGT is being phased out of the Australian Army)
7. Warrant Officer Class Two (WO2) – OR-8
8. Warrant Officer Class One (WO1) – OR-9
9. Regimental Sergeant Major of the Army (RSM-A) – OR-9 (This is an appointment rather than a rank)
10. Second Lieutenant (2LT) – OF-1
11. Lieutenant (LT) – OF-2
12. Captain (CAPT) – OF-3
13. Major (MAJ) – OF-4
14. Lieutenant Colonel (LTCOL) – OF-5
15. Colonel (COL) – OF-6
16. Brigadier (BRIG) – OF-7. Like the United Kingdom, prior to 1922 Australia used the rank Brigadier General
17. Major General (MAJGEN) – OF-8
18. Lieutenant General (LTGEN) – OF-9
19. General (GEN) – OF-10
20. Field Marshal (FM) – OF-11. This rank is generally reserved for wartime and ceremonial purposes; there are no regular appointments to the rank. Sir Thomas Blamey is the only Australian-born officer promoted to the rank. Prince Philip, Duke of Edinburgh, is currently the only living holder of the rank of Field Marshal in the Australian Army. The Duke, however, does not have any active role in the Australian command structure.

Equipment

Small arms	F88 Austeyr (service rifle), F89 Minimi (support weapon), Browning Hi-Power (sidearm), MAG-58 (general purpose machine gun), SR-25 designated marksman rifle, SR-98 (sniper rifle), Mk48 Maximi, AW50F
Special forces	M4 carbine, Heckler & Koch USP, SR-25, F89 Minimi, MP5, SR-98, Mk48, HK416, HK417, Blaser R93 Tactical, Barrett M82, Mk14 EBR
Main battle tanks	59 M1A1 Abrams
Armored recovery vehicle	13 M88A2 Hercules armored recovery vehicles

Australian Army

Infantry fighting vehicles	257 ASLAV
Armoured Personnel Carriers	431 M113 Armored Vehicles upgraded to M113AS3/4 standard (around 100 of these will be placed in reserve)
Infantry Mobility Vehicles	1,052 Bushmaster PMVs,; 31 HMT Extenda Mk1 Nary vehicles and 89 HMT Extenda Mk2 on order
Light Utility Vehicles	2,268 G-Wagon 4 × 4 and 6x6, 1,500 Land Rover FFR and GS, 1,295 Unimog 1700L
Artillery	112 L118/L119 105 mm Hamel Guns (In reserve), 36 M198 155 mm Howitzer (In reserve), 54 M777A2 155 mm Howitzer, 36 RBS-70 surface-to-air missile systems.Wikipedia:Citation needed
Radar	AN/TPQ-36 Firefinder radar, AMSTAR Ground Surveillance RADAR, AN/TPQ-48 Lightweight Counter Mortar Radar, GIRAFFE FOC, Portable Search and Target Acquisition Radar – Extended Range.
Unmanned Aerial Vehicles	Insitu Aerosonde, Elbit Systems Skylark and Boeing ScanEagle

Aircraft	Type	Versions	Number in service	Notes
		Helicopters		
Bell 206B-1 Kiowa	Light observation helicopter	206B-1	27	To be replaced by the Eurocopter Tiger and Eurocopter EC135. 56 originally in service.
Boeing CH-47 Chinook	Transport helicopter	CH-47D	2	One CH-47D lost in Afghanistan on 30 May 2011. From an initial fleet of six; two additional CH-47Ds were ordered in December 2011 as attrition replacement and to boost heavy lift capabilities until the delivery of seven CH-47Fs, which will replace the CH-47Ds. All seven Chinooks were delivered in August 2015. The US State Department has approved the possible sale of three more CH-47F aircraft as of December 2015. The 2016 Defence White Paper confirmed the order of three CH-47F aircraft.
		CH-47F	10	
Eurocopter EC135	Training helicopter	EC135T2+	1	15 Helicopter Aircrew Training System (HATS) are on order to be shared with the Navy.
Eurocopter Tiger	Attack helicopter	Tiger ARH	22	Delivery completed early July 2011. Achieved Final Operational Capability on 14 April 2016.

Sikorsky S-70 Black Hawk	Utility helicopter	S-70A-9	34	Will be replaced by the MRH 90 by June 2018. 18 to be kept in operational service for special forces until the end of 2021 due to issues with MRH 90 with an additional 2 retained.
NHIndustries MRH-90 Taipan	Utility helicopter	TTH: Tactical Transport Helicopter	39 (41)	45 in service as of June 2017. Total of 47 on order (including 6 for Royal Australian Navy)

Figure 85: *SR-25 rifle, Heckler & Koch USP sidearm*

Figure 86: *Australian M1 Abrams, the main battle tank used by the Army*

Figure 87: *Australian Army Sikorsky S-70 Black Hawk*

Figure 88: *An Australian Army MRH-90*

Figure 89: *Australian Army Tiger ARH*

Bases

The Army's operational headquarters, Forces Command, is located at Victoria Barracks in Sydney. The Australian Army's three regular brigades are based at Robertson Barracks near Darwin, Lavarack Barracks in Townsville and Gallipoli Barracks in Brisbane. The Deployable Joint Force Headquarters is also located at Gallipoli Barracks.

Other important Army bases include the Army Aviation Centre near Oakey, Queensland, Holsworthy Barracks near Sydney, Lone Pine Barracks in Singleton, New South Wales and Woodside Barracks near Adelaide, South Australia. The SASR is based at Campbell Barracks Swanbourne, a suburb of Perth, Western Australia.

Puckapunyal north of Melbourne houses the Australian Army's Combined Arms Training Centre, Land Warfare Development Centre, and three of the five principal Combat Arms schools. Further barracks include Steele Barracks in Sydney, Keswick Barracks in Adelaide, and Irwin Barracks at Karrakatta in Perth. Dozens of Australian Army Reserve depots are located across Australia.

Australian Army Journal

Since 1947, the Australian Army has published its own journal titled the *Australian Army Journal*. Covering a broad range of topics including essays, book reviews and editorials, with submissions from serving members as well as professional authors, the journal's stated goal is to provide "...the primary forum for Army's professional discourse... [and to facilitate]... debate within the Australian Army ...[and raise] ...the quality and intellectual rigor of that debate by adhering to a strict and demanding standard of quality". In 1976, the journal was placed on hiatus; however, publishing began again in 1999 and since then the journal has been published largely on a quarterly basis, with only minimal interruptions.

Future procurement

This list includes equipment currently on order or a requirement which has been identified:

- A replacement for the Tiger ARH helicopter was identified in the 2016 Defence White Paper. The Army is set to retire the helicopter earlier than expected after encountering numerous issues with sustainment and serviceability rates. While the Tigers were initially supposed to get a $1–2 billion mid-life upgrade, a new type of helicopter—either manned, unmanned or a combination of both—is set to enter service from the mid 2020s.
- A new deployable short-range ground-based air defence missile system is slated to replace the RBS-70 MANPADS by the early 2020s.
- A new medium-range air defence system is also to be acquired in the late 2020s. The new system will help defend deployed airfields, command centres and other valuable assets from enemy air attack. The Army has lacked a medium-range air defence system capability since the Rapier's retirement in 2005.
- Land-based anti-ship missiles were outlined as a new requirement in the 2016 Defence White Paper to defend deployed forces as well as offshore assets such as oil and natural gas platforms.
- The Australian Government committed to improving the systems that individual soldiers use. Items outlined in the DWP include "weapons and targeting equipment, digital communications systems, body armour and self protection equipment (including for chemical, biological and radiological threats), and night fighting equipment."
- 1,100 Hawkei protected mobility vehicles are currently being procured at a cost of around $1.3 billion.
- The Bushmaster PMV is to be replaced beginning in 2025 by a new platform.
- Land 400 replacement program is set to replace the existing 257 ASLAVs and 700 M113 APCs with new platforms.

- To complement current artillery, a new class of long-range rocket artillery is to be introduced in the mid 2020s. The new system, yet to be named, will be able to provide fire support for troops at three hundred kilometres.
- A riverine patrol capability is to be re-established in 2022. The capability will be established around a fleet of small, lightly armed patrol vessels to allow access to a range of different environments.
- The Army has outlined a need for enhanced intelligence, surveillance and reconnaissance capability. With this, they plan to acquire a fleet of armed, medium-range unmanned aerial vehicles along with regular capability updates. They will provide enhanced firepower and ISR as well as a counter-terrorism ability overseas. They will also assist in humanitarian and relief missions.

References

<templatestyles src="Template:Refbegin/styles.css" />

- Grey, Jeffrey (2008). *A Military History of Australia* (3rd ed.). Melbourne, Victoria: Cambridge University Press. ISBN 978-0-521-69791-0.
- Horner, David (2001). *Making the Australian Defence Force*. Melbourne, Victoria: Oxford University Press. ISBN 0-19-554117-0.
- Jobson, Christopher (2009). *Looking Forward, Looking Back: Customs and Traditions of the Australian Army*. Wavell Heights, Queensland: Big Sky Publishing. ISBN 978-0-9803251-6-4.
- Odgers, George (1988). *Army Australia: An Illustrated History*. Frenchs Forest, New South Wales: Child & Associates. ISBN 0-86777-061-9.

Further reading

<templatestyles src="Template:Refbegin/styles.css" />

- Australian Department of Defence (2009). *Defence Annual Report 2008–09*[481]. Canberra, Australian Capital Territory: Defence Publishing Service. ISBN 978-0-642-29714-3.
- Grey, Jeffrey (2001). *The Australian Army*. South Melbourne, Victoria: Oxford University Press. ISBN 978-0-19554-114-4.
- Palazzo, Albert (2001). *The Australian Army: A History of its Organisation 1901–2001*. Melbourne, Victoria: Oxford University Press. ISBN 0195515072.
- Terrett, Leslie; Taubert, Stephen (2015). *Preserving our Proud Heritage: The Customes and Traditions of the Australian Army*. Newport, New South Wales: Big Sky Publishing. ISBN 9781925275544.

External links

 Wikimedia Commons has media related to *Australian Army*.

- Australian Army website[471]

List of equipment of the Australian Army

This is a list of the equipment currently used by the Australian Army.

Armoured vehicles

Model	Image	Origin	Type	Number	Notes
					Armoured vehicles
M1 Abrams		United States	Main Battle Tank	59	59 M1A1 Abrams and seven M88 Hercules were purchased to replace the Leopard AS1 in service with the 1st Armoured Regiment. The first M1 equipped sub-units of the regiment became operational in mid-2007. In 2016 an additional six M88A2 Hercules were acquired. Beginning in around 2025 Australia is slated to upgrade its M1 fleet under LAND 907 Phase 2, which is currently the most advanced M1 Abrams variant in US service.
ASLAV		Canada Australia	Eight-wheeled Armored Personnel Carrier	257	The Army operates 257 ASLAV-25 vehicles, in a variety of roles including formation reconnaissance, as an infantry fighting vehicle, armoured ambulance or recovery vehicle. Under LAND 400 Phase 2 the ASLAV is slated to be replaced by a new Armored Reconnaissance Vehicle (ARV) beginning in 2021. To be replaced by the Boxer (armoured fighting vehicle).

List of equipment of the Australian Army 147

Model	Image	Origin	Type	Number	Notes
M113 armoured personnel carrier		United States	Armoured personnel carrier	431	The Army now has 340 M113AS4 and 91 M113AS3 in service in seven variants. The vehicles are used in the armoured reconnaissance and armoured personnel carrier roles. The Army had operated 840 M113A1 vehicles in nine variants. The M113 family of vehicles is scheduled to be replaced under LAND 400 Phase 3 beginning in around 2025.
Boxer (armoured fighting vehicle)		Germany Netherlands	Multi-role armoured fighting vehicle	211 on order	211 vehicles planned to be acquired under the Land 400 Phase 2 program (plus 12 additional modules)

Utility, Reconnaissance and Support vehicles

Model	Image	Origin	Type	Number	Notes
Bushmaster PMV		Australia	4×4 MRAP Cat. II	1052	The Army has ordered a total of 1,052 Bushmaster Protected Mobility Vehicles to date, with deliveries commencing in mid-2005. Bushmasters primarily equip the Motorised Infantry 7th Brigade, B Squadron, 3rd/4th Cavalry Regiment also operate armoured vehicles in support of the 3rd Brigade, 1st Combat Engineer Regiment, 2nd Combat Engineer Regiment, and 3rd Combat Engineer Regiment, as well as the heavy weapons and support elements of two mechanised battalions and three light infantry battalions.
Hawkei PMV		Australia	Armoured car	1100 on order	The Army has ordered 1,100 Hawkei Protected Mobility Vehicles – Light (PMV-L) to partially replace the Land Rover Perentie. It is smaller and around half the weight of the Bushmaster. It is able to be carried underslung by the CH-47F Chinook helicopter.
Land Rover Perentie		United Kingdom Australia	Armoured car	5000+	5,000+ Land Rovers were originally acquired as a fleet of light duty vehicles for transporting stores, equipment and personnel. As of 2017 fewer than 1,500 remain in service.

Name	Image	Origin	Type	Quantity	Details
G-Wagen		▇▇ Germany	Multi-purpose/-light assault vehicle	2268	The Army has purchased a total of 2,268 G-Wagons to partially replace the Land Rover Perentie. There are eight G-Wagon variants including several in a specialized 6X6 configuration, including Mobile Command Post, Surveillance and Reconnaissance, and Ambulance. Some 4X4 variants are transportable by the RAAF's Alenia C-27J Spartan battlefield airlifters.
RMMV HX		▇▇ Germany	Tactical military trucks	2536	Under Project LAND 121 Phase 3B Army is in process of acquiring a comprehensive fleet of Rheinmetall MAN medium and heavy military trucks to replace its Unimog, Mack R and IH S vehicles. In 2016 a total of 2,536 trucks were ordered, configured for a wide variety of roles and in a mix of standard and protected (armored cab) variants. Configurations include: Medium 4X4 - Tray (766 standard + 616 protected), Tray w/Crane (96 + 141), Tipper (15 + 24); Medium 6X6 – Recovery (14 + 15); Heavy 8X8 – Integrated Load Handling System (ILHS) (323 + 236), Tipper (66 + 33), Tanker (22 + 0), Tractor (Heavy Trailer Hauler) (89 + 21); Super-Heavy 10X10 – Recovery (22 + 37). In addition to personnel and general cargo medium Tray trucks are able to carry the following specialized mission pallets: Special Stores, Maintenance, Personnel & Cargo (protected and secured), and Combat Engineer. Heavy ILHS trucks are also capable of transporting those pallets as well as the following larger mission modules: Water Storage, Water Storage w/Pump, Fuel Storage, Fuel Storage w/Pump, Heavy Stores, Flatrack (portable open cargo platform), Gun Stores, Gun Ammunition, Command Post, Bridge Erection, and Propulsion Boat and Floating Support Bridge. Beginning in 2018 a total of 1,070 additional medium and heavy MAN military trucks are likely to be acquired under LAND 121 Phase 5B, primarily for use as training vehicles.
HMT Extenda		🇬🇧 United Kingdom	High Mobility Transporter	31	The Army purchased 31 HMT Extenda MK1 Nary patrol vehicles for use by the Special Air Service Regiment to replace the Long Range Patrol Vehicle to provide armoured protection from IEDs. Its namesake comes from Warrant Officer David Nary who was the killed during pre-deployment training in Kuwait for the Iraq War. In addition, 89 HMT Extenda MK2 have been ordered for the 2nd Commando Regiment that will be reconfigurable in four configurations.

List of equipment of the Australian Army   149

Watercraft

Model	Image	Origin	Type	Number	Notes
LARC-V		United States	Amphibious cargo vehicle	15	15 medium size coastal /- inland waterway landing craft fitted with 2 x 12.7mm HMG to be in service until 2027.
LCM-8		United States	River boat and mechanized landing craft	12	12 amphibious vehicles to be in service until 2027. Withdrawn from service in 1993 and reintroduced in 1998 after upgrade.

Artillery

Model	Image	Origin	Type	Number	Notes
M777 howitzer		United Kingdom	155mm Towed Howitzer	54	Thirty-five 155 mm M777s were ordered as part of the first phase of the Land 17 project to replace the Army's inventory of towed artillery, with initial deliveries beginning in late 2010. An additional 19 guns were purchased in late 2012 instead of the self-propelled guns previously planned, bringing the total order to 54.

Air defence

Model	Image	Origin	Type	Number	Notes
RBS 70		Sweden	Short-range Air Defense (SHORAD) Man-portable air-defence system (MANPADS)	30	Thirty upgraded RBS-70 short range air defence weapon systems are currently divided between two Air Defence Batteries within the 16th Air Land Regiment. More sophisticated Bolide missiles have now been purchased.

NASAMS 2		Norway	Medium Range Surface-to-air missile	-	In April 2017 the Australian Government awarded Raytheon a contract to produce an unspecified number of NASAMS systems for use with the Australian Army. The batteries, possibly mounted on Hawkei PMVs, will be used by the 16th Air Land Regiment.

Aircraft

Name	Origin	Type	Number	Notes
Airbus Helicopters ARH Tiger	France	Armed reconnaissance helicopter	22	Modified and upgraded version of the Tiger HAP. These helicopters are planned to be phased out by the mid-2020s by the formal Tiger ARH replacement project.
NHIndustries MRH-90 Taipan	France	Medium lift/utility helicopter	41 (+ 6 joint with Navy)	Replaced the UH-1 Iroquois in 2008, and the Black Hawks in 2017.
UH-60 Black Hawk	United States	Medium lift/utility helicopter	20	The Sikorsky UH-60 Black Hawk was the Army's primary battlefield lift/utility helicopter. The helicopters were assembled by Hawker de Havilland. Replaced in utility and transport roles by the MRH-90, with 20 aircraft remaining in service with the 6th Aviation Regiment until 2021 to support special forces missions.
Boeing CH-47F Chinook	United States	Heavy lift helicopter	10	
Bell 206 Kiowa	United States	Training Helicopter	12	To be replaced by the Eurocopter EC135 in 2018
Eurocopter EC135 T2+	France Germany	Training helicopter	15 (Joint with Navy)	Helicopter Aircrew Training System (HATS) shared with the Navy

Unmanned aerial vehicles

Name	Origin	Type	Number	Notes
AAI RQ-7 Shadow	United States	Reconnaissance and battlefield surveillance	18Wikipedia:Citation needed	
ScanEagle	United States	Reconnaissance and battlefield surveillance		

Infantry weapons

Assault rifles and carbines

Name	Origin	Type	Calibre	Photo	Notes
F88 Austeyr	Austria / Australia	Bullpup assault rifle	5.56×45mm NATO		A derivative of the Austrian Steyr AUG STG-77 assault rifle. It is the ADF's standard individual weapon, which replaced the L1A1 SLR and the M16A1 rifle from front-line service in the late 1980s. The weapon is manufactured under licence in Australia by Thales Australia (formerly Australian Defence Industries Ltd). Enhanced F88 (EF88), The Latest variant to improve modularity featuring extended accessories rail, a fixed barrel and bolt catch release. 1RAR will begin to re-equip with the EF88 from June 2015 with a wider roll out from 2016. The ADF has ordered 30,000 of these rifles.
M4 carbine	United States	Carbine	5.56×45mm NATO		Used by various Australian special forces units. Its official designation in Australia is the **M4A5**.
HK416	Germany	Assault rifle	5.56×45mm NATO		Also used by various Australian special forces units.
L1A1 Self-Loading Rifle	Belgium / United Kingdom / Australia	Battle rifle	7.62×51mm NATO		Used by the Australian Federation Guard with bayonet attachment.

Precision rifles

Name	Origin	Type	Calibre	Photo	Notes
SR-98	United Kingdom	Bolt action sniper rifle	7.62×51mm		An Australian variant of the bolt action Accuracy International Arctic Warfare rifle, it is the standard-issue sniper rifle in the Australian Army and is chambered for 7.62×51mm. It replaced the Parker Hale Model 82 rifle in the late 1990s. Manufactured under licence in Australia by Thales Australia.
AW50F	United Kingdom	Anti-materiel rifle	.50 BMG		The AW50F is the largest-bore variant of the Arctic Warfare sniper rifles suited to the anti-materiel role. It is chambered for the .50 BMG cartridge, and is primarily used with Raufoss Mk211 HEIAP rounds. The AW50F was designed with an Australian-designed and manufactured barrel.
Blaser 93 Tactical 2	Belgium	Bolt Action Sniper rifle	.338 Lapua Magnum		a straight-pull bolt-action sniper rifle chambered in .338 Lapua Magnum. The rifle has been observed in service with special forces and infantry units in Afghanistan.
Heckler & Koch HK417	Germany	Marksman Rifle System	7.62×51mm NATO		'Marksman Rifle System' used by infantry and special forces units to fill the gap between a sniper rifle and 5.56mm derivatives.
SR-25	United States	semi-automatic	7.62×51mm		A semi-automatic 7.62×51mm sniper rifle. It has recently been observed in service with reconnaissance and special forces units of the Australian Army. It has seen service in Iraq, Afghanistan and East Timor.

List of equipment of the Australian Army 153

Name	Origin	Type	Calibre	Photo	Notes
Mk 14 Enhanced Battle Rifle (M14EBR)	United States	Designated marksman rifle	7.62×51mm NATO		Small numbers borrowed from American forces were used by Australian special forces in Afghanistan.
Barrett M82	United States	Anti-materiel Sniper Rifle	.50 BMG		A semi-automatic sniper and anti-materiel rifle chambered in .50 BMG

Machine guns

Name	Origin	Type	Calibre	Photo	Notes
F89 Minimi	Belgium	Light machine gun	5.56×45 mm NATO		The Army's standard light machine gun chambered for 5.56×45 mm NATO. The F89 is also manufactured under licence in Australia by Thales Australia.
Maximi	Belgium	Light machine gun	7.62×51mm NATO		The 7.62×51mm NATO model of the Minimi is also in limited service.
FN MAG 58	Belgium	General-purpose machine gun	7.62×51mm NATO		The Army's general purpose machine gun chambered for 7.62 × 51 mm NATO. It replaced the M60 machine gun.
Browning M2HB-QCB	United States	Heavy machine gun	.50 BMG		Heavy machine gun not used at the infantry section level but rather as a heavy support weapon usually mounted on vehicles. It uses the .50 BMG cartridge and has an effective range in excess of 2,000 metres.

Pistols

Name	Origin	Type	Calibre	Photo	Notes
Self-Loading Pistol 9 millimetre Mark 3	Belgium	Semi-automatic pistol	9mm		The Self-Loading Pistol 9 millimetre Mark 3 is the standard issue service pistol of the Australian Defence Force.
Heckler & Koch USP	Germany	Semi-automatic pistol	9mm		The Heckler & Koch USP is used by various special forces units.

Submachine guns

Name	Origin	Type	Calibre	Photo	Notes
Heckler & Koch MP5	Germany	Submachine gun	9mm		Primarily used by special forces units.

Shotguns

Name	Origin	Type	Calibre	Photo	Notes
Remington Model 870 and 870P	United States	Shotgun	12-gauge		Used by both Special Forces and Military Police personnel. It is also used in specific roles within the infantry.

Grenade launchers

Name	Origin	Type	Calibre	Photo	Notes
M203 grenade launcher	United States	grenade launcher	40×46mm		Attaches to the F88 (RM Equipment M203PI) and M4 (Colt M203-A1) rifles.
Mk 19 AGL	United States	automatic grenade launcher	40×53mm		Automatic grenade launcher that fires grenades at a cyclic rate of 325-375 rounds per minute, giving a practical rate of fire of 60 rounds per minute (rapid) and 40 rounds per minute (sustained). Usually vehicle mounted by Australian special forces units.
Mk 47 Striker LWAGL	United States	automatic grenade launcher	40×53mm		Mk 47 Mod 1 Lightweight automatic grenade launcher (LWAGL) is 36% of the weight of the Mk 19, has a further range than the Mk 19 and is fitted with Lightweight Video Sight (LVS2) sighting system. It will be issued to infantry battalions from late 2016 and to Special Operation Command units from early 2017.

List of equipment of the Australian Army 155

Anti-armour

Name	Origin	Type	Calibre	Photo	Notes
66 mm Short-Range Anti-Armour Weapon (M72 LAW)	United States	anti-tank rocket launcher	66mm		A single shot disposable anti-armour weapon
L14A1 Carl Gustav Medium Direct Fire Support Weapon	Sweden	recoilless rifle	84mm		Primarily used in the anti-armour role.
Javelin Anti-Tank Guided Missile (ATGM)	United States	guided anti-armour missile	127mm		

Mortars

Name	Origin	Type	Calibre	Photo	Notes
F2 81mm Mortar	United Kingdom, Canada	Mortar	81mm		

Grenades and anti personnel mines

Name	Origin	Type	Detonation	Photo	Notes
F1 fragmentation hand grenade	Australia	Frag grenade	Fuse		Manufactured by Thales Australia. It has a lethal range of 6 m (20 ft) and has a fuse time of 4.5 to 5.5 seconds.
M18A1 Claymore Antipersonnel Mine	United States	Anti-personnel mine	Remote		It is called an "Anti-Personnel Device" due to the Commonwealth of Australia agreeing not to use mines of any type. Wikipedia:Citation needed

Bayonets

Name	Origin	Type	Photo	Notes
M9 Bayonet	Australia	Bayonet		The Army's primary combat knife used by all personnel and attached on the F88 Austeyr and the M4 carbine.

Combat uniform of the Australian Army

There are three major combat uniforms worn by the Australian Defence Force, they are:

- **Disruptive Pattern Combat Uniform** - DPCU is the standard combat uniform worn in terrains that feature green and brown-shaded flora. The pattern has been in service since the late 1980s.
- **Disruptive Pattern Desert Uniform** - DPDU is the Desert Combat uniform worn by Australian Defence Force personnel in theatres where the terrain is arid. It uses the same pattern as DPCU, but with the colours changed to suit the desert terrain. This uniform was instituted in the early 2000s, to meet the need for personnel serving overseas in Southwest Asia
- **MultiCam** - in late 2010, the ADF announced that Multicam will be the standard pattern for all regular Australian Army personnel in Afghanistan after trials were conducted by special operations units. Multicam, it is said, provided *"... troops with greater levels of concealment across the range of terrains in Afghanistan – urban, desert and green."* Previously, depending upon the terrain, Australian troops had to alternate between green and desert colored DPCUs.[482,483] Furthermore, the Defence Material Organisation has since announced that they had obtained a licence from Crye Associates to locally produce Multicam and for a new uniquely Australian pattern to be developed by Crye to replace DPCU uniforms.[484]

The current issue of DPCU is known as 'DPCU-NIR' - or Disruptive Pattern Combat Uniform - Near Infra-Red. The Defence Science and Technology Organisation has developed materials for use in combat uniforms which will reduce night-vision detection, and it has been integrated into this uniform, which also sports a new cut and shape, the NATO-style front rank epaulette, zip-fastening, sleeve pockets and Velcro tabs.[485]

Figure 90: *F88A2 rifle and the Australian Multicam Pattern (AMP) combat uniform*

Future equipment

Infantry weapons

The Army has begun to roll out their new state of the art rifle, the Enhanced F88 (EF88). The new rifle has several new features including improved modularity featuring extended accessories rail, a fixed barrel, bolt catch release and a black paint scheme. It was confirmed in July 2015 that the contract for 30,000 EF88 rifles had been approved with full roll out starting in 2016. 2,500 Steyr Mannlicher SL40 grenade launchers have also been ordered.

The Army had previously planned on replacing the F88 with the Advanced Individual Combat Weapon (AICW) by 2010–2012. The most notable feature of the AICW is a grenade launcher with 3 stacked rounds that uses electricity to fire off the grenade. The AICW had aimed to provide the infantry soldier with the ability to fire multiple grenades without having to reload, and to switch between 5.56 mm ballistic rounds and 40 mm grenades without changing sights, trigger or stance, giving the operator more versatility and reduced reaction times in combat.Wikipedia:Citation needed The AICW has all but disappeared from the Army's sights and it is unlikely to ever make a return. The company responsible for the ACIW, Metal Storm Limited was placed in voluntary administration in 2012.

The Army decided to procure the Mk 47 Striker 40 mm lightweight automatic grenade launcher in mid-2015, and plans to begin receiving units within one year.[486]

Armoured vehicles

In December 2011, the Thales Hawkei PMV (Protected Military Vehicle) was selected as the preferred tender for the Army's requirement of a light 4x4 armored car with a potential order for 1300 vehicles. The seven-tonne Hawkei has been described as a 'baby' variant of the Bushmaster having been developed by the same manufacturer.

Under LAND 400 the ASLAV and M113s will be replaced, with the project to acquire a Combat Reconnaissance Vehicle (CRV), an Infantry Fighting Vehicle (IFV), a Manoeuvre Support Vehicle (MSV) and an Integrated Training System (ITS). The ASLAV fleet is planned to be replaced from 2020, and the M113s from 2025. On 19 February 2015 the tender was opened for the replacement of the ASLAV, listing a requirement for up to 225 armored vehicles to provide the future mounted combat reconnaissance capability. The remaining requirements of the project will be confirmed by the upcoming Defence White Paper; however, it is expected to include an infantry fighting vehicle—a capability currently only partly provided by the in-service M113AS4 Armoured Personnel Carrier—as well as a manoeuvre support vehicle, and an integrated training system. The project is valued at more than $10 billion and is expected to acquire approximately 700 vehicles.

Aircraft

The Army is reorganising its aviation element, through the purchase of 22 ARH Tiger attack helicopters and 30 MRH 90 Taipan utility helicopters (30 helicopters out of a total purchase of 46, which will be divided between Army, Fleet Air Arm and a joined MRH 90 training base). Furthermore, 7 CH-47F Chinook heavy lift helicopters will be purchased to replace the Army's five remaining CH-47D Chinook helicopters. In addition, the Army will also acquire a number of UAVs (including a number of Boeing ScanEagles and 18 RQ-7 Shadow) which will equip the 20th Surveillance and Target Acquisition Regiment, at Enoggera Barracks, Queensland. Smaller UAVs being trialed include the AeroVironment Wasp III and Black Hornet Nano.

Previously it was planned that the MRH-90 would eventually replace all of the Army's Black Hawks, with the Black Hawk fleet planned to be reduced to 18 operational aircraft in 2014–15 as part of the phased withdrawal of the type from service. However, in December 2015 it was announced that 20 Black

Hawks will remain in service with the 6th Aviation Regiment until the end of 2021 to provide aviation support to special forces.

The Army as part of a joint program with the RAN under Air 9000 Phase 7B[487] are seeking future advanced training and light support helicopters. The helicopters being offered by industry are: Eurocopter EC-135 (from Boeing-Thales), Bell 429 (Raytheon-Bell) and Agusta A109 (from BAE-CAE-AgustaWestland).

External links

 Wikimedia Commons has media related to *Weapons of Australia*.

- Manufacturing process of the F88 rifle[488] - *Army News*, 6 September 2007.
- "Improving In-Service Small Arms Systems – An Australian Experience"[489] (PDF). *Defense Technical Information Center (dtic.mil)*. Thales Australia Limited. 1 June 2011. Archived from the original[490] (PDF) on 20 October 2016. Retrieved 13 January 2012.

|}

Navy

History of the Royal Australian Navy

The **history of the Royal Australian Navy** traces the development of the Royal Australian Navy (RAN) from the colonisation of Australia by the British in 1788. Until 1859, vessels of the Royal Navy made frequent trips to the new colonies. In 1859, the Australia Squadron was formed as a separate squadron and remained in Australia until 1913. Until Federation, five of the six Australian colonies operated their own colonial naval force, which formed on 1 March 1901 the Australian Navy's (AN) Commonwealth Naval Force which received Royal patronage in July 1911 and was from that time referred to as Royal Australian Navy (RAN).[491] On 4 October 1913 the new replacement fleet for the foundation fleet of 1901 steamed through Sydney Heads for the first time.

The Royal Australian Navy has seen action in every ocean of the world.Wikipedia:Citation needed It first saw action in World War I, in the Pacific, Indian and Atlantic oceans. Between the wars the RAN's fortunes shifted with the financial situation of Australia: it experienced great growth during the 1920s, but was forced to reduce its fleet and operations during the 1930s. Consequently, when it entered World War II, the RAN was smaller than it had been at the start of World War I. During the course of World War II, the RAN operated more than 350 fighting and support ships; a further 600 small civilian vessels were put into service as auxiliary patrol boats. (Contrary to some claims, however, the RAN was not the fifth-largest navy in the world at any point during World War II.[492])

Following World War II, the RAN saw action in Korea, Vietnam, and other smaller conflicts. Today, the RAN consists of a small but modern force, widely regarded as one of the most powerful forces in the Asia Pacific Region.

Figure 91: *A Sopwith 1½ Strutter aircraft taking off from a temporary flight deck on the first HMAS Australia, a battle cruiser, in 1918.*

Australia Station

In the years following the establishment of the British colony of New South Wales in 1788, Royal Navy ships of the East Indies Squadron under the command of the East Indies Station would be station in or visit Australian waters. From the 1820s, a ship was sent annually to New South Wales, and occasionally to New Zealand.[493]

In 1848, an Australian Division of the East Indies Station was established,[494] and in 1859 the British Admiralty established an independent command, the Australia Station, under the command of a Commodore who was assigned as Commander-in-Chief, Australia Station.[495] The Australian Squadron was created to which British naval ships serving on the Australia Station were assigned. The changes were partially in recognition of the fact that a large part of the East Indies Station had been detached to Australian waters, and also reflecting growing concern for the strategic situation in the western Pacific in general, and in Tahiti and New Zealand in particular. In 1884, the commander of the Australia Station was upgraded to the rank of rear admiral.

At its establishment, the Australia Station encompassed Australia and New Zealand, with its eastern boundary including Samoa and Tonga, its western edge in the Indian Ocean, south of India and its southern edge defined by the

Figure 92: *An aerial view of the second HMAS Australia – a heavy cruiser – passing through the Panama Canal in March 1935. Australia saw extensive combat in World War II.*

Figure 93: *HMAS Melbourne (R21) steams in San Diego Harbor, California (USA), in 1977.*

Figure 94: *The gunboat HMQS Paluma in 1889*

Antarctic Circle. The boundaries were modified in 1864, 1872 and 1893.[496] At its largest, the Australia Station reached from the Equator to the Antarctic in its greatest north-south axis, and covered $1/4$ of the Southern Hemisphere in its extreme east-west dimension, including Papua New Guinea, New Zealand, Melanesia and Polynesia.[497]

In 1911 the Australia Station passed to the Commonwealth Naval Forces (initially under the command of RN officers) and the Australian Squadron was disbanded. The Station, now under nominal Australian command, was reduced to only cover Australia and its island dependencies to the north and east. In 1911, the Commonwealth Naval Forces was renamed the Royal Australian Navy, which in 1913 came under Australian command. The Royal Navy's Australia Station's Sydney based depots, dockyards and structures were gifted to the Commonwealth of Australia. The Royal Navy continued to support the RAN and provided additional blue-water defence capability in the Pacific up to the early years of World War II.

Colonial navies and federation

Before the Federation of Australia in 1901, five of the six self-governing colonies in Australia operated a navy, the exception being Western Australia which did not have a naval force. The colonial navies were supported by the ships of the Royal Navy's Australian Station which was established in 1859. In 1856, Victoria received its own naval vessel, HMCSS *Victoria*, which in 1860 was deployed to assist the New Zealand colonial government during the First Taranaki War. When *Victoria* returned to Australia, the vessel had taken part in several minor actions, with the loss of one crew member. The deployment of *Victoria* to New Zealand marked the first occasion that an Australian warship had been deployed overseas. In the years leading up to Federation, Victoria had the most powerful of the colonial navies. Victoria had HMVS *Cerberus* since 1870, as well as HMVS *Nelson*, three small gunboats and five torpedo-boats. NSW had two very small torpedo boats, and the corvette *Wolverine*. The colonial navies were expanded greatly in the mid-1880s and usually consisted of gunboats and torpedo-boats for coastal defence of harbours and rivers, and naval brigades to man vessels and forts.

On 1 January 1901, Australia became a federation of six States, as the Commonwealth of Australia, which on 1 March 1901 took over the defence forces from the States, to form the Commonwealth Naval Forces.[498] The Australian and New Zealand governments agreed with the Imperial government to help fund the Royal Navy's Australian Squadron, while the Admiralty committed itself to maintain the Squadron at a constant strength. In 1902, the commander of the Australia Station was upgraded to the rank of vice admiral. The boundaries were again modified in 1908.

Formation

A growing number of people, among them Captain William Rooke Creswell, the director of the Commonwealth Naval Forces, demanded an autonomous Australian navy, financed and controlled by Australia. In 1907 Prime Minister Alfred Deakin and Creswell, while attending the Imperial Conference in London, sought the British Government's agreement to end the subsidy system and develop an Australian navy. The Admiralty rejected and resented the challenge, but suggested diplomatically that a small fleet of destroyers and submarines would be sufficient. Deakin was not impressed with the Admiralty, and in 1908 invited the United States Great White Fleet to visit Australia. The visit prompted public enthusiasm for a modern navy and led to the order of two 700-ton River-class torpedo-boat destroyers, a purchase that angered the British. The surge in German naval construction in 1909 led the Australian admiralty to change its position on an Australian navy, which resulted in the *Naval Defence Act* of 1910 being passed which created the Australian navy.

The first Australian warship, the destroyer HMAS *Parramatta*, was launched at Govan in Scotland on Wednesday 9 February 1910. Sister ship HMAS *Yarra*

Figure 95: *The official welcome to the new units of the Royal Australian Navy*

was launched at Dumbarton in Scotland on Saturday 9 April 1910. Both ships were commissioned into the Royal Navy on 19 September 1910 and sailed for Australia, arriving at Port Phillip on 10 December 1910. The event was marred by the death of Engineer Lieutenant W. Robertson, RN, who suffered a heart attack 8 miles (13 km) outside Port Phillip Heads whilst onboard HMAS *Yarra*, and drowned.[499]

The British Australia Station passed to the Commonwealth Naval Forces in 1911 and the Australian Squadron was disbanded. On 10 July 1911, King George V granted the title of "Royal Australian Navy" to the Commonwealth Naval Forces, and RAN ships could carry the prefix *"His Majesty's Australian Ship"* (HMAS). The Station was reduced to cover Australia and its island dependencies to the north and east, excluding New Zealand and its surrounds, which became part of the China Station and called the New Zealand Naval Forces. The Navy was to operate under the authority of the Australian Commonwealth Naval Board, which functioned from 1 March 1911.

At the 1911 Imperial Conference Australia expressed concern about Japan's growing naval power and it was agreed that the British government would consult Australia when negotiating renewal of the Anglo-Japanese Alliance. It was also decided that the Royal Navy would continue to support the RAN and provide blue-water defence capability in the Pacific and that if there was war the ships of the RAN would be transferred to British Admiralty control. Under the *Naval Defence Act* (1912) the power to make the transfer was conferred in the Governor-General. The RAN would become the Australia Squadron of the Royal Navy with all ships and personnel under the direct control of the British Admiralty, while the RAN remained responsible for the upkeep of the ships and training.

In 1913, responsibility for the reduced Australia Station passed to the new Royal Australian Navy under nominal Australian command, with the Australia Squadron of the Royal Navy's Australia Station coming to an end and its Sydney based depots, dockyards and structures being gifted to the Commonwealth of Australia. The first commanding officer was Admiral George Edwin Patey, Rear Admiral Commanding HM Australian Fleet, on loan from the Royal Navy. On Saturday 4 October 1913 the Australian fleet, consisting of the battle cruiser *Australia*, the cruisers *Melbourne* and *Sydney*, the protected cruiser *Encounter*, and the torpedo-boat destroyers *Parramatta*, *Yarra* and *Warrego*, entered Sydney Harbour for the first time. The manpower of the fleet stood at four hundred officers and men and, for the next two years, ships were built for the fledgling navy.

The Royal Navy continued to support the RAN and provide blue-water defence capability in the Pacific up to the early years of World War II. In 1958, the boundaries of Australia Station was redrawn again, now to include Papua New Guinea.

World War I

On 3 August 1914, as the prospect of war with the German Empire loomed, the Australian Government sent the following message to the Admiralty.[500]

> *In the event of war Government prepared place vessels of Australian Navy under control British Admiralty when desired.*

The United Kingdom declared war on Germany the next day, and on 8 August, the Australian Government received a reply, requesting that the transfer be made immediately, if not already done. Two days later, on 10 August, the Governor-General officially transferred control of the Royal Australian Navy to the British Admiralty, which would retain control until 19 August 1919.[501]

At the outbreak of war, the RAN stood at 3,800 personnel and consisted of sixteen ships, including the battlecruiser *Australia*, the light cruisers *Sydney* and *Melbourne*, the destroyers *Parramatta*, *Yarra*, and *Warrego*, and the submarines *AE1* and *AE2*. The light cruiser *Brisbane* and three destroyers were under construction, and a small fleet of auxiliary ships was also being maintained. As a consequence the Royal Australian Navy at the start of the war was a small but formidable force.

Figure 96: *The wrecked German raider Emden*

Figure 97: *The Australian squadron entering Simpson Harbour, Rabaul, September 1914*

Australian ships first saw action Asian and Pacific theatre; assisting in the attack on German New Guinea by the Australian Naval and Military Expeditionary Force (AN&MEF). Germany had colonised the northeastern part of New Guinea and several nearby island groups in 1884, and the colony was currently used as a wireless radio base, Britain required the wireless installations to be destroyed because they were used by the German East Asia Squadron which threatened merchant shipping in the region. The objectives of the force were the German stations at Yap in the Caroline Islands, Nauru, and Rabaul in New Britain. On 30 August 1914, the AN&MEF left Sydney under the protection of *Australia* and *Melbourne* for Port Moresby, where the force met the Queensland contingent, aboard the transport HMAHS *Kanowna*. The force then sailed for German New Guinea on 7 September, leaving *Kanowna* behind when her stokers refused to work. *Sydney* and her escorting destroyers met the AN&MEF off the eastern tip of New Guinea. *Melbourne* was detached to destroy the wireless station on Nauru, while on 14 September, *Encounter* bombarded a ridge near Rabaul, while half a battalion advanced towards the town. The only major loss of the campaign was the disappearance of the submarine *AE1* during a patrol off Rabaul on 14 September 1914.[502,503]

On 9 November 1914, the German light cruiser SMS *Emden* attacked the Allied radio and telegraph station at Direction Island in the Cocos (Keeling) Islands. The inhabitants of the island managed to transmit a distress signal, which was received by *Sydney*, only 50 miles (80 km) away. *Sydney* arrived within two hours, and was engaged by *Emden*. *Sydney* was the larger, faster and better armed of the two, and eventually overpowered *Emden*, with captain Karl von Müller running the ship aground on North Keeling Island at 11:15 am. At first, *Emden* refused to strike its colours and surrender; *Sydney* fired on the stationary *Emden* until it eventually struck its colours. The Battle of Cocos was the first battle the RAN participated in.

On 6 February 1915, the obsolescent light cruiser HMAS *Pioneer* joined the East African campaign. On 6 July, she engaged the German cruiser SMS *Königsberg* and German shore batteries, during the Battle of Rufiji Delta. *Pioneer* remained off East Africa and took part in many bombardments of German East Africa, including Dar-es-Salaam on 13 June 1916. *Pioneer* then returned to Australia, to be decommissioned in October 1916.

During the Naval operations in the Dardanelles Campaign the Australian submarine *AE2* became the first Allied warship to breach the Turkish defences of the Dardanelles. *AE2* spent five days in the area, was unsuccessfully attacked several times, but was unable to find any large enemy troop transports. On 29 April 1915, she was damaged in an attack by the Turkish torpedo-boat *Sultan Hisar* in Artaki Bay and was scuttled by her crew. The wreck of *AE2* remained undiscovered until June 1998.

Figure 98: *HMAS Pioneer off East Africa in 1916*

Ships of the Royal Australian Navy also assisted the Royal Navy in the blockade of the German High Seas Fleet. In February 1915, HMAS *Australia* joined the British Grand Fleet, and was made flagship of the 2nd Battle Cruiser Squadron. *Australia* was not involved in the Battle of Jutland; in April, the battlecruiser was damaged in a collision with sister ship HMS *New Zealand*, and she did not return to service until June.[504] Three RAN ships were present during the surrender of the German High Seas Fleet; *Australia*, *Sydney*, and *Melbourne*, with *Australia* leading the port division of the Grand Fleet as it sailed out to meet the Germans.[505,506]

The most decorated Australian Naval unit of World War One, however was not a ship at all, but the Royal Australian Navy Bridging Train, a land-based unit composed mostly of reservists which landed at Suvla Bay with the British IX Corps and was responsible for receiving, storing and distributing the supplies, including potable water, of the British troops at Suvla. Due to their position working the piers and landings at Suvla, the Train was the last Australian unit to depart the Gallipoli Peninsula. After Gallipoli, the Train was sent to the Middle East, where they made a second amphibious landing at the Battle of Magdhaba, before returning to Australia and being disbanded after a series of miscommunications during May 1917.

Expansion during the war had been limited, with the RAN growing to include thirty-seven ships and more than 5,000 personnel by 1918.[507] The RAN's losses had also been modest, only losing the two submarines *AE1* and *AE2*, whilst casualties included 171 fatalities – 108 Australians and 63 officers and men on loan from the Royal Navy, with less than a third the result of enemy action.[508]

The 1918–19 influenza pandemic

Between April 1918 and May 1919, the Spanish Flu killed approximately 25 million people worldwide, far more than had been killed in four years of war. A rigorous quarantine policy was implemented in Australia; although this reduced the immediate impact of the flu, the nation's death toll surpassed 11,500.

When the pandemic struck in 1918, the ships of the Royal Australian Navy were dispersed throughout the world. The speed at which the flu spread, coupled with the cramped mess decks and poorly ventilated living spaces on early 20th century warships, created a favourable environment for the disease. The pandemic swept through the British Grand Fleet in 1918; the Australian cruisers assigned to the fleet suffered high casualties, with up to 157 casualties in one ship alone. Outbreaks in the Mediterranean fleets were more severe than those in the Atlantic. HMAS *Brisbane* recorded 183 casualties between November and December 1918, of those casualties 2 men died of pneumonia. The RAN lost a total of 26 men to the disease; further loss prevented primarily by the ready availability of professional medical treatment.

South Pacific aid mission

The disease arrived in the South Pacific on the cargo vessel SS *Talune*, which sailed from Auckland on 30 October 1918 whilst knowingly carrying sick passengers. *Talune* stopped in Fiji, Samoa, Tonga and Nauru: the first outbreaks in these locations occurred within days of the ships visits. The local authorities were generally unprepared for the size of the outbreak, allowing the infection to spread uncontrollably. The German territory of Samoa was the worst affected of the small islands, the New Zealand administration carried out no efforts to lessen the outbreak and rejected offers of assistance from nearby American Samoa. The New Zealand government officially apologised to Samoa in 2002 for their reaction to the outbreak. On 29 November 1918 the military governor of Apia requested assistance from Wellington; the request was turned down because all doctors were needed in New Zealand. Australia offered the only alternate source of aid.

The Commonwealth Naval Board was aware of the worsening situation in the region; the sloop HMAS *Fantome* reported its first case on 11 November 1918 while stationed in Fiji, with half her complement eventually affected. On 20 November 1918, the Naval Board began forming a joint relief expedition from available military medical personnel. The commanding officer of

Figure 99: *Portside view of the Challenger-class light cruiser HMAS Encounter*

HMAS *Encounter* was then ordered to embark the expedition in Sydney and sail as soon as possible. *Encounter* departed Sydney on 24 November 1918, ten minutes after completing loading. As a precaution, all 450 members of *Encounter*'s crew were doubly inoculated; the ship had suffered 74 cases earlier in the year at Fremantle and the captain did not want a repeat. *Encounter* arrived in Suva on 30 November and took on half of the available coal and 39 tonnes of water.[509] Spanish flu was rampant in Suva; Captain Thring implemented a strict quarantine, placed guards on the wharf, and ordered that coaling be carried out by the crew instead of native labour. *Encounter* departed Suva in the evening of the same day and arrived off Apia on 3 December. Within six hours, the medical landing party assigned to Apia and their stores were ashore. *Encounter* then departed for the Tongan capital of Nuku'alofa, arriving on 5 December. The last of the medical staff and supplies were unloaded, and *Encounter* sailed for Suva on 7 December to re-coal. On arriving in Suva, *Encounter* received orders to return to Sydney, where reached on 17 December and was immediately placed into quarantine. The South Pacific aid mission is regarded as Australia's first overseas relief expedition, and set a precedent for future relief missions conducted by the RAN.

Figure 100: *Australia on her side and sinking during her scuttling in April 1924*

Between the Wars

Following the end of World War I, the Australian Government believed that an immediate evaluation of the RAN was necessary. Australia had based its naval policy on the Henderson *Recommendations* of 1911, developed by Sir Reginald Henderson. The government sent an invitation to Admiral John Jellicoe, he arrived in Australia in May 1919. Jellicoe remained in Australia for three months, before returning to England via New Zealand and Canada. Jellicoe submitted his findings in August 1919, titled the *Report on the Naval Mission to the Commonwealth*. The report outlined several policies designed to strengthen British naval strength in the Pacific Ocean. The report heavily stressed a close relationship between the RAN and the Royal Navy. This would be achieved by strict adherence to the procedures and administration methods of the Royal Navy. The report also suggested constant officer exchange between the two forces. Jellicoe also called for the creation of a large Far East Imperial Fleet, which would be based in Singapore and include capital ships and aircraft carriers. The creation cost for this fleet was to be divided between Great Britain, Australia and New Zealand: contributing 75%, 20%, and 5% respectively. The suggested makeup of the RAN would include; one aircraft carrier, two battlecruisers, eight light cruisers, one flotilla leader, twelve destroyers, a destroyer depot ship, eight submarines, one submarine depot ship, and a small number of additional auxiliary ships. The annual cost and depreciation of the fleet was estimated to be £4,024,600. Except for implementing closer tier with the Royal Navy, none of Jellicoe's major recommendations were carried out.[510]

With the end of World War I, the Australian Government began to worry about the threat Japan posed to Australia. Japan had extended its empire 3,000 kilometres (1,900 mi) to the south, bringing it right to Australia's doorstep. Japan had continued to build up its naval force, and had reached the point where it outgunned the Royal Navy in the Pacific. The RAN and the government believed that the possibility of a Japanese invasion was highly likely. In his report, Admiral Jellicoe believed that the threat of a Japanese invasion of Australia would remain as long as the White Australia Policy remained in place. Due to the perceived threat, and bilateral support in Australia for the White Australia Policy, the Australian Government became a vocal supporter of the continuance of the 1902 Anglo-Japanese Alliance. Australia was joined in its support for the alliance by New Zealand but was heavily opposed by Canada, which believed that the alliance had hindered the British Empire's relationship with China and the United States. No decision on the alliance was agreed on, and the discussion was shelved pending the outcome of the Washington Naval Treaty. The results of the treaty, which allowed the British to retain naval supremacy in the Pacific Ocean, created a sense of security in Australia. Many Australians saw the Four Powers Pact as replacing the Anglo-Japanese Alliance. This sense of security became known as the *Ten Year Rule*. This led to defence retrenchments in Australia, following the international trend, and a £500,000 reduction in expenditure. The Governor-General Henry Forster when opening parliament on 22 June 1922 was quoted as saying:

> *In view of the result of attained at the Washington Treaty which, my advisors believe, guarantee peace in the Pacific for some time to come, it is proposed to reduce the establishment of the navy and army, and postpone the expansion of the air force.*

Between World War I and World War II, the Royal Australian Navy underwent a severe reduction in ships and manpower. As a result of the Washington Naval Treaty, the flagship HMAS *Australia* was scrapped with her main armaments and sunk outside Sydney Heads in 1924. In the same year, the RAN began a five-year program of obtaining new ships from Britain: the heavy cruisers *Australia* and *Canberra* and the seaplane carrier *Albatross*. This purchase was partly paid for by scrapping *Brisbane*, *Melbourne*, *Sydney*, and most of the destroyers. The Great Depression of 1929 led to another reduction of manpower; although reduced in size, the available posts were easily filled as many men were unemployed and the offered pay was greater than most jobs. The RAN's personnel strength fell to 3,117 personnel, plus 131 members of the Naval Auxiliary Services. By 1932, the strength of the Reserves stood at 5,446. In the early 1930s, lack of funds forced the transfer of the Royal

Figure 101: *HMAS Canberra entering Sydney Harbour in 1930*

Australian Naval College from Jervis Bay to Flinders Naval Depot in Victoria. In 1933 the Australian Government ordered three light cruisers; HMA Ships *Perth*, *Hobart*, and *Sydney*; selling the seaplane carrier *Albatross* to fund *Hobart*. During this time, the RAN also purchased destroyers of the V and W destroyer classes, the ships that would become known as the Scrap Iron Flotilla. With the ever-increasing threat of Germany and Japan in the late 1930s, the RAN was not in the position it was at the outbreak of World War I.[511]

World War II

Australia declared war on Nazi Germany one hour after the United Kingdom's declaration of war on 3 September 1939. Unlike the arrangements with the British Admiralty at the start of the First World War, during World War II RAN ships remained under Australian command.

Ship type	Sept. 1939	June 1945
Heavy cruisers	2	2
Light cruisers	4	2
Destroyers	5	11
Frigates	0	6
Sloops	2	2
Corvettes	0	53

Landing ship infantry	0	3
Anti-submarine auxiliaries	0	3
Auxiliary Minesweepers	0	6
Minelayers	0	1
Fleet Oilers	0	1
Store ships	0	12
Repair ships	0	3
Boom defence vessels	0	4
Boom gate vessels	0	6
Tugs	0(?)	6
Cable repair ships	0	2
Survey ships	0(?)	9
Motor Launches	0	33
Harbour defence launches	0	28
Air sea rescue vessels	0	20
Naval auxiliary patrol vessels	0	75
Services reconnaissance	0	8
Miscellaneous vessels	0(?)	41
Total	**13(?)**	**337**

At the onset of war the RAN was relatively modest, even if it was arguably the most combat-ready of the three services. Major units included:[512]

- two County-class heavy cruisers; *Australia* and *Canberra*, both carried 8-inch (203 mm) guns and had entered service in the 1920s
- three modern Modified Leander-class light cruisers; *Hobart*, *Perth*, and *Sydney*, which mounted 6-inch (152 mm) guns
- the older Town-class cruiser *Adelaide*
- four sloops, *Parramatta*, *Swan*, *Warrego*, and *Yarra*; although only *Swan* and *Yarra* were in commission
- five V-class destroyers
- a variety of support and ancillary craft

Following the call up of reserves in 1939 the permanent forces grew from 5,440 to 10,259.[513]

During the war the men and vessels of the RAN served in every theatre of operations, from the tropical Pacific to the frigid Russian convoys and grew exponentially. The table illustrates the growth of the RAN between the outbreak of war on 3 September 1939 and 30 June 1945.[514]

Operations against Italy, Vichy France and Germany

From mid-1940, ships of the RAN, at the request of the Admiralty, began to deploy to the Mediterranean Sea to take part in the Battle of the Mediterranean against Nazi Germany and Fascist Italy. In September 1939, the Admiralty and the Australian Commonwealth Naval Board agreed to deploy the RAN Destroyer Flotilla outside the Australia Station; the five ships of what was to become known as the Scrap Iron Flotilla arrived at Malta in mid-December.[515] HMAS *Sydney* deployed in May 1940 and was later joined by *Hobart*. When Italy declared war on 10 June 1940, the Australian warships made up five of the twenty-two Allied destroyers and one of the five modern light cruisers on station in the Mediterranean. The RAN then offered the services of *Australia* to the Admiralty, and was accepted. When *Australia* arrived in the Mediterranean, the RAN had sent nearly the entire combat fleet to the Northern Hemisphere, leaving Australia open to possible attack.[516]

The entry of Italy into the war also lead to a far more active role for the few remaining RAN vessels on the Australian Station. Indeed, on 12 June 1940, after a prolonged chase, the Armed Merchant Cruiser (AMC) HMAS *Manoora* forced the Italian merchant ship *Romolo* (9,780 tons) to scuttle south-west of Nauru.[517]

On 27 June 1940, Admiral Cunningham commander of the Mediterranean Fleet ordered the 7th Cruiser Squadron, which included HMAS *Sydney*, to rendezvous with an Egypt-bound convoy near Cape Matapan. The cruiser squadron sighted three Italian destroyers at 18.00 on 28 June 1940 and immediately engaged them.[518] Within an hour, the *Espero* was incapacitated and *Sydney* was signalled to sink her. As *Sydney* approached, *Espero* launched torpedoes, but failed to hit any targets. *Sydney* fired four salvos, scoring ten direct hits on *Espero*. *Sydney* remained at the scene for two hours picking up survivors.

Also on 27 June 1940, the *Console Generale Liuzzi* was scuttled south of Crete after being depth-charged by HMAS *Voyager* and the British destroyers *Dainty*, *Ilex*, *Decoy*, and *Defender*. On 29 June 1940, another Italian submarine, the *Uebi Scebeli*, was sunk west of Crete by the same ships.[519]

On 7 July 1940, a 25-ship fleet departed Alexandria, intending to meet a convoy east of Malta.[520] The next day, a submarine sighted an Italian fleet 500 miles (800 km) away; the Allied fleet altered course to intercept.[521] The two fleets sighted each other at 15.00 on 9 July 1940, and a battle that became known as the Battle of Calabria began.[522] Four vessels of the RAN took part in the battle; HMA Ships *Sydney*, *Stuart*, *Vampire*, and *Voyager*. *Sydney* was the first RAN vessel to engage the enemy, and at 15.20 opened fire on an Italian cruiser. When the Italian fleet began to withdraw, the Allied destroyer

Figure 102: *Bartolomeo Colleoni sinking, 19 July 1940*

squadron was ordered forward. *Stuart*, leading the destroyer force, was the first to open fire; her opening salvo was a direct hit at a range of 12,600 yards (11,500 m). Both fleets retired, with the Italians withdrawing under smoke, but Italian aircraft continued to attack Allied ships.[523] *Sydney*, which came under heavy air attack, was believed to have sunk.[524] The fleet arrived back in Alexandria on 13 July.

On 17 July 1940, HMAS *Sydney* and the destroyer HMS *Havock* were ordered to support a Royal Navy destroyer squadron on a sweep north of the island of Crete.[525] At 07.20 on 19 July, the Italian cruisers *Giovanni dalle Bande Nere* and *Bartolomeo Colleoni*, which opened fire seven minutes later.[526] The four British destroyers retreated to the north-east, while *Sydney* and *Havock*, 40 miles (60 km) away, began to close in.[527] *Sydney* sighted the cruisers at 08.29, and fired the first shots of the Battle of Cape Spada at a range of 17,360 metres (56,960 ft).[528] Within minutes, *Sydney* had successfully damaged *Bande Nere*, and when the Italians withdrew to the south, the six Allied ships pursued.[529] At 0848, with *Bande Nere* hiding behind a smoke screen, *Sydney* shifted her fire to *Bartolomeo Colleoni*, which was disabled by 0933.[530] The Australian cruiser left to pursue *Bande Nere*, but broke off at 10.27 as the Italian warship was out of range, and *Sydney* was dangerously low on ammunition.[531] The only damage to *Sydney* during the battle was caused by a shell at 09.21, which knocked a hole in the forward funnel, and wounded a sailor through splinter damage.[532]

Figure 103: *Sailors from Sydney posing around and in the forward funnel shellhole*

On 30 September 1940, HMAS *Stuart* destroyed the Italian 600-Serie Adua class submarine *Gondar*, killing two of its crew. Twenty-eight survivors was subsequently rescued by *Stuart*, with a further nineteen picked up by other vessels.[533]

On 27 March 1941, an Allied fleet under Admiral Cunningham was ambushed by an Italian naval force off Cape Matapan, Greece.[534] Three vessels of the RAN took part in the battle; HMA Ships *Perth*, *Stuart*, and *Vampire*. The victory at Cape Matapan allowed the evacuation of thousands of Allied troops from Crete.[535]

HMAS *Parramatta* was torpedoed and sunk on 27 November 1941 by *U-559* whilst escorting transports resupplying the Allied garrison at Tobruk. There were 24 survivors, but 138 men, including all officers, lost their lives.[536]

The Australians experienced further success on 15 December 1941 when HMAS *Nestor* attacked and sank the German submarine *U-127* off Cape St. Vincent, Portugal.[537]

West Africa

On 6 September 1940, HMAS *Australia* was ordered to sail to Freetown, Sierra Leone to join Operation Menace, the invasion of Vichy French-controlled Dakar in French West Africa. On 19 September, *Australia* and the cruiser HMS *Cumberland* sighted three Vichy cruisers heading south and shadowed them. When the French cruiser *Gloire* developed engine trouble, *Australia* escorted her towards Casablanca and returned to the fleet two days later. On 23 September *Australia* came under heavy fire from shore batteries, then drove two Vichy destroyers back into port. *Australia* then engaged and sunk the destroyer *L'Audacieux* with eight salvos in sixteen minutes. Over the next two days French and Allied forces exchanged fire; *Australia* was struck twice and lost her Walrus amphibian. *Australia* and the rest of the fleet retired on 25 September the battle became known as the Battle of Dakar.[538,539]

The "Scrap-Iron Flotilla"

The Scrap Iron Flotilla was an Australian destroyer group that operated in the Mediterranean and Pacific during World War II. The name was bestowed upon the group by Nazi Propaganda Minister Joseph Goebbels who described the fleet as a *"consignment of junk"* and *"Australia's Scrap-Iron Flotilla"*. The flotilla consisted of five vessels; *Scott*-class destroyer HMAS *Stuart*, which acted as flotilla leader, and four V-class destroyers; *Vampire, Vendetta, Voyager, Waterhen*. The ships were all built to fight in World War I, and were slow and poorly armed compared to newer ships.[540] The five destroyers—the entirety of the RAN's destroyer force—departed Australia in November 1939 destined for Singapore where they carried out anti-submarine exercises with the Royal Navy submarine HMS *Rover*.[541] On 13 November 1939, the flotilla left Singapore for the Mediterranean Sea, following a request from the Admiralty for assistance.

The Australian destroyer flotilla took part in multiple actions while in the Mediterranean, including the Allied evacuation following the battle of Greece in April 1941, though the flotilla came to fame in the mission to resupply the besieged city of Tobruk. The resupply routes from Alexandria and Mersa Matruh to Tobruk became known as *"Bomb Alley"* and was subject to constant Axis air attacks. The flotilla, which by this time was in poor condition, managed to make 138 supply runs to Tobruk, carrying in ammunition and stores and taking out wounded soldiers. On 28 May 1941 *Vampire* became the first of the flotilla to leave the Mediterranean. *Vendetta*, the last to leave, sailed in October 1941.

Of the five destroyers, three were lost during the war; *Waterhen* was sunk in the Mediterranean on 30 June 1941, *Vampire* was sunk by Japanese aircraft during the Indian Ocean Raid and *Voyager* ran aground at Betano, during the Timor campaign and was abandoned.[542]

Figure 104: *HMAS Waterhen*

Red Sea

As well as serving in the Mediterranean Sea, ships of the RAN also served in the Red Sea. In August 1940, Italian forces invaded British Somaliland. After a fighting withdrawal, the small British garrison was evacuated from Berbera, with HMAS *Hobart* assisting in the destruction of the port and its facilities. To aid in the delaying action, *Hobart* sent a 3-pounder gun ashore, operated by volunteers from the crew. The seamen were captured by the Italians, but were later liberated. Two RAN sloops joined the Red Sea force in 1940: *Parramatta* on 30 July and *Yarra* in September. In October, *Yarra* engaged and drove off two Italian destroyers attempting to raid a convoy. Although vessels of the RAN served in the Red Sea throughout the war, after 1941 the larger RAN ships were deployed to Australian waters in response to the threat from Japan.[543]

Loss of HMAS *Sydney*

On 19 November 1941, the Australian light cruiser HMAS *Sydney* and the German auxiliary cruiser *Kormoran* engaged each other in the Indian Ocean, off Western Australia. The two ships sank each other: *Sydney* was lost with all 645 hands, while the majority of the *Kormoran*'s crew were rescued and became prisoners of war. The location of both wrecks remained a mystery to many and subject to much controversy until 16–17 March 2008, when both ships were found.

Figure 105: *Memorial to HMAS Sydney at the state war memorial in Western Australia*

North Africa

RAN units continued to serve in the Mediterranean campaign, with HMAS *Quiberon*, taking part in Operation Torch, the invasion of North Africa. On 28 November 1942 Quiberon assisted in sinking the Italian submarine Dessiè and three days later also took part in the destruction of a four-ship convoy and a destroyer.[544]

Sicily 1943

During early 1943, eight Australian-designed and built *Bathurst*-class corvettes were transferred to Egypt from the Indian Ocean, in preparation for Operation Husky, the Allied invasion of Sicily. They were part of a 3,000-ship Allied force. The corvettes arrived in the Mediterranean in May and were formed into the 21st and 22nd Minesweeping Flotillas. All eight ships survived the campaign without damage or casualties sustained in action, although HMAS *Maryborough* experienced a near-miss from a German bomber. When the captain of HMAS *Gawler* enquired what damage had been sustained, the response from *Maryborough* read: "no damage except to my underpants".

Figure 106: *Australian sailors with a Bathurst-class corvette in the background. The RAN commissioned 56 of this class of corvettes during World War II.*

War with Japan

After the Imperial Japanese Navy's attacks on the Allies in December 1941, the RAN redeployed its larger ships to home waters to protect the Australian mainland from Japanese attack, while several smaller ships remained in the Mediterranean. From 1940 onwards, there was considerable Axis naval activity in Australian waters first from German commerce raiders and submarines and later by the Imperial Japanese Navy.

Initially, RAN ships served as part of the British-Australian component of the American-British-Dutch-Australian Command (ABDACOM) naval forces or in the ANZAC Force. ABDACOM was wound up following the fall of the Netherlands East Indies and was succeeded by the South West Pacific Area (command) (SWPA). The United States Seventh Fleet was formed at Brisbane on 15 March 1943, for service in the SWPA. RAN ships in the Pacific generally served at part of Seventh Fleet taskforces.

Timor

From February 1942, the RAN played a critical role in resupplying Australian and Dutch commandos on Timor. *Voyager* was not the only loss during the campaign. On 1 December 1942, HMAS *Armidale* was attacked by thirteen Japanese aircraft while attempting to land Dutch soldiers off Betano, Portuguese Timor. *Armidale* sank with the loss of 40 of her crew and 60 Dutch personnel. During the engagement, Ordinary Seaman Teddy Sheean operated an Oerlikon anti-aircraft gun and was wounded by strafing Japanese planes, he went down with the ship, still strapped into the gun and still shooting at the attacking aircraft.

Java Sea

On 28 February 1942, a joint ABDA naval force met a Japanese invasion force in the Java Sea. The *Leander*-class cruiser HMAS *Perth* and the American heavy cruiser USS *Houston* fought in and survived the Battle of the Java Sea.

On 1 March 1942, the *Perth* and *Houston* attempted to move through the Sunda Strait to Tjilatjap however they found their path blocked by the main Japanese invasion fleet from western Java. The Allied ships were engaged by at least three cruisers and several destroyers and in a ferocious night action, known as the Battle of Sunda Strait, both Perth and Houston were torpedoed and sunk. Casualties aboard *Perth* included 350 crew and 3 civilians killed, while 324 survived the sinking and were taken prisoner by the Japanese (106 of whom later died in captivity). The loss of *Perth* so soon after the sinking of her sister *Sydney*, had a major psychological effect on the Australian people. Japanese losses included a minesweeper and a troop transport sunk by friendly fire, whilst three other transports were damaged and had to be beached.[545]

Coral Sea

On 2 May 1942, two ships of the RAN were part of the Allied force in the Battle of the Coral Sea; HMA Ships *Australia* and *Hobart* as part of Task Force 44. Both ships came under intense air attack, while part of a force guarding the approaches to Port Moresby.[546]

The defence of Australian shipping

In late May and early June 1942, a group of five Imperial Japanese Navy submarines made a series of attacks on Sydney and the nearby port of Newcastle. On the night of 31 May – 1 June, the submarines launched three *Kohyoteki*-class midget submarines against Allied shipping in Sydney Harbour. A torpedo intended for the cruiser USS *Chicago* exploded under the depot ship HMAS *Kuttabul*, killing 21. On 8 June, two of the submarines shelled

Figure 107: *A Japanese Ko-hyoteki-class midget submarine, believed to be Midget No. 14, is raised from Sydney Harbour*

Sydney and Newcastle, with little effect. In response, the RAN instituted convoys between Brisbane and Adelaide. All ships of over 1,200 tons and with speeds of less than 12 knots (22 km/h; 14 mph) were required to sail in convoy when travelling between cities on the east coast.

The attack on Sydney and Newcastle marked the start of a sustained Japanese submarine campaign against Australia. During 1942, Japanese submarines sank 17 ships in Australian waters, although none of these ships were sailing as part of a convoy.[547] 16 ships were sunk in Australian waters during 1943, before the Japanese ended the campaign in July. Five of these ships were sunk while sailing in escorted convoys.[548] The Australian naval authorities gradually dismantled the coastal convoy system between December 1943 and March 1944.[549] By the end of the war, the RAAF and RAN had escorted over 1,100 convoys along the Australian coastline.

While the scale of the Japanese naval offensive directed against Australia was small compared to other naval campaigns of the war such as the Battle of the Atlantic, these attacks were "the most comprehensive and widespread series of offensive operations ever conducted by an enemy against Australia".[550] Although the RAN only sank a single full-sized Japanese submarine in Australian waters (*I-124* in January 1942) convoy escorts may have successfully reduced

Figure 108: *American destroyers evacuating the crew of HMAS Canberra after the Battle of Savo Island*

the threat to shipping in Australian waters by making it harder for Japanese submarines to carry out attacks.[551]

Whilst escorting convoys between Australia and New Guinea, HMAS *Arunta* attacked and sank the Japanese *Kaichu* type submarine *RO-33* off Port Moresby on 24 August 1942, killing all 42 men aboard.[552]

Loss of HMAS *Canberra*

The loss of HMAS *Canberra* at the Battle of Savo Island in August 1942 was the largest single ship loss the RAN experienced during World War II. In the early hours of the morning of 9 August 1942, *Canberra* was severely damaged off Guadalcanal in a surprise attack by a powerful Japanese naval force. *Canberra* was hit by 24 shells in less than two minutes, with 84 of her crew killed, including Captain Frank Getting. Following an order to abandon ship, *Canberra* was sunk the next day by a torpedo from a US destroyer, to prevent it being captured.

The loss of *Canberra*, following the losses of *Sydney* and *Perth*, attracted unprecedented international attention and sympathy for the RAN. US President Franklin D. Roosevelt wished to commemorate the loss of *Canberra* and requested that a US heavy cruiser under construction be named *Canberra*. USS *Canberra* was launched on 19 April 1943.[553] The British Government approved the transfer of HMS *Shropshire* to the RAN as a replacement, and the ship was commissioned as HMAS *Shropshire* on 20 April 1943.

Figure 109: *The light cruiser HMAS Hobart showing torpedo damage inflicted by a Japanese submarine on 20 July 1943. Hobart did not return to service until December 1944.*

Leyte Gulf and Lingayen Gulf

Between 23–25 October 1944 four RAN warships – HMA Ships *Australia*, *Shropshire*, *Arunta*, and *Warramunga* – took part in the Battle of Leyte Gulf, one of the largest naval battles in history. In the lead-up, on 21 October, *Australia* became the first Allied ship to be hit by a kamikaze aircraft near Leyte Island.[554] Gunners from *Australia* and *Shropshire* fired at, and reportedly hit, an unidentified Japanese aircraft. The plane then flew away from the ships, before turning and flying into *Australia*, striking the ship's superstructure above the bridge, and spewing burning fuel and debris over a large area, before falling into the sea. A 200-kilogram (440 lb) bomb carried by the plane failed to explode; if it had, the ship might have been effectively destroyed. At least 30 crew members died as a result of the attack, including the commanding officer, Captain Emile Dechaineux; among the wounded was Commodore John Collins, the Australian force commander. *Australia* remained on duty, but on 25 October, was hit again and was forced to retire to the New Hebrides for repairs.

Shropshire and *Arunta* remained at Leyte and were part of the United States Seventh Fleet Support Force at the Battle of Surigao Strait on 25 October.

During this action both ships contributed to the sinking of the Japanese battleship *Yamashiro*, with *Shropshire* firing thirty-two eight-gun broadsides into the battleship with her 8-inch guns in a period of 14 minutes.[555]

HMAS *Australia* returned to combat at the Battle of Lingayen Gulf in January 1945. During the battle *Australia* was repeatedly attacked between 5–9 January, suffering significant damage which forced it to retire once more.[556]

Ships with British fleets 1942–45

In 1940–42, five N class and two Q class were built in the UK and commissioned into the RAN for service with the British Eastern Fleet: HMA Ships *Napier*, *Nepal*, *Nestor*, *Nizam*, *Norman*, *Quiberon*, and *Quickmatch*. These ships were predominantly crewed by RAN personnel, although they were often commanded by British officers and remained the property of the British government.

Following the Japanese raid on Ceylon of March–April 1942, the Eastern Fleet was transferred from its base at Trincomalee, to the other side of the Indian Ocean: Kilindi in Kenya. From there the fleet undertook local patrols, escorted convoys and occasionally despatched ships to operations in the Mediterranean. During Operation Vigorous, a convoy to Malta in June 1942, *Nestor* was serious damaged in an air raid and slowly sank.

On 11 February 1944 the corvettes HMA Ships *Ipswich* and *Launceston*, in conjunction with the Indian sloop *Jumna*, sank the Japanese submarine *Ro-110* in the Bay of Bengal after the latter had torpedoed a ship in a Calcutta-bound convoy.

From late 1944, *Nepal*, *Norman* and *Quiberon* were transferred, along with many other Eastern Fleet ships, to the new British Pacific Fleet (BPF). Among other operations with the BPF, they took part in the Battle of Okinawa.

In late 1945, following the end of hostilities, the RAN acquired three more Q-class destroyers: *Queenborough*, *Quality*, and *Quadrant*.

The End of the War 1945

By the end of World War II, the RAN's combat strength numbered 150 ships with an additional 200 auxiliary craft with the service reaching its peak in June 1945, when it ranks swelled to 39,650 personnel. During the six years of war, the RAN lost three cruisers, four destroyers, two sloops, a corvette, and an auxiliary minesweeper to enemy action. Casualties included 1,740 personnel from the 19 ships sunk, and another 436 personnel killed aboard other ships or at other posts. By most measures, such losses were heavy for such a small service, representing over half its pre-war strength in ships and one-fifth in

Figure 110: *30 August 1945. Yokosuka Naval Base, Tokyo Bay. Commander Yuzo Tanno hands over the keys of Yokosuka Naval Base to Captain H. J. Buchanan, Royal Australian Navy. Buchanan led the first Commonwealth party to go ashore in Japan.*

men. Against this the RAN destroyed one cruiser, an armed merchant raider, three destroyers or torpedo boats, a minesweeper, many light craft and seven submarines. It also destroyed or captured more than 150,000 tons of Axis merchant shipping and shot down more than a hundred aircraft. Although difficult to quantify the RAN also played a role in numerous other successes.

Surrender and occupation of Japan

Ten RAN vessels were present at the signing of the Japanese surrender in Tokyo Bay on 2 September 1945; HMA Ships *Ballarat, Cessnock, Gascoyne, Hobart, Ipswich, Napier, Nizam, Pirie, Shropshire,* and *Warramunga*. Following the surrender ceremony, the majority of the RAN vessels left Japanese waters for other duties. As part of the surrender agreement, Japan agreed to an Allied occupation and disarmament. On 17 August 1945, the Australian Government agreed to provide two cruisers and two destroyers for service with the British Commonwealth Occupation Force (BCOF). A total of 15 RAN ships served with the BCOF, the ships performed a variety of tasks but were mainly employed on the Kyushu Patrol, preventing Korean nationals from illegally entering Japan.

Figure 111: *Australian sailors take possession of a midget submarine at a Japanese naval base near Tokyo in September 1945.*

The RAN also played a role in the disarmament of Japan, assisting in the scuttling of former Imperial Japanese Navy ships, in one instance *Quiberon* took part in the sinking of seven submarines of Kyushu as part of Operation Bottom. When Indian and New Zealand contingents began to withdraw from the BCOF, the operation became a predominantly Australian operation. In 1948, Kure naval base was turned over to Australia, and became known as HMAS *Commonwealth*. When North Korea invaded South Korea on 25 June 1950, one RAN ship was on station as part of BCOF. The Australian Government immediately offered HMAS *Shoalhaven* for United Nations service. Eventually, all RAN ships in the area were transferred to the command of British Commonwealth Forces Korea (BCFK).[557]

Clearing mines from Australian and New Guinean waters was another focus for the RAN in the years after the war. Minesweeping began in December 1945 and was conducted by HMAS *Swan*, eight *Bathurst*-class corvettes and several smaller craft from a base at Cairns. The work was arduous and dangerous, and HMAS *Warrnambool* was sunk with the loss of four men killed and another 25 wounded when she struck a mine off North Queensland on 13 September 1947. The RAN completed this task in August 1948 after sweeping 1,816 mines.

Figure 112: *Fairey Firefly aircraft on board HMAS Sydney off Korea, during the Korean War.*

Cold War

Following World War II, the RAN reduced its surface fleet but continued to expand in other ways, acquiring two Royal Navy *Majestic*-class aircraft carriers then under construction (HMAS *Melbourne* and HMAS *Sydney*) to build up a Fleet Air Arm. In the 1960s, the RAN began to move away from British-designed ships; the last major British design used was the Type 12 frigate, which formed the basis of the River-class frigates.

When it was decided that the RAN should commission a destroyer armed with guided missiles, the obvious British design was the County class; however, the RAN had reservations regarding the gas turbine propulsion, the Seaslug missile system, and the ability to adapt the design to Australian needs. Instead, the Australian government chose the United States-built, steam turbine-powered *Charles F. Adams*-class destroyer, armed with the Tartar missile as the basis for its *Perth* class, the first major US warship design chosen for the RAN.[558]

By the mid-late 1960s, the RAN was at the zenith of its operational capabilities; it was capable of dispatching a full carrier battle group in support of major operations by having in service an aircraft carrier (HMAS *Melbourne*), three large area defence destroyers of the *Perth* class, six modern River-class frigates and four *Oberon*-class submarines.

Figure 113: *HMAS Sydney leading HMAS Melbourne*

With the retreat of British forces west of the Suez Canal in the 1960s, the RAN began to take a more defensive role, and in co-operation with the United States, allied though the ANZUS treaty. The RAN saw service in many of the world's post war conflicts, including Korea, Vietnam, and the Indonesian Confrontation.

Korea

On 27 June 1950, the United Nations Security Council called on member nations to aid South Korea. On 29 June, Prime Minister Robert Menzies announced that the frigate HMAS *Shoalhaven*, stationed in Japan, and the destroyer HMAS *Bataan*, in Hong Kong, would be placed under UN command in Korea. On 1 July, one day after President Truman committed American ground forces to Korea, the first Australian operation in Korea took place; *Shoalhaven* escorted an American ammunition ship from Japan to Pusan.

The destroyer *Warramunga* was deployed in July 1950, and provided gunfire support during the X Corps landing at Wonsan in October. In December, *Bataan* and *Warramunga* assisted the mass evacuation of troops and refugees from Hungnam. The aircraft carrier *Sydney* was deployed to Korea between September 1951 and January 1952—the first carrier owned by a Commonwealth Dominion to see wartime service.[559] During this time, 2,366 sorties were flown from *Sydney*, with only fifteen aircraft lost and three pilots killed.

Over the course of the Korean War, nine ships of the RAN participated in the naval blockade of North Korea.[560]

Malaya

The Malayan Emergency was declared on 18 June 1948, prompted by a rise in Malayan Communist guerrillas in Malaya (later Malaysia). Australia, as a member of the Southeast Asia Treaty Organization, first deployed two RAAF squadrons to the region in 1950. In 1955, the Far East Strategic Reserve was created as a concentration of Commonwealth military forces (primarily British, New Zealand, and Australian) in Malaya for the protection of that nation from communist threats. Australia's commitment included two destroyers or frigates on station at any time, plus an annual visit by an aircraft carrier, and additional ships as needed. Training for the potentiality of war was the main occurrence for ships deployed to the Strategic Reserve, with RAN personnel gaining experience in working as part of a larger naval organisation.

The first ships of the RAN to arrive in the area were the Tribal-class destroyers *Warramunga* and *Arunta* in June 1955. Between 1955 and 1960, eleven other ships of the RAN operated with the Strategic Reserve: *Anzac*, *Melbourne*, *Quadrant*, *Queenborough*, *Quiberon*, *Quickmatch*, *Sydney Tobruk*,*Vampire*, *Vendetta*, and *Voyager*.

Indonesia

In response to the Indonesian invasion of Borneo and Malaya in 1963, Australia increased its presence in the region. At the outbreak of hostilities, the RAN frigates *Yarra* and *Parramatta* were on duty in the area. As tension mounted, Australia increased its presence by sending *Sydney*, *Vampire*, *Vendetta*, *Duchess*, and *Derwent* to the area. On 19 May 1964, the 16th Minesweeping Squadron, comprising six Ton-class minesweepers, was also deployed.

On 13 December 1964, the minesweeper HMAS *Teal* was fired upon with automatic weapons by an unlit vessel whilst operating as part of the Singapore Strait patrol. The vessel was overpowered and arrested by *Teal*, following a further small arms engagement that resulted in the deaths of three Indonesian crew members. On 23 February 1965, *Teal* was again involved in another engagement, she detected an unlit vessel off Cape Rachado. The suspicious vessel was closed on and illuminated, and revealed nine armed men in uniform who surrendered immediately upon challenge. On 13 March 1964, HMAS *Hawk* became the second vessel of the 16th Minesweeping Squadron to see action, when she was fired on by an Indonesian shore battery while patrolling off Raffles Lighthouse. Eleven high-explosive rounds were fired at the

Figure 114: *Melbourne with Vendetta, Voyager and Queenborough, circa 1962*

ship, some landing within 200 yards (200 m) of the vessel, and *Hawk* withdrew from the area at speed. The following morning, *Hawk* intercepted a sampan with five Indonesians on board who were promptly arrested.

When Indonesian forces crossed the border into Sebatik Island, Sabah on 28 June 1965, HMAS *Yarra* was called on to carry out bombardments disrupting the withdrawal of the Indonesians. *Yarra* carried out two more bombardments of the border area on 5 and 10 July. During three runs, *Yarra* fired a total of 70 rounds on the enemy. On 13 August 1966, an agreement between Indonesia and Malaysia brought an end to the conflict.

Melbourne-Voyager collision

During the night of 10 February 1964, the worst peacetime disaster in the RAN's history occurred when the destroyer HMAS *Voyager* was cut in two by the bow of the aircraft carrier HMAS *Melbourne*, killing 82 of the 293 men on board *Voyager*.[561,562] *Melbourne* was conducting air group exercises off Jervis Bay with *Voyager* acting as the plane guard destroyer. After a series of manoeuvres to reverse the course of the ships, *Voyager* ended up to starboard of *Melbourne*, and was ordered to resume her position (behind the carrier and to port) at 20.52.[563] Instead of turning away from *Melbourne*, *Voyager* unexpectedly turned towards the carrier, and did not alter course until it was too late.[564] At 20.56, *Melbourne*'s bow hit the destroyer just behind the bridge, and cut her in half, with the bow sinking quickly.[565] The search for survivors went on through the night; of the 314 aboard, 14 officers, 67 sailors, and 1 civilian dockyard worker were killed, including Captain Duncan Stevens.[566]

Following the collision Prime Minister Menzies ordered a Royal Commission to investigate the event.[567] The Commissioner concluded that the collision was primarily the fault of *Voyager*'s bridge crew not maintaining an effective lookout, but also placed blame on *Melbourne*'s Captain John Robertson (who resigned shortly after) and two other officers for failing to alert *Voyager* or take effective measures to avoid collision.[568,569] The handing of the Royal Commission was seen as poor, and after a combination of public pressure and claims that Stevens had a drinking problem, a second Royal Commission was announced: the only time two Commissions have been held for the same incident.[570] The second Royal Commission found that Stevens was likely medically unfit for command, that some of the first Commission's conclusions were therefore incorrect, and the *Melbourne* officers were not at fault.[571] The two commissions caused great anguish in the hierarchy of the RAN, which was not accustomed to such tight scrutiny, and led to the eventual dismantling of the Naval Board's isolation from the civilian world.

Vietnam War

Ships of the Royal Australian Navy were stationed on continuous operational service in Vietnam between 1965 and 1972; a total 18 ships served in Vietnam waters during the war. During this period, the navy performed a wide variety of operational tasks at sea, ashore, and in the air. The RAN's primary contribution consisted of destroyers, Fleet Air Arm personnel attached to a United States Army helicopter company and No. 9 Squadron RAAF, a Clearance Diving Team, and a logistical support force consisting of transport and escort ships. Other RAN personnel served ashore in medical teams or performed staff duties at the Australian Embassy in Saigon or the 1st Australian Task Force Headquarters at Nui Dat.

The RAN did not deploy operationally until 1965, but in 1962 HMAS *Vampire* and HMAS *Quickmatch* made goodwill visits to Saigon. They were followed a year later by similar visits by HMAS *Quiberon* and HMAS *Queenborough*. In 1967, HMAS *Hobart* became the first RAN destroyer to be operationally deployed to Vietnam. *Hobart* served three tours in Vietnam from March to September in 1967, 1968, and 1970. During her operations, she fired 10,000 rounds at 1,000 shore targets and came under fire around 10 times, including on one occasion by a United States F-4

Figure 115: *HMAS Hobart refuels from a US Navy tanker during Operation Sea Dragon off Vietnam in 1967.*

Phantom. *Hobart* was awarded the United States Navy Unit Commendation in recognition of her service in Vietnam, while sister ship *Perth* received both the United States Navy Unit Commendation and the Meritorious Unit Commendation. Clearance Diving Team 3 was awarded the US Presidential Citation, two US Navy Unit Commendations and a US Meritorius Unit Commendation. The only non US Unit to ever receive all 3 awards. After their five years of service in Vietnam, the four gunline destroyers; *Perth*, *Brisbane*, *Hobart* and *Vendetta* steamed over 397,000 miles and fired 102,546 rounds.

The aircraft carrier HMAS *Sydney* was converted for troopship duties in the early 1960s, and began her first voyage to Vietnam in May 1965, transporting the 1st Battalion, Royal Australian Regiment, from Sydney to Vung Tau in southern Vietnam. Sydney became known as the *Vung Tau Ferry* and made 25 voyages to Vietnam: carrying 16,094 troops, 5,753 deadweight tons (5,845 t) of cargo and 2,375 vehicles.

In 1969, the aircraft carrier HMAS *Melbourne* rammed and sank another destroyer.[572] During the night of 2–3 June, USS *Frank E. Evans* was escorting the carrier during multinational wargames in the South China Sea. Ordered to the plane guard station, *Evans* crosses the carrier's bows and was cut in two, killing 74 United States personnel.[573] A Joint RAN-USN Board of Inquiry was established, which found *Melbourne*'s Captain John Stevenson and three officers from *Evans* at fault. Despite being cleared by a RAN court-martial,

Stevenson resigned after receiving similar treatment to Robertson in the first collision.⁵⁷⁴ HMAS *Melbourne* is believed to be the only warship to sink two friendly vessels in peacetime.

In April 1971, Prime Minister John Gorton announced that Australian forces in Vietnam would be reduced. This led to the withdrawal of the clearance divers in May and the Fleet Air Arm in June. The final RAN destroyer on the gunline, *Brisbane*, returned to Sydney on 15 October 1971. The Whitlam government withdrew all Australian forces from and stopped military aid to South Vietnam. HMAS *Jeparit* returned to Sydney on 11 March 1972 and was followed the next day by HMAS *Sydney*. During the 10 years that the RAN was involved in the war, eight officers and sailors were killed, and another 46 were either wounded or suffered other injuries.⁵⁷⁵

Cyclone Tracy

During the morning of 25 December 1974, Tropical Cyclone Tracy struck the city of Darwin, killing 71 people and causing $4 billion of damage (1998 A$). In response to the cyclone, the RAN embarked upon Operation Navy Help Darwin; the largest peacetime disaster relief operation in its history, involving 13 ships, 11 aircraft and some 3,000 personnel.

When Tracy struck Darwin, the RAN had a total of 351 personnel based in the city, along with four *Attack*-class patrol boat; the small number of men limited the capability of the RAN to render immediate assistance to the citizens of Darwin.⁵⁷⁶ All four patrol boats were damaged in some way: *Advance* and *Assail* were able to weather the cyclone with minor damage, but *Attack* was forced aground, and *Arrow* sank after colliding with Stokes Hill Wharf, killing two personnel. Land-based naval installations were also heavily damaged by the cyclone, Darwin Naval Headquarters was destroyed, as were large sections of the patrol boat base and the married quarters. The oil fuel supply installation and naval communications station at HMAS *Coonawarra* were also damaged. The initial RAN relief which was limited to search and rescue in the area of Darwin Harbour and Melville Island, which was hindered by the lack of reliable communications.

As the severity of the disaster was realised, a naval task force was established to render aid to the people of Darwin; Operation Navy Help Darwin. A general recall was issued to all personnel; volunteers from shore bases and ships unable to sail were used to replace those who could not return to their ships in time. The first RAN assets arrived in Darwin on 26 December, a HS 748 aircraft carrying blood transfusion equipment and Red Cross workers, followed shortly by another HS 748 carrying Clearance Diving Team 1 (CDT1). Ships also began departing for Darwin on 26 December: *Balikpapan* and *Betano* departed from Brisbane, *Flinders* sailed from Cairns, while *Melbourne* (with Rear Admiral Wells aboard), *Brisbane*, and *Stuart* left Sydney. The next day, *Hobart*, *Stalwart*, *Supply*, and *Vendetta* left Sydney, while *Brunei* and *Tarakan* sailed from Brisbane. The last ship, *Wewak*, left Brisbane on 2 January.

The first vessels, HMA Ships *Brisbane* and *Flinders*, arrived in Darwin on 31 December. *Flinders* surveyed the approaches to Darwin, ensuring the safety of the taskforce, while *Brisbane* landed working parties and established communications. The entire 13-ship task force had arrived in Darwin by 13 January 1975, bringing over 3,000 personnel. RAN personnel was primarily assigned to clear the suburbs of Nightcliff, Rapid Creek, Northern Territory, and Casuarina, while aircraft and helicopters were used to move evacuees and supplies, and CDT1 inspected ships in the harbour for damage and cleared several wharves. Vessels of the task force began to depart Darwin as early as 7 January, with HMA Ships *Brisbane* and *Stalwart* the last to depart on 31 January, after command of the relief operation was turned over to the Commandant of the Army's 7th Military District.

Pacific patrol boat program

Following the introduction of the 1982 United Nations Convention on the Law of the Sea (UNCLOS) the exclusive economic zone (EEZ) of many coastal nations was increased from 12 to 200 Nmi. The sudden expansion of responsibility dramatically increased the area of ocean requiring surveillance, monitoring and policing by these nations, increasing the strain on existing maritime patrol resources, and highlighting the need for countries without a maritime patrol force to obtain one, especially in the South West Pacific area.

In 1979, the Australian and New Zealand Governments, at the request of Pacific Island nations, sent defence representatives into the South-West Pacific region to assess surveillance and maritime patrol requirements. The governments of a number of the Pacific nations expressed their concern about the need for a suitable naval patrol force to meet their new surveillance requirements. The Australian government responded by creating the Defence Cooperation Project (DCP), to provide suitable patrol vessels, training and infrastructure to island nations in the region. The Pacific Patrol Boat Systems Program Office was created within the Minor War Vessels Branch of the RAN procurement organisation.

The tender for the vessels was released in August 1984, and was awarded to Australian Shipbuilding Industries Pty Ltd (now Tenix Western Australia) in September 1985. The first of ten vessels was to be delivered in early 1987. The first vessel, HMPNGS *Tarangau*, was officially handed over to the Papua New Guinea Defence Force on 16 May 1987. Over the course of the project the

Figure 116: *HMAS Melbourne launches a Grumman S2G Tracker, 1980*

number of participating countries increased. By the end of the construction phase of the project, a total of 22 boats had been delivered to 12 countries, compared to the original order of 10 boats for 8 countries. In total, the project cost for 22 vessels and associated support was A$155.25 million.

The RAN never operated the Pacific-class patrol boat (PPB), although the project has given the RAN a number of advantages in the Pacific region. The introduction of self-reliant patrol forces throughout the region has eased the strain on Australia's own maritime patrol force. Cooperation between Australia and its Pacific neighbours has allowed for a greater allocation of RAN patrol boats to protecting Australia's maritime resources, patrolling the Sea Lines of Communication (SLOC), and conducting border protection operations. The PPB's have recently undergone a mid life refit which could potentially see them operating in the region until at least 2027.

Two-Ocean Policy

The main role of the Royal Australian Navy in the two decades following the end of Australia's involvement in the Vietnam War was supporting Australian diplomatic initiatives. In line with this goal the RAN exercised with the navies of Australia's allies and provided support to civil authorities in Australia and the South Pacific.[577] The RAN's main military concern from the 1970s was the activities of the Soviet Navy in the Indian Ocean. These concerns lead to

Figure 117: *HMAS Success refuelling HMAS Canberra in 1988*

increased co-operation with the United States Navy and the development of the RAN's main base in Western Australia, HMAS *Stirling*.[578]

During the late 1970s, the RAN replaced many of its ageing ships with modern equivalents. While it planned to purchase the British aircraft carrier HMS *Invincible* to replace *Melbourne*, Britain's offer of the carrier was withdrawn after the Falklands War. As a result, *Melbourne* was decommissioned without replacement in 1982 and the Fleet Air Arm retired almost all of its fixed wing aircraft on 30 June 1983.[579]

In 1987, the Hawke Government's Defence White Paper called for the RAN to become a more self-reliant *two-ocean* navy with major fleet bases in New South Wales and Western Australia. The plan called for the expansion of *Stirling* on Garden Island and Jervis Bay to accommodate an expanded RAN combat surface and submarine fleets. The plan originally called for the major combat units and submarines to be split between the two fleet bases, providing similar capabilities on both sides of the continent. The proposed Jervis Bay naval base never became a reality; Fleet Base East was built up around HMAS *Kuttabul* in Sydney while HMAS *Stirling* is home to half the surface fleet and the entire submarine fleet.

The rationale behind the policy included the possibility of savings in fuel and maintenance that would result from Indian Ocean deployments beginning their journey from Western Australia rather than New South Wales. The report also classed the Indian Ocean as an area where contingencies might arise. The new facilities would increase Australia's worth to the United States, particularly to do with maintenance of submarines. Expansion at Jervis Bay would allow intensified east coast visits by the United States Pacific Fleet, and its nuclear warship visits would not run into as much opposition as they do in Sydney and Melbourne.[580]

The 1987 White Paper was seen by many as an attempt to strengthen Australia's relationship with the United States, which had been damaged by New Zealand's stance against nuclear weapons in its ports. In line with this policy, the RAN was structured to become more self-reliant and its activities during the late 1980s were focused on operating within Australia's local region.[581]

The Two Ocean Policy remains in place today and is supported by the current Australian Government and the opposition. The success of the policy is especially evident at HMAS *Stirling*. The base is thriving and its location both in a global and local context gives it an advantage over Fleet Base East. It has been suggested that all eight *Anzac* class ships be relocated to *Stirling*, this would create an easier training environment for sailors and would lead to significant cost savings.

Post Cold-War

The Gulf Wars

Australia's contribution to the 1991 Gulf War centred on a Naval Task Group, initially Task Group 627.4, which formed part of the multi-national fleet in the Persian Gulf and Gulf of Oman. In addition, medical teams were deployed aboard a US hospital ship and a naval clearance diving team took part in de-mining Kuwait's port facilities at the end of the war. Over the period from 6 September 1990 to 4 September 1991 the RAN deployed a total of six ships to the area: HMA Ships *Adelaide*, *Brisbane*, *Darwin*, *Success*, *Sydney*, and *Westralia*. Clearance Diving Team 3 operated in the theatre from 27 January 1991 to 10 May 1991. It was involved in mine clearing operations in Kuwait from 5 March to 19 April 1991.[582]

After the end of the first Gulf War the Royal Australian Navy periodically deployed a ship to the Gulf or Red Sea to assist in maintaining sanctions against Iraq. Until the outbreak of the Second Gulf War the Australian naval force in the Persian Gulf continued to enforce the sanctions against Iraq. These operations were conducted by boarding parties from the RAN warships.[583]

Upon the outbreak of war, the RAN's focus shifted to supporting the coalition land forces and clearing the approaches to Iraqi ports. HMAS *Anzac* provided gunfire support to Royal Marines during fighting on the Al-Faw Peninsula and

Figure 118: *HMAS Anzac and HMAS Darwin with United States and British warships in late 2002*

Figure 119: *A sailor from HMAS Adelaide inspecting a ship in the Persian Gulf during 2004*

the Clearance Diving Team took part in clearing the approaches to Umm Qasr. Boarding operations continued during the war, and on 20 March, boarding parties from HMAS *Kanimbla* seized an Iraqi ship carrying 86 naval mines.[584]

Since the end of the war the RAN has continuously maintained a frigate in the Persian Gulf to protect Iraq's oil infrastructure and participate in counter-smuggling operations. Twelve Australian sailors were deployed to Umm Qasr, Iraq between January and October 2004 to join the multi-national training team working with the Iraqi Coastal Defense Force.[585] The RAN has also assumed command of coalition forces in the Persian Gulf on two occasions; Combined Task Force 58 in 2005[586] and Combined Task Force 158 in 2006.[587]

HMAS *Westralia* fire

On 5 May 1998, a fire broke out onboard HMAS *Westralia* while off the Western Australia coast. The fire was caused by the rupture of a flexible fuel line (one of a number used to replace rigid hoses) on cylinder number nine, starboard engine. This sprayed diesel fuel onto a hot indicator cock, which ignited a spray fire, resulting in the deaths of four crew. Following the fire, the Australian Government and the RAN began a major investigation known as the *Westralia Board of Inquiry*. The enquiry found that the RAN and the contractor Australian Defence Industries (ADI) did not critically examine their course of action and that key personnel in both the RAN and the contractor were insufficiently trained and qualified. The inquiry also found that the hoses were not properly designed and were unfit for the intended purpose. In 2005, ADI was fined $75,000 for failing to provide a safe workplace. Seven sailors who were severely traumatised by the fire have also sued ADI and subcontractor Jetrock. In August 2006, the Australian Government decided to accept liability after it reached settlement with the ADI and Jetrock. The seven sailors stand to receive compensation totalling up to $10 million.[588]

East Timor

During the Australian-led United Nations peacekeeping mission to East Timor in 1999 known as INTERFET, the RAN deployed a total of 16 ships to the mission: HMA Ships *Adelaide, Anzac, Balikpapan, Brunei, Darwin, Farncomb, Jervis Bay, Labuan, Success, Sydney, Tarakan, Tobruk, Waller, Westralia, Newcastle* and *Melbourne*.[589] The RAN played a vital role in transporting troops and providing protection to transports and were vital to the success of INTERFET.

The RAN returned to East Timor in 2006 under Operation Astute the United Nations-authorised, Australian-led military deployment to East Timor to quell unrest and return stability during the 2006 East Timor crisis. The Royal Australian Navy deployed the Amphibious Ready Group, including the ships; *Kanimbla*, *Manoora*, *Tobruk* (until approximately 8 June), *Balikpapan*, *Tarakan* and *Success* (until 28 May). The RAN also deployed the *Adelaide*-class frigate HMAS *Adelaide* (until 28 May). The Fleet Air Arm contributed one S-70B-2 Seahawk helicopter from 816 Squadron RAN (until 28 May) and two Sea King helicopters from 817 Squadron RAN. The Royal Australian Navy force committed to Operation Astute is apparently the largest amphibious task force in the navy's history.[590]

Solomon Islands

On 24 July 2003, HMAS *Manoora* arrived off Honiara, marking the beginning of Operation Anode, Australia's contribution to the Regional Assistance Mission to the Solomon Islands (RAMSI). The deployment of a 2,200 strong multinational force followed several years of unrest in the Solomon Islands. Manoora was soon joined by HMA Ships *Hawkesbury*, *Labuan*, *Wewak* and *Whyalla*. Following the initial deployment, two vessels were generally kept on station in the area. By the time the RAN deployment ended, 19 Australian warships had taken part. The last ship to leave was *Fremantle*, which sailed home in October 2004.

Operation Anode was not the first time units of the RAN had been deployed to the Solomon Islands; Anode was unique in that the navy's primary role was to support and facilitate the work of the Participating Police Force (PPF). Moreover, along with being the first time the RAN had supported a police-led mission,[591]

Fiji

On 2 November 2006, in response to the Fijian military threats to overthrow the Fijian Government, the Australian government began Operation Quickstep by deploying military resources to support Australian citizens in Fiji in the event of a coup d'état. The contribution from the RAN was the deployment of three vessels; HMA Ships *Kanimbla*, *Newcastle*, and *Success* to international waters south of Fiji. The three vessels were deployed to Fiji to evacuate the estimated 7,000 Australian citizens present in Fiji if the need arose.[592] Along with the three vessels a detachment of the Special Air Service Regiment (SASR), helicopters from the 171st Aviation Squadron, and an evacuation team were also deployed.

On 29 November 2006, an Australian Army S-70A Black Hawk helicopter operating from *Kanimbla*, and carrying ten Army personnel on board, crashed whilst attempting to land on the ship's deck, killing 1 person, injuring 7 more and leaving one missing (later confirmed dead).[593] HMAS *Melville* arrived on task the morning of 15 December 2006, equipped with a Towed Pinger Locating Drone supplied from the United States Navy set about locating the downed Black Hawk. *Melville* detected the locator beacon during its first pass over the crash site and pinpointed its exact location in subsequent passes. The helicopter is sitting in around 2900 metres of water.[594]

The coup took place on 5 December, but was bloodless and almost completely without violence. The evacuation of Australians was deemed unnecessary, and vessels of the task force began arriving back in Australia on 17 December, with *Kanimbla* docking in Townsville, and both *Newcastle* and *Success* returning to Sydney. *Melville* returned to Australia in late December. The RAN has decided to attempt to recover the downed Black Hawk and has identified the United States Navy Supervisor of Salvage (SUPSALV) as the preferred organisation. MV *Seahorse Standard* recovered the remains of Trooper Joshua Porter on 5 March and the Blackhawk helicopter on 9 March, with the assistance of specialist equipment provided by the SUPSALV team. The soldier's body was repatriated on 13 March, escorted by members of the SASR. *Seahorse Standard* arrived in Australia with the aircraft wreckage at the end of March. The wreckage will become evidence in the Board of Inquiry into the crash.

Battle honours

Prior to 1989, the battle honour system of the Royal Australian Navy (RAN) was linked to that of the Royal Navy. The British Ministry of Defence and the Admiralty were responsible for approving and assigning battle honours, although from 1947, this was done on advice from the RAN Badges, Names and Honours Committee.[595] The only uniquely Australian battle honour during this time was "Vietnam 1965–72" (and smaller date units thereof) for deployments to the Vietnam War.[596] Ships of the RAN inherited honours from British ships of the same name, in addition to Australian predecessors.

In 1989, the RAN Chief of Naval Staff, Admiral Michael Hudson approved a decision to have Australian warships only carry battle honours earned by previous Australian vessels. The creation and awarding of battle honours came completely under RAN control.

A complete overhaul of the RAN battle honours system was unvelied on 1 March 2010, to celebrate the navy's 109th anniversary of creation. New honours were created for operations during the 1990s and 2000s—the last approved honour prior to this was "Kuwait 1991", for Gulf War service—and the service history of previous vessels was updated to include 'due recognition' of previous actions.

Figure 120: *Women are expected to play a greater role in the RAN in the future*

Women in the RAN

From 1911 to 1941 women were forbidden from serving in the RAN; the demands World War II placed on personnel and resources led to a change of policy. On 21 April 1941, the Australian Naval Board sent a letter authorising the entry of women into the RAN to the Commodore-in-Charge, Sydney. The letter led to the formation of the Women's Royal Australian Naval Service (WRANS) and the Royal Australian Naval Nursing Service (RANNS). The two separate women's services existed until 1984, when they were incorporated into the permanent force. Today, female members of the RAN have a wide variety of roles open to them; women serve on submarines, command ships and shore postings and are expected to play an increasingly important role in the future of the RAN.[597]

The current navy

The Royal Australian Navy today is a medium-sized modern navy in world terms but is one of the strongest navies in the Asia Pacific Region. Today, the combat fleet of the RAN is made up of eight *Anzac*-class frigates, four *Adelaide*-class frigates, fourteen patrol boats of the *Armidale* class, and six *Collins*-class submarines. The RAN also comprises an amphibious and supply force to transport the Australian Army and to resupply the combat arm of the navy.[598] The RAN is divided into seven Force Element Groups (FEGs):

Figure 121: *HMAS Sheean at Fremantle Harbour*

Surface Combatants, Amphibious Warfare Forces and Afloat Support Force, Naval Aviation, Submarine Force, Mine Warfare and Clearance Diving, Patrol Boat Force and the Hydrographic Force. The FEG's were formed to manage the operations of the separate sections of the RAN in a more efficient way.[599] Wikipedia:Manual of Style/Dates and numbers#Chronological items

The modern RAN began to form during the late 1970s when the Fraser Government announced the purchase of four *Oliver Hazard Perry*-class frigates, all to be built in America; in 1980 they announced an additional two vessels both to be built in Australia. The fifteen Australian-built vessels of the *Fremantle* class made up Australia's patrol boat from 1979 to 2007; they have now been replaced by the fourteen *Armidale*-class patrol boats.

The *Collins* class is the newest class of Australian submarines, built in Australia for the Royal Australian Navy. They were constructed by the Australian Submarine Corporation in Adelaide, South Australia, and replace the six *Oberon*-class submarines in the Australian fleet. The first vessel, HMAS *Collins*, was laid down in 1990 and commissioned in 1996, with all six vessels of the class in service and based at HMAS *Stirling* in Western Australia.

The *Anzac* class is the current main fleet unit of the Royal Australian Navy; the class has eight vessels. The lead vessel of the class, HMAS *Anzac*, was commissioned in 1996 and the final vessel, HMAS *Perth*, was commissioned

Figure 122: *HMAS Anzac operating in support of Operation Enduring Freedom*

on 26 August 2006. Along with the eight Australian vessels, two *Anzac*s were also constructed for the Royal New Zealand Navy. The *Anzac* class were jointly constructed in New Zealand and Australia with the final fitout in Williamstown, Victoria.

The amphibious and supply arm of the RAN is made up of; one *Kanimbla*-class landing platform, one heavy landing ship (HMAS *Tobruk*), six *Balikpapan*-class landing craft, two *Leeuwin*-class survey vessels, four *Paluma*-class motor launches, the fleet oiler HMAS *Sirius*, and the Dual Stores Replenishment Vessel HMAS *Success*. The RAN also has six *Huon*-class minehunters.

The Royal Australian Navy maintains several bases around Australia. Under the RAN's Two-Ocean Policy, HMAS *Stirling* (Fleet Base West) and HMAS *Kuttabul* (Fleet Base East) are the primary bases for all major fleet unit of the RAN. The majority of the patrol boat and amphibious forces are located at HMAS *Cairns* and HMAS *Coonawarra*, while all Fleet Air Arm squadrons are based at HMAS *Albatross*.

The future of the RAN

In 2000, a major white paper was produced by the Australian Government, which set out a program of defence spending that will see significant improvements to the RAN's fleet and capabilities.

The most significant current project is *SEA 4000* the procurement of three *Hobart*-class destroyers, which will replace the *Adelaide* class.[600] These ships will be fitted with the Aegis combat system, and will be based on the Spanish F100 design. The class has a planned in service date of 2013, with the three units to be named *Hobart*, *Brisbane*, and *Sydney*.

In August 2005 the Australian Government passed approval for the acquisition of two *Canberra*-class landing helicopter dock ships; these will displace over 20,000 tonnes, can carry over 1,000 troops, and will potentially be able to operate fixed wing aircraft. The project is expected to cost between A$1.5 and A$2 billion, and be completed by around 2014. The new ships will be named *Canberra* and *Adelaide*.[601]

References

- Burnell, Frederick. (1914). How Australia took German New Guinea : An illustrated record of the Australian Naval & Military Expeditionary Force. Australasian News, Sydney.
- Cassells, Vic (2000). *The Capital Ships: their battles and their badges*. East Roseville, NSW: Simon & Schuster. ISBN 0-7318-0941-6. OCLC 48761594[602].
- Cassells, Vic (2000). *The Destroyers: their battles and their badges*. East Roseville, NSW: Simon & Schuster. ISBN 0-7318-0893-2. OCLC 46829686[603].
- Frame, Tom (2004). *No Pleasure Cruise: the story of the Royal Australian Navy*. Crows Nest, NSW: Allen & Unwin. ISBN 1-74114-233-4. OCLC 55980812[604].
- Frame, Tom (2005). *A Cruel Legacy: the HMAS Voyager tragedy*. Crows Nest, NSW: Allen & Unwin. ISBN 1-74115-254-2. OCLC 61213421[605].
- Macdougall, A. (1991). Australians at War A Pictorial History, The Five Mile Press, ISBN 1-86503-865-2
- Nash, Greg and David Stevens (2006). *Australia's Navy in the Gulf. From Countenance to Catalyst, 1941-2006*. Topmill, Sydney.
- Stevens, David (1996). *The Royal Australian Navy in World War II*. Allen & Unwin, Sydney, ISBN 1-74114-184-2

- Stevens, David (2005). *A Critical Vulnerability: the impact of the submarine threat on Australia's maritime defense 1915–1954*[606]. Papers in Australian Maritime Affairs. No. 15. Canberra: Sea Power Centre Australia. ISBN 0-642-29625-1. ISSN 1327-5658[607]. OCLC 62548623[608]. Archived from the original[609] on 2011-06-13.
- Stevens, David, ed. (2001). *The Royal Australian Navy*. The Australian Centenary History of Defence (vol III). South Melbourne, VIC: Oxford University Press. ISBN 0-19-555542-2. OCLC 50418095[610].
- Stevens, David *Japanese submarine operations against Australia 1942–1944*[611]
- Jenkins, David (1992). *Battle Surface! Japan's Submarine War Against Australia 1942–44*. Milsons Point, NSW: Random House Australia. ISBN 0-09-182638-1. OCLC 0091826381[612].
- Official History of Australia in the War of 1914–1918
  - Jose, A.W. (1941). *Volume IX – The Royal Australian Navy, 1914 – 1918 (9th edition, 1941)*[613]. Australian War Memorial, Canberra.
- Australia in the War of 1939–1945
  - Gill, G. Hermon (1957). *Australia in the War of 1939 – 1945. Series 2 – Navy. Volume I – Royal Australian Navy, 1939–1942*[614]. Australian War Memorial, Canberra.
  - Gill, G. Hermon (1968). *Australia in the War of 1939 – 1945. Series 2 – Navy. Volume II – Royal Australian Navy, 1942–1945*[615]. Australian War Memorial, Canberra.
  - Long, Gavin (1973). *The Six Years War. A Concise History of Australia in the 1939–45 War*. Australian War Memorial and Australian Government Publishing Service, Canberra.
- Royal Australian Navy Sea Power Centre
  - Semaphore Series – Newsletter of the Sea Power Centre – Australia[616]
  - Australian Maritime Doctrine[617]
  - RAN Histories[618]

Further reading

- Haken, John (2015). "The Formation of Naval Forces in the Commonwealth of Australia". *Sabretache*. Garran, Australian Capital Territory: Military Historical Society of Australia. Volume LVI (No. 3, September): 54. ISSN 0048-8933[619].

External links

- Royal Australian Navy Articles[620] from ADF-History.com

<indicator name="good-star"> ⊕ </indicator>

Royal Australian Navy

Royal Australian Navy	
Active	1911–present
Country	Australia
Type	Navy
Size	14,215 Permanent personnel 8,493 Reserve personnel 47 commissioned ships 3 non-commissioned ships
Part of	Australian Defence Force
Headquarters	Russell Offices, Canberra
Motto(s)	*Serving Australia with Pride*
March	"Royal Australian Navy"
Anniversaries	10 July
Engagements	- World War I - World War II - Korean War - Malayan Emergency - Indonesian Confrontation - Vietnam War - Gulf War - War in Afghanistan - Iraq War
Website	www<wbr/>.navy<wbr/>.gov<wbr/>.au[621]
Commanders	
Commander-in-chief	General Sir Peter Cosgrove As Governor-General of Australia
Chief of the Defence Force	General Angus Campbell
Vice Chief of the Defence Force	Vice Admiral David Johnston
Chief of Navy	Vice Admiral Michael Noonan
Deputy Chief of Navy	Rear Admiral Mark Hammond
Commander Australian Fleet	Rear Admiral Jonathan Mead

Insignia	
Naval Ensign (1967–present)	
Naval Jack	
Aircraft flown	
Reconnaissance	Sikorsky MH-60R
Trainer	Bell 429 GlobalRanger
Transport	NHIndustries NH90

The **Royal Australian Navy** (**RAN**) is the naval branch of the Australian Defence Force. Following the Federation of Australia in 1901, the ships and resources of the separate colonial navies were integrated into a national force: the **Commonwealth Naval Forces**. Originally intended for local defence, the navy was granted the title of 'Royal Australian Navy' in 1911, and became increasingly responsible for defence of the region.

Britain's Royal Navy continued to support the RAN and provided additional blue-water defence capability in the Pacific up to the early years of World War II. Then, rapid wartime expansion saw the acquisition of large surface vessels and the building of many smaller warships. In the decade following the war, the RAN acquired a small number of aircraft carriers, the last of these paying off in 1982.

Today, the RAN consists of 47 commissioned vessels, 3 non-commissioned vessels and over 16,000 personnel. The navy is one of the largest and most sophisticated naval forces in the South Pacific region, with a significant presence in the Indian Ocean and worldwide operations in support of military campaigns and peacekeeping missions. The current Chief of Navy is Vice Admiral Tim Barrett.

History

The Commonwealth Naval Forces were established on 1 March 1901, two months after the federation of Australia, when the naval forces of the separate Australian colonies were amalgamated. A period of uncertainty followed as the policy makers sought to determine the newly established force's requirements and purpose, with the debate focusing upon whether Australia's naval force would be structured mainly for local defence or whether it would be designed to serve as a fleet unit within a larger imperial force, controlled centrally by the British Admiralty.[622] In 1908–09, the decision was made to pursue a compromise solution, and the Australian government agreed to establish a force that would be used for local defence but which would be capable of forming a fleet unit within the imperial naval strategy, albeit without central control. As a result, the navy's force structure was set at "one battlecruiser, three light cruisers, six destroyers and three submarines".[623]

On 10 July 1911, King George V granted the service the title of "Royal Australian Navy". The first of the RAN's new vessels, the destroyer *Yarra*, was completed in September 1910 and by the outbreak of the First World War the majority of the RAN's planned new fleet had been realised. The Australian Squadron was placed under control of the British Admiralty,[624] and initially it was tasked with capturing many of Germany's South Pacific colonies and protecting Australian shipping from the German East Asia Squadron. Later in the war, most of the RAN's major ships operated as part of Royal Navy forces in the Mediterranean and North Seas, and then later in the Adriatic, and then the Black Sea following the surrender of the Ottoman Empire.

In 1919, the RAN received a force of six destroyers, three sloops and six submarines from the Royal Navy,[625] but throughout the 1920s and early 1930s, the RAN was drastically reduced in size due to a variety of factors including political apathy and economic hardship as a result of the Great Depression.[626] In this time the focus of Australia's naval policy shifted from defence against invasion to trade protection,[627] and several fleet units were sunk as targets or scrapped. By 1923, the size of the navy had fallen to eight vessels, and by the end of the decade it had fallen further to five, with just 3,500 personnel. In the late 1930s, as international tensions increased, the RAN was modernised and expanded, with the service receiving primacy of funding over the Army and Air Force during this time as Australia began to prepare for war.

Early in the Second World War, RAN ships again operated as part of Royal Navy formations, many serving with distinction in the Mediterranean, the Red Sea, the Persian Gulf, the Indian Ocean, and off the West African coast.[628] Following the outbreak of the Pacific War and the virtual destruction of British naval forces in south-east Asia, the RAN operated more independently, or as part of United States Navy formations. As the navy took on an even greater role, it was expanded significantly and at its height the RAN was the fourth-largest navy in the world, with 39,650 personnel operating 337 warships. A total of 34 vessels were lost during the war, including three cruisers and four destroyers.[629]

After the Second World War, the size of the RAN was again reduced, but it gained new capabilities with the acquisition of two aircraft carriers, *Sydney* and *Melbourne*.[630] The RAN saw action in many Cold War–era conflicts in the Asia-Pacific region and operated alongside the Royal Navy and United States Navy off Korea, Malaysia, and Vietnam.[631] Since the end of the Cold War, the RAN has been part of Coalition forces in the Persian Gulf and Indian Ocean, operating in support of Operation Slipper and undertaking counter piracy operations. It was also deployed in support of Australian peacekeeping operations in East Timor and the Solomon Islands.

RAN today

Command structure

The strategic command structure of the RAN was overhauled during the New Generation Navy changes. The RAN is commanded through Naval Headquarters (NHQ) in Canberra. The professional head is the Chief of Navy (CN), who holds the rank of vice admiral. NHQ is responsible for implementing policy decisions handed down from the Department of Defence and for overseeing tactical and operational issues that are the purview of the subordinate commands.Wikipedia:Citation needed

Beneath NHQ are two subordinate commands:

- **Fleet Command**: fleet command is led by Commander Australian Fleet (COMAUSFLT). COMAUSFLT holds the rank of rear admiral; previously, this post was Flag Officer Commanding HM's Australian Fleet (FOCAF), created in 1911,[632] but the title was changed in 1988 to the Maritime Commander Australia. On 1 February 2007, the title changed again, becoming Commander Australian Fleet. The nominated at-sea commander is Commodore Warfare (COMWAR), a one-star deployable task group commander. Fleet command has responsibility to CN for the full command of assigned assets, and to Joint Operations command for the provision of operationally ready forces.
- **Navy Strategic Command**: the administrative element overseeing the RAN's training, engineering and logistical support needs. Instituted in 2000, the Systems Commander was appointed at the rank of commodore; in June 2008, the position was upgraded to the rank of rear admiral.

Fleet Command was previously made up of seven Force Element Groups, but after the New Generation Navy changes, this was restructured into four Force Commands:

- Fleet Air Arm, responsible for the navy's aviation assets

- Mine Warfare, Hydrographic and Patrol Boat Force, an amalgamation of the previous Patrol Boat, Hydrographic, and Mine Warfare and Clearance Diving Forces, operating what are collectively termed the RAN's "minor war vessels"
- Submarine Force, operating the *Collins*-class submarines
- Surface Force, covering the RAN's surface combatants (generally ships of frigate size or larger)

Fleet

As of September 2017, the RAN fleet consisted of 47 warships, including destroyers, frigates, submarines, patrol boats and auxiliary ships. Ships commissioned into the RAN are given the prefix HMAS (His/Her Majesty's Australian Ship).[633]

The RAN has two primary bases for its fleet:

- Fleet Base East, located at HMAS *Kuttabul*, Sydney; and
- Fleet Base West, located at HMAS *Stirling*, near Perth.

In addition, three other bases are home to the majority of the RAN's minor war vessels:

- HMAS *Cairns*, at Cairns;
- HMAS *Coonawarra*, at Darwin; and
- HMAS *Waterhen*, at Sydney.

Current ships

The RAN currently operates 47 commissioned vessels, made up of eight ship classes and three individual ships, plus three non-commissioned vessels. In addition, DMS Maritime operates a large number of civilian-crewed vessels under contract to the Australian Defence Force.

Commissioned vessels					
Image	Class/name	Type	Number	Entered service	Details
	Collins class	Submarine	6	2000	Anti-shipping, intelligence collection. Diesel-electric powered.

	Class	Type	No.	Year	Notes
	Canberra class	Landing helicopter dock	2	2014	Amphibious warfare ships.
	Hobart class	Destroyer	1 (2)	2017	Air Warfare Destroyer. Two more to be commissioned.
	Anzac class	Frigate	8	1996	Anti-submarine and anti-aircraft frigate with 1 helicopter. Two more were built for the Royal New Zealand Navy.
	Adelaide class	Frigate	2	1985	General-purpose guided-missile frigate with 2 helicopters. Four more ships have been decommissioned.
	Armidale class	Patrol boat	13	2005	Coastal defence, maritime border, and fishery protection
	Huon class	Minehunter	6	1997	Minehunting. Four active, two laid up.
	Leeuwin class	Survey ship	2	2000	Hydrographic survey

Royal Australian Navy

	Paluma class	Survey launch	4	1989	Hydrographic survey
	HMAS Choules (Bay class)	Landing Ship Dock	1	2011	Heavy sealift and transport
	HMAS Success (Durance class)	Replenishment ship	1	1986	Replenishment at sea and afloat support
	HMAS Sirius	Replenishment ship	1	2006	Replenishment at sea and afloat support. Modified commercial tanker.
Non-commissioned vessels					
	Cape class	Patrol boat	2	2015	Cape Byron and Cape Nelson were leased from the Australian Border Force to supplement Armidales during classwide remediation maintenance. ADV (Australian Defence Vessel) ship prefix.
	STS Young Endeavour	Tall Ship	1	1988	Sail training ship

Aviation

Fleet Air Arm

The Fleet Air Arm (previously known as the Australian Navy Aviation Group) provides the RAN's aviation capability. As of 2013, the FAA consists of three active squadrons plus a fourth being activated, operating five helicopter types in the anti-submarine warfare and maritime support roles. The Fleet Air Arm is based at HMAS *Albatross* in Nowra, New South Wales, and operates from the RAN's frigates, large amphibious warfare vessels, and large support ships.

LADS Flight

In addition to the helicopter squadrons of the Fleet Air Arm, the RAN operates an additional flying unit that comes under the operational responsibility of the Australian Hydrographic Service. The Laser Airborne Depth Sounder Flight contains the sole remaining fixed-wing aircraft operated by the RAN, and is based at HMAS *Cairns* in Cairns, Queensland.

Gallery

Figure 123: *MRH-90 of 808 Squadron*

Figure 124: *S-70 Seahawk of 816 Squadron*

Figure 125: *Bombardier Dash 8 of the LADS Flight*

Clearance Diving Branch

The Clearance Diving Branch is composed of two *Clearance Diving Teams* (CDT) that serve as parent units for naval clearance divers:

- Clearance Diving Team 1 (AUSCDT ONE), based at HMAS *Waterhen* in New South Wales; and

Figure 126: *Clearance Divers during a ship boarding exercise in 2006 as a part of RIMPAC exercises.*

- Clearance Diving Team 4 (AUSCDT FOUR), based at HMAS *Stirling* in Western Australia.

When clearance divers are sent into combat, Clearance Diving Team Three (AUSCDT THREE) is formed.

The CDTs have two primary roles:

- Mine counter-measures (MCM) and explosive ordnance disposal (EOD); and
- Maritime tactical operations.

Future

There are currently several major projects underway that will see upgrades to RAN capabilities:

- *Project SEA 1180 Phase 1* will replace the Armidale-class patrol boat with twelve new Offshore Patrol Vessels to be constructed by Lürssen. Construction will commence in Q4 2018, with the first vessel to enter service in Q4 2021.
- *Project SEA 1429 Phase 2* will upgrade the *Collins*-class submarines with state-of-the-art heavyweight torpedoes.

Figure 127: *HMAS Canberra, a Canberra-class landing helicopter dock, being fitted out in 2013*

Figure 128: *Hobart, the lead ship of the RAN's new class of air-warfare destroyers, under construction in 2015*

- *Project SEA 1439 Phase 3* will upgrade the *Collins*-class submarine platform systems and improve 'reliability, sustainability, safety and capability'.
- *Project SEA 1439 Phase 4A* will equip the *Collins*-class submarines with the United States Navy Combat and Weapon Control System, as well as improvements to the combat system augmentation sonar system. Shore facilities relating to integration, training, and testing will also be upgraded. Expected to achieve Final Operating Capability in December 2018.
- *Project SEA 1654 Phase 3* is a project to acquire a Sea Logistic Support and Replenishment Support vessel to replace the supply ship HMAS *Success*.
- *Project SEA 4000 Phase 3*, under which the RAN will acquire three *Hobart*-class air warfare destroyers, built around the United States Navy Aegis air and surface combat management system. The vessels are to be based on the Spanish *Álvaro de Bazán*-class frigate. As of June 2018, one is in active service and two are currently under construction.
- *Project SEA 5000 Phase 1*, where nine *Hunter*-class frigates to replace the *Anzac*-class frigates. The vessels will be built in Adelaide by BAE Systems and will be a variation of the Type 26 Global Combat Ship to be operated by the Royal Navy.

Future procurement plans include:

- Twelve Future Submarines, under *Project SEA 1000*, to replace the *Collins*-class (up to 4,000 tons, potentially equipped with cruise missiles and minisubs).

Current operations

The RAN currently has forces deployed on four major operations:

- Operation Highroad: Australia's commitment to the International Coalition forces in Afghanistan;
- Operation Resolute: border protection;
- Operation Manitou: counter-piracy, counter-terrorism and maritime stability in the Middle East; and
- Operation Accordion: support operation to provide sustainment to forces deployed on Operations Highroad and Manitou.

Figure 129: *A female RAN officer in 2014. Women serve in the RAN in combat roles and at sea.*

Personnel

As of June 2011, the RAN has 14,215 permanent full-time personnel, 161 gap year personnel, and 2,150 reserve personnel. The permanent full-time force consisted of 3,357 commissioned officers, and 10,697 enlisted personnel. In June 2010, male personnel made up 82% of the permanent full-time force, while female personnel made up 18%. The RAN has the highest percentage of women in the ADF, compared to the RAAF's 17.8% and the Army's 9.7%.

The following are the current senior Royal Australian Navy officers:

- Vice Admiral David Johnston – Vice Chief of the Defence Force
- Vice Admiral Michael Noonan – Chief of Navy
- Rear Admiral Mark Hammond – Deputy Chief of Navy
- Rear Admiral Jonathan Mead – Commander Australian Fleet
- Rear Admiral Peter Quinn – Head Navy Capability
- Rear Admiral Colin Lawrence – Head Navy Engineering
- Rear Admiral Bruce Kafer – Director-General Australian Navy Cadets and Reserves
- Commodore Brett Brace – Hydrographer of Australia
- Warrant Officer Gary Wight – Warrant Officer of the Navy

Figure 130: *Royal Australian Navy sailors in 2010*

Ranks and uniforms

The uniforms of the Royal Australian Navy are very similar in cut, colour and insignia to their British Royal Navy forerunners. However, beginning with the Second World War, all RAN personnel began wearing shoulder flashes reading *Australia*, a practice continuing today. These are cloth arcs at shoulder height on uniforms, metallic gold on officers' shoulder boards, and embroidered on shoulder slip-ons.

Commissioned officers

Commissioned officers of the Australian Navy have pay grades ranging from S-1 to O-11. The only O-11 position in the navy is honorary and has only ever been held by royalty, currently being held by HRH The Duke of Edinburgh. The highest position occupied in the current Royal Australian Navy structure is O-9, a vice admiral who serves as the Chief of the Navy. O-8 (rear admiral) to O-11 (admiral of the fleet) are referred to as flag officers, O-5 (commander) and above are referred to as senior officers, while S-1 (midshipman) to O-4 (lieutenant commander) are referred to as junior officers. All officers of the navy receive a commission from Her Majesty Queen Elizabeth II, Queen of Australia. The commissioning scroll issued in recognition of the commission is signed by the Governor General of Australia as Commander-in-Chief and the serving Minister for Defence.Wikipedia:Citation needed

Naval officers are trained at the Royal Australian Naval College (HMAS *Creswell*) in Jervis Bay, New South Wales and the Australian Defence Force Academy in Canberra.

Commissioned officer rank structure of the Royal Australian Navy						
Admiral of the Fleet	Admiral	Vice Admiral	Rear Admiral	Commodore		Captain
O-11	O-10	O-9	O-8	O-7		O-6
AF	ADML	VADM	RADM	CDRE		CAPT

Commander	Lieutenant Commander	Lieutenant	Sub Lieutenant	Acting Sub Lieutenant	Midshipman
O-5	O-4	O-3	O-2	O-1	S-1
CMDR	LCDR	LEUT	SBLT	ASLT	MIDN

Figure 131: *depiction of RAN Chaplains shoulder rank slide*

Chaplain

Chaplains in the Royal Australian Navy are commissioned officers who complete the same training as other officers in the RAN at the Royal Australian Naval College, HMAS Creswell. RAN regulations group RAN chaplains with commanders for purposes of protocol such as marks of respect (saluting); however, RAN chaplains have no other rank other than "chaplain", and their rank emblem is identifiable by a Maltese cross with gold anchor. Senior chaplains are grouped with captains, and principal chaplains are grouped with commodores, but their chaplain rank slide remains the same. Principal chaplains, however, have gold braid on the peak of their white service cap.Wikipedia:Citation needed

Other ranks

Other ranks								
Warrant Officer of the Navy	Warrant Officer	Chief Petty Officer		Petty Officer	Leading Seaman		Able Seaman	Seaman
E-9		E-8	E-7	E-6	E-5	E-4	E-3	E-2

WO-N	WO	CPO	(No rank)	PO	LS	(No rank)	AB	SMN

Royal Australian Navy Other Ranks wear "right arm rates" insignia, called "Category Insignia" to indicate speciality training qualifications.WP:NOTRS The use pattern mirrors that of the Royal Navy, and has since formation.Wikipedia:Citation needed Stars or a Crown are added to these to indicate higher qualifications.Wikipedia:Citation needed

Special insignia

The Warrant Officer of the Navy (WO-N) is an appointment held by the most senior sailor in the RAN, and holds the rank of warrant officer (WO). However, the WO-N does not wear the WO rank insignia; instead, they wear the special insignia of the appointment. The WO-N appointment has similar equivalent appointments in the other services, each holding the rank of warrant officer, each being the most senior sailor/soldier/airman in that service, and each wearing their own special insignia rather than their rank insignia. The Australian Army equivalent is the Regimental Sergeant Major of the Army (RSM-A) and the Royal Australian Air Force equivalent is the Warrant Officer of the Air Force (WOFF-AF).

References

Bibliography

- Dennis, Peter; Grey, Jeffrey; Morris, Ewan; Prior, Robin (1995). *The Oxford Companion to Australian Military History*. Melbourne: Oxford University Press. ISBN 0-19-553227-9.
- Frame, Tom (2004). *No Pleasure Cruise: The Story of the Royal Australian Navy*. Crows Nest, New South Wales: Allen & Unwin. ISBN 1-74114-233-4.
- Gillett, Ross; Graham, Colin (1977). *Warships of Australia*. Adelaide, South Australia: Rigby. ISBN 0-7270-0472-7.
- Whitley, M. J. (2000) [1988]. *Destroyers of World War Two: An International Encyclopedia*. London: Cassell. ISBN 1-85409-521-8.

Figure 132: *Royal Australian Navy sailors from HMAS Sydney during Operation Northern Trident 2009*

External links

 Wikimedia Commons has media related to ***Royal Australian Navy***.

- Royal Australian Navy home page[621]
  - Historical listing of RAN ships[634]
- Maritimequest Royal Australian Navy photo gallery[635]
- Biographies of senior RAN officers[636]
- Royal and Dominion Navies in World War II, Campaigns, Battles, Warship losses[637]

List of active Royal Australian Navy ships

The Royal Australian Navy (RAN) fleet is made up of 49 commissioned warships as of December 2017[638].

The main strength is the ten frigates and one destroyer of the surface combatant force: eight *Anzac* class frigates, two *Adelaide* class frigates, and one *Hobart* class destroyer. Six *Collins*-class boats make up the submarine service, although due to the maintenance cycle not all submarines are active at any time. The issues have now been fixed and five submarines are available for service. Amphibious warfare assets include two *Canberra*-class landing helicopter dock ships and the landing ship HMAS *Choules*. Thirteen *Armidale*-class patrol boats perform coastal and economic exclusion zone patrols, and four *Huon*-class vessels are used for minehunting and clearance (another two are commissioned but in reserve since October 2011). Replenishment at sea is provided by two ships, *Sirius* and *Success*, while the two *Leeuwin*-class and four *Paluma*-class vessels perform survey and charting duties.

In addition to the commissioned warships, the RAN operates the sail training ship *Young Endeavour* and two Cape-class patrol boats acquired from the Australian Border Force. Other auxiliaries and small craft are not operated by the RAN, but by DMS Maritime, who are contracted to provide support services.[639]

The lion's share of the RAN fleet is divided between Fleet Base East (HMAS *Kuttabul*, in Sydney) and Fleet Base West (HMAS *Stirling*, near Perth). Mine warfare assets are located at HMAS *Waterhen* (also in Sydney), while HMAS *Cairns* in Cairns and HMAS *Coonawarra* in Darwin host the navy's patrol and survey vessels.

Figure 133: *HMAS Collins, lead ship of her class*

Submarines

Collins class

Australia operates a single class of diesel-electric submarines, the six *Collins*-class boats which began entering service in 1993. The *Collins* was designed by the Swedish submarine builder Kockums as the Type 471 specifically to meet Australian requirements, many of which were derived from Australia's need for great range without utilizing a nuclear propulsion system. The ships themselves were built in Australia by the Australian Submarine Corporation in Adelaide, South Australia. The submarines are classified by the RAN as guided missile submarines (SSG), but are often referred to as hunter-killer submarines (SSK) in the international press. While these vessels represented a major increase in capability for the RAN, they have found themselves mired in numerous technical and operational problems. Meanwhile, the RAN has struggled to sufficiently crew their submarine fleet, with at times no more than two qualified crews available.[640] The twelve-boat strong Future Submarine Program (SEA 1000) was initiated to replace the existing six Collins-class boats. The Shortfin Barracuda, the conventional-powered variant of the French Barracuda-class submarine, proposed by French shipbuilder DCNS, was chosen by the Australian government as the design for the new boats.

Size	Performance	Armament	Other features
Displacement: 3051 t surfaced 3353 t submerged	Submerged speed: 21 knots (39 km/h; 24 mph)	6 × 21-inch (530 mm) torpedo tubes, firing: Mark 48 Mod 7 CBASS torpedoes, UGM-84C Sub-Harpoon anti-ship missiles, or Stonefish Mark III mines	Sonars: Scylla, SHORT-TAS
	Surfaced speed: 10.5 knots (19.4 km/-h; 12.1 mph)		Radar: Type 1007
Length: 77.4 metres (254 ft)			
Complement: 58	Surfaced range: 11,000 nautical miles (20,000 km; 13,000 mi)		Periscope: CK043, CH093
	Submerged range: 480 nautical miles (890 km; 550 mi)		

Name	Pennant number	Commissioned	Homeport	Notes
Collins	SSG 73	27 July 1996	Fleet Base West	
Farncomb	SSG 74	31 January 1998	Fleet Base West	
Waller	SSG 75	10 July 1999	Fleet Base West	
Dechaineux	SSG 76	23 February 2001	Fleet Base West	
Sheean	SSG 77	23 February 2001	Fleet Base West	
Rankin	SSG 78	29 March 2003	Fleet Base West	

Amphibious warfare

Canberra class

The *Canberra* class are landing helicopter dock ships based on the design of Spanish ship *Juan Carlos I*. The hull of each ship was built by the designer, Navantia, then was transported to Australia by heavy lift ship for internal fitout and installation of the superstructure by BAE Systems Australia. Designed to transport and land an amphibious force of up to 1,600 soldiers by landing craft and helicopter, the *Canberra*s are the largest ships ever operated by the RAN. Lead ship HMAS *Canberra* was commissioned into the RAN in late 2014. The second ship of the class, *Adelaide*, was commissioned at the end of 2015.

Figure 134: *HMAS Adelaide*

Size	Performance	Armament	Other features
Displacement: 27,500 t full load Length: 230.82 metres (757.3 ft) Complement: 358 personnel (293 RAN, 62 Army, 3 RAAF) 1,046-1,600 troops	Maximum speed: Over 20 knots (37 km/h; 23 mph) Range: 9,000 nautical miles (17,000 km; 10,000 mi)	4 × Rafael Typhoon 25 mm 6 × 12.7 mm machine guns	Aviation: 6-spot helicopter deck 8 × helicopters (standard load) Boats carried: 4 × LLC in well deck Vehicle deck: Up to 110 vehicles

List of active Royal Australian Navy ships 233

Name	Pennant number	Commissioned	Homeport	Notes
Canberra	L02	28 November 2014	Fleet Base East	RAN Flagship
Adelaide	L01	4 December 2015	Fleet Base East	

Surface combatants

Hobart Class

The Australian Air Warfare Destroyer (AWD) project commenced in 2000, to replace the *Adelaide*-class frigates and restore the capability last exhibited by the *Perth*-class destroyers. The ship was assembled from 31 pre-fabricated modules ('blocks'): 12 for the hull, 9 for the forward superstructure, and 10 for the aft superstructure. The *Hobarts* are built around the Aegis combat system. The first ship HMAS Hobart was ordered on 4 October 2007 and commissioned on 23 September 2017.

Size	Performance	Armament	Other features
Displacement: 7,000 t full load	Maximum speed: 28 knots (52 km/h; 32 mph)	48-cell Mark 41 Vertical Launch System	Aviation: 1 x MH-60R Seahawk
Length: 147.2 metres (483 ft)	Range: 5,000 nautical miles (9,300 km; 5,800 mi)	2 × 4-canister Harpoon missile launchers	Radar: Lockheed Martin AN/SPY-1D(V) S-band radar
Complement: 186 + 16 aircrew		1 × Mark 45 Mod 4 5-inch gun	
		2 × Mark 32 Mod 9 two-tube torpedo launchers	Sonar: Ultra Electronics Sonar Systems' Integrated Sonar System
		1 × Phalanx CIWS	
		2 × 25mm M242 Bushmaster autocannons in Typhoon mounts	

Name	Pennant number	Commissioned	Homeport	Notes
Hobart	DDG 39	23 September 2017	Fleet Base East	

Figure 135: *HMAS Hobart in December 2017*

Anzac class

There are eight frigates of the *Anzac* class. These were commissioned from 1996 to 2006 as part of a joint program with New Zealand, whose navy operates an additional two examples. Derived from Blohm + Voss' MEKO modular ship family and designated the MEKO 200 ANZ by that company, the ships were built in Australia by Tenix in Williamstown, Victoria. They are designated as helicopter frigates (FFH) by the RAN, and are designed to be capable of both mid-level patrol and blue water operations. In 2010, these vessels began to receive upgrades to their anti-ship missile defence (ASMD) capabilities.

Size	Performance	Armament	Other features
Displacement: 3600 t full load	*Maximum speed:* 27 knots (50 km/h; 31 mph)	5-inch/54 Mk 45 DP gun	*Aviation:* 1 × S-70B-2 Seahawk helicopter
Length: 118 metres (387 ft)	*Range:* 6,000 nautical miles (11,000 km; 6,900 mi)	8-cell Mk 41 VLS	*Radar:* SPS-49(V)8 CEAFAR (part of ASMD upgrade being rolled out across the class)
Complement: 22 officers + 141 sailors		8 × Harpoon Block II	
		2 × 3-tube Mk 32 torpedo tubes	*Sonar:* Spherion B

Figure 136: *Anzac-class frigate HMAS Perth (post-ASMD configuration)*

Name	Pennant number	Commissioned	Homeport	Notes
Anzac	FFH 150	18 May 1996	Fleet Base East	
Arunta	FFH 151	12 December 1998	Fleet Base West	
Warramunga	FFH 152	31 March 2001	Fleet Base West	
Stuart	FFH 153	17 August 2002	Fleet Base West	
Parramatta	FFH 154	4 October 2003	Fleet Base East	
Ballarat	FFH 155	26 June 2004	Fleet Base East	
Toowoomba	FFH 156	8 October 2005	Fleet Base West	
Perth	FFH 157	26 August 2006	Fleet Base West	
Two additional ships built for and operated by the Royal New Zealand Navy				

Figure 137: *Adelaide-class frigate HMAS Darwin*

Adelaide class

The Australian variant of the American *Oliver Hazard Perry*-class guided missile frigate, six *Adelaide*-class frigates were built for the RAN. Four were built by Todd Pacific Shipyards in Seattle, Washington, while the final two were built by AMECON in Williamstown, Victoria. They first entered service in 1980, and with the retirement of the *Perth*-class destroyers, have become the RAN's primary air defence asset. Four of the frigates received upgrades to their weapons and systems during the 2000s, of which three remain in service. The other three ships have been paid off: the first two in the late 2000s to free up funds for the modernisation, and the third in 2015.

Size	Performance	Armament	Other features
Displacement: 4100 t full load	*Maximum speed:* 29 knots (54 km/h; 33 mph)	3-inch OTO Melara DP gun	*Aviation:* 2 × S-70B-2 Seahawk helicopters
Length: 139 metres (456 ft) overall	*Range:* 4,500 nautical miles (8,300 km; 5,200 mi)	8-cell Mk 41 VLS	*Radars:* AN/SPS-49, AN/SPS-55
		Mk 13 missile launcher	
Complement: 176-221		2 × 3-tube Mk 32 torpedo tubes	*Sonar:* AN/SQS-56
		Phalanx CIWS	

Name	Pennant number	Commissioned	Homeport	Notes
Melbourne	FFG 05	15 February 1992	Fleet Base East	
Newcastle	FFG 06	11 December 1993	Fleet Base East	

Four additional ships (*Adelaide*, *Canberra*, *Sydney*, and *Darwin*) retired from service

Patrol and mine warfare

Armidale class

For patrol of Australia's vast coastline, territorial waters, and offshore territories, the RAN operates thirteen *Armidale*-class patrol boats. These replaced the *Fremantle* class from 2005 as the navy's primary asset for border protection, fisheries patrols, and interception of unauthorised arrivals by sea. Based on the *Bay*-class customs vessels, the *Armidale*s are significantly enlarged to allow for better range and seakeeping ability. Originally, twelve boats were to be built by Austal Ships, but the establishment of a dedicated patrol force for the North West Shelf Venture saw another two ordered. The Australian Patrol Boat Group has divided the class into four divisions, with three ships' companies assigned for every two vessels to achieve higher operational availability. HMAS *Bundaberg* was decommissioned in December 2014 after being extensively damaged by an onboard fire. Ongoing problems with the patrol boats, including wear from high operational use and structural issues, prompted the RAN to acquire two Cape-class patrol boats from the Australian Border Force.

Size	Performance	Armament	Other features
Displacement: 270 t	Maximum speed: 25 knots (46 km/h; 29 mph)	1 × 25 mm M242 Bushmaster	2 × Zodiac 7.2 m (24 ft) RHIBs
Length: 56.8 metres (186 ft)	Range: 3,000 nautical miles (5,600 km; 3,500 mi)	2 × 12.7 mm machine guns	
Complement: 21			

Name	Pennant number	Commissioned	Homeport	Notes
Armidale	ACPB 83	24 June 2005	HMAS *Coonawarra*	
Larrakia	ACPB 84	10 February 2006	HMAS *Coonawarra*	
Bathurst	ACPB 85	10 February 2006	HMAS *Coonawarra*	
Albany	ACPB 86	15 July 2006	HMAS *Coonawarra*	
Pirie	ACPB 87	29 July 2006	HMAS *Coonawarra*	

Maitland	ACPB 88	29 September 2006	HMAS *Coonawarra*
Ararat	ACPB 89	13 November 2006	HMAS *Coonawarra*
Broome	ACPB 90	10 February 2007	HMAS *Coonawarra*
Wollongong	ACPB 92	23 June 2007	HMAS *Cairns*
Childers	ACPB 93	7 July 2007	HMAS *Cairns*
Launceston	ACPB 94	22 September 2007	HMAS *Cairns*
Maryborough	ACPB 95	8 December 2007	HMAS *Coonawarra*
Glenelg	ACPB 96	22 February 2008	HMAS *Coonawarra*
One additional ship (*Bundaberg*) destroyed by fire			

Huon class

Mine countermeasures at sea are handled by the *Huon*-class minehunters, which began to enter RAN service from 1999. The class was based on the Italian Navy's *Gaeta*-class minehunter developed by Intermarine SpA. Development was undertaken in partnership between Intermarine and Australian Defence Industries (ADI). The first hull was built in Italy, with fitting out the first and construction of the remaining five vessels of the class done by ADI in Newcastle, New South Wales, replacing the problematic Bay-class minehunters. In addition to the mine warfare role, individual have been deployed on occasion to support patrol and border protection operations. Four vessels operate out of HMAS *Waterhen*, in Sydney, New South Wales. An additional two ships were placed in reserve in October 2011.

Size	Performance	Armament	Other features
Displacement: 720 t full load	*Maximum speed:* 14 knots (26 km/h; 16 mph)	1 × 30 mm DS30B autocannon	2 × Double Eagle mine disposal vehicles
Length: 52.5 metres (172 ft)	*Range:* 1,500 nautical miles (2,800 km; 1,700 mi)	2 × 12.7 mm machine guns	Type 1007 navigational radar
			Type 2093M mine-hunting sonar
Complement: 6 officers + 33 sailors			Type 133 PRISM radar warning
			2 × Wallop Super Barricade decoy launchers

List of active Royal Australian Navy ships

Figure 138: *Armidale-class patrol boat HMAS Broome*

Figure 139: *Huon-class minehunter HMAS Gascoyne*

Name	Pennant number	Commissioned	Homeport	Notes
Huon	M 82	15 May 1999	HMAS *Waterhen*	
Hawkesbury	M 83	12 February 2000	HMAS *Waterhen*	In reserve
Norman	M 84	26 August 2000	HMAS *Waterhen*	In reserve
Gascoyne	M 85	2 June 2001	HMAS *Waterhen*	
Diamantina	M 86	4 May 2002	HMAS *Waterhen*	
Yarra	M 87	1 March 2003	HMAS *Waterhen*	

Choules

The Bay-class landing ship dock HMAS *Choules* was acquired by the RAN in 2011. The ship was originally built by Swan Hunter for the British Royal Fleet Auxiliary, and entered British service in 2006 as RFA *Largs Bay*. She was made redundant in the 2011 Strategic Defence and Security Review and sold to Australia. *Choules* represents a major increase in sealift capability for the RAN, particularly after mechanical issues in 2010 and 2011 forced the early retirement of the navy's two *Kanimbla*-class vessels, and put HMAS *Tobruk* in dock for an extensive refit.

Size	Performance	Armament	Other features
Displacement: 16,190 t full load	*Maximum speed:* 18 knots (33 km/h; 21 mph)	Unarmed	*Aviation:* Helicopter deck, no hangar
Length: 176.6 metres (579 ft)	*Range:* 8,000 nautical miles (15,000 km; 9,200 mi)		*Boats carried:* 1 × LCU, 1 × LCM-8, or 2 × LCVP in well deck 2 × Mexeflotes on flanks
Complement: 158 personnel 356-700 troops			*Vehicle deck:* 32 tanks or 150 trucks

Name	Pennant number	Commissioned	Homeport	Notes
Choules	L100	13 December 2011	Fleet Base East	In Royal Fleet Auxiliary service 2006-2011

Figure 140: *HMAS Choules in 2012*

Replenishment

Sirius

HMAS *Sirius* was initially built as a civilian oil tanker, but was purchased by the RAN during construction and converted into a replenishment ship for the west coast. Built by Hyundai Mipo Dockyard in South Korea, she was launched in 2004 and commissioned in 2006; costing half the price and becoming active three years before the RAN's original plan of a purpose-build ship.

Size	Performance	Armament	Other features
Displacement: 25,016.53 t	*Maximum speed:* 16 knots (30 km/h; 18 mph)	Small arms only	34,806 cz fuel capacity
Length: 191.3 metres (628 ft)	*Range:* -		*Aviation:* Helicopter deck, no hangar
Complement: 60			

Figure 141: *HMAS Sirius in 2006*

Name	Pennant number	Commissioned	Homeport	Notes
Sirius	O 266	16 September 2006	Fleet Base West	

List of active Royal Australian Navy ships

Figure 142: *HMAS Success underway in 2009*

Success

The *Durance*-class replenishment oiler HMAS *Success* is the only example of the class not built for the French Navy. Launched in 1984, the vessel was the largest ever built in Australia for military service, and the last major construction project undertaken by Cockatoo Island Dockyard.

Size	Performance	Armament	Other features
Displacement: 17,993 t full load	*Maximum speed:* 19 knots (35 km/h; 22 mph)	2 × Phalanx Mk 15 close-in weapon systems	
Length: 157.2 metres (516 ft)	*Range:* -	4 × 12.7 mm machine guns	
Complement: 220			

Name	Pennant number	Commissioned	Homeport	Notes
Success	OR 304	23 April 1986	Fleet Base East	

Hydrographic survey

Leeuwin class

Two *Leeuwin*-class survey ships were built for the RAN by NQEA Australia of Cairns. Ordered in 1996, the ships were commissioned in a joint ceremony in 2000. They are capable of charting waters up to 6,000 metres (20,000 ft) deep, and carry three *Fantome*-class survey boats for shallow-water work. In addition to hydrographic surveying duties, since 2001 both vessels have also operated in support of the RAN patrol force.

Size	Performance	Armament	Other features
Displacement: 2,170 t Length: 71.2 metres (234 ft) Complement: 10 officers + 46 sailors	Maximum speed: 18 knots (33 km/h; 21 mph) Range: 18,000 nautical miles (33,000 km; 21,000 mi) at 9 knots (17 km/h; 10 mph)	2 × × 12.7 mm machine guns	*Sonars:* C-Tech CMAS 36/39 hull mounted high frequency active sonar Atlas Fansweep-20 multi-beam echo sounder Atlas Hydrographic Deso single-beam echo sounder Klein 2000 towed sidescan sonar array
			Radar STN Atlas 9600 ARPA navigation radar
			Aviation: Helicopter deck, no hangar

Name	Pennant number	Commissioned	Homeport	Notes
Leeuwin	A 245	27 May 2000	HMAS *Cairns*	
Melville	A 246	27 May 2000	HMAS *Cairns*	

Paluma class

The *Paluma*-class survey motor launches are large catamarans designed for survey operations around northern and eastern Australia. Four ships were built by Eglo Engineering at Port Adelaide, South Australia between 1988 and 1990. The vessels normally operate in pairs.

Figure 143: *Leeuwin-class survey vessel HMAS Leeuwin*

Figure 144: *Paluma-class survey motor launch HMAS Benalla*

Size	Performance	Armament	Other features
Displacement: 320 t	Maximum speed: 12 knots (22 km/h; 14 mph)	None fitted	Radar: JRC JMA-3710-6 navigational radar
Length: 36.6 metres (120 ft)	Range: 1,800 nautical miles (3,300 km; 2,100 mi) at 10 knots (19 km/h; 12 mph)		Sonars: ELAC LAZ 72 side-scan mapping sonar Skipper 113 hull-mounted scanning sonar
Complement: 3 officers + 11 sailors			

Name	Pennant number	Commissioned	Homeport	Notes
Paluma	A 01	27 February 1989	HMAS *Cairns*	
Mermaid	A 02	4 December 1989	HMAS *Cairns*	
Shepparton	A 03	24 January 1990	HMAS *Cairns*	
Benalla	A 04	2 June 2001	HMAS *Cairns*	

Non-commissioned vessels

Young Endeavour

The Sail Training Ship *Young Endeavour* was built as a gift from the United Kingdom to Australia for the latter's 1988 bicentenary of colonisation. Built by British shipbuilder Brooke Marine, the brigantine rig vessel is operated by the RAN, but is used to facilitate the Young Endeavour Youth Scheme; a sail training program for Australian youth aged between 16 and 23. A 10-strong RAN crew is supplemented by 24-30 youth on ten-day voyages, with 500 applicants selected every year through two ballots.

Name	Pennant number	In service	Homeport	Notes
Young Endeavour	-	25 January 1988	HMAS *Waterhen*	

Figure 145: *The youth crew of Young Endeavour manning the mast after the ship's arrival at the Australian National Maritime Museum*

Cape class

Eight Cape-class patrol boats were built for the Australian Customs and Border Protection Service (now the Australian Border Force) by Austal Ships between 2012 and 2015, as replacements for the Bay class.[641] Following the loss of HMAS *Bundaberg* and hull issues with the *Armidale* class requiring an intense remedial maintenance program, two Cape-class patrol boats were leased to the RAN from late 2015 until the end of 2016. In naval service, the two rotating crew groups for each of the two vessel are made up of RAN personnel, the patrol boats operate from HMAS *Cairns*, and are identified with the Australian Defence Vessel (ADV) prefix, but retain the blue-and-red customs colour scheme.

Size[642]	Performance	Armament	Other features
Length: 57.8 metres (190 ft)	*Maximum speed:* 25 knots (46 km/h; 29 mph)	2 x .50 calibre machine guns	2 × 7.3 m (24 ft) Gemini RHIBs
Complement: 18	*Range:* 4,000 nautical miles (7,400 km; 4,600 mi) at 12 knots (22 km/h; 14 mph)		

Figure 146: *ABFC Cape St. George, a Cape-class patrol boat in service with the Australian Border Force*

Name	Pennant number	In service	Homeport	Notes
ADV *Cape Byron*	20	July 2015	HMAS *Cairns*	
ADV *Cape Nelson*	40	October 2015	HMAS *Cairns*	
Six additional ships built for and operated by the Australian Border Force				

References

Citations

Bibliography

- Defense Industry Daily (23 April 2012). "Australia's Submarine Program In the Dock"[643]. *Defense Industry Daily*. Retrieved 27 May 2012.
- Defense Industry Daily (5 May 2012). "Australia's Next Generation Submarines"[644]. *Defense Industry Daily*. Retrieved 27 May 2012.
- Matterson Marine Pty Ltd (10 March 2007). "Australia: Submarines"[645]. *Warships*. Archived from the original[646] on 27 December 2010. Retrieved 22 May 2012.
- Matterson Marine Pty Ltd (3 July 2007). "Australia: Support Ships"[647]. *Warships*. Archived from the original[648] on 27 December 2010. Retrieved 22 May 2012.
- Matterson Marine Pty Ltd (1 December 2007). "Australia: Minor Warships"[649]. *Warships*. Archived from the original[650] on 27 December 2010. Retrieved 22 May 2012.
- Matterson Marine Pty Ltd (19 January 2008). "Australia: Major Warships"[651]. *Warships*. Archived from the original[652] on 21 June 2012. Retrieved 22 May 2012.
- Royal Australian Navy. "Current Ships"[653]. Retrieved 30 November 2014.
- Saunders, Stephen; Philpott, Tom, eds. (7 August 2015). *IHS Jane's Fighting Ships 2015-2016*. Jane's Fighting Ships (116th Revised ed.). Coulsdon: IHS Jane's. ISBN 9780710631435. OCLC 919022075[654].

Air Force

History of the Royal Australian Air Force

The Royal Australian Air Force (RAAF) traces its history back to the Imperial Conference held in London in 1911, where it was decided aviation should be developed within the Armed Forces of the British Empire. Australia implemented this decision, the only country to do so, by approving the establishment of the Central Flying School (CFS) in 1912. The location for the proposed school was initially to be at Duntroon, Australian Capital Territory, but in July 1913 Point Cook, Victoria, was announced as the preferred location. The first flights by CFS aircraft took place there in March 1914.

The Australian Flying Corps (AFC) was formed as a Militia unit, with staff and students to be selected from the Citizen Forces. After an abortive deployment to German New Guinea at the end of 1914 as part of the Australian Naval and Military Expeditionary Force, it earned a most creditable reputation in both Palestine and France during World War I as a part of the Australian Imperial Force (AIF). The Australian Flying Corps remained part of the Australian Army until 1919, when it was disbanded along with the AIF. Although the Central Flying School continued to operate at Point Cook, military flying virtually ceased until 1920, when the Australian Air Corps was formed. The Australian Air Force was formed on 31 March 1921. King George V approved the prefix "Royal" in June 1921 and it became effective on 31 August 1921. The RAAF then became the second Royal air arm to be formed in the British Commonwealth, following the British Royal Air Force.

The service was rapidly expanded during World War II and at its height, it was the fourth largest air force in the world, consisting of 53 squadrons based in the Pacific and a further 17 in Europe.

Figure 147: *An Australian Flying Corps aircraft c. 1918*

Formation, 1912

In 1911, the Imperial Conference that was held in London determined that the armed forces of the British Empire needed to develop an aviation branch. At the time, aircraft were a newly emerging technology, but nevertheless Australia implemented the decision, the only country to do so. The first step taken by the government was to approve the establishment of the Central Flying School (CFS) in 1912. Initially, it had been proposed to establish the school at Duntroon, in the Australian Capital Territory, where the Royal Military College had been established in 1911, but in July 1913 it was determined that Point Cook, Victoria, was the preferred location. The Australian Flying Corps (AFC) was subsequently formed as a Militia unit, with staff and students to be selected from the Citizen Forces, and the first flights by CFS aircraft took place in March 1914.[655]

World War I and the Inter-war years

Soon after the outbreak of World War I in August 1914, the AFC sent aircraft to assist the Australian Naval and Military Expeditionary Force in capturing German colonies in what is now north-west New Guinea. These colonies surrendered quickly however, before the planes were even unpacked.[656] The first operational flights did not occur until 27 May 1915, when the Mesopotamian Half Flight was called upon to assist the Indian Army in protecting British oil interests in what is now Iraq. The corps later saw action in Egypt, Palestine and on the Western Front throughout the remainder of World War I. By the end of the war, four squadrons – Nos. 1, 2, 3 and 4 – had seen active service; another four squadrons – Nos. 5, 6, 7, and 8 – had also been raised to provide training in the United Kingdom. The AFC was disbanded along with the rest of the Australian Imperial Force in 1919, following the end of hostilities. Although the Central Flying School continued to operate at Point Cook, military flying virtually ceased until 1920, when the Australian Air Corps was formed. The following year, this was separated from the Army on 31 March 1921, when the Australian Air Force was formed as an independent service; in June that year King George V gave his assent for the service to use the prefix "Royal" and this came into effect on 31 August 1921.[657]

Upon formation, the RAAF had more aircraft than personnel, with 21 officers and 128 other ranks,[658] and just 170 aircraft.Wikipedia:Citation needed Initially, it had been planned to expand the force to 1,500 personnel – three-quarters permanent staff and one quarter reserves – who would serve in six squadrons: two of fighter aircraft, two of reconnaissance aircraft, and two squadrons of seaplanes. These plans were scuttled a year after formation due to budget constraints and until 1924, the service's strength remained steady at just 50 officers and 300 other ranks; of the six planned squadrons, only five had been raised, albeit cadre strength, and these were subsequently merged into a single mixed squadron until 1925.[659] A slightly improved economic situation in 1925 allowed the re-raising of Nos. 1 and 3 Squadrons, which were initially composite units equipped with fighters and bombers. Later in the decade, they were reorganised with No. 1 Squadron becoming a solely bomber formation, while No. 3 focused on army co-operation roles; smaller squadrons – in reality only flights – of fighters and seaplanes were formed within the RAAF's flying training unit, No. 1 Flying Training School, which had been raised at Point Cook.

Throughout the inter-war years the fledgling RAAF focused on local defence and providing training opportunities to Australia's naval and military forces. It also undertook aerial survey missions, meteorological flights, public displays, and provision of defence aid to the civil community, undertaking search and rescue missions and bush fire patrols. In the late 1930s, the force was expanded amidst concerns about a future war in Europe. Additional squadrons were raised and bases established away from the south-east coast, including airbases in Western Australia, Queensland and the Northern Territory. This expansion saw the RAAF increase its personnel from under 1,000 in 1935 to around 3,500 in 1939, and the establishment of a force of 12 squadrons, with plans for a further six, by the outbreak of World War II in September 1939.

World War II

Shortly after the declaration of war in Europe, although Australia's air force was small – consisting of just 246 aircraft – the Australian government offered to send six squadrons to Britain to fight, in addition to the 450 Australians who were already serving in the ranks of the Royal Air Force at the time.[660] The RAAF already had one squadron in the United Kingdom, No. 10 Squadron

Figure 148: *An Australian Hampden from No. 455 Squadron RAAF at RAF Leuchars in May 1942.*

RAAF, which had been dispatched earlier in the year to take ownership of nine Short Sunderland flying boats and return them to Australia. They subsequently took place in their first operational mission on 10 October 1939, when they carried out a sortie to Tunisia. To rapidly expand, Australia joined the Empire Air Training Scheme,[661] under which flight crews received basic training in Australia before travelling to Canada or Rhodesia for advanced training. These crews were then posted to operational units. A total of 17 RAAF bomber, fighter, reconnaissance and other squadrons served initially in Britain, and/or with the Desert Air Force, in North Africa and the Mediterranean.[662]

With British manufacturing targeted by the *Luftwaffe*, the Australian government created the Department of Aircraft Production (DAP), which was later known as the Government Aircraft Factories, to supply Commonwealth air forces and the RAAF was eventually provided with large numbers of locally-built versions of British designs like the Beaufort torpedo bomber.Wikipedia:Citation needed

In the European Theatre of World War II, RAAF personnel were especially notable in RAF Bomber Command: although they represented only two percent of all RAAF personnel during the war, they accounted for 23% of the total number killed in action. This statistic is further illustrated by the fact that No. 460 Squadron RAAF, mostly flying Avro Lancasters, had an official

Figure 149: *An Australian Halifax from No. 462 Squadron RAAF at RAF Foulsham in 1945.*

establishment of about 200 aircrew and yet had 1,018 combat deaths. The squadron was therefore effectively wiped out five times over.[663]

The beginning of the Pacific War—and the rapid advance of Japanese forces—threatened the Australian mainland for the first time. The RAAF was quite unprepared for the emergency, and initially had negligible forces available for service in the Pacific. Its four squadrons based in Malaya – Nos. 1, 8, 21 and 453 – equipped with a mixture of Hudsons, Wirraways and Buffalos, were the first to go into combat, but they suffered heavily against Japanese during the Malayan Campaign and the subsequent fighting on Singapore, highlighting the fact that the Japanese held the upper hand in the air.[664] The devastating air raids on Darwin on 19 February 1942 – launched from four aircraft carriers stationed in the Timor Sea – drove the point home. Defended by a small force of just 18 Wirraways and 14 Hudsons from two squadrons – Nos. 12 and 13 – the town was heavily damaged with the loss of 10 ships, 23 aircraft and a death toll of several hundred.[665] In response, some RAAF squadrons – such as No. 452 Squadron.[666] – were transferred from the northern hemisphere—although 15 remained there until the end of the war.[667] Shortages of fighter and ground attack planes led to the acquisition of US-built P-40 Kittyhawks, and the rapid design and manufacture of the first Australian fighter, the CAC Boomerang.[668] RAAF Kittyhawks, such as those operated by Nos. 75, 76 and 77 Squadrons, came to play a crucial role in the New Guinea and

Figure 150: *An Australian Beaufighter flying over the Owen Stanley Range in New Guinea in 1942*

Solomon Islands campaigns, especially in the Battle of Milne Bay and in the Kokoda Track campaign.

In the Battle of the Bismarck Sea, imported Bristol Beaufighters proved to be highly effective ground attack and maritime strike aircraft. Beaufighters were later made locally by the DAP. Although it was much bigger than Japanese fighters, the Beaufighter had the speed to outrun them. The RAAF's heavy bomber force predominantly comprised 287 B-24 Liberators, which could bomb Japanese targets as far away as Borneo and the Philippines from airfields in Australia and New Guinea.Wikipedia:Citation needed

In September 1942 most Australian squadrons were grouped under RAAF Command. The only Australian air combat units in the SWPA not under RAAF Command were those based in New Guinea as No. 9 Operational Group RAAF, which was controlled by Fifth Air Force.[669,670,671] RAAF Command was charged with defending Australia, except in the north-east, protecting the sea lanes to New Guinea, and conducting operations against Japanese shipping, airfields and other installations in the Dutch East Indies.[672,673] Its role was thus "mainly defensive" at the outset, with the expectation that "in the event of developments in the North and North-West of Australia, this would be altered".[674] Bostock was to exercise control of air operations through the

RAAF area command system, comprising North-Western, Western, Southern, Eastern, and North-Eastern Area Commands.[675]

By late 1945, the RAAF had received or ordered about 500 P-51 Mustangs, for fighter/ground attack purposes. The Commonwealth Aircraft Corporation initially assembled US-made Mustangs, but later manufactured most of those used. The RAAF's main operational formation, the First Tactical Air Force, comprised more than 18,000 personnel and 20 squadrons; it had taken part in the Philippines and Borneo campaigns and was scheduled to participate in the invasion of the Japanese mainland, Operation Downfall. So too were the RAAF bomber squadrons in Europe, as part of the proposed Tiger Force. However, the war was brought to a sudden end by the US nuclear attacks on Japan. As a result of the Empire Air Training Scheme, about 20,000 Australian personnel had served with other Commonwealth air forces in Europe during World War II. A total of 216,900 men and women served in the RAAF, of whom 9,780 lost their lives. At war's end, a total of 53 RAAF squadrons were serving in the Pacific and a further 17 in Europe. With over 152,000 personnel operating nearly 6,000 aircraft it was the world's fourth largest air force, after those of the USA, the USSR and the UK.[676]

Post-World War II service

Korean War

In the Korean War, Mustangs from No. 77 Squadron (77 Sqn), stationed in Japan with the British Commonwealth Occupation Force, were among the first United Nations aircraft to be deployed, in ground support, combat air patrol, and escort missions. When the UN planes were confronted by MiG-15 jet fighters, 77 Sqn acquired Gloster Meteors, which enabled some success against the Soviet pilots flying for North Korea. However, the MiGs were superior aircraft and the Meteors were relegated to ground support missions, as the North Koreans gained experience. The air force also operated transport aircraft during the conflict.[677]

Vietnam War

During the Vietnam War, from 1966–1972, the RAAF contributed squadrons of Caribou STOL transport aircraft (No. 35 Squadron), UH-1 Iroquois helicopters (No. 9 Squadron) and English Electric Canberra bombers (No. 2 Squadron).

The Canberras flew a large number of bombing sorties, two were lost (in 1970 and 1971). Two crew members were killed, two squadron members died of disease, and three from accidents during the war. One of the Canberras lost (*A84-228*) was brought down by a surface-to-air missile from which the crew (including the squadron commander, W/C Frank Downing) safely ejected and were rescued by helicopter. The other (*A84-231*) was lost near Da Nang,[678] during a bombing run. Its exact location and fate of its crew (FlgOff. Michael Herbert and Plt Off. Robert Carver) were unknown for 28 years, when it was located and their remains were returned to Australia.[679])

RAAF transport aircraft also supported anti-communist ground forces. The UH-1 helicopters were used in many roles including Dustoff (medical evacuation) and Bushranger Gunships for armed support.Wikipedia:Citation needed

Peacekeeping and Iraq

Military airlifts were conducted for a number of purposes in the intervening decades, such as the peacekeeping operations in East Timor from 1999. Australia's combat aircraft were not used again in anger until the Iraq War in 2003, when F/A-18s from No. 75 Squadron operated in the escort and ground attack roles.Wikipedia:Citation needed

References

Citations

Bibliography

- Armstrong, John. "History of the RAAF: 20 Years of Warfighting 1939–1959, Part 2". *Air Power International*. Vol. 4 (No. 6): 42–48.
- Ashworth, Norman (2000). *How Not to Run an Air Force! The Higher Command of the Royal Australian Air Force During the Second World War: Volume 1*[680]. Canberra: Air Power Studies Centre. ISBN 0-642-26550-X.
- Barrett, Rees D. (2009). *Significant People in Australia's History*. South Yarra, Victoria: Macmillan. ISBN 9781420266221.
- Barnes, Norman (2000). *The RAAF and the Flying Squadrons*. St Leonards, New South Wales, Australia: Allen & Unwin. ISBN 1-86508-130-2.
- Dennis, Peter; Grey, Jeffrey; Morris, Ewan; Prior, Robin (2008) [1995]. *The Oxford Companion to Australian Military History*. South Melbourne: Oxford University Press. ISBN 0-19-551784-9.
- Eather, Steve (1996). *Odd Jobs: RAAF Operations in Japan, the Berlin Airlift, Korea, Malaya & Malta, 1946–1960*[681]. RAAF Williams, Victoria: RAAF Museum. ISBN 0-642-23482-5.

- Gillison, Douglas (1962). *Australia in the War of 1939–1945: Series Three (Air) Volume I – Royal Australian Air Force 1939–1942*[682]. Canberra: Australian War Memorial. OCLC 2000369[683]. Archived from the original[684] on 7 June 2011.
- Horner, David (2002). "The Evolution of Australian Higher Command Arrangements"[685]. *Command Papers*. Canberra: Centre for Defence Leadership Studies, Australian Defence College. Archived from the original[686] on 9 November 2014.
- Odgers, George (1968) [1957]. *Australia in the War of 1939–1945: Series Three (Air) Volume II – Air War Against Japan 1943–1945*[687]. Canberra: Australian War Memorial. OCLC 246580191[688]. Archived from the original[689] on 14 October 2013.
- Odgers, George (1996) [1984]. *Air Force Australia*. Frenchs Forest, New South Wales: National. ISBN 1-86436-081-X.
- Stephens, Alan (2006) [2001]. *The Royal Australian Air Force: A History*. London: Oxford University Press. ISBN 0-19-555541-4.

Royal Australian Air Force

Royal Australian Air Force	
Royal Australian Air Force insignia	
Active	31 March 1921 – present
Country	Australia
Type	Air force
Size	14,120 Active personnel 4,273 Reserve personnel 259 aircraft
Part of	Australian Defence Force
Headquarters	Canberra
Motto(s)	Latin: *Per Ardua ad Astra* "Through Adversity to the Stars"
March	Royal Australian Air Force March Past
Anniversaries	RAAF Anniversary Commemoration – 31 March
Engagements	• World War I • World War II • Berlin Airlift • Korean War • Malayan Emergency • Indonesia–Malaysia Confrontation • Vietnam War • East Timor • War in Afghanistan • Iraq War • Military intervention against ISIL
Website	www<wbr/>.airforce<wbr/>.gov<wbr/>.au[690]
Commanders	
Commander-in-chief	Sir Peter Cosgrove As Governor-General of Australia
Chief of Air Force	Air Marshal Gavin "Leo" Davies
Deputy Chief of Air Force	Air Vice Marshal Warren McDonald
Air Commander Australia	Air Vice Marshal Steven Roberton
Warrant Officer of the Air Force	Warrant Officer Robert Swanwick
Insignia	
Logo	AIR F◉RCE

Ensign	
Roundels	
Aircraft flown	
Electronic warfare	Boeing EA-18G, E-7A Wedgetail
Fighter	F/A-18 Hornet (A and B), F/A-18F Super Hornet, F-35
Patrol	AP-3C Orion, P8-A Poseidon
Trainer	PC-9,
Transport	C-130 Hercules, C-17 Globemaster III, Boeing 737, B300, Challenger 600, Airbus A330 MRTT, C-27J Spartan

The **Royal Australian Air Force** (**RAAF**), formed March 1921, is the aerial warfare branch of the Australian Defence Force (ADF). It operates the majority of the ADF's fixed wing aircraft, although both the Australian Army and Royal Australian Navy also operate aircraft in various roles. It directly continues the traditions of the Australian Flying Corps (AFC), formed on 22 October 1912. The RAAF provides support across a spectrum of operations such as air superiority, precision strikes, intelligence, surveillance and reconnaissance, air mobility, and humanitarian support.

The RAAF took part in many of the 20th century's major conflicts. During the early years of the Second World War a number of RAAF bomber, fighter, reconnaissance and other squadrons served in Britain, and with the Desert Air Force located in North Africa and the Mediterranean. From 1942, a large number of RAAF units were formed in Australia, and fought in South West Pacific Area. Thousands of Australians also served with other Commonwealth air forces in Europe, including during the bomber offensive against Germany. By the time the war ended, a total of 216,900 men and women served in the RAAF, of whom 10,562 were killed in action.[691]

Later the RAAF served in the Berlin Airlift, Korean War, Malayan Emergency, Indonesia–Malaysia Confrontation and Vietnam War. More recently, the RAAF has participated in operations in East Timor, the Iraq War, the War in Afghanistan, and the military intervention against the Islamic State of Iraq and the Levant (ISIL).

The RAAF has 259 aircraft, of which 110 are combat aircraft.

Figure 151: *A Royal Australian Air Force B-737 taxies at Sydney Airport*

History

Formation, 1912

The RAAF traces its history back to the Imperial Conference held in London in 1911, where it was decided aviation should be developed within the armed forces of the British Empire. Australia implemented this decision, the first dominion to do so, by approving the establishment of the "Australian Aviation Corps". This initially consisted of the Central Flying School at Point Cook, Victoria, opening on 22 October 1912. By 1914 the corps was known as the "Australian Flying Corps".

First World War

Soon after the outbreak of war in 1914, the Australian Flying Corps sent aircraft to assist in capturing German colonies in what is now north-east New Guinea. However, these colonies surrendered quickly, before the planes were even unpacked. The first operational flights did not occur until 27 May 1915, when the Mesopotamian Half Flight was called upon to assist the Indian Army in protecting British oil interests in what is now Iraq.[692]

The corps later saw action in Egypt, Palestine and on the Western Front throughout the remainder of the First World War. By the end of the war, four squadrons—Nos. 1, 2, 3 and 4—had seen operational service, while another four training squadrons—Nos. 5, 6, 7 and 8—had also been established. A total of 460 officers and 2,234 other ranks served in the AFC, whilst another 200 men served as aircrew in the British flying services.[693] Casualties included 175 dead, 111 wounded, 6 gassed and 40 captured.[694]

Inter-war period

The Australian Flying Corps remained part of the Australian Army until 1919, when it was disbanded along with the First Australian Imperial Force (AIF). Although the Central Flying School continued to operate at Point Cook, military flying virtually ceased until 1920, when the Australian Air Corps (AAC) was formed. The Australian Air Force was formed on 31 March 1921. King George V approved the prefix "Royal" in June 1921 and became effective on 31 August 1921. The RAAF then became the second Royal air arm to be formed in the British Commonwealth, following the British Royal Air Force. When formed the RAAF had more aircraft than personnel, with 21 officers and 128 other ranks and 153 aircraft.

Second World War

Europe and the Mediterranean

In September 1939, the Australian Air Board directly controlled the Air Force via RAAF Station Laverton, RAAF Station Richmond, RAAF Station Pearce, No. 1 Flying Training School RAAF at Point Cook, RAAF Station Rathmines and five smaller units.

In 1939, just after the outbreak of the Second World War, Australia joined the Empire Air Training Scheme, under which flight crews received basic training in Australia before travelling to Canada for advanced training. A total of 17 RAAF bomber, fighter, reconnaissance and other squadrons served initially in Britain and with the Desert Air Force located in North Africa and the Mediterranean. Thousands of Australians also served with other Commonwealth air forces in Europe during the Second World War. About nine percent of the personnel who served under British RAF commands in Europe and the Mediterranean were RAAF personnel.

With British manufacturing targeted by the German Luftwaffe, in 1941 the Australian government created the Department of Aircraft Production (DAP; later known as the Government Aircraft Factories) to supply Commonwealth air forces,[695] and the RAAF was eventually provided with large numbers of locally built versions of British designs such as the DAP Beaufort torpedo bomber, Beaufighters and Mosquitos, as well as other types such as Wirraways, Boomerangs, and Mustangs.[696]

Figure 152: *Curtiss Kittyhawk Mk IA of 75th Squadron RAAF, which F/O Geoff Atherton flew over New Guinea in August 1942.*

Figure 153: *The Brewster F2A Buffalo participated in air campaigns over Malayan, Singapore and Dutch East Indies*

In the European theatre of the war, RAAF personnel were especially notable in RAF Bomber Command: although they represented just two percent of all Australian enlistments during the war, they accounted for almost twenty percent of those killed in action. This statistic is further illustrated by the fact that No. 460 Squadron RAAF, mostly flying Avro Lancasters, had an official establishment of about 200 aircrew and yet had 1,018 combat deaths. The squadron was therefore effectively wiped out five times over.[697] Total RAAF casualties in Europe were 5,488 killed or missing.

Figure 154: *RAAF volunteers from Brisbane leaving for training*

Pacific War

The beginning of the Pacific War—and the rapid advance of Japanese forces—threatened the Australian mainland for the first time in its history. The RAAF was quite unprepared for the emergency, and initially had negligible forces available for service in the Pacific. In 1941 and early 1942, many RAAF airmen, including Nos. 1, 8, 21 and 453 Squadrons, saw action with the RAF Far East Command in the Malayan, Singapore and Dutch East Indies campaigns. Equipped with aircraft such as the Brewster Buffalo, and Lockheed Hudsons, the Australian squadrons suffered heavily against Japanese Zeros.[698]

During the fighting for Rabaul in early 1942, No. 24 Squadron RAAF fought a brief, but ultimately futile defence as the Japanese advanced south towards Australia.[699] The devastating air raids on Darwin on 19 February 1942 increased concerns about the direct threat facing Australia. In response, some RAAF squadrons were transferred from the northern hemisphere—although a substantial number remained there until the end of the war. Shortages of fighter and ground attack planes led to the acquisition of US-built Curtiss P-40 Kittyhawks and the rapid design and manufacture of the first Australian fighter, the CAC Boomerang. RAAF Kittyhawks came to play a crucial role in the New Guinea and Solomon Islands campaigns, especially in operations like the Battle of Milne Bay. As a response to a possible Japanese chemical warfare threat the RAAF imported hundreds of thousands of chemical weapons into Australia.

In the Battle of the Bismarck Sea, imported Bristol Beaufighters proved to be highly effective ground attack and maritime strike aircraft. Beaufighters were later made locally by the DAP from 1944.[700] Although it was much bigger than Japanese fighters, the Beaufighter had the speed to outrun them.[701] The RAAF operated a number of Consolidated PBY Catalina as long range bombers and scouts. The RAAF's heavy bomber force was predominantly made up of 287 B-24 Liberators, equipping seven squadrons, which could bomb Japanese targets as far away as Borneo and the Philippines from airfields in Australia and New Guinea. By late 1945, the RAAF had received or ordered about 500 P-51 Mustangs, for fighter/ground attack purposes. The Commonwealth Aircraft Corporation initially assembled US-made Mustangs, but later manufactured most of those used.

By mid-1945, the RAAF's main operational formation in the Pacific, the First Tactical Air Force (1st TAF), consisted of over 21,000 personnel, while the RAAF as a whole consisted of about 50 squadrons and 6,000 aircraft, of which over 3,000 were operational.[702] The 1st TAF's final campaigns were fought in support of Australian ground forces in Borneo,[703] but had the war continued some of its personnel and equipment would likely have been allocated to the invasion of the Japanese mainland, along with some of the RAAF bomber squadrons in Europe, which were to be grouped together with British and Canadian squadrons as part of the proposed Tiger Force. However, the war was brought to a sudden end by the US nuclear attacks on Japan. The RAAF's casualties in the Pacific were around 2,000 killed, wounded or captured.

By the time the war ended, a total of 216,900 men and women served in the RAAF, of whom 10,562 were killed in action; a total of 76 squadrons were formed. With over 152,000 personnel operating nearly 6,000 aircraft it was the world's fourth largest air force.[704]

Service since 1945

During the Berlin Airlift, in 1948–49, the RAAF Squadron Berlin Air Lift aided the international effort to fly in supplies to the stricken city; two RAF Avro York aircraft were also crewed by RAAF personnel. Although a small part of the operation, the RAAF contribution was significant, flying 2,062 sorties and carrying 7,030 tons of freight and 6,964 passengers.[705]

In the Korean War, from 1950–53, North American Mustangs from No. 77 Squadron RAAF, stationed in Japan with the British Commonwealth Occupation Force, were among the first United Nations aircraft to be deployed, in ground support, combat air patrol, and escort missions. When the UN planes were confronted by North Korean Mikoyan-Gurevich MiG-15 jet fighters, 77 Sqn acquired Gloster Meteors, however the MiGs remained superior

Figure 155: *Two RAAF Mirage III fighters in 1980*

and the Meteors were relegated to ground support missions as the North Koreans gained experience. The air force also operated transport aircraft during the conflict. No. 77 Squadron flew 18,872 sorties, claiming the destruction of 3,700 buildings, 1,408 vehicles, 16 bridges, 98 railway carriages and an unknown number of enemy personnel. Three MiG-15s were confirmed destroyed, and two others probably destroyed. RAAF casualties included 41 killed and seven captured; 66 aircraft – 22 Mustangs and 44 Meteors – were lost.[706]

In July 1952, No. 78 Wing RAAF was deployed to Malta in the Mediterranean where it formed part of a British force which sought to counter the Soviet Union's influence in the Middle East as part of Australia's Cold War commitments. Consisting of No. 75 and 76 Squadrons equipped with de Havilland Vampire jet fighters, the wing provided an air garrison for the island for the next two and half years, returning to Australia in late 1954.[707]

In 1953, a Royal Air Force officer, Air Marshal Sir Donald Hardman, was brought out to Australia to become Chief of the Air Staff.[708] He reorganised the RAAF into three commands: Home Command, Maintenance Command, and Training Command. Five years later, Home Command was renamed Operational Command, and Training Command and Maintenance Command were amalgamated to form Support Command.[709]

In the Malayan Emergency, from 1950–60, six Avro Lincolns from No. 1 Squadron RAAF and a flight of Douglas Dakotas from No. 38 Squadron

Figure 156: *An RAAF F/A-18 with a USAF KC-135 Stratotanker, two F-15Es, an F-117, two F-16s and a RAF Tornado over Iraq*

RAAF took part in operations against the communist guerrillas (labelled as "Communist Terrorists" by the British authorities) as part of the RAF Far East Air Force. The Dakotas were used on cargo runs, in troop movement and in paratroop and leaflet drops within Malaya. The Lincolns, operating from bases in Singapore and from Kuala Lumpur, formed the backbone of the air war against the CTs, conducting bombing missions against their jungle bases. Although results were often difficult to assess, they allowed the government to harass CT forces, attack their base camps when identified and keep them on the move. Later, in 1958, Canberra bombers from No. 2 Squadron RAAF were deployed to Malaya and took part in bombing missions against the CTs.[710]

During the Vietnam War, from 1964–72, the RAAF contributed Caribou STOL transport aircraft as part of the RAAF Transport Flight Vietnam, later redesignated No. 35 Squadron RAAF, UH-1 Iroquois helicopters from No. 9 Squadron RAAF, and English Electric Canberra bombers from No. 2 Squadron RAAF. The Canberras flew 11,963 bombing sorties, and two aircraft were lost. One went missing during a bombing raid. The wreckage of the aircraft was recovered in April 2009, and the remains of Flying Officer Michael Herbert and Pilot Officer Robert Carver were found in late July 2009. The other was shot down by a surface-to-air missile, although both crew were

Figure 157: *A Royal Australian Air Force F/A-18F Super Hornet at the 2013 Avalon Airshow*

rescued. They dropped 76,389 bombs and were credited with 786 enemy personnel confirmed killed and a further 3,390 estimated killed, 8,637 structures, 15,568 bunkers, 1,267 sampans and 74 bridges destroyed.[711] RAAF transport aircraft also supported anti-communist ground forces. The UH-1 helicopters were used in many roles including medical evacuation and close air support. RAAF casualties in Vietnam included six killed in action, eight non-battle fatalities, 30 wounded in action and 30 injured.[712] A small number of RAAF pilots also served in United States Air Force units, flying F-4 Phantom fighter-bombers or serving as forward air controllers.[713]

Military airlifts were conducted for a number of purposes in the intervening decades, such as the peacekeeping operations in East Timor from 1999. Australia's combat aircraft were not used again in combat until the Iraq War in 2003, when 14 F/A-18s from No. 75 Squadron RAAF operated in the escort and ground attack roles, flying a total of 350 sorties and dropping 122 laser-guided bombs.[714] A detachment of AP-3C Orion maritime patrol aircraft were deployed in the Middle East between 2003 and 2012. These aircraft conducted maritime surveillance patrols over the Persian Gulf and North Arabian Sea in support of Coalition warships and boarding parties, as well as conducting extensive overland flights of Iraq and Afghanistan on intelligence, surveillance and reconnaissance missions, and supporting counter-piracy operations in Somalia. From 2007 to 2009, a detachment of No. 114 Mobile

Figure 158: *A leading aircraftwoman from No. 75 Squadron wearing Auscam DPCU, 2008*

Control and Reporting Unit RAAF was on active service at Kandahar Airfield in southern Afghanistan. Approximately 75 personnel deployed with the AN/TPS-77 radar assigned the responsibility to co-ordinate coalition air operations. A detachment of IAI Heron unmanned aerial vehicles has been deployed in Afghanistan since January 2010.

In late September 2014, an Air Task Group consisting of up to eight F/A-18F Super Hornets, a KC-30A Multi Role Tanker Transport, a E-7A Wedgetail Airborne Early Warning & Control aircraft and 400 personnel was deployed to Al Minhad Air Base in the United Arab Emirates as part of the coalition to combat Islamic State forces in Iraq. Operations began on 1 October. A number of C-17 and C-130J Super Hercules transport aircraft based in the Middle East have also been used to conduct airdrops of humanitarian aid and to airlift arms and munitions since August.

In June 2017 two RAAF AP-3C Orion maritime patrol aircraft were deployed to the southern Philippines in response to the Marawi crisis.[715]

Ranks and uniform

The rank structure of the nascent RAAF was established within the context of the desire to ensure that the service remained separate from both the Army and Navy.[716] While the service's predecessor formations, the AFC and the AAC, had used the Army's rank structure, in November 1920, just prior to the

RAAF's foundation, it was decided by the Air Board that the RAAF would adopt the rank structure that had been implemented in the RAF the previous year. As a result, the RAAF's rank structure came to be: Aircraftsman, Leading Aircraftsman, Corporal, Sergeant, Flight Sergeant, Warrant Officer, Officer Cadet, Pilot Officer, Flying Officer. Flight Lieutenant, Squadron Leader, Wing Commander, Group Captain, Air Commodore, Air Vice Marshal, Air Marshal, Air Chief Marshal, Marshal of the RAAF.

In 1922, the colour of the RAAF winter uniform was determined by Williams on a visit to the Geelong Wool Mill. He asked for one dye dip fewer than the RAN blue (three indigo dips rather than four). There was a change to a lighter blue when an all-seasons uniform was introduced in the 1970s. The original colour and style were re-adopted around 2005.[717] Slip-on rank epaulettes, known as "Soft Rank Insignia" (SRI), displaying the word "AUSTRALIA" are worn on the shoulders of the service dress uniform. When not in the service dress or "ceremonial" uniform, RAAF personnel wear the Auscam DPCU as a working dress. Commencing in mid-2014 DPCU began to be replaced, only in the non-deployed environment, with the General Purpose Uniform (GPU) which is a blue version of the Australian Multicam Pattern.

Roundel

Originally, the air force used the existing red, white and blue roundel of the Royal Air Force. However, during the Second World War the inner red circle, which was visually similar to the Japanese *hinomaru*, was removed after a No. 11 Squadron Catalina was mistaken for a Japanese aircraft and attacked by a Grumman Wildcat of VMF-212 of the United States Marine Corps on June 27, 1942.

After the war, a range of options for the RAAF roundel were proposed, including the Southern Cross, a boomerang, a sprig of wattle, and the red kangaroo. On 2 July 1956, the current version of the roundel was formally adopted. This consists of a white inner circle with a red kangaroo surrounded by a royal blue circle. The kangaroo faces left, except when used on aircraft or vehicles, when the kangaroo should always face in the direction of travel. Low visibility versions of the roundel exist, with the white omitted and the red and blue replaced with light or dark grey.

Badge

The RAAF badge was accepted by the Chester Herald in 1939. The badge is composed of the imperial crown mounted on a circle featuring the words Royal Australian Air Force, beneath which scroll work displays the Latin motto *Per*

Figure 159: *A F-35 taking off during the Australian International Airshow*

Ardua Ad Astra, which it shares with the Royal Air Force. Surmounting the badge is a wedge-tailed eagle. *Per Ardua Ad Astra* is attributed with the meaning "Through Adversity to the Stars" and is from Sir Henry Rider Haggard's novel *The People of the Mist*.

Current strength

Personnel

As of 2014, the RAAF had 13,991 permanent full-time personnel and 4,316 part-time active reserve personnel.

Current inventory

Aircraft	Origin	Type	Variant	In service	Notes
Combat Aircraft					
Boeing F/A-18	United States	multirole	F/A-18A/B	54 / 16	some B variants tasked with training
Boeing F/A-18E/F	United States	multirole	F/A-18F	24	

Aircraft	Origin	Role	Variant	In Service	Notes
F-35 Lightning II	United States	multirole	F-35A	6	94 on order
AWACS					
Boeing 737 AEW&C	United States	AEW&C	E-7A	6	
Gulfstream G550	United States	SIGINT /- ELINT	SEMA		Up to 5 to be purchased
Electronic Warfare					
Boeing EA-18G	United States	radar jamming		12	
Maritime Patrol					
Boeing P-8	United States	ASW / patrol		11	7 on order
AP-3C Orion	United States	maritime patrol		15	
MQ-4C Triton	United States	unmanned aerial vehicle			6 on order
Tanker					
Airbus A330 MRTT	France	refueling / transport	KC-30A	6	1 on order
Transport					
Boeing 737	United States	VIP		2	
Boeing C-17	United States	strategic airlifter		8	
C-27J Spartan	Italy	utility transport		10	
Super King Air	United States	utility / transport	350	8	
Challenger CL-600	Canada	VIP	604	3	
C-130J Super Hercules	United States	tactical airlifter	C-130J-30	12	
Helicopter					
Sikorsky S-76	United States	SAR / utility		6	contracted with CHC Helicopter
Trainer Aircraft					
BAE Hawk	United Kingdom	primary trainer	Hawk 127	33	
Pilatus PC-9	Switzerland	trainer	PC-9/A	59	produced under license by de Havilland Australia.
Pilatus PC-21	Switzerland	trainer		10	39 on order
Super King Air	United States	multi-engine trainer	350	8	4 on order

Figure 160: *A RAAF C-130J departing Point Cook*

Figure 161: *A C-17A Globemaster III*

Figure 162: *A 79 Sqn BAe Hawk on approach*

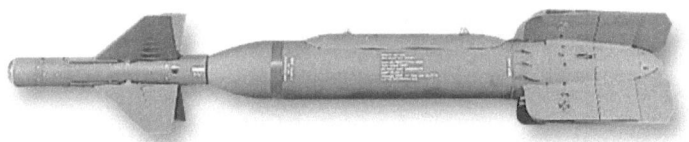

Figure 163: *Paveway II laser guided bomb*

Armament

Name	Origin	Type	Notes
Air-to-air missile			
ASRAAM	United Kingdom	IR guided missile	200 units
AIM-120 AMRAAM	United States	beyond-visual-range missile	360 units[718]
AIM-9 Sidewinder	United States		1297 units of which 47 were AIM-9X
Air-to-surface missile			
AGM-154	United States	joint standoff weapon	50 units
AGM-158	United States		260 units

General-purpose bomb			
JDAM	United States	precision guided munition	100 units
GBU-15	United States	precision guided munition	100 units
GBU-10 Paveway II	United States	laser-guided bomb	100 units
Anti-ship missile			
Mark 46 torpedo	United States	anti-sub weapon	250
AGM-84 Harpoon	United States		305

Flying squadrons

List of flying squadrons
No. 1 Squadron – Boeing F/A-18F Super Hornet (Multi-Role Fighter)
No. 2 Squadron – Boeing E-7A Wedgetail (AEW&C)
No. 3 Squadron – McDonnell Douglas F/A-18A Hornet (Multi-Role Fighter)
No. 4 Squadron – Pilatus PC9/A (JTAC Training)
No. 6 Squadron – Boeing E/A-18G Growler (Electronic Warfare)
No. 10 Squadron – Lockheed AP-3C Orion (Maritime Patrol)
No. 11 Squadron – Boeing P-8 Poseidon (Maritime Patrol)
No. 32 Squadron – Beechcraft King Air 350 (School of Air Warfare Support)
No. 33 Squadron – Airbus KC-30A MRTT (Air Refueling/Transport)
No. 34 Squadron – Boeing 737 BBJ, Bombardier Challenger 604 (VIP Transport)
No. 35 Squadron – Alenia C-27J Spartan (Transport)
No. 36 Squadron – Boeing C-17A Globemaster III (Transport)
No. 37 Squadron – Lockheed C-130J-30 Super Hercules (Transport)
No. 38 Squadron – Beechcraft King Air 350 (Transport)
No. 75 Squadron – McDonnell Douglas F/A-18A Hornet (Multi-Role Fighter)
No. 76 Squadron – BAE Systems Hawk 127 (Lead-in Fighter Training/ADF Support)
No. 77 Squadron – McDonnell Douglas F/A-18A Hornet (Multi-Role Fighter)
No. 79 Squadron – BAE Systems Hawk 127 (Hawk Conversion/ADF Support)
No. 285 Squadron – Lockheed C-130H/C-130J-30 Hercules (C-130 Conversion)
No. 292 Squadron – Lockheed AP-3C Orion (AP-3C Conversion)
CFS – Pacific Aerospace CT4B, Pilatus PC9/A (Flying Instructor Training)
ADFBFTS – Pacific Aerospace CT4B (Basic Tri-Service Flying Training)
No. 2 FTS – Pilatus PC9/A (Advanced RAAF and RAN Flying Training)

Royal Australian Air Force 277

No. 2 OCU – McDonnell Douglas F/A-18A/B Hornet (F/A-18A Conversion)

ARDU – Various Aircraft Types (Flight Testing)

Non-flying squadrons

List of non-flying squadrons No. 1 SECFOR SQN – Airbase Force Protection No. 1 EHS – Health Operations No. 1 CCS – Combat Communications No. 1 RSU – Wide Area Surveillance No. 1 RTU – Airman Ab Initio Training No. 2 SECFOR SQN – Airbase Force Protection No. 2 EHS – Health Operations No. 3 EHS – Health Operations No. 3 CRU – Surveillance and Air Battle Management No. 3 SECFOR SQN – Airbase Force Protection No. 4 EHS – Health Operations No. 13 Squadron – RAAF Darwin Airbase Operations No. 17 Squadron – RAAF Tindal Airbase Operations No. 19 Squadron – RMAF Butterworth Airbase Operations No. 20 Squadron – RAAF Woomera Airbase Operations No. 21 Squadron – RAAF Williams Airbase Operations No. 22 Squadron – RAAF Richmond Airbase Operations No. 23 Squadron – RAAF Amberley Airbase Operations No. 24 Squadron – RAAF Edinburgh Airbase Operations No. 25 Squadron – RAAF Pearce Airbase Operations No. 26 Squadron – RAAF Williamtown Airbase Operations No. 27 Squadron – RAAF Townsville Airbase Operations No. 28 Squadron – Administrative Support Operations No. 29 Squadron – Administrative Support Operations No. 30 Squadron – RAAF East Sale Airbase Operations No. 31 Squadron – RAAF Wagga Airbase Operations No. 65 Squadron – Airfield Engineering and Explosive Ordnance Disposal (EOD) No. 87 Squadron – Intelligence Operations No. 114 MCRU – Deployable Surveillance, Air Battle Management and Air Traffic Control No. 278 Squadron – Operational Training No. 381 SQN – Contingency Response Squadron No. 382 SQN – Contingency Response Squadron No. 452 Squadron – Air Traffic Control No. 453 Squadron – Air Traffic Control No. 460 Squadron – Intelligence Operations No. 462 Squadron – Information Warfare Operations ASCENG SQN – Aircraft/Stores Compatibility Engineering Development AMTDU – Air Movements Training and Development ASES – Aircraft Systems Engineering Development CSTS – Combat Survival Training RAAF AIS – Aeronautical Information RAAF BAND – RAAF Ceremonial Band DEOTS – Explosive Ordnance Training AVMED – Aviation Medicine Research and Development JEWOSU – Electronic Warfare Operations and Development OTS – Officer Ab Initio Training RAAF Museum – Royal Australian Air Force Museum RAAF SFS – Security and Fire Training SAW – Air Combat Officer and Observer Training RAAFSALT – Administrative and Logistics Training RAAFSATC – Air Traffic Control Training RAAFSPS – Officer and Airman Post Graduate Professional Training RAAFSTT – Air Technical Training SACTU – Air Defence Training Woomera Test Facility – Augmented Testing Range

Figure 164: *AIM 9L Sidewinder*

Figure 165: *Mark 84 general purpose bomb*

Wings

List of current wings
No. 41 Wing (Surveillance & Air Battle Management)
No. 42 Wing (AEW&C)
No. 44 Wing (ATC)
No. 78 Wing (Lead-in Fighter Training)
No. 81 Wing (Multi-Role Fighter)
No. 82 Wing (Multi-Role Fighter)
No. 84 Wing (Airlift & VIP transport)
No. 86 Wing (Airlift & AAR)

No. 92 Wing (Maritime Patrol)
No. 95 Wing (Expeditionary Combat Support)
No. 96 Wing (Fixed Base Combat Support)
Air Mobility Control Centre – central combat airlift tasking control centre
ATW – Flying Training
DTWG – Aerospace Systems Development
CSCC – Combat Support Coordination
GTW – Ground Training
HSW – Health Operations
IWD – Information Warfare and Intelligence
RAAFCOL – Ab initio, career development, promotion and leadership training

Force Element Groups

Current force element groups

- Air Combat Group – air combat capability
- Air Mobility Group – air lift and aerial refuelling capability
- Air Warfare Centre – information warfare, intelligence and capability development
- Combat Support Group – combat support and air base operations capability
- Surveillance and Response Group – surveillance and reconnaissance capability
- Air Force Training Group – air force training capability and development

Headquarters

- Air Force Headquarters RAAF – Air Force Executive
- RAAF Air Command – Air Force Combat Forces

Roulettes

The Roulettes are the RAAF's formation aerobatic display team. They perform around Australia and South-east Asia, and are part of the RAAF Central Flying School (CFS) at RAAF Base East Sale, Victoria. The Roulettes use the Pilatus PC-9 and formations for shows are done in a group of six aircraft. The pilots learn many formations including loops, rolls, corkscrews, and ripple roles. Most of the performances are done at the low altitude of 500 feet (150 metres).

Figure 166: *Roulette aircraft in formation*

Future procurement

This list includes aircraft on order or a requirement which has been identified:

- Up to 100 Lockheed Martin F-35A Lightning II (CTOL variant)—are scheduled to be delivered from 2020. In a first stage not fewer than 72 aircraft will be acquired to equip three operational squadrons. The remaining aircraft will be acquired in conjunction with the withdrawal of the F/A-18F Super Hornets after 2020 to ensure no gap in Australia's overall air combat capability occurs. On 25 November 2009, Australia committed to placing a first order for 14 aircraft at a cost of A$3.2 billion with deliveries to begin in 2014.[719] In May 2012, the decision to purchase 12 F-35s from the initial 14 order was deferred until 2014 as part of wider ADF procurement deferments to balance the Federal Government budget. On 23 April 2014, Australia confirmed the purchase of 58 F-35A Lightning II fighters in addition to the 14 already ordered. Up to a further 28 more aircraft may be acquired. The first two Australian F-35A Lightning II fighters were rolled out in July 2014, and began flying training flights with the USAF 61st Fighter Squadron in December 2014.
- Eight Boeing P-8 Poseidon to replace the Lockheed AP-3C Orions. A further seven to be purchased and brought into service by the late 2020s, bringing the total number of aircraft to fifteen.
- Six MQ-4C unmanned aerial vehicles (UAVs) to expand the surveillance of Australia's maritime approaches, with the possibility of purchasing a

Figure 167: *The first Australian F-35A takes off from Luke AFB on a test sortie in 2015*

seventh air frame. The drones will cost approximately A$6.9 billion over their entire life-time, with the fleet expected to be in service by late 2025. They will be based at RAAF Base Edinburgh however will regularly conduct missions from RAAF Base Tindal.
- Forty-nine Pilatus PC-21 training aircraft under Project AIR 5428.
- Two more KC-30As, one in full VIP configuration. The Australian Government is also looking at a further two to support the incoming P-8A fleet, which would bring the total number of aircraft to nine.
- The RAAF has shown interest in acquiring armed unmanned drones. Air Marshal Geoff Brown stated that "it is certainly something we have put forward" and that the Reaper was one of the force's highest priorities. As of February 2015 six ADF personnel are currently training on the General Atomics MQ-9 Reaper in two USAF bases. The RAAF is willing to spend A$300 million on the platform and is believed to be preparing to purchase eight drones and two ground stations. In March 2017, it was reported that the acquisition program had been singled down to two UAV platforms: the MQ-9 Reaper and the IAI Heron. In September 2017, IAI accused the Australian government of giving preferential treatment to General Atomics.
- A$4–5 billion project to replace the RAAFs 33 Hawk lead-in fighter trainers announced in the 2016 Defence White Paper. The project has a timeframe of 2022 to 2033.

References

Citations

Bibliography

<templatestyles src="Template:Refbegin/styles.css" />

- Armstrong, John. "History of the RAAF: 20 Years of Warfighting 1939–1959, Part 2". *Air Power International*. Strike Publications. **4** (6): 42–48. ISSN 1326-1533[720].
- Barnes, Norman (2000). *The RAAF and the Flying Squadrons*. St Leonards, New South Wales: Allen & Unwin. ISBN 1-86508-130-2.
- Beaumont, Joan (2001). *Australian Defence: Sources and Statistics*. The Australian Centenary History of Defence. Volume VI. Melbourne: Oxford University Press. ISBN 0-19-554118-9.
- Coulthard-Clark, Chris (1995). *The RAAF in Vietnam. Australian Air Involvement in the Vietnam War 1962–1975*. The Official History of Australia's Involvement in Southeast Asian Conflicts 1948–1975. Volume Four. Sydney: Allen and Unwin in association with the Australian War Memorial. ISBN 1-86373-305-1.
- Dennis, Peter; Grey, Jeffrey; Morris, Ewan; Prior, Robin; Bou, Jean (2008). *The Oxford Companion to Australian Military History* (2nd ed.). Melbourne, Victoria: Oxford University Press. ISBN 978-0-19-551784-2.
- Eather, Steve (1995). *Flying Squadrons of the Australian Defence Force*. Weston Creek, Australian Capital Territory: Aerospace Publications. ISBN 1-875671-15-3.
- Eather, Steve (1996). *Odd Jobs: RAAF Operations in Japan, the Berlin Airlift, Korea, Malaya and Malta, 1946–1960*[721]. RAAF Williams, Victoria: RAAF Museum. ISBN 0-642-23482-5.
- Grey, Jeffrey (1999). *A Military History of Australia* (2nd ed.). Port Melbourne: Cambridge University Press. ISBN 0-521-64483-6.
- Grey, Jeffrey (2008). *A Military History of Australia* (3rd ed.). Port Melbourne, Victoria: Cambridge University Press. ISBN 978-0-521-69791-0.
- Millar, Thomas Bruce (1969). *Australia's Defence* (2nd ed.). Carlton: Melbourne University Press. OCLC 614049220[722].
- McLaughlin, Andrew (June 2010). "Dingo Airlines". *Australian Aviation*. No. 272. pp. 40–43. ISSN 0813-0876[723].
- Moclair, Tony; McLaughlin, Andrew (2014). *Hornet Country*. Fyshwick, ACT: Phantom Media. ISBN 9780992343200.
- Pittaway, Nigel (March 2010). "ADF pilot training under contract". *Defence Today*. Amberley: Strike Publications. **8** (2): 20–21. ISSN 1447-0446[724].

- Sandler, Stanley (2001). *World War II in the Pacific: An Encyclopedia*. Military History of the United States Series. Taylor & Francis. ISBN 9780815318835.
- Stephens, Alan (2006) [2001]. *The Royal Australian Air Force: A History*. London: Oxford University Press. ISBN 0-19-555541-4.
- Taylor, Michael John Haddrick; Taylor, John William Ransom (1978). *Encyclopedia of Aircraft*. New York: Putnam. ISBN 0399122176.

Further reading

<templatestyles src="Template:Refbegin/styles.css" />

- Ashworth, Norman (1999). *How Not To Run An Air Force! The Higher Command of the Royal Australian Air Force During the Second World War*. Australia: Royal Australian Air Force Air Power Development Centre. ISBN 0-642-26550-X.
- McPhedran, Ian (2011). *Air Force: Inside the New era of Australian Air Power*. Australia: Harper Collins Publishers. ISBN 978-0-7322-9025-2.
- Royal Australian Air Force (September 2013). *The Air Power Manual - 6th Edition*[725]. Canberra: Department of Defence, Air Power Development Centre. ISBN 978-1-9208-0090-1. <q>reprinted with corrections May 2014</q>.

External links

Wikimedia Commons has media related to *Royal Australian Air Force*.

- RAAF official site[726]
- RAAF Air Power Doctrine[727]
- ADF Aircraft Serial Number[728]
- RAAF YouTube channel[729]

Women in Military

Women in the Australian military

Part of a series on
Women in society
• ♀ Feminism portal
• v • t • e[730]

Women have served in Australian armed forces since 1899. Until World War II women were restricted to the Australian Army Nursing Service. This role expanded in 1941–42 when the Royal Australian Navy (RAN), Australian Army and Royal Australian Air Force established female branches in which women took on a range of support roles. While these organisations were disbanded at the end of the war, they were reestablished in 1950 as part of the military's permanent structure. Women were integrated into the services during the late 1970s and early 1980s and can now serve in most positions in the Australian Defence Force (ADF), including combat roles.

Figure 168: *A female member of No. 75 Squadron RAAF in 2008*

History

Separate branches

Female service in the Australian military began in 1899 when the Australian Army Nursing Service was formed as part of the New South Wales colonial military forces. Army nurses formed part of the Australian contribution to the Boer War, and their success led to the formation of the Australian Army Nursing Reserve in 1902. More than 2000 members of the Australian Army Nursing Service (AANS) served overseas during World War I as part of the Australian Imperial Force. At the end of the war the AANS returned to its pre-war reserve status.[731] In addition to the military nurses, a small group of civilian nurses dubbed the "Bluebirds" were recruited by the Australian Red Cross Society and served in French hospitals.

Australian women during World War II

Australian women played a larger role in World War II. Many women wanted to play an active role, and hundreds of voluntary women's auxiliary and paramilitary organisations had been formed by 1940. These included the Women's Transport Corps, Women's Flying Club, Women's Emergency Signalling Corps and Women's Australian National Services.[732] In Brisbane alone there were six different organisations providing women with war-related training in July 1940, the largest of which was the Queensland-based Women's National Emergency Legion. The Federal Government and military did not

Figure 169: *The leaders of the female branches of the Australian military in 1942*

initially support women being trained to serve in the armed forces, however, and these organisations were not taken seriously by the general public.

A shortage of male recruits forced the military to establish female branches in 1941 and 1942. The RAAF established the Women's Auxiliary Australian Air Force (WAAAF) in March 1941, the Army formed the Australian Women's Army Service (AWAS) in October 1941 and the Australian Army Medical Women's Service in December 1942 and the Women's Royal Australian Naval Service (WRANS) came into being in July 1942. In 1944 almost 50,000 women were serving in the military and thousands more had joined the civilian Australian Women's Land Army (AWLA). Many of these women were trained to undertake skilled work in traditionally male occupations in order to free servicemen for operational service. Women were also encouraged to work in industry and volunteer for air raid precautions duties or clubs for Australian and Allied servicemen.[733] The female branches of the military were disbanded after the war.

Figure 170: *Male and female sailors on board HMAS Tobruk in 2010*

Korean War

Manpower shortages during the Korean War led to the permanent establishment of female branches of the military. In 1951 the WRANS was reformed and the Army and Air Force established the Women's Australian Army Corps (WAAC) and Women's Royal Australian Air Force (WRAAF) respectively. The proportion of women in the services was initially limited to four percent of their strength, though this was ignored by the RAAF.[734] The quota was lifted to 10 percent in the RAAF and RAN during the 1960s and 1970s while the Army recruited only on a replacement basis.[735]

Integration

The role of women in the Australian military began to change in the 1970s. In 1975, which was the International Year of Women, the service chiefs established a committee to explore opportunities for increased female participation in the military. This led to reforms which allowed women to deploy on active service in support roles, pregnancy no longer being grounds for automatic termination of employment and changes to leave provisions. The WRAAF and WAAC were abolished in 1977 and 1979 respectively, with female soldiers being merged into the services. Equal pay was granted to servicewomen in 1979 and the WRANS was abolished in 1985.

Figure 171: *Wing Commander Linda Corbould, the first woman to command a Royal Australian Air Force flying squadron.*

Despite being integrated into the military, there were still restrictions on female service. The ADF was granted an exemption from the *Sexual Discrimination Act* when it was introduced in 1984 so that it could maintain gender-based restrictions against women serving in combat or combat-related positions, which limited women to 40 percent of positions in the ADF. As a result of personnel shortages in the late 1980s the restriction against women in combat-related positions was dropped in 1990, and women were for the first time allowed to serve in warships, RAAF combat squadrons and many positions in the Army. Women were banned from positions involving physical combat, however, and were unable to serve in infantry, armoured, artillery and engineering units in the Army and clearance diving and ground defence positions in the RAN and RAAF respectively.

The ADF was not sufficiently prepared for integrating women into all units. Integration was hindered by entrenched discriminatory attitudes, sexual harassment and a perception that less demanding standards were applied to women. This led to a number of scandals, including allegations of sexual harassment on board HMAS *Swan*, and the RAN's mishandling of these complaints. These scandals did great harm to the ADF's reputation at the time when it most needed servicewomen. The Defence Equality Organisation was established in 1997 in response to these problems, and it developed frameworks to facilitate the acceptance of women throughout the ADF.[736]

Figure 172: *Female Australian soldiers in Afghanistan*

Women have formed part of ADF deployments around the world since the early 1990s. Female sailors were sent into a combat zone for the first time on board HMAS *Westralia* in 1991, female medical personnel were deployed to Iraq, Western Sahara and Rwanda during the early 1990s and 440 of the 5,500 Australians deployed to East Timor in November 1999 were women.[737] Women also began to be promoted to command units in the late 1990s, and Air Commodore Julie Hammer became the first woman to reach one-star rank in 2000.[738]

Despite the expansion in the number of positions available to women, there has been only limited growth in the percentage of female permanent defence personnel. In the 1989–1990 financial year women filled 11.4% of permanent ADF positions. In the 2005–2006 financial year women occupied 13.3% of permanent positions and 15.6% of reserve positions. During the same period the proportion of civilian positions filled by women in the Australian Defence Organisation increased from 30.8% to 40.3%.[739] The percentage of female members of the Australian labour force increased from approximately 41% to 45% between June 1989 and June 2006.[740] In 2008 defence minister, Joel Fitzgibbon instructed the ADF to place a greater emphasis on recruiting women and addressing barriers to women being promoted to senior roles.

On 27 September 2011, Defence Minister Stephen Smith announced that women will be allowed to serve in frontline combat roles by 2016. Women became able to apply for all positions other than special forces roles in the Army on 1 January 2013; it is planned that this remaining restriction will be removed in 2014 once the physical standards required for service in these units are determined. Women will be directly recruited into all frontline combat positions from late 2016.

While women have been eligible for all flying roles in the RAAF since 1987, only 42 had qualified as pilots up to 2016 and none have passed the training courses for the force's fighter jets. A 2016 Australian Human Rights Commission report found that "the absence of female fast jet pilots is remarkable" given that the air forces of many comparable countries have had female fighter pilots since the 1990s. The report judged that there was no single factor responsible for this, and made a range of recommendations to address barriers to women becoming fighter pilots. The first two female RAAF fighter pilots completed training in December 2017.

References

- Adam-Smith, Patsy (1984). *Australian Women at War*. Melbourne: Thomas Nelson Australia. ISBN 0-17-006408-5.
- Darian-Smith, Kate (1996). "War and Australian Society". In Beaumont, Joan. *Australia's War, 1939–1945*. Sydney: Allen & Unwin. ISBN 1-86448-039-4.
- Dennis, Peter; et al. (2008). *The Oxford Companion to Australian Military History* (Second ed.). Melbourne: Oxford University Press Australia & New Zealand. ISBN 978-0-19-551784-2.
- Horner, David (2001). *Making the Australian Defence Force*. Melbourne: Oxford University Press. ISBN 0-19-554117-0.
- Khosa, Raspal (2004). *Australian Defence Almanac 2004–05*. Canberra: Australian Strategic Policy Institute.
- Parliamentary Library Foreign Affairs, Defence and Trade Group (2000). "Women in the armed forces: the role of women in the Australian Defence Force"[741]. Parliament of Australia Parliamentary Library. Retrieved 2009-02-15.

External links

 Wikimedia Commons has media related to *Women in the Australian military*.

- "Australian Women in War"[742]. National Foundation for Australian Women.

Sexual Orientation in Military

Sexual orientation and gender identity in the Australian military

Sexual orientation and gender identity in the Australian military are no longer relevant considerations in the 21st century, with the Australian Defence Force (ADF) allowing LGBT people to serve openly and access the same entitlements as other personnel. The ban on gay and lesbian personnel was lifted by the Keating Government in 1992, with a 2000 study finding no discernible negative impacts on troop morale. In 2009, the First Rudd Government introduced equal entitlements to military retirement pensions and superannuation for the domestic partners of LGBTI personnel. Since 2010, transgender personnel may serve openly and may undergo gender transition with ADF support while continuing their military service. LGBTI personnel are also supported by the charity DEFGLIS, the Defence Force Lesbian Gay Bisexual Transgender and Intersex Information Service.

Gay, lesbian and bisexual personnel

Historical prohibition

Homosexuals were not permitted to join the Australian armed forces until 1992. Gay and lesbian personnel who evaded this ban ran the risk of being dismissed from the military if their sexual orientation was discovered; this tended to be more strictly enforced during peacetime than wartime. Nevertheless, many homosexual personnel served in the military during the world wars, Korean War and Vietnam War, with their comrades often being aware of their orientation and accepting of it.[743]

Figure 173: *Members of the Australian Army marching in the 2013 Sydney Gay and Lesbian Mardi Gras*

The Australian military prohibited "unnatural offences" or "conduct prejudicial to good order and discipline" from the time of the Boer War, with the Australian Army introducing a specific anti-homosexuality policy after World War II at the urging of the United States military, who had witnessed homosexual acts between Australian troops in Papua New Guinea. From 1974 to 1992, the Australian military services had consistent policies against LGB personnel, who could be subject to surveillance, interviews, secret searches and discharge from the military.

The ban on homosexuals reflected both social attitudes at the time and British military law, which directly governed discipline in the armed forces until 1985. An Australian *Defence Force Discipline Act* was enacted in 1985, and the Australian Defence Force (ADF) set out its position on homosexuality the next year. This statement maintained the ban on homosexual behaviour among service personnel, on the grounds that it would erode command relationships and morale, raise risks of blackmail, create health problems and endanger minors. However, it did not require that homosexual personnel be automatically dismissed, with their commanding officer having a degree of discretion in the matter. Few homosexual personnel were dismissed during the period this statement was in force.[743]

Lifting the ban

During the 1980s and early 1990s, gay and human rights activists sought to have the ban on homosexuals serving in the ADF lifted. In 1992 a female reservist in the Australian Army made a complaint to the Human Rights and Equal Opportunities Commission on the basis that she was dismissed on the grounds of homosexuality. The Commission called for a review of the long-standing ban on LGBT military personnel, leading to extensive debate among politicians and members of the ADF.[743]

In June 1992, Defence Minister Senator Robert Ray responded by instead reaffirming the prohibition on homosexuality in Australia's armed forces, accepting a recommendation by service chiefs and strengthening the existing ban on LGBT personnel by including the definition of "unacceptable sexual acts" as inclusive of sexual harassment and offences under civil and military law. Adrian d'Hagé, a public relations officer in the Defence Department told media that the presence of an admitted homosexual in defence units could be divisive.

Senator Ray's decision led to significant outrage and was opposed by several Labor party politicians of the day, including Attorney-General Michael Duffy. In response Prime Minister Paul Keating established a special Labor Caucus Committee to examine the possibility of removing the ban on LGBT personnel in the military, to be chaired by Senator Terry Aulich. The Caucus Committee heard from many stakeholders including the Defence Chiefs.[744][745] By September 1992, the committee had returned with a recommendation to remove the ban by four votes to two, with support from Aulich, Stephen Loosley, Olive Zakharov and Duncan Kerr and opposition from Ted Grace and Brian Courtice. Despite opposition to change from certain military groups and the RSL, this recommendation received support from Human Rights Commissioner Brian Burdekin and Attorney General Michael Duffy.

On 23 November 1992, the First Keating Ministry met to consider whether the military ban on homosexuals should be lifted, despite Senator Ray's opposition within Cabinet. Following the meeting, Prime Minister Paul Keating announced that the Government had decided to end discrimination preventing homosexual people serving in the defence forces, effective immediately. Keating, who had supported overturning the ban, stated that the decision "reflected community support for the removal of employment discrimination and brings the ADF into line with tolerant attitudes of Australians generally ... The ADF acknowledges there are male and female homosexuals among its members and has advised the Government that these members are no longer actively sought out or disciplined because of their sexual orientation." This outcome was heavily influenced by a perception in Cabinet that if they did not lift the ban, the issue would continue to be raised and the ADF needed to adapt to the changing social attitudes towards homosexuality as soon as possible.[743]

Opposition defence spokesman Alexander Downer told media that, if elected, the Coalition would immediately reinstate the ban if the service chiefs were to advise for it: at that time the chiefs remained in favour of such a ban.

Military benefits

In 2003, the Howard Government blocked same-sex partners of military personnel from receiving the benefits of a support program that partners in heterosexual relationships were able to access. Since 1 January 2009, same-sex couples within the Australian Military, are treated the same as de facto mixed-sex couples, that extends many military benefits (e.g. Defence housing and superannuation).

Growing inclusion

By the 2000s the ADF was seeking to actively engage the gay and lesbian community. An official defence contingent joined the Sydney Gay and Lesbian Mardi Gras for the first time in 2008 and the contingent marched in uniform for the first time in 2013. Unofficial support groups had marched in the parade from 1996, initially against the wishes of the ADF's headquarters.

Acknowledging the 20th anniversary of the lifting of the ban in November 2012, Chief of the Defence Force David Hurley said he was proud of the diversity of Australia's military. Hurley also noted that he regards diversity as being an asset for the ADF. Nevertheless, the ADF continued to have a reputation at this time for homophobia. A 2013 survey of gay Army personnel found that 59 per cent of respondents had not experienced harassment due to their sexuality, but 30 per cent hid their sexuality from other soldiers.

In 2013 the Department of Defence commissioned Army pride cufflinks and lapel pins which combine the Rising Sun badge with a rainbow flag.

Transgender and gender-neutral personnel

In 2010 ADF policy was amended to allow transgender Australians to openly serve without the risk of being discharged. The policy was updated following the advocacy of Bridget Clinch, who sought to transition from male to female while serving in the Australian Army.

The free medical services all members of the ADF receive as part of their service contract includes treatment for gender dysphoria. A Department of Defence spokesperson stated in 2015 that this can include meeting the costs of "some but not all aspects of the management of gender dysphoria, including surgery", with the level of assistance provided generally being set at a level equivalent to that available to all Australians through Medicare.

In 2017, from ADF records between November 2012 and March 2016, 27 ADF members received treatment for gender dysphoria. Seventeen had sex-change surgery. Ten of those were male-to-female reassignments at a cost of $1,052,330, not including the cost of ADF dispensed pharmaceuticals, or the cost of transition leave. For the ADF, "challenges posed by transgender personnel" include non-deployable periods and the use of toilets and bathrooms. Sex discrimination laws may be exempted by the ADF for gender-neutral personnel who are employed in key roles.

The ADF's financial support for gender dysphoria treatment was criticised in October 2017 by conservative politicians including Pauline Hanson, Cory Bernardi and Andrew Hastie. It was defended by the Defence Minister Marise Payne, Labor Defence Personnel spokesperson Amanda Rishworth, trans former army personnel Cate McGregor and Bridget Clinch.

The RAAF has produced a document for Airforce Cadets entitled *Gender Transition Guidelines* designed to build understanding and respect within the organisation. In conjunction with the International Day Against Homophobia and Transphobia (IDAHOT) the RAAF is creating opportunities to partner with LGBTI-supporting agencies.

Effect of inclusion on troop morale

A study conducted in 2000 by Aaron Belkin and Jason McNichol found that the lifting of the ban on gay service had not led to any identifiable negative effects on troop morale, combat effectiveness, recruitment and retention or other measures of military performance. The study also found that the lifting of the ban may have contributed to improvements in productivity and working environments for service members. Similarly, Hugh Smith states in the *Oxford Companion to Australian Military History* that predictions of damage to the ADF's morale and mass-resignations if the ban was lifted did not eventuate, and the reform did not lead to any widespread or long-lasting problems.[746]

DEFGLIS

The Defence Force Lesbian Gay Bisexual Transgender and Intersex Information Service (DEFGLIS), founded in 2002 by Petty Officer Stuart O'Brien, supports and represents Australian Defence Force LGBTI personnel and their families. It does this through professional networking and peer support, by strengthening defence capability through greater inclusion of LGBTI people, and by educating defence about LGBTI matters.

DEFGLIS is registered with the Australian Charities and Not-for-profits Commission as a charity.

References

Works consulted

- Smith, Hugh (2009). "Homosexuality in the Defence Forces". In Dennis, Peter; Grey, Jeffrey; Morris, Ewan; Prior, Robin; Bou, Jean. *The Oxford Companion to Australian Military History* (2nd ed.). South Melbourne: Oxford University Press. ISBN 9780195517842.

Further reading

- Goldberg, Suzanne B. "Open Service and Our Allies: A Report on the Inclusion of Openly Gay and Lesbian Servicemembers in U.S. Allies' Armed Forces," *William & Mary Journal of Women & Law* (2011) v 17 pp 547–90 online[747]
- Willett, Graham; Smaal, Yorick (2013). "A Homosexual Institution': Same-sex Desire in the Army During World War II"[748] (PDF). *Australian Army Journal*. **X** (3): 23–40.

Defence Industry

Defence industry of Australia

The **defence industry of Australia** provides military equipment, supplies and services for the Australian Defence Force (ADF) and export customers. Definitions of what the defence industry comprises and estimates of its size differ, but it was believed to have employed between 12,000 and 29,000 people as of the mid 2010s.[749] The industry has grown over recent years, and *Australian Defence Magazine* reported that the 40 largest companies had a total revenue of $A 9.2 billion in 2015.

Current scale

As there is no agreed definition of what the Australian defence industry comprises it is difficult to determine the size of the sector. Many of the companies which supply goods and services to the military also have a significant civilian market, and their staff often work on items intended for both military and civilian customers.[750] The Australian Government's 2018 *Defence Export Strategy* provided the following definition:

> *Australian defence industry consists of businesses with an Australian Business Number who are providing or have the capacity to provide defence-specific or dual-use goods or services in a supply chain that leads to the Australian Department of Defence or an international Defence force.*[751]

A 2015 parliamentary inquiry into the defence industry noted that "published estimates of the number of people employed in the defence industry have cited varying figures". The federal government body Skills Australia estimated in 2012 that between 15,000 and 25,000 were employed in the industry. In 2010 the Department of Defence put the figure at up to 29,000 people, and in 2015 it advised the inquiry that around 27,000 people were directly employed in the industry.[749] The *2016 Defence Industry Policy Statement* stated that 25,000

Figure 174: *The Australian-built frigate HMAS Newcastle and other warships at Fleet Base East in Sydney, a major centre for the Australian defence industry*

people were employed in the defence industry, of whom around 50 percent worked in global defence companies.[752] If accurate, this estimate means that the industry represents 0.24% of total employment, and is equivalent to 2.9% of jobs in the total manufacturing sector.[753]

In January 2016 *Australian Defence Magazine* reported that the 40 largest Australian defence companies had a combined revenue of $A 9.2 billion in 2015. A 2017 Australian Strategic Policy Institute report stated that the defence industry "accounts for 0.22% of Australian industry and 1.7% of the manufacturing sector", and "although [the] Australian defence industry is undoubtedly important for our defence force, it represents only a trifling fraction of the overall Australian economy.[753]

Exports and imports

The scale of the Australian defence industry's exports is greatly outweighed by the scale of imports of military goods and services into Australia. Between 2001 and 2016, the total value of defence exports from Australia measured using the Stockholm International Peace Research Institute's methodology represented 6.8 percent of the total value of defence imports into Australia. There was considerable variation in this ratio between years. As of 2018, the total value of Australian defence exports was around $A2 billion per year. While this made Australia the 20th largest exporter of defence goods and services, it represented only around half of one percent of the global arms trade.

A 2010 Australian Strategic Policy Institute report stated that "Defence's principal needs from Australian industry are maintenance, repair and upgrading of the ADF's equipment, most of which is imported". This report also noted that at the time it was estimated that manufacturing represented 20 percent of the Australian defence industry's revenue, with sustainment services making up the remainder.[754]

In 2018 the Australian Government announced a plan to support the Australian defence industry to expand its exports, with the goal of Australia becoming the 10th largest source of military exports. This will include making $A3.8 billion in government funding available for loans to companies and establishing an Australian Defence Export Advocate.

Defence industry media

Several trade journals currently cover the Australian defence industry. These include the *Australian Defence Magazine* and the *Asia-Pacific Defence Reporter*.

References

Citations

Works consulted

- Department of Defence (2016). *2016 Defence Industry Policy Statement*[755] (PDF). Canberra: Department of Defence. ISBN 9780994168078.
- Department of Defence (2018). *Defence Export Strategy*[756]. Canberra: Department of Defence. ISBN 9780648097716.
- Joint Standing Committee on Foreign Affairs, Defence and Trade (2015). *Principles and Practice - Australian Defence Industry and Exports*[757]. Canberra: Parliament of Australia. ISBN 978-1-74366-316-5.
- Thomson, Mark (2017). "The Cost of Defence: ASPI Defence Budget Brief 2017-2018"[758]. Canberra: Australian Strategic Policy Institute. ISSN 2200-6613[759].

Further reading

- Cain, Frank, ed. (1999). *Arming the Nation: A History of Defence Science and Technology in Australia*. Canberra: Australian Defence Studies Centre. ISBN 0-7317-0433-9.
- Davies, Andrew; Layton, Peter (24 November 2009). *Special Report Issue 25 - We'll have six of them and four of those: Off-the-shelf procurement and its strategic implications*[760]. Canberra: Australian Strategic Policy Institute.
- Davies, Mark (February 2018). "Can Australia Fight Alone?". *Australian Foreign Affairs* (2): 43–66.
- Ferguson, Gregor (22 December 2010). *Risks and rewards: Defence R&D in Australia*[761]. Canberra: Australian Strategic Policy Institute.
- Mellor, D.P. (1958). *The Role of Science and Industry*[762]. Australia in the War of 1939–1945. Series 4 – Civil - Volume V. Canberra: Australian War Memorial.
- Ross, A.T. (1994). *Armed and Ready: The Industrial Development and Defence of Australia 1900-1945*. Sydney: Turton and Armstrong. ISBN 0908031637.
- Schaetzel, Stanley S. (1986). *Local Development of Defence Hardware in Australia*. The Strategic and Defence Studies Centre Working Paper No. 100. Canberra: Research School of Pacific Studies, Australian National University. ISBN 0-86784-845-6.

Military Bases

List of Australian military bases

The Australian Defence Force is made up of the Royal Australian Navy, Australian Army and the Royal Australian Air Force. These three military services have numerous military bases situated in all the States and Territories of Australia. Most of Australian Defence Force bases are equipped with Everyman's Welfare Service recreation centres.

Australian Defence Force (Joint)

Australian Capital Territory

- Australian Defence Force Academy - military academy
- Campbell Park Offices/Russell Offices - Headquarters of the Australian Defence Force
- Tuggeranong
- Headquarters Joint Operations Command (HQJOC)

New South Wales

- Defence Establishment Myambat - munitions storage facility
- Defence Plaza, Sydney

Victoria

- Defence Plaza, Melbourne
- Swan Island
- Victoria Barracks, Melbourne

Australian Army

Australian Capital Territory

- Royal Military College, Duntroon

New South Wales

- Holsworthy Barracks – Holsworthy, Liverpool Military Area, Sydney
- Steele Barracks – Moorebank, Liverpool Military Area, Sydney
- Blamey Barracks – Kapooka, Kapooka Military Area, Wagga Wagga
- Randwick Barracks, Sydney
- Victoria Barracks, Sydney
- Lone Pine Barracks, Singleton
- Timor Barracks, Ermington, Sydney[763][764]
- Bullecourt Barracks, Adamstown (Newcastle)
- Lancer Barracks, Parramatta, Sydney

Northern Territory

- Larrakeyah Barracks – Darwin
- Robertson Barracks – Darwin

Queensland

- Victoria Barracks – Brisbane
- Borneo Barracks – Darling Downs Military Area, Cabarlah
- Kokoda Barracks – Canungra
- Gallipoli Barracks – Enoggera
- Lavarack Barracks – Townsville
- Army Aviation Centre – Darling Downs Military Area, Oakey

Rockhampton Army Base, Rockhampton

South Australia

- Hampstead Barracks - Adelaide
- Keswick Barracks - Adelaide
- Warradale Barracks
- Woodside Barracks - Woodside
- RAAF Base Edinburgh

List of Australian military bases 305

Tasmania

- Anglesea Barracks, Hobart
- Derwent Barracks, Glenorchy
- Paterson Barracks, Launceston
- Youngtown Barracks, Launceston
- Kokoda Barracks, Devonport
- Warrane Baracks, Warrane
- Buckland Military Training Area, north of Richmond, Tasmania
- Burnie Army Reserve Burnie

Victoria

- Latchford Barracks, Bonegilla – Albury/Wodonga Military Area
- Gaza Ridge Barracks, Bandiana – Albury/Wodonga Military Area
- Wadsworth Barracks, Bandiana – Albury/Wodonga Military Area
- Tobruk Barracks, Puckapunyal – Puckapunyal Military Area
- Hopkins Barracks, Puckapunyal – Puckapunyal Military Area
- Bridges Barracks, Puckapunyal – Puckapunyal Military Area
- Simpson Barracks, Watsonia – Melbourne
- Maygar Barracks, Broadmeadows – Melbourne
- Oakleigh Barracks, Oakleigh South – Melbourne
- Ringwood Barracks, Ringwood East – Melbourne

Western Australia

- Campbell Barracks – Swanbourne
- Irwin Barracks – Karrakatta
- Leeuwin Barracks – Fremantle

Royal Australian Air Force

Australian Capital Territory

- Defence Establishment Fairbairn

New South Wales

- RAAF Base Glenbrook - Sydney
- RAAF Base Richmond - Sydney
- RAAF Base Wagga - Wagga Wagga
- RAAF Base Williamtown - Newcastle

Northern Territory

- RAAF Base Darwin - Darwin
- RAAF Base Tindal - Katherine

Queensland

- RAAF Base Amberley - Brisbane
- RAAF Base Scherger (bare base)
- RAAF Base Townsville - Townsville

South Australia

- RAAF Base Edinburgh - Adelaide
- RAAF Woomera Range Complex
  - RAAF Base Woomera

Victoria

- RAAF Base East Sale - Sale
- RAAF Base Williams – Point Cook - Melbourne
- RAAF Base Williams – Laverton - Melbourne

Western Australia

- RAAF Base Curtin (bare base)
- RAAF Base Learmonth (bare base)
- RAAF Base Pearce - Perth

Royal Australian Navy

Australian Capital Territory

- HMAS *Harman* – Canberra
- HMAS *Creswell* – Jervis Bay Territory

New South Wales

- HMAS *Albatross* – Nowra
- HMAS *Kuttabul* – Garden Island, Sydney
- HMAS *Penguin* – Balmoral, Sydney
- HMAS *Waterhen* – Waverton, Sydney
- HMAS *Watson* – Watsons Bay, Sydney

Northern Territory

- HMAS *Coonawarra* – Darwin

Queensland

- HMAS *Cairns* – Cairns
- HMAS *Moreton* – Brisbane

South Australia

- NHQ *South Australia* – Adelaide

Tasmania

- NHQ *Tasmania* –Anglesea Barracks, Hobart

Victoria

- HMAS *Cerberus* – Crib Point

Western Australia

- HMAS *Stirling* – Garden Island

Appendix

References

[1] Khosa 2010, p. 2.
[2] McKeown & Jordan 2010, p. 1.
[3] Australian Government 2016, pp. 17–18.
[4] Australian Government 2016, p. 71.
[5] Horner 2001, p. 55.
[6] Grey 2008, p. 67.
[7] Dennis et al 2008, p. 467.
[8] Dennis et al 2008, pp. 61, 457.
[9] Horner 2007, pp. 145–150.
[10] Horner 2001, p. 42.
[11] Horner 2001, p. 44.
[12] Horner 2001, p. 47.
[13] Horner 2001, p. 65.
[14] Tewes, Rayner & Kavanaugh 2004.
[15] Horner 2001, p. 72.
[16] Horner 2001, pp. 225–227.
[17] Horner 2001, pp. 228–255.
[18] Horner 2001, pp. 231–237.
[19] Horner 2001, pp. 95–96.
[20] Horner 2001, pp. 93–95.
[21] Thomson 2005, p. 11.
[22] Thomson 2012, p. 25.
[23] Thomson 2006, pp. 7–8.
[24] Dennis et al 2008, pp. 8–9.
[25] Dennis et al 2008, p. 248.
[26] Bullard 2017, p. 512.
[27] Dennis et al 2008, p. 193.
[28] Edwards 2016, pp. 20–21.
[29] Edwards 2016, p. 21.
[30] Thomson 2016, p. vi.
[31] Thomson 2017, p. 7.
[32] Jennings 2016, pp. 114, 137.
[33] United Nations Command-Rear Fact Sheet http://www.yokota.af.mil/Portals/44/Documents/Units/AFD-150924-004.pdf United States Yokota Air Base
[34] Australian Government 2016, pp. 16–17.
[35] Henry 2005, p. 19.
[36] Henry 2005, pp. 22–23.
[37] Grey 2008, p. 280.
[38] Australian Government 2016, pp. 18–20.
[39] Khosa 2011, pp. 2–3.
[40] Khosa 2010, pp. 50–51.
[41] Khosa 2011, p. 2.
[42] Khosa 2011, p. 3.
[43] Khosa 2011, p. 13.
[44] Khosa 2011, pp. 12–13.
[45] Khosa 2011, p. 14.
[46] Thomson 2017, p. 35.
[47] Khosa 2010, pp. 13–15.
[48] Chief of Navy 2017, pp. 9–11.
[49] Chief of Navy 2017, p. 13.

[50] Australian Army 2014, pp. 9, 16.
[51] Australian Army 2014, pp. 25–30.
[52] Australian Army 2014, pp. 35–36.
[53] Davies 2010, p. 3.
[54] Australian Army 2014, p. 12.
[55] Australian Army 2014, p. 32.
[56] Davies 2010, p. 6.
[57] Davies, Jennings & Schreer 2014, p. 13.
[58] Pittaway 2014, pp. 76–80.
[59] Air Power Development Centre 2015, p. 26.
[60] Air Power Development Centre 2015, p. 40.
[61] Air Power Development Centre 2015, pp. 44–45.
[62] Wilson & Pittaway 2017, p. 15.
[63] Horner 2001, p. 273.
[64] Department of Defence 2017, p. 1.
[65] Horner 2001, pp. 265–279.
[66] Thomson 2005a, pp. 30–32.
[67] Horner 2001, p. 150.
[68] Chief of Navy 2017, pp. 19, 165.
[69] Australian Army 2014, pp. 8–9, 27.
[70] Pittaway 2014, p. 76.
[71] Khosa 2011, pp. 31–35.
[72] Air Power Development Centre 2016, p. 41.
[73] Khosa 2011, p. 125.
[74] Defence People Group 2017, p. 20.
[75] Department of Defence 2017a, p. 88.
[76] Thomson 2016, p. 61.
[77] Thomson 2017, p. 64.
[78] Thomson 2017, p. 65.
[79] Thomson 2005, pp. 4–5.
[80] Thomson 2005, p. 5.
[81] Australian Government 2014, p. 33.
[82] Australian National Audit Office 2001, p. 11.
[83] Australian National Audit Office 2001, p. 29.
[84] Australian National Audit Office 2001, p. 30.
[85] Dennis et al 2008, p. 46.
[86] Australian National Audit Office 2001, p. 31.
[87] Defence People Group 2017, p. 6.
[88] Australian National Audit Office 2001, p. 58.
[89] Defence People Group 2017, p. 11.
[90] Australian National Audit Office 2001, pp. 36, 61, 65, 76.
[91] Smith 2014, pp. 42–43.
[92] Department of Defence 2009, p. 90.
[93] Horner 2001, p. 281.
[94] Horner 2001, pp. 294–301.
[95] Horner 2001, pp. 321–324.
[96] Beaumont 2001, p. 357.
[97] Foreign Affairs, Defence and Trade Group 2000.
[98] Department of Defence 2017, p. 106.
[99] Thomson 2017, p. 80.
[100] Khosa 2010, p. 79.
[101] Department of Defence 2017a, pp. 90–91.
[102] Department of Defence 2016, pp. 5–8.
[103] Thomson 2017, pp. 77–79.
[104] Thomson 2009, pp. 47–49.
[105] Department of Defence 2017a, p. 113.

[106] Department of Defence 2017a, pp. 111–112.
[107] Dennis et al 2008, pp. 3–5.
[108] Thomson 2017, pp. 78–79.
[109] Hoglin 2016, pp. 20–23.
[110] Grey 2008, p. 275.
[111] Dennis et al 2008, p. 264.
[112] Dennis et al 2008, pp. 264–265.
[113] Belkin & McNichol 2000, pp. 2–3.
[114] Thomson 2016, pp. 51–52.
[115] Thomson 2017, p. 42.
[116] Thomson 2017, p. 180.
[117] Thomson 2017, pp. 174–175.
[118] Thomson 2016, pp. 139–140.
[119] Thomson 2016, p. 141.
[120] Thomson (2011), p. vi
[121] Thomson 2005, pp. 9–10.
[122] Khosa 2011, p. 39.
[123] Khosa 2011, pp. 98–99.
[124] Wilson & Pittaway 2017, p. 34.
[125] Australian Army 2014, p. 4.
[126] //en.wikipedia.org/w/index.php?title=Australian_Defence_Force&action=edit
[127] International Institute for Strategic Studies 2016, p. 233.
[128] Wilson & Pittaway 2017, p. 100.
[129] Khosa 2010, pp. 16–35.
[130] International Institute for Strategic Studies 2016, p. 235.
[131] Chief of Navy 2017, pp. 195–203.
[132] Australian Army 2014, pp. 52–54.
[133] Air Power Development Centre 2015, pp. 31, 44–45, 57.
[134] Peacock & von Rosenbach 2011, p. 28.
[135] Dennis et al 2008, p. 178.
[136] Australian National Audit Office 2014, pp. 11–13, 39.
[137] Australian National Audit Office 2014, pp. 30–31.
[138] Australian National Audit Office 2014, p. 39.
[139] Sutton 2017, pp. 42.
[140] Dennis et al 2008, p. 179.
[141] Council of Australian Governments 2015, p. 17.
[142] Smith & Bergin 2006, p. 7.
[143] Australian Government 2016, p. 72.
[144] Smith & Bergin 2006, p. 13.
[145] Khosa 2010, p. 97.
[146] Blaxland 2014, p. 12.
[147] Australian Government 2016, pp. 117–120.
[148] Beaumont 2001, p. 457.
[149] Australian Government 2016, pp. 118–120.
[150] Ball, Robinson & Tranter 2016, pp. 53–54.
[151] Joint Standing Committee on Treaties 2014, p. 3.
[152] Khosa 2010, p. 111.
[153] http://airpower.airforce.gov.au/Publications/Details/628/Air-Force---Serving-Australias-Interests.aspx
[154] http://airpower.airforce.gov.au/Publications/Air-Force-Capability-Guide
[155] //www.worldcat.org/oclc/950573401
[156] https://www.army.gov.au/sites/g/files/net1846/f/aide_memoire.pdf
[157] http://www.defence.gov.au/WhitePaper/docs/DefenceIssuesPaper2014.pdf
[158] http://www.defence.gov.au/Whitepaper/
[159] https://www.anao.gov.au/work/performance-audit/australian-defence-force-reserves
[160] https://www.anao.gov.au/sites/g/files/net616/f/AuditReport_2013-2014_24.pdf

[161] http://nautilus.org/wp-content/uploads/2016/06/Australias-Participation-in-the-Pine-Gap-Enterprise.pdf
[162] https://web.archive.org/web/20120207062427/http://www.aph.gov.au/library/intguide/fad/women_armed.htm
[163] http://www.aph.gov.au/library/intguide/fad/women_armed.htm
[164] http://www.palmcenter.org/wp-content/uploads/2017/12/Australia_Final_Report.pdf
[165] http://www.navy.gov.au/sites/default/files/documents/Australian_Maritime_Operations_2017.pdf
[166] https://www.nationalsecurity.gov.au/Media-and-publications/Publications/Documents/Australias-Counter-Terrorism-Strategy-2015.pdf
[167] https://www.aspi.org.au/report/army-capability-review-2010
[168] https://www.aspi.org.au/report/versatile-force-future-australias-special-operations-capability
[169] http://www.defence.gov.au/adf-totalworkforcemodel/Docs/FAQs-170314FINAL.pdf
[170] http://www.defence.gov.au/whitepaper/
[171] http://www.defence.gov.au/AnnualReports/15-16/Downloads/Women-in-ADF-Report-2015-16-online-only.pdf
[172] https://www.aph.gov.au/Parliamentary_Business/Committees/Joint/Public_Works/EOLRPproject/Submissions
[173] http://www.defence.gov.au/AnnualReports/16-17/
[174] //www.worldcat.org/issn/1323-5036
[175] https://www.aspi.org.au/report/defence-white-papers-40
[176] https://www.aph.gov.au/About_Parliament/Parliamentary_Departments/Parliamentary_Library/Publications_Archive/archive/womenarmed
[177] http://www.defence.gov.au/adc/adfj/Documents/issue_199/199_2016_Mar_Apr.pdf
[178] https://press.anu.edu.au/publications/series/strategic-and-defence-studies-centre-sdsc/history-policy
[179] https://press.anu.edu.au/publications/geography-power-strategy-and-defence-policy
[180] https://www.aph.gov.au/Parliamentary_Business/Committees/Joint/Treaties/2_September_2014/Report_145
[181] https://www.aspi.org.au/report/australian-defence-almanac-2010-2011
[182] //www.worldcat.org/issn/1449-9355
[183] https://www.aspi.org.au/report/australian-defence-almanac-2011-2012
[184] http://www.aph.gov.au/binaries/library/pubs/bn/pol/parliamentaryinvolvement.pdf
[185] //www.worldcat.org/issn/1748-2526
[186] https://www.aspi.org.au/report/strategic-insights-31-australian-domestic-security-role-defence
[187] http://www.defence.gov.au/adc/adfj/Documents/issue_193/193_2014_Mar_Apr.pdf
[188] http://www.defence.gov.au/adc/adfj/Documents/issue_202/Sutton_July_2017.pdf
[189] http://parlinfo.aph.gov.au/parlInfo/download/library/prspub/3L7F6/upload_binary/3l7f66.pdf
[190] https://www.aspi.org.au/report/strategic-insights-18-punching-above-our-weight-australia-middle-power
[191] https://www.aspi.org.au/publications/strategic-insights-18-punching-above-our-weight-australia-as-a-middle-power/SI_Strategic_weight.pdf
[192] https://www.aspi.org.au/report/war-and-profit-doing-business-battlefield
[193] https://www.aspi.org.au/publications/war-and-profit-doing-business-on-the-battlefield/20937-ASPI-War-and-Profit.pdf
[194] https://www.aspi.org.au/report/cost-defence-aspi-defence-budget-brief-2009-2010
[195] //www.worldcat.org/issn/2200-6613
[196] https://www.aspi.org.au/report/cost-defence-aspi-defence-budget-brief-2012-2013
[197] https://www.aspi.org.au/report/cost-defence-aspi-defence-budget-brief-2016-2017
[198] https://www.aspi.org.au/report/cost-defence-aspi-defence-budget-brief-2017-2018
[199] //www.worldcat.org/issn/1448-8086
[200] http://www.defence.gov.au/
[201] //en.wikipedia.org/w/index.php?title=Template:History_of_Australia&action=edit
[202] This figure represents military casualties only and does not include those that died during the frontier conflict. See Coulthard-Clark 1998, p. v.

[203] Australian War Memorial 2010, p. 14
[204] Evans 2005.
[205] Millar 1978, p. 49.
[206] White 2002, p. 257.
[207] Grey 1999, pp. 265–266.
[208] Millar 1978, pp. 25–26.
[209]
[210] Dennis et al 1995, p. 121.
[211] Although unknown by the British at the time, in 2015 it was reported that recent research had revealed that Spain had planned to invade the fledgling Australian colony in the 1790s with a 100-ship armada. The operation, which was intended to challenge the growth of British influence in the Pacific, would have included an attack on Sydney mounted from Spanish colonies in South America; however, it was subsequently deferred and ultimately abandoned. See
[212] Dennis et al 1995, pp.121–124.
[213] Dennis et al 1995, p. 59.
[214] Dennis et al 1995, p. 9.
[215] Macintyre 1999, p. 62.
[216] Grey 1999, pp. 31–34.
[217] Dennis et al 1995, p. 12.
[218] Grey 1999, p. 31.
[219] Grey 1995, p. 12.
[220] Dennis et al 1995, p. 5.
[221] Grey 1999, p. 30.
[222] Dennis et al 1995, pp. 12–13.
[223] Dennis et al 1995, pp. 7–8.
[224] Grey 1999, p. 32.
[225] Dennis et al 1995, p. 11.
[226] Dennis et al 1995, p. 435.
[227] Coulthard-Clark 1998, pp. viii–ix.
[228] Grey 1999, p. 22.
[229] Dennis et al 1995, pp. 159–165.
[230] Dennis et al 1995, p. 584.
[231] Grey 1999, 50–51.
[232] Frame 2004, p. 54.
[233] Dennis et al 1995, pp. 166–167.
[234] Grey 1999, p. 64.
[235] Dennis et al 1995, p. 575.
[236] Coulthard-Clark 2001, pp. 53–54.
[237] Turner 2014, pp. 40–53.
[238] Odgers 1994, pp. 28–31.
[239] Odgers 1994, p. 32.
[240] Odgers 1994, p. 33.
[241] Odgers 1994, p. 34.
[242] Odgers 1994, pp. 34–35.
[243] Odgers 1994, p. 40.
[244] Odgers 1994, pp. 40–43.
[245] Odgers 1994, p. 48.
[246] Odgers 1994, pp. 46–47.
[247] Odgers 1994, p. 47.
[248] Grey 2008, p. 62.
[249] Grey 2008, p. 62
[250] Grey 1999, p. 61.
[251] Grey 2008, p. 57 and pp. 63–64.
[252] Dennis et al 1995, p. 117.
[253] Nicholls 1986, pp. 32–33.
[254] Dennis et al 2008, p. 179.

[255] The land forces of Australia have held a number of titles during their history. From 1901 to 1916 they were called the Commonwealth Military Forces, after which they were renamed the Australian Military Forces (AMF). In 1980 the AMF was renamed the Australian Army, see
[256] Laffin 1996, p. 8.
[257] Macdougall 1991, p. 23.
[258] Dennis et al 2008, pp. 466–470.
[259] Stephens 2001, p. 29.
[260] Horner 2001, p. 42.
[261] Odgers 1994, p. 58.
[262] Dennis 1999, p. 85.
[263] Dennis et al 2008, p. 63.
[264] Grey 1999, p. 81.
[265] Beaumont 1995, pp. 1–28.
[266] Grey 1999, p. 83.
[267] Dennis et al 2008, p. 521.
[268] Grey 1999, p. 88.
[269] Despite temporarily being disembarked when the convoy reached the Suez Canal at the end of November in order to assist with the defence of the canal against Turkish forces, it had always been intended that the Australians and New Zealanders would eventually go to the Western Front like the Canadians; however, issues involving the availability of accommodation and equipment in the training areas of the Salisbury Plain made the arrival of further troops during the winter impossible, and they remained in Egypt as a result. See Grey 1999, p. 88.
[270] Grey 1999, p. 89.
[271] Dennis et al 1995, p. 261.
[272] Walhert 2008, p. 28.
[273] Grey 1999, p. 112.
[274] Bean 1946, p. 188.
[275] Coulthard-Clark 2001, pp. 118–119.
[276] Dennis et al 2008, p. 405.
[277] Coulthard-Clark 2001, pp. 134–135.
[278] Grey 1999, p. 114.
[279] Dennis et al 2008, pp. 61–62.
[280] Grey 2008, p. 100.
[281] Grey 2008, p. 102.
[282] Grey 2008, 103.
[283] Odgers 1994, pp. 93–94.
[284] Odgers 1994, p. 95.
[285] Coulthard-Clark 1998, p. 126.
[286] Coulthard-Clark 1998, pp.127–128.
[287] Odgers 1994, p. 96.
[288] Coulthard-Clark 1998, p. 129.
[289] Coulthard-Clark 1998, p. 130.
[290] Odgers 1994, p. 100.
[291] Odgers 1994, p. 117.
[292] Coulthard-Clark 1998, p. 138.
[293] Odgers 1994, p. 121.
[294] Coulthard-Clark 1998, pp. 137–149.
[295] Coulthard-Clark 1998, p. 148.
[296] Grey 2008, p. 108.
[297] Odgers 1994, p. 122.
[298] Coulthard-Clark 1998, p. 152.
[299] Coulthard-Clark 1998, pp. 152–164.
[300] Odgers 1994, p. 127.
[301] Grey 1999, p. 116.
[302] South Africa was the only other nation not to implement conscription during the war. See Dennis et al 1995, p. 176.

[303]

[304] Grey 1985, pp. 12–17.
[305] Muirden 1990, p. 8.
[306] Dennis et al 1995, p. 437.
[307] Muirden 1990, p. 78.
[308] Cassells 2000, p. 6.
[309] Coulthard-Clark 2001, pp. 167–168.
[310] Dennis et al 1995, p. 81.
[311] Grey 1999, p. 133.
[312] Such service was technically illegal under the *Foreign Enlistment Act 1870*—an act of British Parliament. Notably Australia did not possess similar legislation until the *Crimes (Foreign Incursions and Recruitment) Act 1978* was passed. See Dennis et al 2008, p. 81.
[313] Dennis et al 2008, p. 72.
[314] Grey 2008, p. 144.
[315] Beaumont 1996a, pp. 7–9.
[316] Stevens 2006, pp. 60–64, 75.
[317] Frame 2004, pp. 153–157.
[318] Long 1973, pp. 54–63.
[319] Coates 2006, p. 132.
[320] Grey 2008, pp. 159–161.
[321] Grey 2008, pp. 161–162.
[322] Grey 2008, p. 162.
[323] Grey 2008, p. 163.
[324] Coates 2006, pp. 168–172.
[325] Odgers 1999, pp. 183–194.
[326] Stevens 2006, p. 107.
[327] Odgers 1999, pp. 187–191.
[328] Stevens 2006, p. 96.
[329] Long 1973. pp. 379–393
[330] Odgers 1999, p. 187.
[331] Dennis et al 2008, pp. 339–340.
[332] Horner 1993, pp. 2–3.
[333] Grey 2008, pp 169–172.
[334] Grey 2008, p. 172.
[335] Coulthard-Clark 2001, pp. 204–206.
[336] Beaumont 1996b, pp. 48–49.
[337] Horner 1993, pp. 4–5.
[338] Beaumont 1996b, pp. 34–36.
[339] Beaumont 1996b, pp. 36–39.
[340] Grey 2008, p. 181.
[341] Grey 2008, pp. 187–188.
[342] Dennis et al 2008, p. 124.
[343] Dennis et al 2008, pp. 288–289.
[344] Grey 2008, p. 188.
[345] Grey 2008, pp. 188–191.
[346] 27,073 Australians were killed and 23,477 were wounded by enemy action during the war, however when non-battle casualties are included these figures are 39,767 killed and another 66,553 wounded. See
[347] Grey 1999, pp. 195–196.
[348] Kuring 2004, pp. 219–220.
[349] Dennis et al 2008, p. 111.
[350] Eather 1996, p. 1.
[351] Grey 2008, p. 203
[352] Long 1963, p. 578.
[353] Kuring 2004, p. 219.
[354] Eather 1996, pp. 1–19.

[355] Dennis et al 2008, pp. 111–112.
[356] Kuring 2004, p. 223.
[357] Eather 1996, p. 38 and pp. 172–183.
[358] Kuring 2004, p. 224.
[359] Grey 1999, p. 200.
[360] Dennis et al 2008, p. 302.
[361] Coulthard-Clark 2001, p. 258.
[362] Kuring 2004, p. 232.
[363] Coulthard-Clark 2001, pp. 259–260.
[364] O'Neill 1985, pp. 55–56.
[365] Kuring 2004, p. 233.
[366] Breen 1992, p. 9.
[367] Kuring 2004, p. 236.
[368] Coulthard-Clark 2001, pp. 263–265.
[369] Coulthard-Clark 2001, pp. 266–268.
[370] Grey 1999, pp.207–208.
[371] Coulthard-Clark 2001, p. 269.
[372] Odgers 1999, p. 147.
[373] Dennis et al 2008, p. 345.
[374] Dennis et al 2008, p. 347.
[375] Eather 1996, pp. 70–76.
[376] Macdougall 1991, p. 327.
[377] Stevens 2001, pp. 181–194.
[378] Stephens 2001, pp. 200 and 291.
[379] Dennis et al 1995, p. 171.
[380] Dennis et al 1995, p. 173.
[381] Horner 1989
[382] Dennis and Grey 1996, p. 196.
[383] A number of contingency plans existed, although none were ever fully implemented. For instance: Plan Spillikin, Plan Hemley, Plan Shalstone (renamed Mason), Plan Addington, and Plan Althorpe. These plans called for different levels of commitment depending on different contingencies, including using the majority of Australian air, land and naval forces in the Strategic Reserve, such as the Canberra bombers already based at Butterworth, as well involvement in the defence of Malaysian airspace from Indonesian attacks, air attacks on Indonesian bases by Australian aircraft flying from Australian bases and even the use of facilities in Darwin by the RAF Strategic V Bomber Force. See Dennis and Grey 1996, p. 196.
[384] Ham 2007, pp. 48–49.
[385] Dennis et al 2008, p. 555.
[386] Dennis et al 2008, p. 556.
[387] Dennis 1995, p. 619.
[388] McNeill 2003, p. 126.
[389] McNeill and Ekins 2003, p. 303.
[390] Coulthard-Clark 2001, pp. 288–289.
[391] Dennis et al 1995, p. 620.
[392] Horner 2008, p. 231.
[393] Dennis et al 2008, p. 557.
[394] Horner 2001, p. 44.
[395] Horner 2001, p. 47.
[396] Horner 2001, p. 41.
[397] Horner 2001, p. 112.
[398] Tewes, Rayner and Kavanaugh 2004.
[399] Horner 2001, p. 72.
[400] Horner 2001, pp. 225–227.
[401] Dennis et al 2008, pp. 208–209.
[402] Horner and Bou 2008, pp. 256 and 340.
[403] Kirkland 1991, p. 160.

[404] Horner 2001, pp. 231–237.
[405] Horner 2001, pp. 228–255.
[406] Australian Army 2008, p. 81.
[407] Horner 2001, pp. 20–23.
[408] Dennis et al 2008, p. 193.
[409] Thomson 2005, p. 11.
[410] Dennis et al 2008, pp. 7–8.
[411] Dennis et al 2008, p. 9.
[412] Connery, Cran and Evered 2012, pp. 9–17.
[413] These ships are deployed as part of the US-led Combined Maritime Forces. Headquartered in Bahrain, the coalition operates three naval task forces in the Red Sea, Gulf of Aden, Arabian Sea, Indian Ocean and Gulf of Oman, being Combined Task Force 150 (CTF 150) – maritime security and counter-terrorism, Combined Task Force 151 (CTF 151) – counter-piracy, and Combined Task Force 152 (CTF 152) – maritime security operations in the Persian Gulf. See
[414] Dennis et al 2008, p. 248.
[415] Holmes 2006, pp. 38–39.
[416] Dennis et al 2008, p. 250.
[417] Londey 2004, p. xxi.
[418] Bullard 2017, pp. 491–499.
[419] http://www.awm.gov.au/about/annual_report/ann_rep09-10.pdf
[420] //www.worldcat.org/issn/1441-4198
[421] https://web.archive.org/web/20081206212730/http://www.defence.gov.au/army/PUBS/downloads/LWD_1_The_Fundamentals_of_Land_Warfare_Full.pdf
[422] //www.worldcat.org/oclc/223250226
[423] http://www.defence.gov.au/ARMY/PUBS/downloads/LWD_1_The_Fundamentals_of_Land_Warfare_Full.pdf
[424] https://www.awm.gov.au/collection/RCDIG1069750/
[425] //www.worldcat.org/oclc/251999955
[426] https://www.awm.gov.au/collection/RCDIG1069871/
[427] //www.worldcat.org/oclc/220477286
[428] //www.worldcat.org/oclc/48761594
[429] //www.worldcat.org/oclc/39097011
[430] //www.worldcat.org/oclc/48793439
[431] //www.worldcat.org/oclc/187450156
[432] http://airpower.airforce.gov.au/Publications/Details/237/Odd-Jobs---RAAF-Operations-in-Japan-The-Berlin-Airlift-Korea-Malaya-and-Malta-1946-1970.aspx
[433] //www.worldcat.org/issn/0813-0876
[434] //www.worldcat.org/oclc/23828245
[435] //www.worldcat.org/issn/0729-2473
[436] //www.worldcat.org/oclc/27614090
[437] //www.worldcat.org/oclc/57212671
[438] https://www.awm.gov.au/collection/RCDIG1070206/
[439] //www.worldcat.org/oclc/1297619
[440] //www.worldcat.org/oclc/260164058
[441] //www.worldcat.org/oclc/31743147
[442] //www.worldcat.org/oclc/50315481
[443] //www.worldcat.org/oclc/47367004
[444] //www.worldcat.org/oclc/52647129
[445] https://web.archive.org/web/20080930070253/http://www.aph.gov.au/library/pubs/rb/2004-05/05rb04.htm
[446] //www.worldcat.org/oclc/224183782
[447] http://www.aph.gov.au/library/pubs/rb/2004-05/05rb04.htm
[448] http://www.aspi.org.au/publications/publication_details.aspx?ContentID=78&pubtype=6
[449] //www.worldcat.org/oclc/224546956
[450] //www.worldcat.org/issn/0048-8933
[451] //doi.org/10.1080/10357710220147451

[452] //www.worldcat.org/issn/1465-332X
[453] https://www.awm.gov.au/
[454] Dennis et al 2008, p. 47.
[455] Nicholls 1986, pp. 32–33.
[456] Grey 2008, p. 141.
[457] Grey 1999, pp. 195–196.
[458] Kuring 2004, pp. 219–220.
[459] Hall 2000, p. 58.
[460] Cameron Stewart and Milanda Rout, 5 August 2009. "Somali extremists on a 'fatwa order' from God" http://www.theaustralian.news.com.au/story/0,25197,25884512-601,00.html. *The Australian*, Retrieved on 5 August 2009
[461] Melissa Iaria, 4 August 2009. "Terror suspects 'sought holy approval'" http://www.news.com.au/story/0,27574,25883085-29277,00.html. News.com.au, Retrieved on 4 August 2009
[462] //www.worldcat.org/oclc/500113513
[463] http://103.11.78.168/~/media/Army/Our%20future/Publications/AAJ/2010s/2012/AAJ_2012_1.pdf
[464] //www.worldcat.org/issn/1448-2843
[465] //www.worldcat.org/issn/0048-8933
[466] https://www.army.gov.au/sites/g/files/net1846/f/aaj_291_aug_1973.pdf
[467] //www.worldcat.org/oclc/30798241
[468] https//web.archive.org
[469] http//www.army.gov.au
[470] https://www.army.gov.au/sites/g/files/net1846/f/aaj_165_feb_1963.pdf
[471] http://www.army.gov.au
[472] Grey 2008, pp. 88 & 147.
[473] Odgers 1988, p. 5.
[474] Grey 2008, pp. 200–201.
[475] Odgers 1988.
[476] Grey 2008, pp. 284–285.
[477] Horner 2001, p. 195.
[478] Jobson 2009, p. 53.
[479] Jobson 2009, pp. 55–56.
[480] Jobson 2009, p. 58.
[481] http://www.defence.gov.au/budget/08-09/dar/index.htm
[482] New combat uniform makes troops job easier http://www.defence.gov.au/defencenews/stories/2010/Nov/1119.htm, *Australian Department of Defence*, 19 November 2010.
[483] Land Warfare Conference - Minister for Defence Materiel http://www.minister.defence.gov.au/clarespeechtpl.cfm?CurrentId=11103 , *Australian Department of Defence*, 19 November 2010.
[484] New defence uniforms on the way http://news.smh.com.au/breaking-news-national/new-defence-uniforms-on-the-way-20110530-1fcay.html, The Sydney Morning Herald, 30 May 2011
[485] *Cloak of invisibility* http://www.defence.gov.au/news/armynews/editions/1095/topstories/story04.htm. Army News 22 April 2004.
[486] NIOA wins 40mm grenade launcher contracts http://www.australiandefence.com.au/news/nioa-wins-40mm-grenade-launcher-contracts - Australiandefence.com.au, 28 July 2015
[487] http://www.defence.gov.au/dmo/id/dcp/html/air/AIR9000_7.html
[488] http://www.defence.gov.au/news/armynews/editions/1174/features/feature01.htm
[489] https://web.archive.org/web/20161020204550/http://www.dtic.mil/ndia/2011smallarms/WednesdayInter12397Evenden.pdf
[490] http://www.dtic.mil/ndia/2011smallarms/WednesdayInter12397Evenden.pdf
[491] John M Wilkins, Australian Naval Reserve publication
[492] The peak strength of the Royal Canadian Navy was 95,000 personnel on VE day, whereas the peak strength of the RAN, in mid-1945, was less than 40,000 personnel. While the RAN surpassed the RCN in terms of the number of vessels operated during 1939–45, both navies were dwarfed by the wartime fleets of the US, British, Soviet, Japanese, German, French and probably other navies. (Rob Stuart, 2009, "Was the RCN ever the Third Largest

Navy?", *Canadian Naval Review*, vol. 5, no. 3, pp. 5–9. http://www.navalreview.ca/wp-content/uploads/public/vol5num3/vol5num3art2.pdf)

[493] Nicholls 1988, p. 2.
[494] Graham 1967, p. 459.
[495] Dennis et. al 2008, p.53.
[496] Dennis et al. 2008, p. 54.
[497] Blunt 2002, p. 16–17.
[498] Australian Naval Reserves by John M Wilkins RFD*.
[499] "Death of a Bluejacket" http://www.brightoncemetery.com/HistoricInterments/Crimes/robertsonw.htm. Retrieved 24 September 2007.
[500] Official History of Australia in the War of 1914 – 1918 Volume XI Chapter 1 http://www.awm.gov.au/cms_images/histories/10/chapters/01.pdf.
[501] Official History of Australia in the War of 1914 – 1918 Volume XI Chapter 1 Appendix 27 http://www.awm.gov.au/cms_images/histories/10/chapters/41.pdf.
[502] Official History of Australia in the War of 1914–1918 Vol. X: The Australians at Rabaul, S.S. Mackenzie, 1927.
[503] Burnell 1914.
[504] Jose, *The Royal Australian Navy 1914–1918*, p. 274
[505] Stevens, in Stevens, *The Royal Australian Navy*, pp. 52–3
[506] Official History of Australia in the War of 1914–1918 Vol. IX The Royal Australian Navy, 1914–1918.
[507] Stevens 2001, pp. 29—30.
[508] Stevens 2001, p. 318.
[509] Report of cruise to render assistance in the influenza outbreak, 14 December 1918, HMAS Encounter file, SPC-A.
[510] Australia in the War of 1939–1945, Volume I – Royal Australian Navy, 1939 – 1942 (1st edition, 1957) Chapter 1 Accessed 3 September 2006 http://www.awm.gov.au/cms_images/histories/24/chapters/01.pdf.
[511] Macdougall 1991, p. 158.
[512] Stevens 2001, p. 105
[513] Stevens 2001, p. 104
[514] Sourced from Gavin Long (1973), *The Six Years War. A Concise History of Australia in the 1939–45 War*. Australian War Memorial and Australian Government Publishing Service, Canberra. p 16. and G. Herman Gill (1968). *Australia in the War of 1939 – 1945. Series 2 – Navy. Volume II – Royal Australian Navy, 1942 – 1945* http://www.awm.gov.au/histories/chapter.asp?volume=25. Australian War Memorial, Canberra. p 710.
[515] Stevens (1996) pp. 38–39.
[516] Macdougall 1991, p. 170.
[517] Stevens 2001, p. 111.
[518] Gill, *Royal Australian Navy, 1939–1942*, p. 165
[519] Stevens 2001, p. 121.
[520] Gill, *Royal Australian Navy, 1939–1942*, pp. 172–3
[521] Gill, *Royal Australian Navy, 1939–1942*, p. 173
[522] Gill, *Royal Australian Navy, 1939–1942*, p. 176
[523] Gill, *Royal Australian Navy, 1939–1942*, p. 177
[524] Macdougall 1991, p. 180.
[525] Gill, *Royal Australian Navy, 1939–1942*, p. 184
[526] Gill, *Royal Australian Navy, 1939–1942*, pp. 185–6
[527] Macdougall pg. 180
[528] Macdougall 1991, p. 181.
[529] Cassells, *The Capital Ships*, pp. 149–50
[530] Cassells, *The Capital Ships*, p. 150
[531] Gill, *Royal Australian Navy, 1939–1942*, pp. 192–3
[532] Gill, *Royal Australian Navy, 1939–1942*, p. 191
[533] Gill 1957, pp. 223–224.
[534] Macdougall pg. 193

[535] Dakar: Operation Menace http://users.swing.be/navbat/bataille/68.html . Retrieved 21 August 2006.
[536] Stevens 2001, p. 124.
[537] Stevens 2001, p. 151.
[538] Macdougall 1991, p. 176.
[539] Book review: *The Guns of Dakar* and *Operation Menace* http://stonebooks.com/archives/960425.shtml.
[540] Macdougall 1991, p. 216.
[541] Stevens 1996, p. 54.
[542] The Gun Plot http://www.gunplot.net/. Retrieved 21 August 2006.
[543] Macdougall 1991, p. 182.
[544] Stevens 2001, p. 141.
[545] van Oosten, F. C. (1976). The Battle of the Java Sea (Sea battles in close-up; 15). Naval Institute Press.
[546] AWM Battle of the Coral Sea http://www.awm.gov.au/encyclopedia/coral_sea/doc.htm.
[547] Stevens 2005, pp. 205–207.
[548] Gill 1968, pp. 253–262.
[549] Stevens 2005, pp. 247–248.
[550] David Stevens. *Japanese submarine operations against Australia 1942–1944* http://ajrp.awm.gov.au/AJRP/AJRP2.nsf/437f72f8ac2c07238525661a00063aa6/225b90b97196e29bca256a1d00130203?OpenDocument. Retrieved 1 September 2006.
[551] Stevens (2005). Page 281.
[552] Jenkins 1992, p. 265.
[553] AWM HMAS Canberra – Sinking of HMAS Canberra in Battle of Savo Island http://www.awm.gov.au/encyclopedia/ww2_navy/savo.htm. Retrieved 21 August 2006.
[554] H. P. Willmott, The Battle of Leyte Gulf: The Last Fleet Action
[555] Stevens 2001, p. 148.
[556] Gill 1968, p. 590
[557] Frame 2004, pp. 198–199 and Stevens 2001, pp. 156–157.
[558] Macdougall 1991, p. 327.
[559] p. 66
[560] Macdougall 1991, pp. 321–323.
[561] Stevens 2001, p. 201
[562] Macdougall 1991, p. 332.
[563] Frame, *A Cruel Legacy*, pp. 11–12
[564] Frame, *A Cruel Legacy*, pp. 12–13
[565] Frame, *A Cruel Legacy*, pp. 1–3, 14–15
[566] Frame, *A Cruel Legacy*, p. 5
[567] Frame, *Where Fate Calls*, pp. 27, 43–6
[568] Frame, *A Cruel Legacy*, pp. 67–9
[569] Stevens 2001, p. 202.
[570] Frame, *A Cruel Legacy*, pp. 68, 82, 88, 114–7
[571] Frame, *A Cruel Legacy*, pp. 159–60
[572] Frame, *Pacific Partners*, p. 126.
[573] Frame, *Pacific Partners*, p. 127.
[574] Frame, *Pacific Partners*, pp. 130–131.
[575] Macdougall 1991, p. 338.
[576] Johnson. E, Operation Navy help: Disaster operations by the RAN post Cyclone-Tracy, Northern Territory Library Service, Darwin, 1987, p. 2.
[577] Tom Frame (2004), *No Pleasure Cruise. The Story of the Royal Australian Navy*. Allen & Unwin, Sydney. p. 251.
[578] Frame. Pg. 257.
[579] Frame 2004, p. 262.
[580] Analysis of the 1987 Defence White Paper Accessed on 27 August 2006 http://www.agitprop.org.au/lefthistory/1987_booker_new_pacific_policeman.php.
[581] Frame 2004, pp. 267–272.

[582] Australian War Memorial. Gulf War 1990–1991 and Commander J.P. Hodgman (editor) (1991). *Australia's Navy 1991 – 92.* Australian Department of Defence. Canberra.
[583] Greg Nash and David Stevens (2006) *Australia's Navy in the Gulf. From Countenance to Catalyst, 1941–2006.* Topmill, Sydney. pp. 61–63.
[584] Nash and Stevens (2006). pp. 66–72.
[585] Nash and Stevens (2006). Pages 80–81.
[586] Journalist Seaman Joseph Ebalo, *Australian-Led Command Patrols Persian Gulf* http://www.news.navy.mil/search/display.asp?story_id=18240 . Navy newsstand. 10 May 2005.
[587] Lt. Karen E. Eifert *U.S. Navy Takes the Reins of CTF 158 from Royal Australian Navy* http://www.news.navy.mil/search/display.asp?story_id=26621 . Navy newsstand. 15 November 2006.
[588] Westralia sailors set for $10m compo http://www.theage.com.au/news/National/Govt-opens-way-for-Westralia-payouts/2006/08/29/1156617313071.html The Age Newspaper Accessed 13 September 2006.
[589] INTERFET Military Personnel Chart accessed 27 August 2006 http://www.britains-smallwars.com/RRGP/EastTimor.html .
[590] Navy News http://www.defence.gov.au/news/navynews/editions/4909/topstories/story01.htm.
[591] C. Woods, 'Bikfala Sip: Aussies come to Help our Pacific Friends', Navy News, 14 August 2003. Retrieved 14 September 2006.
[592] Aussie Navy vessels ready for Fiji evacuation http://www.fijitimes.com/story.aspx?id=52286. *Fiji Times*, 24 November 2006.
[593] and
[594] and
[595] Cassells, *The Destroyers*, p. 233
[596] Cassells, *The Destroyers*, p. 1
[597] "Women in the RAN".
[598] Royal Australian Navy Official Website http://www.navy.gov.au/. Retrieved 10 August 2013.
[599] Royal Australian Navy Website http://www.navy.gov.au/Force_Element_Groups Accessed 5 November 2006.
[600] Sea 4000 http://www.defence.gov.au/dmo/msd/sea4000/sea4000.cfm .
[601] Defence Materiel Organisation website. Retrieved 4 November 2006. http://www.defence.gov.au/dmo/lsp/amphibs.cfm/
[602] //www.worldcat.org/oclc/48761594
[603] //www.worldcat.org/oclc/46829686
[604] //www.worldcat.org/oclc/55980812
[605] //www.worldcat.org/oclc/61213421
[606] https://web.archive.org/web/20110613221149/http://www.navy.gov.au/w/index.php/Publication:Papers_in_Australian_Maritime_Affairs_No._15
[607] //www.worldcat.org/issn/1327-5658
[608] //www.worldcat.org/oclc/62548623
[609] http://www.navy.gov.au/w/index.php/Publication:Papers_in_Australian_Maritime_Affairs_No._15
[610] //www.worldcat.org/oclc/50418095
[611] http://ajrp.awm.gov.au/AJRP/AJRP2.nsf/437f72f8ac2c07238525661a00063aa6/225b90b97196e29bca256a1d00130203?OpenDocument
[612] //www.worldcat.org/oclc/0091826381
[613] https://www.awm.gov.au/collection/RCDIG1069926/
[614] https://www.awm.gov.au/collection/RCDIG1070207/
[615] https://www.awm.gov.au/collection/RCDIG1070208/
[616] http://www.navy.gov.au/media-room/publications/semaphore
[617] http://www.navy.gov.au/media-room/publications/australian-maritime-doctrine
[618] http://www.navy.gov.au/History
[619] //www.worldcat.org/issn/0048-8393
[620] https://web.archive.org/web/20090123072727/http://www.adf-history.com/ran.html
[621] http://www.navy.gov.au/
[622] Dennis et al 1995, p. 516.

[623] Whitley 2000, p. 17.
[624] Dennis et al 1995, p. 517.
[625] Gillett & Graham 1977, p. 193.
[626] Gillett & Graham 1977, p. 61.
[627] Dennis et al 1995 p. 518.
[628] Gillett & Graham 1977, pp. 69–76.
[629] Gillett & Graham 1977, p. 93.
[630] Gillett & Graham 1977, p. 94.
[631] Dennis et al 1995, pp. 519–520.
[632] C L Cumberlege http://homepage.ntlworld.com/bob.cumberbatch/C%20L%20Cumberlege.htm
[633] Frame 2004, p. 96.
[634] http://www.navy.gov.au/fleet/ships-boats-craft/available-ship-histories
[635] http://www.maritimequest.com/warship_directory/australia/royal_australian_navy_main_page.htm
[636] http://www.navy.gov.au/about/senior-leadership-group
[637] http://www.naval-history.net/
[638] //en.wikipedia.org/w/index.php?title=List_of_active_Royal_Australian_Navy_ships&action=edit
[639] Saunders & Philpott (eds.), *IHS Jane's Fighting Ships* 2015-2016, p. 35
[640] Defense Industry Daily, 23 April 2012
[641] Australian Security Magazine, *Govt to buy new border patrol vessels*
[642] Saunders (ed.), *IHS Jane's Fighting Ships 2012–2013*, p. 39
[643] http://www.defenseindustrydaily.com/Australias-Submarine-Program-In-the-Dock-06127/
[644] http://www.defenseindustrydaily.com/Australias-Next-Generation-Submarines-05917/
[645] https://web.archive.org/web/20101227054134/http://worldwarships.com/warships_australia_submarines.htm
[646] http://www.worldwarships.com/warships_australia_submarines.htm
[647] https://web.archive.org/web/20101227055640/http://worldwarships.com/warships_australia_support.htm
[648] http://www.worldwarships.com/warships_australia_support.htm
[649] https://web.archive.org/web/20101227070832/http://worldwarships.com/warships_australia_minor.htm
[650] http://www.worldwarships.com/warships_australia_minor.htm
[651] https://web.archive.org/web/20120621102756/http://www.worldwarships.com/warships_australia_major.htm
[652] http://www.worldwarships.com/warships_australia_major.htm
[653] http://www.navy.gov.au/fleet/ships-boats-craft/current-ships
[654] //www.worldcat.org/oclc/919022075
[655] Odgers, *Air Force Australia*, pp. 13–14
[656] Dennis et al, *The Oxford Companion to Australian Military History*, p. 67
[657] Dennis et al, *The Oxford Companion to Australian Military History*, pp. 68–69; 507
[658] Dennis et al, *The Oxford Companion to Australian Military History*, p. 507
[659] Dennis et al, *The Oxford Companion to Australian Military History*, p. 508
[660] Armstrong, "History of the RAAF: 20 Years of Warfighting 1939–1959, Part 2", p. 43
[661] Armstrong, "History of the RAAF: 20 Years of Warfighting 1939–1959, Part 2", p. 42
[662] Dennis et al, *The Oxford Companion to Australian Military History*, p. 509
[663] Barnes, *The RAAF and the Flying Squadrons*, p. 299
[664] Armstrong, "History of the RAAF: 20 Years of Warfighting 1939–1959, Part 2", p. 44
[665] Armstrong, "History of the RAAF: 20 Years of Warfighting 1939–1959, Part 2", p. 45
[666] Barnes, *The RAAF and the Flying Squadrons*, pp. 260–261
[667] Armstrong, "History of the RAAF: 20 Years of Warfighting 1939–1959, Part 2", p. 46
[668] Barrett, *Significant People in Australia's History, Issue 7*, pp. 21–22
[669] Gillison, *Royal Australian Air Force*, pp.585–588 http://www.awm.gov.au/cms_images/histories/26/chapters/28.pdf

[670] Odgers, *Air War Against Japan*, pp.4–6 http://www.awm.gov.au/cms_images/histories/27/chapters/01.pdf
[671] Ashworth, *How Not to Run an Air Force*, pp.143–146
[672] Bostock, William Dowling (1892–1968) http://www.adb.online.anu.edu.au/biogs/A130255b.htm at Australian Dictionary of Biography. Retrieved on 26 December 2010.
[673] Horner, "The Evolution of Australian Higher Command Arrangements", pp.17–18
[674] Ashworth, *How Not to Run an Air Force*, pp.147–151
[675] Stephens, *The Royal Australian Air Force*, p.144
[676] Eather, *Odd Jobs*, p. xv.
[677] Armstrong, "History of the RAAF: 20 Years of Warfighting 1939–1959, Part 2", p. 47
[678] Barnes 2000, p. 17.
[679] Bell, T.E. (2011). *B-57 Canberra Units of the Vietnam War*. Oxford, UK; Osprey, p.80.
[680] http://airpower.airforce.gov.au/Publications/Details/241/How-Not-To-Run-An-Air-Force-Volume-1.aspx
[681] http://airpower.airforce.gov.au/Publications/Details/237/Odd-Jobs---RAAF-Operations-in-Japan-The-Berlin-Airlift-Korea-Malaya-and-Malta-1946-1970.aspx
[682] https://web.archive.org/web/20110607140547/http://www.awm.gov.au/histories/second_world_war/volume.asp?levelID=67912
[683] //www.worldcat.org/oclc/2000369
[684] http://www.awm.gov.au/histories/second_world_war/volume.asp?levelID=67912
[685] https://web.archive.org/web/20141109220745/http://www.defence.gov.au/adc/cdclms/Command%20evolution.doc
[686] http://www.defence.gov.au/adc/cdclms/Command%20evolution.doc
[687] https://web.archive.org/web/20131014171352/http://www.awm.gov.au/histories/second_world_war/volume.asp?levelID=67913
[688] //www.worldcat.org/oclc/246580191
[689] http://www.awm.gov.au/histories/second_world_war/volume.asp?levelID=67913
[690] http://www.airforce.gov.au
[691] Eather 1995, p. 18.
[692] Dennis et al 2008, pp. 61–62.
[693] Grey 1999, pp. 114–115.
[694] Beaumont 2001, p. 214.
[695] Dennis et al 2008, p. 277.
[696]
[697] Stephens 2006, p. 96.
[698] Armstrong, p. 44.
[699] Armstrong, p. 45.
[700] Dennis et al 2008, p. 81.
[701] Taylor and Taylor 1978, p. 48.
[702] Sandler 2001, pp. 21–22
[703] Sandler 2001, p. 22.
[704] Eather 1996, p. xv.
[705] Eather 1996, p. 38.
[706] Eather 1996, p. 162.
[707] Eather 1996, pp. 172–183
[708] Millar 1969, pp. 114–115.
[709] Dennis et al 2008, pp. 150–151.
[710] Eather 1996, pp. 40–77.
[711] Coulthard-Clark 1995, p. 215.
[712] Coulthard-Clark 1995, p. 351.
[713] Barnes 2000, p. 5.
[714] Tony Holmes, 'RAAF Hornets at War' in *Australian Aviation*, January/February 2006, No. 224. pp. 38–39.
[715] Valente, Catherine (June 24, 2017). "Australia sending spy planes to Marawi" http://www.manilatimes.net/australia-sending-spy-planes-marawi/334543/. *The Manila Times*. Retrieved June 25, 2017. <q>As soon as the AFP and the Australian military finalize operational details,

[716] the AP-3C Orion aircraft [of Australia] "will immediately assist in the ongoing operations" in Marawi City, he added.</q>

[716] Grey 2008, p. 132.

[717] Williams, Air Marshal Sir Richard, *These are the Facts*, Australian War Memorial, Canberra, 1977.

[718]

[719] Walters, Patrick. "Kevin Rudd signs off on purchase of 14 F-35 joint strike fighters." http://www.theaustralian.com.au/news/kevin-rudd-signs-off-on-purchase-of-14-f-35-joint-strike-fighters/story-e6frg8yo-1225803790418 *The Australian*, 25 November 2009. Retrieved: 16 December 2009.

[720] //www.worldcat.org/issn/1326-1533

[721] http://airpower.airforce.gov.au/Publications/Details/237/Odd-Jobs---RAAF-Operations-in-Japan-The-Berlin-Airlift-Korea-Malaya-and-Malta-1946-1970.aspx

[722] //www.worldcat.org/oclc/614049220

[723] //www.worldcat.org/issn/0813-0876

[724] //www.worldcat.org/issn/1447-0446

[725] http://airpower.airforce.gov.au/Publications/Details/534/The-Air-Power-Manual---6th-Edition.aspx

[726] http://www.airforce.gov.au/

[727] http://airpower.airforce.gov.au/Contents/About-APDC/Doctrine/Doctrine/158/Current-Doctrine.aspx

[728] http://www.adf-serials.com/

[729] https://www.youtube.com/user/AirForceHQ

[730] //en.wikipedia.org/w/index.php?title=Template:Women_in_society_sidebar&action=edit

[731] Dennis et al. (2008), p. 605.

[732] Darian-Smith (1996), p. 62.

[733] Darian-Smith (1996), pp. 62–63.

[734] Horner (2001), pp. 321–324.

[735] Horner (2001), p. 324.

[736] Horner (2001), p. 325.

[737] Horner (2001), p. 326.

[738] Horner (2001), pp. 325–326.

[739] Khosa (2004). Page 52 and Australian Department of Defence (2006). *2005–06 Defence Annual Report* http://www.defence.gov.au/budget/05-06/dar/downloads/2005-2006_Defence_DAR_07_v1append.pdf. Page 281.

[740] Australian Bureau of Statistics Labour Force, Australia http://www.abs.gov.au/AUSSTATS/abs@.nsf/productsbyCatalogue/362607CA0519045ACA25712B000D0425?OpenDocument.

[741] http://www.aph.gov.au/library/intguide/fad/women_armed.htm

[742] http://www.womenaustralia.info/exhib/war/war.html

[743] Smith 2009, p. 264.

[744] Report of the Caucus Joint Working Group on Homosexual Policy in the Australian Defence Force September 1992.

[745] The Committee's approach was outlined in *Outmanoeuvring Defence: The Australian Debates Over Gay and Lesbian Military Service 1992* by Noah Riseman, Australian Journal of Politics and History Volume 61, Number 4 2015.

[746] Smith 2009, pp. 264-265.

[747] http://scholarship.law.wm.edu/wmjowl/vol17/iss3/3

[748] https://www.army.gov.au/sites/g/files/net1846/f/aaj_2013_3.pdf

[749] Joint Standing Committee on Foreign Affairs, Defence and Trade 2015, p. 4.

[750] Joint Standing Committee on Foreign Affairs, Defence and Trade 2015, p. 6.

[751] Department of Defence 2018, p. 11.

[752] Department of Defence 2016, p. 6.

[753] Thomson 2017, p. 209.

[754] Ferguson 2010, p. 5.

[755] http://www.defence.gov.au/WhitePaper/Docs/2016-Defence-Industry-Policy-Statement.pdf

[756] http://www.defence.gov.au/SPI/Industry/ExportStrategy/Default.asp

[757] https://www.aph.gov.au/Parliamentary_Business/Committees/Joint/Foreign_Affairs_Defence_and_Trade/Defence_Industry_Exports/Report
[758] https://www.aspi.org.au/report/cost-defence-aspi-defence-budget-brief-2017-2018
[759] //www.worldcat.org/issn/2200-6613
[760] https://www.aspi.org.au/report/special-report-issue-25-well-have-six-them-and-four-those-shelf-procurement-and-its
[761] https://www.aspi.org.au/report/risks-and-rewards-defence-rd-australia
[762] https://www.awm.gov.au/collection/RCDIG1070217/
[763] http://www.parracity.nsw.gov.au/council/on_exhibition/?a=9650
[764] http://www.parracity.nsw.gov.au/__data/assets/pdf_file/0008/6569/Attachment_3.pdf

Article Sources and Contributors

The sources listed for each article provide more detailed licensing information including the copyright status, the copyright owner, and the license conditions.

Australian Defence Force *Source:* https://en.wikipedia.org/w/index.php?oldid=851190290 *License:* Creative Commons Attribution-Share Alike 3.0 *Contributors:* 0211 SKDGAKUCHO, 2018slorenzen, ANDREVV, Anotherclown, AussieLegend, AustralianRupert, Bender235, BilCat, Birdy1234, Brutannica, CLCStudent, Ceannlann gorm, Charles lindberg, Chocoholic2017, ClueBot NG, Cobatfor, ColRad85, CommonsDelinker, Coreydragon, Cyberbot II, Dcirovic, DrKay, Gadget593, GenQuest, Gilliam, Greenshed, GünniX, HandsomeFella, HueSatLum, Hugopako, Hydrargyrum, IVORK, Ian Rose, Iazyges, Iehviehge123, JJMC89, Jacarandacounsel, JackofOz, Jarble, JennyOz, Jim1138, Josve05a, Kbooth1102, Kind Tennis Fan, KylieTastic, LordHello1, LtNOWIS, Magioladitis, Markab1975, Mattew124, Mbrandall, Melbguy05, Mr Stephen, Nford24, Nick-D, Noclador, Ohconfucius, Opencooper, Oshwah, Peacemaker67, Piledhigheranddeeper, Plastikspork, Rangasyd, Redalert2fan, Rodw, Saberwyn, ScottDavis, Serols, SoloWing3844, Squiresy92, Superegz, Teracide, The Drover's Wife, TheSturgenator, TinTin, Trappist the monk, Triptothecottage, WOSlinker, Wheelz71, WikiesDad, Yuvraj kinger, Zzaakkaa, 74 anonymous edits 1

Military history of Australia *Source:* https://en.wikipedia.org/w/index.php?oldid=851822090 *License:* Creative Commons Attribution-Share Alike 3.0 *Contributors:* 1exec1, Adavidb, Aeonx, Anotherclown, AustralianRupert, BD2412, Bananapeelt, Bender235, Bethaso, Bobobaggins2030, Buckshot06, BurnAfterReading, Catmando999, Chris the speller, ClueBot NG, Colonies Chris, CommonsDelinker, Derekbridges, Discospinster, Dl2000, Dom3084, Download, Eumolpo, Euryalus, Fifelfoo, Foofbun, Gaius Cornelius, Gfcan777, Gilliam, Graham87, Grant65, HarDNox, Hmains, Holdoffhunger, Hummerrocket, JHCaufield, JaconaFrere, Jennica, Jguy, John of Reading, Kamran the Great, Leventio, LilHelpa, Mandarax, Materialscientist, Nedrutland, Nevwik, Niceguyedc, Nick-D, Ohconfucius, Pharaoh of the Wizards, Psydneyj, Ralph S Lawrence, Rinconsoleao, Rjensen, Rjwilmsi, RomanSpa, Rudolph89, Saberwyn, Shudde, Socrates2008, Spy007au, Squids and Chips, Srednuas Lenoroc, StAnselm, TaqPol, Timrollpickering, Trappist the monk, UESPArules, WereSpielChequers, Woohookitty, Zachlipton, ÄDA - DÄP, 97 anonymous edits 43

History of the Australian Army *Source:* https://en.wikipedia.org/w/index.php?oldid=808796799 *License:* Creative Commons Attribution-Share Alike 3.0 *Contributors:* 42° South, Aeonx, Afrank, Anotherclown, Anthony Staunton, Apodeictic, Art LaPella, AustralianRupert, BD2412, Bendono, Berichard, Betacommand, Bidgee, Bielenberg, Bobblehead, Booksworm, Buckshot06, Canley, Chris j wood, ClueBot NG, Colonies Chris, Cryptic, Cuddy Wifter, Curpsbot-unicodify, Darwinek, Davehi1, Davidcannon, Desertsky85451, Deville, Dl2000, Durova, Foofbun, Gaius Cornelius, Ged UK, Giraffedata, GreatWhiteNortherner, Greenshed, Hammersfan, Hawkeye7, Hossen27, Hunarian, Indon, Ipatrol, Iridescent, Jazzahammer, Josephus37, Karl Barnfather, Kisefau, Koalabearoo7, Lawrencema, Legotech, M-le-mot-dit, Macesito, Majormax, Marudubshinki, Mogism, Nick-D, Noclador, Noveltyghost, Ohconfucius, PBS, Paul foord, Plasticup, QuiteUnusual, Qwerty900009, R'n'B, Risker, SMC, Silverxxx, StAnselm, Steven J. Anderson, Surtsicna, Sus scrofa, Tim!, Tobby72, Tonyob, Viprile, Wintonian, Xfiles82, 50 anonymous edits 109

Australian Army *Source:* https://en.wikipedia.org/w/index.php?oldid=852068279 *License:* Creative Commons Attribution-Share Alike 3.0 *Contributors:* Abraham, B.S., Adam9007, Aeonx, Andrewa, Anotherclown, Atethnekos, AussieLegend, AustralianRupert, B19892014, Ben Dawid, Bender235, BilCat, Bob1960evens, Bobrayner, Bongomanrae, Braeden kersey, Brandon.hargraves, Bsawakig, Buckshot06, Bunnyman78, C.Fred, Ceannlann gorm, ChamithN, Chris the speller, ChrisGualtieri, Chronodm, ClueBot NG, CommonsDelinker, Cstan77, Cyberbot II, David.moreno72, Davidcannon, Dawkeye, De728631, Deathstroke21, DerbyCountyinNZ, Dewritech, Doc9871, Donkeybollocks69, Dormskirk, F1freak78, FlieGerFaUstMe262, Fnlayson, Frietjes, Fry1989, Gbawden, General Ization, Godsavethequeen001, Hammersfan, Hammersoft, Hawkeye7, Hedwig in Washington, Hsinchong, IVORK, Jackfork, Jason Quinn, Jeff G., Jennica, Jim1138, Jprg1966, Julthep, KH-1, Kbog, Kbooth1102, Klemen Kocjancic, LiL BROOMSTiCKKKKK, Lightlowemon, Loppoptop01, LordHello1, Magioladitis, Markdukes21, Materialscientist, Melbguy05, Melonkelon, Mitch Ames, Mosessuccar3, Mr Stephen, MrDolomite, MusikAnimal, Muzi, Nford24, Niceguyedc, Nick-D, Nihiltres, Noclador, Ohconfucius, Oshwah, Pdfpdf, Phildy65, Pocketjacks, PraetorianD, Quercus solaris, Randomdonate, Rjensen, SOTGMichael, Sam Sofi, Scout MLG, Scriberius, Scythia, Shellwood, Snarbydog, Steve92341, Suzuki Auto, TenthEagle, Thane, Thespaceninja3, This lousy T-shirt, Toby6250, Tucoxn, UnbiasedVictory, Whoop whoop pull up, Zappa123, Zyxw, Zzaakkaa, 176 anonymous edits 130

List of equipment of the Australian Army *Source:* https://en.wikipedia.org/w/index.php?oldid=852896989 *License:* Creative Commons Attribution-Share Alike 3.0 *Contributors:* Adnan bogi, Aeonx, AirWave 800S1, America789, Anonaus, Anotherclown, AussieLegend, AustralianRupert, Baron Dewy 94, Bmon94, Brayneeah360, Bsawakig, ChoraPete, Chris the speller, ClueBot NG, CommonsDelinker, Crossyroaders552, Dewritech, Dobby669, Faceless Enemy, Gilliam, GraemeLeggett, Hayman30, Hpeterswald, Hsinchong, Humayun1919, IVORK, Intratecc, Jason Quinn, John Lunney, John of Reading, Krassotkin, LAsast, LordHello1, Luck in the Sky, MORNINGSIDE, Mandarax, Maoenlai, Markdukes21, Melbguy05, Mft2000, MilborneOne, Mojoworker, Mongoose Army, Muhandes, Newm30, Niceguyedc, Nick Number, Nick-D, Nickel nitride, Ohconfucius, Onbvy, Orenburg1, Phildy65, PraetorianD, Rabbigon, RadiculousJ, Randomdonate, RichardMills65, Russavia, SCARECROW, Saberwyn, Sharpiee, Snarbydog, Solid State Survivor, Stephen Hui, Tentinator, Thatwikiman1, The Showgun Master, Thekillerpenguin, Thelawlollol, UndateableOne, Wbm1058, 木の枝, 229 anonymous edits ... 146

History of the Royal Australian Navy *Source:* https://en.wikipedia.org/w/index.php?oldid=850579420 *License:* Creative Commons Attribution-Share Alike 3.0 *Contributors:* 1exec1, 564dude, Aircorn, Alansplodge, America789, Andrew in Darwin, Anotherclown, Ashley Pomeroy, Australian Matt, AustralianRupert, Basetornado, Bazonka, Benea, Bidgee, Blake-, Boing! said Zebedee, Breno, Brian1979, Buckshot06, Cardamon, Cavalryman V31, Chewings72, Chris the speller, Citation bot 1, Cla68, ClueBot NG, Cobatfor, CommonsDelinker, Davidcannon, Dawkeye, Dcirovic, Derekbridges, Dl2000, Dolphin51, Dormskirk, Download, Drpickem, Enthusiast01, Esemono, Euchiasmus, Eynbein, Ged UK, Gene Nygaard, Giraffedata, Gnangarra, Graham87, Grahamec, Grant65, GrindtXX, GroveGuy, Hammersfan, HandsomeFella, Hossen27, Iridescent, Janggeom, John of Reading, Joshua Scott, KTo288, Khazar2, Kisefau, Kjp993, Kobalt64, Kozuch, Lacrimosus, Lightmouse, LilHelpa, Logan, LtNOWIS, LukeSearle, Lyndaship, Magioladitis, MartinDK, Materialscientist, Mogism, MoondyneAWB, Nachoman-au, Neddyseagoon, Newm30, Niceguyedc, Nick-D, Nono64, NorthBySouthBaranof, Northumbrian, Noveltyghost, Noyster, Ohconfucius, Onco p53, OscarSierraGolf, Parsecboy, Pauly04, Pdfpdf, Peter Ellis, Prezbo, Pyrotec, Quasar G., R'n'B, R. A. Hicks, Rcbutcher, Rjwilmsi, RomanSpa, Rorschach, Russavia, Saberwyn, SchreiberBike, ScottDavis, Shem1805, Skyhawk805, SpookyMulder, Tabletop, Talon Artaine, The Bushranger, The Dart, Thiseye, Tim!, Tony1, Topbanana, Tpbradbury, Trappist the monk, Travyola, Trofflement, Ubersejanus, Viprile, WOSlinker, Wbm1058, Welsh, Widr, WolfgangFaber, Xdamr, Xezbeth, Xt828, Xyl 54, Ynhockey, 51 anonymous edits 161

Royal Australian Navy *Source:* https://en.wikipedia.org/w/index.php?oldid=852213594 *License:* Creative Commons Attribution-Share Alike 3.0 *Contributors:* 113727b, Abraham, B.S., Adamgerber80, Adnan bogi, Alpha3031, Anotherclown, Anthonyra3, AusTerrapin, AussieLegend, AustralianRupert, Bamyers99, BeastyCollin, Bender235, Bgwhite, BilCat, Boreas74, Breno, Callanecc, Ceannlann gorm, Chris the speller, ClueBot NG, Coekon, CommonsDelinker, Crownnino, DerbyCountyinNZ, Dewritech, Dfvj, Dl2000, DocWatson42, Dragnadh, Dunno2014, EditorDB, Editorjohn112, Ejointhehouse, FokkerTISM, Fry1989, Geo Swan, Giraffedata, Graham87, HaeB, Hammersfan, HandsomeFella, Hawkeye7, Hpeterswald, IVORK, IgnorantArmies, Illegitimate Barrister, Itschipino, Jacarandacounsel, Jennica, Jimdgo, Jprg1966, Kistara, KylieTastic, LordHello1, Lovetravel86, Malo95, Markab1975, MayerG, Melbguy05, MilborneOne, Mocky3497, Mogism, Moonraker, Muffin Wizard, Nford24, Nick Thorne, Nick-D, Ohconfucius, Optio1987, Oshwah, Padre1992, Pdfpdf, Pertuan, RAN Web Manager, Rawlangs, Refsmithy, Renzopiano2, Rye85, Saberwyn, Sammartinlai, Sean Clark, Siegfried Nugent, Snarbydog, Sodacan, Solarra, Steve92341, TGCP, Terrymwalsh, Thespaceninja3, Toothpickst, Trappist the monk, UnbiasedVictory, Valetude, Velella, Werddemer, Werieth, Wfh, Wiae, 125 anonymous edits 211

List of active Royal Australian Navy ships *Source:* https://en.wikipedia.org/w/index.php?oldid=848470556 *License:* Creative Commons Attribution-Share Alike 3.0 *Contributors:* 113727b, Aldis90, AlexanderFrancis, AllenYC, Anotherclown, Bromy2004, BrownHairedGirl, Camerong, Champchesse2.0, Chanakyathegreat, Chris j wood, Clare., Coolabahapple, DJGB, Dewritech, Dpaajones, Dunno2014, Epipelagic, Godanov, Gwg hitman, Hammersfan, Haus, Hossen27, Hpeterswald, Inane Imp, Ingolfson, Jez 14, Joshbaumgartner, Josve05a, Kisefau, Kistara, Leandrod, LordHello1, Materialscientist, Maverick007, Merno1976, Meticulo, Mft2000, Mogism, Morzs, Nachoman-au, Newm30, Nford24, Nick-D, Noclador, Nudge67, PDH, PKT, PalawanOz, PrimeHunter, Quadell, Randomdonate, Rb119, Redalert2fan, Saberwyn, Tempest717, The Bushranger, Timothy Titus, Zebde, □, 39 anonymous edits 229

History of the Royal Australian Air Force *Source:* https://en.wikipedia.org/w/index.php?oldid=825062763 *License:* Creative Commons Attribution-Share Alike 3.0 *Contributors:* Anotherclown, AustralianRupert, BD2412, Berichard, Betacommand, Buckshot06, Businessman332211, Charles Matthews, Chris the speller, Cla68, Cryptic, David McIlwain, Dl2000, Dolphin51, Equata32, Eugman, Garion96, Grant65, Greenshed, Hfricke, Hossen27, Hu, Ian Rose, JHunterJ, Kisefau, Lawrencema, Lexysexy, Longhair, Mahanga, MilborneOne, Mogism, Nick-D, Ohconfucius, Rich Farmbrough, Sanguinity, Sus scrofa, The Quixotic Potato, Tim!, Unbuttered Parsnip, Uriber, Vgy7ujm, Viprile, Wdixson, 8 anonymous edits 251

Royal Australian Air Force *Source:* https://en.wikipedia.org/w/index.php?oldid=852869248 *License:* Creative Commons Attribution-Share Alike 3.0 *Contributors:* ARA SANTA FE, Anotherclown, AusTempest, Ausfootball wiki, AustralianRupert, Awweccshon1, B.Velikov, BD2412, Bender235, BilCat, CAPTAIN RAJU, COOPERCR7LOL2, Ceannlann gorm, Cizek Martin, Clare., ClueBot NG, CommonsDelinker, Coolabahapple, Dan100, Dawnseeker2000, Desertferal, Dfadden, Divad500, Dolphin51, Donama, Drslrfrts, Dwo, FOX 52, Fry1989, Garuda28, Godanov, GraemeLeggett, Hammersfan, Hawkeye7, Hmains, Hpeterswald, Huy Victory, IO8ZSGIITI, IVORK, Ian Rose, Josephus37, Joshbaumgartner, Julien1978, Kbooth1102, LiamKasbar, LordHello1, Lucygoose199, Mai353, Markab1975, Markdukes21, Meticulo, MilborneOne, Mongoose Army, Muffin Wizard, MusikAnimal, Mustang137, Mztourist, NYBrook098, Necessary Evil, Newm30, NiD.29, Niceguyedc, Nick-D, Non-dropframe, Ochkev, Ohconfucius, Oshwah, Quercus solaris, Ramaksoud2000, Rcbutcher, Redalert2fan, RichardDG, Rickyrider35, Rsjep1, SamHolt6, ScoreHero, Sl3nderman3006, Smilenw84flash, Snarbydog, Soundofmusicals, Steelpillow, Stepat, TAnthony, The Bushranger, Theinstantmatrix, Thespaceninja3, Toby6250, Trappist the monk, Usernamekiran, Vgy7ujm, WOSlinker, Wargo, Zyxw, Zzaakkaa, 122 anonymous edits 260

Women in the Australian military *Source:* https://en.wikipedia.org/w/index.php?oldid=849347006 *License:* Creative Commons Attribution-Share Alike 3.0 *Contributors:* AnakngAraw, Byerw, ClueBot NG, Colin S, Colonies Chris, Courcelles, HandsomeFella, I dream of horses, Ian Rose, JaneSwifty, Kwamikagami, Mentifisto, Nick-D, Queenmomcat, Rich Farmbrough, ShipFan, Trappist the monk, VMS Mosaic, 14 anonymous edits 285

Sexual orientation and gender identity in the Australian military *Source:* https://en.wikipedia.org/w/index.php?oldid=851456641 *License:* Creative Commons Attribution-Share Alike 3.0 *Contributors:* Arado, B20097, Bewtiful, Callinus, Carbon Caryatid, Certes, Clare., Davidcannon, Goldcactus, JennyOz, Loopy30, Lor, Newsoas, Nick-D, RayneVanDunem, Rjensen, Terry Aulich, Viennese Waltz, Vincentunpack, 9 anonymous edits 293

Defence industry of Australia *Source:* https://en.wikipedia.org/w/index.php?oldid=852325768 *License:* Creative Commons Attribution-Share Alike 3.0 *Contributors:* Aeonx, Anotherclown, Nick-D 299

List of Australian military bases *Source:* https://en.wikipedia.org/w/index.php?oldid=839419062 *License:* Creative Commons Attribution-Share Alike 3.0 *Contributors:* 113727b, Adamdaley, Anotherclown, AusTerrapin, AustralianRupert, Berichard, Bidgee, Botiffity, Brenont, CAPTAIN RAJU, CarolGray, Chris j wood, ClueBot NG, Commking, DJGB, Dan 4RAR, Dan arndt, Dbenbenn, Epistemos, Flyer22 Reborn, FoCuSandLeArN, GPS73, Great republic of williamland, GreatWhiteNortherner, Hammersfan, Hossen27, Ian Rose, JBazza, JarrahTree, Jevansen, John Dalton, Josh Parris, Justinbrett, Longhair, Markhurd, Mitch Ames, Neelix, Newm30, Nick-D, Pdfpdf, Peter Ellis, Pkoz, Rangasyd, Rich Farmbrough, ScottDavis, Seamus733, Theslider09, TinTin, Williamlandgov, 58 anonymous edits 303

Image Sources, Licenses and Contributors

The sources listed for each image provide more detailed licensing information including the copyright status, the copyright owner, and the license conditions.

Image *Source:* https://en.wikipedia.org/w/index.php?title=File:Cscr-featured.svg *License:* GNU Lesser General Public License *Contributors:* Anomie ... 1

Figure 1 *Source:* https://en.wikipedia.org/w/index.php?title=File:HMAS_Melbourne_(R21)_and_USS_Midway_(CV-41)_underway,_16_May_1981_(6380752).jpg *License:* Public Domain *Contributors:* User:Felix Stember ... 4

Figure 2 *Source:* https://en.wikipedia.org/w/index.php?title=File:Kangaroo_89.jpg *License:* Public Domain *Contributors:* US gov ... 5

Figure 3 *Source:* https://en.wikipedia.org/w/index.php?title=File:Australian_C-130_H_being_unloaded_at_Tallil_Air_Base_in_April_2003.jpeg *License:* Public Domain *Contributors:* Bidgee, Ian Rose, Lineagegeek, Nick-D, Ruff tuff cream puff ... 6

Figure 4 *Source:* https://en.wikipedia.org/w/index.php?title=File:Five_ASLAVs_in_Afghanistan_during_March_2011.jpg *License:* Public Domain *Contributors:* U.S. Army photo by Spc. Edward A. Garibay, 16th Mobile Public Affairs Detachment ... 8

Figure 5 *Source:* https//en.wikipedia.org *License:* Public Domain *Contributors:* Nick-D ... 10

Figure 6 *Source:* https//en.wikipedia.org *Contributors:* Elisfkc, Nick-D ... 11

Figure 7 *Source:* https://en.wikipedia.org/w/index.php?title=File:Russell_Offices_in_November_2006.jpg *Contributors:* User:Nick-D ... 12

Figure 8 *Source:* https://en.wikipedia.org/w/index.php?title=File:Soldiers_with_a_LHD_Landing_Craft_in_May_2018.jpg *License:* Public Domain *Contributors:* Nick-D ... 13

Figure 9 *Source:* https://en.wikipedia.org/w/index.php?title=File:Australia_Land_Forces_2018.png *License:* Public Domain *Contributors:* User:Noclador ... 15

Figure 10 *Source:* https://en.wikipedia.org/w/index.php?title=File:CHC_Helicopter_S-76_helicopter_during_Exercise_Pitch_Black_in_August_2016.jpg *License:* Public Domain *Contributors:* Elisfkc, Nick-D ... 16

Figure 11 *Source:* https://en.wikipedia.org/w/index.php?title=File:A9-757_Lockheed_AP-3C_Orion_RAAF_(9687341571).jpg *Contributors:* Achim55, Articseahorse, Fæ, NiD.29, Rcbutcher, Russavia ... 18

Figure 12 *Source:* https://en.wikipedia.org/w/index.php?title=File:16th_Air_Defence_Regiment_soldiers_posing_with_RBS-70_July_2011.jpg *License:* Public Domain *Contributors:* U.S. Navy Petty Officer 1st Class Thomas E. Coffman ... 19

Figure 13 *Source:* https://en.wikipedia.org/w/index.php?title=File:Australian_Defence_Force_permanent_force_personnel_strengths_2002-03_to_2015-16.jpg *Contributors:* User:Nick-D ... 21

Figure 14 *Source:* https://en.wikipedia.org/w/index.php?title=File:5-6_RVR_ANZAC_Day_2008.JPG *License:* Public Domain *Contributors:* Paul Perrottet ... 22

Figure 15 *Source:* https://en.wikipedia.org/w/index.php?title=File:ADFA_Aerial.jpg *License:* Creative Commons Attribution-Sharealike 3.0 *Contributors:* A.schinzinger, King of Hearts, Rangasyd, VernoWhitney ... 23

Figure 16 *Source:* https://en.wikipedia.org/w/index.php?title=File:RAAF_airwoman_performing_preflight_checks_of_a_C-130.jpg *License:* Public Domain *Contributors:* U.S. Air Force Photo/Tech. Sgt. Jason W. Edwards ... 24

Figure 17 *Source:* https://en.wikipedia.org/w/index.php?title=File:RAAF_airman_constructing_a_Joint_Direct_Attack_Munition_in_February_2017.jpg *License:* Public Domain *Contributors:* Elisfkc, Nick-D ... 25

Figure 18 *Source:* https://en.wikipedia.org/w/index.php?title=File:Sydney_Mardi_Gras_2013_-_8522985059.jpg *License:* Creative Commons Attribution 2.0 *Contributors:* Bidgee, 1 anonymous edits ... 27

Figure 19 *Source:* https://en.wikipedia.org/w/index.php?title=File:HMAS_Canberra_arrives_at_Joint_Base_Pearl_Harbor-Hickam_for_RIMPAC_2016.jpg *Contributors:* Elisfkc, Nick-D ... 29

Figure 20 *Source:* https://en.wikipedia.org/w/index.php?title=File:Three_RAAF_FA-18_Hornets_in_flight_at_Red_Flag_2012.JPG *Contributors:* Avron, Bidgee, Nick-D ... 30

Figure 21 *Source:* https://en.wikipedia.org/w/index.php?title=File:HMAS_Kuttabul,_2007_(03).JPG *Contributors:* User:Bahnfrend ... 31

Figure 22 *Source:* https://en.wikipedia.org/w/index.php?title=File:HMAS_Albany_2010.jpg *License:* Creative Commons Attribution 2.0 *Contributors:* kenhodge13 ... 33

Figure 23 *Source:* https://en.wikipedia.org/w/index.php?title=File:RAF_RAAF_USAF_C-17s_2007.jpg *License:* Public Domain *Contributors:* U.S. Air Force photo by Master Sgt. Wendy Weidenhamer ... 35

Figure 24 *Source:* https//en.wikipedia.org *Contributors:* Beko, Melbguy05, SantiLak, Sajaleer, 木の枝 ... 36

Image *Source:* https://en.wikipedia.org/w/index.php?title=File:Commons-logo.svg *License:* logo *Contributors:* Anomie, Callanecc, CambridgeBayWeather, Jo-Jo Eumerus, RHaworth ... 41

Image *Source:* https://en.wikipedia.org/w/index.php?title=File:Symbol_support_vote.svg *License:* Public Domain *Contributors:* Anomie, Fastily, Jo-Jo Eumerus ... 43

Image *Source:* https://en.wikipedia.org/w/index.php?title=File:Coat_of_Arms_of_Australia.svg *License:* Creative Commons Attribution-Sharealike 3.0 *Contributors:* Erlenmeyer, Gunnex, JotaCartas, Jürgen Krause, Sarang, Sodacan, 星際漫遊, 2 anonymous edits ... 43

Image *Source:* https://en.wikipedia.org/w/index.php?title=File:Flag_of_Australia.svg *License:* Public Domain *Contributors:* Anomie, Jo-Jo Eumerus, Mifter ... 44

Figure 25 *Source:* https://en.wikipedia.org/w/index.php?title=File:AWM_canberra_1.jpg *License:* Creative Commons Attribution-Sharealike 3.0 *Contributors:* Capital photographer (talk) ... 45

Figure 26 *Source:* https://en.wikipedia.org/w/index.php?title=File:Battle_of_VinegarHill.jpg *License:* Public Domain *Contributors:* Acad Ronin, Gareth, HappyWaldo, Rangasyd, Zhuyifei1999, 1 anonymous edits ... 47

Figure 27 *Source:* https://en.wikipedia.org/w/index.php?title=File:Gov_Davey's_proclamation-edit2.jpg *Contributors:* Government of Van Diemen's Land, original conception by Surveyor General George Frankland (edited from original scan by ... 48

Figure 28 *Source:* https://en.wikipedia.org/w/index.php?title=File:Mounted_police_and_blacks.jpg *License:* Public Domain *Contributors:* W.Walton after Louisa and Godfrey Charles Mundy ... 50

Figure 29 *Source:* https://en.wikipedia.org/w/index.php?title=File:HMCSS_Victoria_300060.jpg *License:* Public Domain *Contributors:* 293.xx.xxx.xx, BotMultichill, Docu, Finavon, Ghouston, Mattinbgn, McZusatz, Metilsteiner, Notnarayan, Rcbutcher, Saberwyn, Stunteltje ... 51

Figure 30 *Source:* https://en.wikipedia.org/w/index.php?title=File:Hobart_Town_Volunteer_Artillery_members_1869.jpg *Contributors:* photographer not identified ... 52

Figure 31 *Source:* https://en.wikipedia.org/w/index.php?title=File:Avernus_(AWM_306823).jpg *License:* Public Domain *Contributors:* photographer not identified ... 53

Figure 32 *Source:* https://en.wikipedia.org/w/index.php?title=File:Departure_of_NSW_Contingent_Sydeny_1885_(ART19713).jpg *License:* Public Domain *Contributors:* Breckmann Brothers, London. ... 54

Figure 33 *Source:* https://en.wikipedia.org/w/index.php?title=File:Australians_and_New_Zealanders_at_Klerksdorp_24_March_1901_by_Charles_Hammond.jpg *License:* Public Domain *Contributors:* Charles Hammond ... 56

Figure 34 *Source:* https://en.wikipedia.org/w/index.php?title=File:ACH_South_Africa_1902.jpg *Contributors:* photographer not identified ... 57

Figure 35 *Source:* https://en.wikipedia.org/w/index.php?title=File:Protector_crew.jpg *License:* Public Domain *Contributors:* photographer not identified ... 59

Figure 36 *Source:* https://en.wikipedia.org/w/index.php?title=File:HMAS_Australia_Sydney_Oct_1913.jpg *Contributors:* photographer not identified. ... 61

Figure 37 *Source:* https://en.wikipedia.org/w/index.php?title=File:Trumpetcallsa.jpg *License:* Public Domain *Contributors:* . Printed by William GullickW.A. Gullick, government printer ... 62

Figure 38 *Source:* https://en.wikipedia.org/w/index.php?title=File:Anzac_Beach_4th_Bn_landing_8am_April_25_1915.jpg *License:* Public Domain *Contributors:* Photographer: L-Cpl. Arthur Robert Henry Joyner (1st Division Signal Company, killed 5 December 1916 at Bazentin, Somme) ... 64

Figure 39 *Source:* https://en.wikipedia.org/w/index.php?title=File:4th_Light_Horse_Brigade_Beersheba.jpg *License:* Public Domain *Contributors:* 1989, AustralianRupert, Docu, Eman, Gsl~commonswiki, Rcbutcher, 1 anonymous edits ... 65

Figure 40 *Source:* https://en.wikipedia.org/w/index.php?title=File:Chateauwood.jpg *Contributors:* Frank Hurley ... 67

Figure 41 *Source:* https://en.wikipedia.org/w/index.php?title=File:Battle_of_the_hindenburg_line.jpg *License:* Public Domain *Contributors:* Athaenara, J'adore, Jcb, Mtsmallwood, Nick-D, OgreBot 2, Rcbutcher ... 68

Figure 42 *Source:* https://en.wikipedia.org/w/index.php?title=File:Aussies_in_Russia_(AWM_A04697).jpg *Contributors:* photographer not identified ... 70

Figure 43 *Source:* https://en.wikipedia.org/w/index.php?title=File:HMAS_Sydney_(AWM_301473)_cropped.jpg *License:* Public Domain *Contributors:* HMAS_Sydney_(AWM_301473).jpg: Fox photos derivative work: Bellhalla (talk) ... 72

Figure 44 *Source:* https://en.wikipedia.org/w/index.php?title=File:AustraliansAtTobruk.jpg *License:* Public Domain *Contributors:* Smith, N (Lt), No 1 Army Film & Photographic Unit ... 73

Figure 45 *Source:* https://en.wikipedia.org/w/index.php?title=File:460_Sqn_(AWM_044167).jpg *License:* Public Domain *Contributors:* photographer not identified ... 74
Figure 46 *Source:* https://en.wikipedia.org/w/index.php?title=File:Darwin_42.jpg *License:* Public Domain *Contributors:* RAN Historical Collection 74
Figure 47 *Source:* https://en.wikipedia.org/w/index.php?title=File:Buna_(AWM_014008).jpg *Contributors:* - ... 76
Figure 48 *Source:* https://en.wikipedia.org/w/index.php?title=File:Boomerangs_Bougainville_OG2064.jpg *License:* Public Domain *Contributors:* John Thomas Harrison ... 77
Figure 49 *Source:* https//en.wikipedia.org *License:* Public Domain *Contributors:* General MacArthur's Tokyo headquarters ... 78
Figure 50 *Source:* https://en.wikipedia.org/w/index.php?title=File:3_RAR_Korea_(AWM_P01813-449).jpg *License:* Public Domain *Contributors:* Robertson, Ian ... 80
Figure 51 *Source:* https://en.wikipedia.org/w/index.php?title=File:Sydney_Korea_(AWM_044274).jpg *License:* Public Domain *Contributors:* 293.xx.xxx.xx, BotMultichill, Docu, Felix Stember, File Upload Bot (Magnus Manske), Keraunoscopia, McZusatz, OgreBot 2, Rcbutcher, Sisyphos23 81
Figure 52 *Source:* https://en.wikipedia.org/w/index.php?title=File:RAAFAvroLincolnMalaya1950.jpg *Contributors:* Australian Government .. 83
Figure 53 *Source:* https://en.wikipedia.org/w/index.php?title=File:HMAS_Perth_(D_38)_fires_on_North_Vietnamese_coastal_defense_sites_in_February_1968.jpg *License:* Public Domain *Contributors:* U.S. Navy ... 84
Figure 54 *Source:* https://en.wikipedia.org/w/index.php?title=File:Australian_soldier_Borneo.jpg *License:* Creative Commons Attribution-Sharealike 2.0 *Contributors:* Steve Swayne from Maleny, Australia ... 85
Figure 55 *Source:* https://en.wikipedia.org/w/index.php?title=File:RAAF_UH1_1964.jpg *License:* Creative Commons Attribution-Sharealike 2.0 *Contributors:* Steve Swayne from Maleny, Australia ... 86
Figure 56 *Source:* https://en.wikipedia.org/w/index.php?title=File:7_RAR_Vietnam_(AWM_EKN-67-0130-VN).jpg *Contributors:* 293.xx.xxx.xx, Durin, Hawkeye7, Keraunoscopia, Nick-D, Ronhjones, ShakespeareFan00, Skier Dude ... 87
Figure 57 *Source:* https://en.wikipedia.org/w/index.php?title=File:RAAF_TFV_(HD-SN-99-02052).jpg *License:* Public Domain *Contributors:* Amada44, AnRo0002, BrokenSphere, J 1982, MECU, Mattes, Nick-D, OgreBot 2, RP88, Verdy p, 2 anonymous edits ... 89
Figure 58 *Source:* https://en.wikipedia.org/w/index.php?title=File:Russell_Offices.JPG *License:* GNU Free Documentation License *Contributors:* BotMultichill, Docu, File Upload Bot (Magnus Manske), Gareth, MGA73bot2, Nick-D, OgreBot 2, Rangasyd ... 90
Figure 59 *Source:* https://en.wikipedia.org/w/index.php?title=File:HMAS_Sydney_1991.jpg *License:* Public Domain *Contributors:* KTo288, Pibwl, Roo72, Tony Wills ... 92
Figure 60 *Source:* https://en.wikipedia.org/w/index.php?title=File:INTERFET_12_Feb_2000.jpg *License:* Public Domain *Contributors:* PH3 Dan Mennuto ... 94
Figure 61 *Source:* https://en.wikipedia.org/w/index.php?title=File:3RAR_Afghanistan_2008.jpg *License:* Public Domain *Contributors:* Petty Officer 1st Class John Collins ... 96
Figure 62 *Source:* https://en.wikipedia.org/w/index.php?title=File:An_ASLAV_in_a_defensive_position_in_Afghanistan_during_2010.jpg *License:* Public Domain *Contributors:* Illegitimate Barrister, Nick-D ... 97
Figure 63 *Source:* https://en.wikipedia.org/w/index.php?title=File:Cavalry_scout_Iraq.jpg *License:* Public Domain *Contributors:* US Army photo/Spc. Robert H. Baumgartner ... 98
Figure 64 *Source:* https://en.wikipedia.org/w/index.php?title=File:A21-36_taking_off_for_a_mission_over_Iraq_during_Operation_Okra.jpg *License:* Public Domain *Contributors:* Nick-D, Themightyquill ... 99
Figure 65 *Source:* https://en.wikipedia.org/w/index.php?title=File:Australian_Peacekeeping.PNG *License:* Public Domain *Contributors:* Nick Dowling ... 100
Figure 66 *Source:* https://en.wikipedia.org/w/index.php?title=File:Boer_War_officers_P03206.001.jpg *License:* Public Domain *Contributors:* User:Rcbutcher ... 110
Figure 67 *Source:* https://en.wikipedia.org/w/index.php?title=File:Trumpetcallsa.jpg *License:* Public Domain *Contributors:* . Printed by William GullickW.A. Gullick, government printer ... 113
Figure 68 *Source:* https://en.wikipedia.org/w/index.php?title=File:Anzac_Beach_4th_Bn_landing_8am_April_25_1915.jpg *License:* Public Domain *Contributors:* Photographer: L-Cpl. Arthur Robert Henry Joyner (1st Division Signal Company, killed 5 December 1916 at Bazentin, Somme) 114
Figure 69 *Source:* https://en.wikipedia.org/w/index.php?title=File:5th_Pioneer_reinforcements_Melbourne_(AWM_image_PB0058).jpg *License:* Public Domain *Contributors:* Barnes, Josiah ... 115
Figure 70 *Source:* https://en.wikipedia.org/w/index.php?title=File:9_Div_Tobruk(AWM_020779).jpg *License:* Public Domain *Contributors:* Not stated at source ... 117
Figure 71 *Source:* https://en.wikipedia.org/w/index.php?title=File:Kaiapit_flags_057510.jpg *License:* Public Domain *Contributors:* Stuckey, Norman Bradford ... 118
Figure 72 *Source:* https://en.wikipedia.org/w/index.php?title=File:37-52_Battalion_soldiers_crossing_a_river_in_New_Britain.jpg *License:* Public Domain *Contributors:* M.B. Rogers ... 119
Figure 73 *Source:* https://en.wikipedia.org/w/index.php?title=File:3RAR_village_(AWM_146980).jpg *License:* Public Domain *Contributors:* 293.xx.xxx.xx, Benchill, BotMultichill, Diannaa, Docu, File Upload Bot (Magnus Manske), Jesper7, Keraunoscopia, MGA73bot2, OgreBot 2, Rcbutcher 121
Figure 74 *Source:* https://en.wikipedia.org/w/index.php?title=File:Troops_of_Royal_Australian_Regiment_After_Arrival_at_Tan_Son_Nhut_Airport.jpg *License:* Public Domain *Contributors:* US military personnel ... 123
Figure 75 *Source:* https://en.wikipedia.org/w/index.php?title=File:C5_Namibia.jpg *License:* Public Domain *Contributors:* Master Sergeant Jose Lopez Jr. ... 124
Figure 76 *Source:* https://en.wikipedia.org/w/index.php?title=File:Op_Solace_DN-ST-93-02615.jpg *License:* Public Domain *Contributors:* BotMultichill, Darz Mol～commonswiki, File Upload Bot (Magnus Manske), Innotata, KTo288, Martin H., OgreBot 2, Quake44, 木の枝, 1 anonymous edits 126
Figure 77 *Source:* https://en.wikipedia.org/w/index.php?title=File:East_timor_independence_un2.jpg *License:* Creative Commons Attribution 3.0 *Contributors:* Geoffrey C. Gunn ... 127
Image *Source:* https://en.wikipedia.org/w/index.php?title=File:Australian_Army_Emblem_Transparent.png *License:* Public Domain *Contributors:* Australian_Army_Emblem.JPG: Ruob derivative work: Aeonx (talk) ... 130
Image *Source:* https://en.wikipedia.org/w/index.php?title=File:Flag_of_Australia_(converted).svg *License:* Public Domain *Contributors:* Unknown (Vector graphics image by Ian Fieggen) (only minor code changes by uploader.) ... 131
Image *Source:* https://en.wikipedia.org/w/index.php?title=File:Roundel_of_Australia_-_Army_Aviation.svg *License:* Creative Commons Attribution-Sharealike 3.0 *Contributors:* User:Fry1989 ... 131
Image *Source:* https://en.wikipedia.org/w/index.php?title=File:Roundel_of_the_Australian_Army.svg *License:* Creative Commons Attribution-Sharealike 3.0 *Contributors:* User:Fry1989 ... 131
Figure 78 *Source:* https://en.wikipedia.org/w/index.php?title=File:Australian_39th_Battalion_after_the_Kokoda_Track_campaign_1942_(AWM_013289).jpg *License:* Public Domain *Contributors:* Parer, Damien Peter ... 132
Figure 79 *Source:* https://en.wikipedia.org/w/index.php?title=File:Australian_SOTG_sniper_team_June_2010.jpg *License:* Creative Commons Attribution 2.0 *Contributors:* NATO International Security Assistance Force Public Affairs Photo Courtesy Corporal Raymond Vance 1st Joint Public Affai 132
Figure 80 *Source:* https://en.wikipedia.org/w/index.php?title=File:Cavalry_scout_Iraq.jpg *License:* Public Domain *Contributors:* US Army photo/Spc. Robert H. Baumgartner ... 133
Figure 81 *Source:* https://en.wikipedia.org/w/index.php?title=File:Australia_Land_Forces_2018.png *Contributors:* User:Noclador ... 133
Figure 82 *Source:* https://en.wikipedia.org/w/index.php?title=File:Machine_gun_team_from_1_RAR_during_RIMPAC_2012.JPG *License:* Public Domain *Contributors:* Nick-D, Quake44 ... 134
Figure 83 *Source:* https://en.wikipedia.org/w/index.php?title=File:1st_Commando_Regiment_soldier_jumping_out_of_an_Australian_Army_blackhawk_helicopter_in_2013.jpg *License:* Public Domain *Contributors:* Anotherclown, Chesipiero, De728631, Nick-D ... 135
Figure 84 *Source:* https://en.wikipedia.org/w/index.php?title=File:Australian_SOTG_patrol_Oct_2009.jpg *License:* Creative Commons Attribution 2.0 *Contributors:* NATO International Security Assistance Force Public Affairs Photo Courtesy Leading Seaman Paul Berry 1st Joint Public Af 136
Figure 85 *Source:* https://en.wikipedia.org/w/index.php?title=File:Australian_SOTG_wait_for_extraction_2011.jpg *License:* Creative Commons Attribution 2.0 *Contributors:* ISAF Headquarters Public Affairs Office from Kabul, Afghanistan ... 141
Figure 86 *Source:* https://en.wikipedia.org/w/index.php?title=File:Australian_Army_Abrams_tanks_during_Exercise_Koolendong_at_Bradshaw_Training_Area,_Aug_21,_2014.jpg *License:* Public Domain *Contributors:* Avron, Nick-D ... 141
Figure 87 *Source:* https://en.wikipedia.org/w/index.php?title=File:Australian_and_US_Army_helicopter_medical_rescue_exercise_in_2011_110712-M-PM709-051.jpg *License:* Public Domain *Contributors:* De728631, Fæ, Lotje, Nick-D, SantiLak, Tokorokoko ... 142
Figure 88 *Source:* https://en.wikipedia.org/w/index.php?title=File:Australian_Army_(A40-003)_NHI_MRH-90_arriving_at_Wagga_Wagga_Airport.jpg *Contributors:* Bidgee ... 142
Figure 89 *Source:* https//en.wikipedia.org *Contributors:* Bidgee ... 142
Image *Source:* https://en.wikipedia.org/w/index.php?title=File:Exercise_Gold_Eagle_smooth_ride_for_Aussie,_Marine_tanks_130914-M-AL626-0138.jpg *License:* Public Domain *Contributors:* Fæ, 木の枝 ... 146

Image *Source:* https://en.wikipedia.org/w/index.php?title=File:Flag_of_the_United_States.svg *License:* Public Domain *Contributors:* Anomie, Jo-Jo Eumerus, MSGJ, Mr. Stradivarius 146
Image *Source:* https://en.wikipedia.org/w/index.php?title=File:ASLAV_in_Afghanistan_2011.jpg *License:* Public Domain *Contributors:* U.S. Army photo by Spc. Edward A. Garibay, 16th Mobile Public Affairs 146
Image *Source:* https://en.wikipedia.org/w/index.php?title=File:Flag_of_Canada.svg *License:* Public Domain *Contributors:* Anomie, Jo-Jo Eumerus 146
Image *Source:* https://en.wikipedia.org/w/index.php?title=File:Side_view_of_a_M113AS4_at_the_2015_ADFA_open_day.jpg *Contributors:* User:Nick-D 147
Image *Source:* https://en.wikipedia.org/w/index.php?title=File:Boxer_Land_400.jpg *Contributors:* User:Teamlang 147
Image *Source:* https://en.wikipedia.org/w/index.php?title=File:Flag_of_Germany.svg *License:* Public Domain *Contributors:* Anomie, Jo-Jo Eumerus 147
Image *Source:* https://en.wikipedia.org/w/index.php?title=File:Flag_of_the_Netherlands.svg *License:* Public Domain *Contributors:* Zscout370 147
Image *Source:* https://en.wikipedia.org/w/index.php?title=File:Bushmaster_at_the_2016_ADFA_Open_Day.jpg *Contributors:* User:Nick-D .. 147
Image *Source:* https://en.wikipedia.org/w/index.php?title=File:Hawkei_DSC02320.JPG *License:* Creative Commons Attribution-Share Alike *Contributors:* User:Pibwl 147
Image *Source:* https://en.wikipedia.org/w/index.php?title=File:Flag_of_the_United_Kingdom.svg *License:* Public Domain *Contributors:* Anomie, Good Olfactory, Jo-Jo Eumerus, MSGJ, Mifter 147
Image *Source:* https://en.wikipedia.org/w/index.php?title=File:Bundeswehr_MB_Wolf.jpg *License:* Creative Commons Attribution-Sharealike 2.5 *Contributors:* user:Darkone 148
Image *Source:* https://en.wikipedia.org/w/index.php?title=File:45M_28_Camo.jpg *Contributors:* Arado, Jianhui67, Mattes, UndateableOne ... 148
Image *Source:* https://en.wikipedia.org/w/index.php?title=File:Extenda.jpg *Contributors:* Brakeet, De728631, HantsAV, Storkk, UndateableOne, Yann, 木の枝 148
Image *Source:* https://en.wikipedia.org/w/index.php?title=File:Australian_Army_LARC-V_in_2013.jpg *License:* Public Domain *Contributors:* Nick-D, OgreBot 2 149
Image *Source:* https://en.wikipedia.org/w/index.php?title=File:Aust._Army_LCM-8.jpg *License:* Creative Commons Attribution 3.0 *Contributors:* Angra (talk) 149
Image *Source:* https://en.wikipedia.org/w/index.php?title=File:Australian_soldiers_from_the_8-12_Field_Regiment_firing_a_M777_155mm_howitzer.jpg *License:* Public Domain *Contributors:* Nick-D 149
Image *Source:* https://en.wikipedia.org/w/index.php?title=File:16th_Air_Defence_Regiment_soldiers_with_RBS-70_July_2011.jpg *License:* Public Domain *Contributors:* U.S. Navy Petty Officer 1st Class Thomas E. Coffman 149
Image *Source:* https://en.wikipedia.org/w/index.php?title=File:Flag_of_Sweden.svg *License:* Public Domain *Contributors:* Anomie, Jo-Jo Eumerus, Mr. Stradivarius 149
Image *Source:* https://en.wikipedia.org/w/index.php?title=File:NASAMS_II_E.T..JPG *License:* Creative Commons Attribution-Sharealike 3.0 *Contributors:* Outisnn 150
Image *Source:* https://en.wikipedia.org/w/index.php?title=File:Flag_of_Norway.svg *License:* Public Domain *Contributors:* Dbenbenn 150
Image *Source:* https://en.wikipedia.org/w/index.php?title=File:Flag_of_France.svg *License:* Public Domain *Contributors:* Anomie, Fastily, Jo-Jo Eumerus 150
Image *Source:* https://en.wikipedia.org/w/index.php?title=File:Flag_of_Austria.svg *License:* Public Domain *Contributors:* User:SKopp 151
Image *Source:* https://en.wikipedia.org/w/index.php?title=File:Tactical_Live_Fire_Demonstration_during_RIMPAC_2014_140729-M-QH615-107.jpg *License:* Public Domain *Contributors:* Fæ, Nick-D, Sanandros, 木の枝 151
Image *Source:* https://en.wikipedia.org/w/index.php?title=File:PEO_M4_Carbine_RAS_M68_CCO.jpg *License:* Public Domain *Contributors:* Photo Courtesy of PEO Soldier 151
Image *Source:* https://en.wikipedia.org/w/index.php?title=File:HK416.jpg *License:* Creative Commons Attribution-Sharealike 2.0 *Contributors:* Dybdal. 151
Image *Source:* https://en.wikipedia.org/w/index.php?title=File:Flag_of_Belgium_(civil).svg *License:* Public Domain *Contributors:* Allforrous, Andres gb.ldc, Bean49, Cathy Richards, David Descamps, Dbenbenn, Denelson83, Evanc0912, FreshCorp619, Fry1989, Gabriel trzy, Howcome, IvanOS, Jdx, Mimich, Ms2ger, Nightstallion, Oreo Priest, Pitke, Ricordisamoa, Rocket000, Rodejong, Sarang, SiBr4, Sir Iain, ThomasPusch, Warddr, Zscout370, 15 anonymous edits 151
Image *Source:* https://en.wikipedia.org/w/index.php?title=File:SLRL1A1.jpg *License:* Public Domain *Contributors:* Jan Hrdonka 151
Image *Source:* https://en.wikipedia.org/w/index.php?title=File:USMC-110507-M-JG138-004.jpg *License:* Public Domain *Contributors:* OgreBot 2, Reguyla, Sanandros, 木の枝 152
Image *Source:* https://en.wikipedia.org/w/index.php?title=File:AW50.png *License:* Creative Commons Attribution-Sharealike 3.0 *Contributors:* Pjedvaj 152
Image *Source:* https://en.wikipedia.org/w/index.php?title=File:Blaser_R93_LRS2_.308_Win_4thNovSniperCompetition06.jpg *Contributors:* User:VitalyKuzmin 152
Image *Source:* https://en.wikipedia.org/w/index.php?title=File:SR-25_pic02.jpg *License:* Creative Commons Attribution 2.0 *Contributors:* User:MathKnight 152
Image *Source:* https://en.wikipedia.org/w/index.php?title=File:PEO_M14_EBR.jpg *License:* Public Domain *Contributors:* Photo Courtesy of PEO Soldier 153
Image *Source:* https://en.wikipedia.org/w/index.php?title=File:Barrett-M82A1-Independence-Day-2017-IZE-048-white.jpg *Contributors:* User:MathKnight 153
Image *Source:* https://en.wikipedia.org/w/index.php?title=File:An_Australian_soldier_with_a_F89_light_machine_gun_in_2010.jpg *License:* Public Domain *Contributors:* Nick-D 153
Image *Source:* https://en.wikipedia.org/w/index.php?title=File:FN_MINIMI_Standard_Right.jpg *License:* Creative Commons Attribution 2.0 *Contributors:* FN Herstal 153
Image *Source:* https://en.wikipedia.org/w/index.php?title=File:Australian_Army_soldier_armed_with_a_FN_MAG_machine_gun_in_Afghanistan_during_2010_-_cropped.jpg *License:* Public Domain *Contributors:* Nick-D 153
Image *Source:* https://en.wikipedia.org/w/index.php?title=File:IDF-M2-Browning-v01-by-Zachi-Evenor.jpg *License:* Creative Commons Attribution 2.0 *Contributors:* FlickreviewR 2, Havang(nl), MathKnight 153
Image *Source:* https://en.wikipedia.org/w/index.php?title=File:Browning_High-Power_9mm_IMG_1526.jpg *License:* Creative Commons Attribution-Sharealike 2.0 *Contributors:* Rama 153
Image *Source:* https://en.wikipedia.org/w/index.php?title=File:HKUSP.png *Contributors:* Dybdal / Miroslav Pragl 153
Image *Source:* https://en.wikipedia.org/w/index.php?title=File:MP5.jpg *Contributors:* Dybdal / Mattes 154
Image *Source:* https://en.wikipedia.org/w/index.php?title=File:Remington_M870_12_Gauge.jpg *License:* Public Domain *Contributors:* Felix Stember, KOKUYO, Leyo, 1 anonymous edits 154
Image *Source:* https://en.wikipedia.org/w/index.php?title=File:Australian_soldiers_Afghanistan_March2010.jpg *License:* Creative Commons Attribution 2.0 *Contributors:* ISAF Headquarters Public Affairs Office from Kabul, Afghanistan 154
Image *Source:* https://en.wikipedia.org/w/index.php?title=File:MK19-02.jpg *License:* Public Domain *Contributors:* BotMultichill, BotMultichillT, Nemo5576 154
Image *Source:* https://en.wikipedia.org/w/index.php?title=File:MK47.jpg *Contributors:* User:Zajje 154
Image *Source:* https://en.wikipedia.org/w/index.php?title=File:M72A2_LAW.png *License:* Creative Commons Zero *Contributors:* User:ZiaLater 155
Image *Source:* https://en.wikipedia.org/w/index.php?title=File:M3E1.jpg *Contributors:* Signaleer, 木の枝 155
Image *Source:* https://en.wikipedia.org/w/index.php?title=File:FGM-148_Javelin_(5160721562).jpg *License:* Creative Commons Attribution 2.0 *Contributors:* U.S. Army Alaska (USARAK) from Anchorage, Alaska, U.S. 155
Image *Source:* https://en.wikipedia.org/w/index.php?title=File:81mmMORT_L16.png *License:* Creative Commons Attribution-Sharealike 3.0,2.5,2.0,1.0 *Contributors:* Hisamikabunomura (talk)Hisamikabunomura 155
Image *Source:* https://en.wikipedia.org/w/index.php?title=File:Australian_Army_soldiers_throw_a_grenade_RIMPAC_Exercise_2014.JPG *License:* Public Domain *Contributors:* Nick-D 155
Image *Source:* https://en.wikipedia.org/w/index.php?title=File:US_M18a1_claymore_mine.jpg *License:* Public Domain *Contributors:* Avron, Harald Hansen, 1 anonymous edits 155
Image *Source:* https://en.wikipedia.org/w/index.php?title=File:Bayonet-Knife_M9_w_Scabbard.jpg *License:* Public Domain *Contributors:* ~Shotgun 156
Figure 90 *Source:* https//en.wikipedia.org *License:* Public Domain *Contributors:* Fæ, Illegitimate Barrister, Nick-D, OgreBot 2 157
Figure 91 *Source:* https://en.wikipedia.org/w/index.php?title=File:HMAS_Australia_launching_aircraft_1918.jpg *License:* Public Domain *Contributors:* Associated News Agency 162
Figure 92 *Source:* https://en.wikipedia.org/w/index.php?title=File:HMAS_Australia_(D84)_passing_through_the_Panama_Canal_in_March_1935.jpg *License:* Public Domain *Contributors:* U.S. Navy 163

Figure 93 *Source:* https://en.wikipedia.org/w/index.php?title=File:HMAS_Melbourne_(R21)_San_Diego_1977.jpeg *License:* Public Domain *Contributors:* U.S. Navy ... 163
Figure 94 *Source:* https://en.wikipedia.org/w/index.php?title=File:Paluma_(AWM_300024).jpg *License:* Public Domain *Contributors:* photographer not identified ... 164
Figure 95 *Source:* https://en.wikipedia.org/w/index.php?title=File:RAN_fleet_review.jpg *Contributors:* photographer not identified. ... 166
Figure 96 *Source:* https://en.wikipedia.org/w/index.php?title=File:Wrecked_SMS_Emden.jpg *License:* Public Domain *Contributors:* photographer not identified. Australian forces. ... 168
Figure 97 *Source:* https://en.wikipedia.org/w/index.php?title=File:Aust_fleet_Rabaul_(AWM_J03326).jpg *License:* Public Domain *Contributors:* photographer not identified ... 168
Figure 98 *Source:* https://en.wikipedia.org/w/index.php?title=File:HMAS_Pioneer_(AWM_P01585009).jpg *License:* Public Domain *Contributors:* 293.xx.xxx.xx, Andy king50, Blue Elf, BotMultichill, Docu, File Upload Bot (Magnus Manske), OgreBot 2, Rcbutcher, Revent ... 170
Figure 99 *Source:* https://en.wikipedia.org/w/index.php?title=File:HMAS_Encounter.jpg *License:* Public Domain *Contributors:* photographer not identified ... 172
Figure 100 *Source:* https://en.wikipedia.org/w/index.php?title=File:HMAS_Australia_sinking_12_April_1924_AWM_300256.jpeg *Contributors:* Carlton Photo, Sydney ... 173
Figure 101 *Source:* https://en.wikipedia.org/w/index.php?title=File:HMAS_Canberra_sailing_into_Sydney_Harbour_in_1930.jpg *Contributors:* photographer not identified ... 175
Figure 102 *Source:* https://en.wikipedia.org/w/index.php?title=File:RNBartolomeo_Colleoni-Capo_Spada.jpg *License:* Public Domain *Contributors:* User:Berichard ... 178
Figure 103 *Source:* https://en.wikipedia.org/w/index.php?title=File:Sydney_battle_damage.jpg *Contributors:* Not specified ... 179
Figure 104 *Source:* https://en.wikipedia.org/w/index.php?title=File:HMAS_Waterhen_(AWM_044789).jpg *Contributors:* photographer not identified ... 181
Figure 105 *Source:* https://en.wikipedia.org/w/index.php?title=File:HMAS_Sydney_memorial_01_gnangarra.jpg *Contributors:* Gnangarra .. 182
Figure 106 *Source:* https://en.wikipedia.org/w/index.php?title=File:RAN_Sailors_(AWM_P00001-418).jpg *Contributors:* RNZAF OFFICIAL PHOTOGRAPH ... 183
Figure 107 *Source:* https://en.wikipedia.org/w/index.php?title=File:Ko-hyoteki_Sydney.jpg *License:* Public Domain *Contributors:* Keam, Ronald Noel ... 185
Figure 108 *Source:* https://en.wikipedia.org/w/index.php?title=File:Sinking_HMAS_Canberra_(D33)_with_US_destroyers_on_9_August_1942.jpg *License:* Public Domain *Contributors:* U.S. Navy ... 186
Figure 109 *Source:* https://en.wikipedia.org/w/index.php?title=File:Torpedo_damage_of_HMAS_Hobart_(D63)_at_Espiritu_Santo_on_23_July_1943.jpg *License:* Public Domain *Contributors:* Bidgee, Cobatfor, D.W., Docu, Finavon, Jochen Burghardt, Methem, Nevfennas, Pibwl, Rcbutcher, Schekinov Alexey Victorovich ... 187
Figure 110 *Source:* https://en.wikipedia.org/w/index.php?title=File:AWM019422_Yokosuka.jpg *License:* Public Domain *Contributors:* Catsmeat, Common Good, Docu, MGA73bot2, Nick-D, OgreBot 2, Rcbutcher, Schekinov Alexey Victorovich, Tonkawa68, あばさー ... 189
Figure 111 *Source:* https://en.wikipedia.org/w/index.php?title=File:New_management_(AWM_019164).jpg *License:* Public Domain *Contributors:* 293.xx.xxx.xx, Athaenara, BotMultichill, Docu, File Upload Bot (Magnus Manske), KTo288, McZusatz, OgreBot 2, Sisyphos23 ... 190
Figure 112 *Source:* https://en.wikipedia.org/w/index.php?title=File:Sydney_Korea_(AWM_044274).jpg *License:* Public Domain *Contributors:* 293.xx.xxx.xx, BotMultichill, Docu, Felix Stember, File Upload Bot (Magnus Manske), Keraunoscopia, McZusatz, OgreBot 2, Rcbutcher, Sisyphos23 191
Figure 113 *Source:* https://en.wikipedia.org/w/index.php?title=File:RAN_Carriers_(AWM_301021).jpg *License:* Public Domain *Contributors:* 293.xx.xxx.xx, Athaenara, BotMultichill, Docu, Felix Stember, File Upload Bot (Magnus Manske), KTo288, Keraunoscopia, McZusatz, OgreBot 2, Rcbutcher ... 192
Figure 114 *Source:* https://en.wikipedia.org/w/index.php?title=File:HMAS_Melbourne_(R21)_with_destroyers_c1962.jpg *License:* Public Domain *Contributors:* USN ... 194
Figure 115 *Source:* https://en.wikipedia.org/w/index.php?title=File:USS_Guadalupe_(AO-32)_refuels_HMAS_Hobart_(D39)_off_Vietnam_in_1967.jpg *License:* Public Domain *Contributors:* Eric Bollin, USN ... 196
Figure 116 *Source:* https://en.wikipedia.org/w/index.php?title=File:Melbourne-S2G-launch.jpg *License:* Creative Commons Attribution 3.0 *Contributors:* Nick Thorne ... 199
Figure 117 *Source:* https://en.wikipedia.org/w/index.php?title=File:Canberra_Success.jpg *License:* Public Domain *Contributors:* BotMultichill, File Upload Bot (Magnus Manske), KTo288, NeverDoING, OgreBot 2 ... 200
Figure 118 *Source:* https://en.wikipedia.org/w/index.php?title=File:US_Aust_UK_warships_Dec_02.jpg *License:* Public Domain *Contributors:* U.S. Navy/PhoM1 Brien Aho ... 202
Figure 119 *Source:* https://en.wikipedia.org/w/index.php?title=File:RAN_ship_inspection.jpg *License:* Public Domain *Contributors:* BotMultichill, File Upload Bot (Magnus Manske), KTo288, MECU, Nick-D, OgreBot 2, Rodhullandemu, 1 anonymous edits ... 202
Figure 120 *Source:* https//en.wikipedia.org *License:* Public Domain *Contributors:* BotMultichill, BotMultichillT, Chyah, Docu, File Upload Bot (Magnus Manske), Tm, 1 anonymous edits ... 206
Figure 121 *Source:* https://en.wikipedia.org/w/index.php?title=File:HMAS_Sheean,_Fremantle.jpg *License:* Creative Commons Attribution-ShareAlike 3.0 Unported *Contributors:* Nachoman-au ... 207
Figure 122 *Source:* https://en.wikipedia.org/w/index.php?title=File:HMAS_Anzac_F-150.jpg *License:* Public Domain *Contributors:* Chanueting, Felix Stember, Ingolfson, OgreBot 2, Zaccarias, 1 anonymous edits ... 208
Image *Source:* https://en.wikipedia.org/w/index.php?title=File:Naval_Ensign_of_Australia.svg *License:* Public Domain *Contributors:* User: David Newton ... 212
Image *Source:* https://en.wikipedia.org/w/index.php?title=File:HMAS_Collins_Kockums_photo.jpg *License:* Attribution *Contributors:* Kockums AB ... 215
Image *Source:* https://en.wikipedia.org/w/index.php?title=File:HMAS_Hobart_December_2017.jpg *Contributors:* User:Nick-D ... 216
Image *Source:* https://en.wikipedia.org/w/index.php?title=File:HMAS_Perth_entering_Pearl_Harbor_in_June_2012.jpg *License:* Public Domain *Contributors:* Nick-D, O484 ... 216
Image *Source:* https//en.wikipedia.org *License:* Public Domain *Contributors:* BotMultichill, BotMultichillT, Cobatfor, Howcheng, Nick-D ... 216
Image *Source:* https://en.wikipedia.org/w/index.php?title=File:HMAS_Broome_(ACPB_90).jpg *License:* Creative Commons Attribution-Sharealike 3.0 *Contributors:* User:Hpeterswald ... 216
Image *Source:* https://en.wikipedia.org/w/index.php?title=File:RAN-IFR_2013_D3_81.JPG *License:* Creative Commons Attribution-Sharealike 3.0 *Contributors:* User:Saberwyn ... 216
Image *Source:* https://en.wikipedia.org/w/index.php?title=File:RAN-IFR_2013_D3_179.JPG *License:* Creative Commons Attribution-Sharealike 3.0 *Contributors:* User:Saberwyn ... 216
Image *Source:* https://en.wikipedia.org/w/index.php?title=File:HMAS_Benalla_(A_04)_at_IFR.jpg *License:* Creative Commons Attribution-Sharealike 3.0 *Contributors:* User:Hpeterswald ... 217
Image *Source:* https://en.wikipedia.org/w/index.php?title=File:HMAS_Choules_FBE_2014.JPG *Contributors:* User:Saberwyn ... 217
Image *Source:* https://en.wikipedia.org/w/index.php?title=File:HMAS_Success_July09.jpg *License:* Public Domain *Contributors:* Casey H. Kyhl, U.S. Navy ... 217
Image *Source:* https://en.wikipedia.org/w/index.php?title=File:HMAS_Sirius_2009.jpg *License:* Creative Commons Attribution 2.0 *Contributors:* L G ... 217
Image *Source:* https://en.wikipedia.org/w/index.php?title=File:Cape_St_George,_on_Darwin_Harbour.jpg *License:* Creative Commons Attribution 2.0 *Contributors:* FlickreviewR 2, Flock, Leoboudv, Saberwyn ... 217
Image *Source:* https://en.wikipedia.org/w/index.php?title=File:Melbourne_International_Tall_Ship_Festival_2013_(9713636920).jpg *License:* Creative Commons Attribution 2.0 *Contributors:* Chris Phutully from Australia ... 217
Figure 123 *Source:* https://en.wikipedia.org/w/index.php?title=File:Australian_MRH-90_lands_on_USS_Green_Bay_(LPD-20)_in_July_2015.JPG *License:* Public Domain *Contributors:* Cobatfor, De728631 ... 218
Figure 124 *Source:* https://en.wikipedia.org/w/index.php?title=File:RAN_S-70B-2_Seahawk_Avalon_2011.jpg *Contributors:* Mehdi Nazarinia 219
Figure 125 *Source:* https://en.wikipedia.org/w/index.php?title=File:De_Havilland_Canada_DHC-8-200_VH-LCL.jpg *License:* GNU Free Documentation License *Contributors:* Bidgee, BotMultichill, BotMultichillT, Bri, Rcbutcher, Uli Elch, 2 anonymous edits ... 219
Figure 126 *Source:* https://en.wikipedia.org/w/index.php?title=File:CDT-1.jpg *License:* Public Domain *Contributors:* U.S. Navy photo by Mass Communication Specialist 2nd Class Jennifer A. Villalovos ... 220
Figure 127 *Source:* https://en.wikipedia.org/w/index.php?title=File:LHD_Canberra_fitting_out.JPG *License:* Creative Commons Attribution-Sharealike 3.0 *Contributors:* User:Saberwyn ... 221
Figure 128 *Source:* https://en.wikipedia.org/w/index.php?title=File:HMAS_Hobart_under_construction_April_2015.JPG *Contributors:* User:Bahudhara ... 221
Figure 129 *Source:* https://en.wikipedia.org/w/index.php?title=File:Royal_Australian_Navy_officer_during_RIMPAC_2014.jpg *License:* Public Domain *Contributors:* Blackcat, GT1976, Illegitimate Barrister, Nick-D ... 223

Figure 130 *Source:* https://en.wikipedia.org/w/index.php?title=File:Safety_briefing_aboard_HMAS_Tobruk_in_2010.jpg *License:* Public Domain *Contributors:* Nick-D 224
Image *Source:* https://en.wikipedia.org/w/index.php?title=File:Royal_Australian_Navy_OF-10.svg *Contributors:* User:Sodacan 225
Image *Source:* https://en.wikipedia.org/w/index.php?title=File:Royal_Australian_Navy_(sleeves)_OF-10.svg *Contributors:* User:Sodacan 225
Image *Source:* https://en.wikipedia.org/w/index.php?title=File:Royal_Australian_Navy_OF-9.svg *Contributors:* User:Sodacan 225
Image *Source:* https://en.wikipedia.org/w/index.php?title=File:Royal_Australian_Navy_(sleeves)_OF-9.svg *Contributors:* User:Sodacan 225
Image *Source:* https://en.wikipedia.org/w/index.php?title=File:Royal_Australian_Navy_OF-8.svg *Contributors:* User:Sodacan 225
Image *Source:* https://en.wikipedia.org/w/index.php?title=File:Royal_Australian_Navy_(sleeves)_OF-8.svg *Contributors:* User:Sodacan 225
Image *Source:* https://en.wikipedia.org/w/index.php?title=File:Royal_Australian_Navy_OF-7.svg *Contributors:* User:Sodacan 225
Image *Source:* https://en.wikipedia.org/w/index.php?title=File:Royal_Australian_Navy_(sleeves)_OF-7.svg *Contributors:* User:Sodacan 225
Image *Source:* https://en.wikipedia.org/w/index.php?title=File:Royal_Australian_Navy_OF-6.svg *Contributors:* User:Sodacan 225
Image *Source:* https://en.wikipedia.org/w/index.php?title=File:Royal_Australian_Navy_(sleeves)_OF-6.svg *Contributors:* User:Sodacan 225
Image *Source:* https://en.wikipedia.org/w/index.php?title=File:Royal_Australian_Navy_(sleeves)_OF-5.svg *Contributors:* User:Sodacan 225
Image *Source:* https://en.wikipedia.org/w/index.php?title=File:Royal_Australian_Navy_(sleeves)_OF-4.svg *Contributors:* User:Sodacan 225
Image *Source:* https://en.wikipedia.org/w/index.php?title=File:Royal_Australian_Navy_(sleeves)_OF-3.svg *Contributors:* User:Sodacan 225
Image *Source:* https://en.wikipedia.org/w/index.php?title=File:Royal_Australian_Navy_(sleeves)_OF-2.svg *Contributors:* User:Sodacan 225
Image *Source:* https://en.wikipedia.org/w/index.php?title=File:Royal_Australian_Navy_(sleeves)_OF-1.svg *Contributors:* User:Sodacan 225
Image *Source:* https://en.wikipedia.org/w/index.php?title=File:UK-Navy-OFD.svg *License:* Public Domain *Contributors:* Greentubing (talk) .225
Figure 131 *Source:* https://en.wikipedia.org/w/index.php?title=File:Royal_Australian_Navy_Chaplain_rank_slide.png *Contributors:* Gbawden, Padre1992 226
Image *Source:* https://en.wikipedia.org/w/index.php?title=File:Royal_Australian_Navy_OR-9b.svg *Contributors:* User:Sodacan 227
Image *Source:* https://en.wikipedia.org/w/index.php?title=File:Royal_Australian_Navy_OR-9a.svg *Contributors:* User:Sodacan 227
Image *Source:* https://en.wikipedia.org/w/index.php?title=File:Royal_Australian_Navy_OR-8.svg *Contributors:* User:Sodacan 227
Image *Source:* https://en.wikipedia.org/w/index.php?title=File:Royal_Australian_Navy_OR-6.svg *Contributors:* User:Sodacan 227
Image *Source:* https://en.wikipedia.org/w/index.php?title=File:Royal_Australian_Navy_OR-5.svg *Contributors:* User:Sodacan 227
Image *Source:* https://en.wikipedia.org/w/index.php?title=File:Royal_Australian_Navy_OR-3.svg *Contributors:* User:Sodacan 227
Image *Source:* https://en.wikipedia.org/w/index.php?title=File:Royal_Australian_Navy_OR-2.svg *Contributors:* User:Sodacan 227
Figure 132 *Source:* https://en.wikipedia.org/w/index.php?title=File:CIS_Department_Halifax.jpg *License:* Public Domain *Contributors:* Merno1976 228
Figure 133 *Source:* https://en.wikipedia.org/w/index.php?title=File:HMAS_Collins_Kockums_photo.jpg *License:* Attribution *Contributors:* Kockums AB 230
Figure 134 *Source:* https://en.wikipedia.org/w/index.php?title=File:HMAS_Adelaide_arriving_at_Pearl_Harbor_in_June_2018.jpg *License:* Public Domain *Contributors:* Cobatfor, Nick-D 232
Figure 135 *Source:* https://en.wikipedia.org/w/index.php?title=File:HMAS_Hobart_December_2017.jpg *Contributors:* User:Nick-D 234
Figure 136 *Source:* https://en.wikipedia.org/w/index.php?title=File:HMAS_Perth_(FFH_157)_near_Garden_Island_Naval_Base.jpg *License:* Creative Commons Attribution-Sharealike 3.0 *Contributors:* User:Hpeterswald 235
Figure 137 *Source:* https://en.wikipedia.org/w/index.php?title=File:HMAS_Darwin_(FFG_04)_at_IFR.jpg *License:* Creative Commons Attribution-Sharealike 3.0 *Contributors:* User:Hpeterswald 236
Figure 138 *Source:* https://en.wikipedia.org/w/index.php?title=File:HMAS_Broome_(ACPB_90).jpg *License:* Creative Commons Attribution-Sharealike 3.0 *Contributors:* User:Hpeterswald 239
Figure 139 *Source:* https://en.wikipedia.org/w/index.php?title=File:HMAS_Gascoyne_(M_85).jpg *License:* Creative Commons Attribution-Sharealike 3.0 *Contributors:* User:Hpeterswald 239
Figure 140 *Source:* https://en.wikipedia.org/w/index.php?title=File:HMAS_Choules_FBE_May_2012.jpg *License:* Creative Commons Attribution-Sharealike 3.0 *Contributors:* User:Saberwyn 241
Figure 141 *Source:* https://en.wikipedia.org/w/index.php?title=File:HMAS_Sirius_01_gnangarra.jpg *Contributors:* Gnangarra 242
Figure 142 *Source:* https://en.wikipedia.org/w/index.php?title=File:HMAS_Success_July09.jpg *License:* Public Domain *Contributors:* Casey H. Kyhl, U.S. Navy 243
Figure 143 *Source:* https://en.wikipedia.org/w/index.php?title=File:RAN-IFR_2013_D3_179.JPG *License:* Creative Commons Attribution-Sharealike 3.0 *Contributors:* User:Saberwyn 245
Figure 144 *Source:* https://en.wikipedia.org/w/index.php?title=File:HMAS_Benalla_(A_04)_at_IFR.jpg *License:* Creative Commons Attribution-Sharealike 3.0 *Contributors:* User:Hpeterswald 245
Figure 145 *Source:* https://en.wikipedia.org/w/index.php?title=File:Young_Endeavour_man_the_mast.jpg *License:* Creative Commons Attribution-Sharealike 3.0 *Contributors:* User:Saberwyn 247
Figure 146 *Source:* https://en.wikipedia.org/w/index.php?title=File:Cape_St_George,_on_Darwin_Harbour.jpg *License:* Creative Commons Attribution 2.0 *Contributors:* FlickreviewR 2, Flock, Leoboudv, Saberwyn 248
Figure 147 *Source:* https://en.wikipedia.org/w/index.php?title=File:R.E.8_(3_sqn_AFC).jpg *License:* Public Domain *Contributors:* AustralianRupert, OgreBot 2, Soundofmusicals, Tamba52 252
Figure 148 *Source:* https://en.wikipedia.org/w/index.php?title=File:Handley_Page_Hampden_in_the_air.jpg *License:* Public Domain *Contributors:* Royal Air Force official photographer; , (original upload date) 254
Figure 149 *Source:* https://en.wikipedia.org/w/index.php?title=File:462_Sqn_(AWM_P01523033).jpg *License:* Public Domain *Contributors:* Hines, Ronald Maxwell 255
Figure 150 *Source:* https://en.wikipedia.org/w/index.php?title=File:Beaufighter_(AWM_OG0001).jpg *License:* Public Domain *Contributors:* AustralianRupert, Dcoetzee, Docu, Johnny Rotten, Labattblueboy, Liftarn, McZusatz, Nick-D, OgreBot 2, PMG, PawelMM, Rcbutcher 256
Image *Source:* https://en.wikipedia.org/w/index.php?title=File:Logo_of_the_Royal_Australian_Air_Force.svg *License:* Public Domain *Contributors:* Allforrous, Fry1989 260
Image *Source:* https://en.wikipedia.org/w/index.php?title=File:Ensign_of_the_Royal_Australian_Air_Force.svg *Contributors:* - 261
Image *Source:* https://en.wikipedia.org/w/index.php?title=File:Roundel_of_Australia.svg *License:* Public Domain *Contributors:* RAAF-Lowvis-Roundel.svg: Liftarn derivative work: Ospalh (talk) 261
Image *Source:* https://en.wikipedia.org/w/index.php?title=File:Roundel_of_Australia_-_Low_Visibility.svg *License:* Public Domain *Contributors:* Liftarn 261
Figure 151 *Source:* https://en.wikipedia.org/w/index.php?title=File:RAAFBBJA36001.JPG *License:* Creative Commons Attribution-Sharealike 3.0 *Contributors:* Apalsola, Ardfern, Benchill, Bidgee, BotMultichill, File Upload Bot (Magnus Manske), MB-one, Nick-D, OgreBot 2 262
Figure 152 *Source:* https://en.wikipedia.org/w/index.php?title=File:Kittyhawk_IA_RAAF.jpg *License:* GNU Free Documentation License *Contributors:* Martin Čížek 264
Figure 153 *Source:* https://en.wikipedia.org/w/index.php?title=File:BrewsterBuffalosMkIRAAFSingaporeOctober1941.jpg *License:* Public Domain *Contributors:* British Government 264
Figure 154 *Source:* https://en.wikipedia.org/w/index.php?title=File:StateLibQld_1_100268.jpg *License:* Public Domain *Contributors:* Billofocham, Butko, PeterWD, Rcbutcher 265
Figure 155 *Source:* https://en.wikipedia.org/w/index.php?title=File:Two_Mirage_III_of_the_Royal_Australian_Air_Force_1.JPEG *License:* Public Domain *Contributors:* TSGT CURT EDDINGS 267
Figure 156 *Source:* https://en.wikipedia.org/w/index.php?title=File:AirForce_over_Iraq.jpg *License:* Public Domain *Contributors:* AdamBMorgan, Ardfern, Bestiasonica, Cobatfor, Denniss, FieldMarine, Greenshed, Ishbane, Joshbaumgartner, Julian Herzog, KTo288, Morio, Nick-D, Rocket000, Slomox, 3 anonymous edits 268
Figure 157 *Source:* https://en.wikipedia.org/w/index.php?title=File:RAAF_(A44-222)_FA_18F_Super_Hornet_landing.jpg *Contributors:* Bidgee 269
Figure 158 *Source:* https://en.wikipedia.org/w/index.php?title=File:Leading_Aircraft_Woman_Patricia_Entwistle_RAAF.jpg *License:* Public Domain *Contributors:* U.S Air Force photo by Tech. Sgt. Eric T. Sheler 270
Figure 159 *Source:* https//en.wikipedia.org *Contributors:* Elisfkc, Nick-D 272
Figure 160 *Source:* https://en.wikipedia.org/w/index.php?title=File:RAAF_Lockheed_Martin_C-130J-30_YPMC_Creek.jpg *Contributors:* Ian Creek 274
Figure 161 *Source:* https://en.wikipedia.org/w/index.php?title=File:A41-206_Boeing_C-17A_Globemaster_III_RAAF_(9639221235).jpg *Contributors:* Achim55, FOX 52, Fæ, JotaCartas, OgreBot 2, Rcbutcher, Russavia 274
Figure 162 *Source:* https://en.wikipedia.org/w/index.php?title=File:RAAF_BAe_Hawk_AVV_Creek.jpg *Contributors:* Ian Creek 275
Figure 163 *Source:* https://en.wikipedia.org/w/index.php?title=File:GBU-24_xxl.jpg *Contributors:* Avron, D-Kuru, Night Gyr 275
Figure 164 *Source:* https://en.wikipedia.org/w/index.php?title=File:AIM_9L_Sidewinder_(modified)_copy.jpg *Contributors:* User:David.Monniaux, User:FOX 52 278
Figure 165 *Source:* https://en.wikipedia.org/w/index.php?title=File:Mk-84_xxl.jpg *Contributors:* Avron, Night Gyr 278
Figure 166 *Source:* https://en.wikipedia.org/w/index.php?title=File:Roulettes_flying_in_formation.jpg *Contributors:* Fir0002 280
Figure 167 *Source:* https://en.wikipedia.org/w/index.php?title=File:A35-001_in_flight.jpg *Contributors:* De728631, Nick-D 281

Figure 168 *Source:* https://en.wikipedia.org/w/index.php?title=File:Leading_Aircraft_Woman_Patricia_Entwistle_RAAF.jpg *License:* Public Domain *Contributors:* U.S Air Force photo by Tech. Sgt. Eric T. Sheier 286
Image *Source:* https://en.wikipedia.org/w/index.php?title=File:Symbol_venus.svg *License:* Creative Commons Attribution-ShareAlike 3.0 Unported *Contributors:* By 285
Image *Source:* https://en.wikipedia.org/w/index.php?title=File:Woman-power_emblem.svg *License:* Public Domain *Contributors:* User:AnonMoos 285
Figure 169 *Source:* https://en.wikipedia.org/w/index.php?title=File:Leaders_of_Australian_Womens_Services_1942.jpg *License:* Public Domain *Contributors:* The Argus Newspaper 287
Figure 170 *Source:* https://en.wikipedia.org/w/index.php?title=File:Sailors_render_honors_as_distinguished_visitors_depart_HMAS_Tobruk.jpg *License:* Public Domain *Contributors:* Nick-D 288
Figure 171 *Source:* https://en.wikipedia.org/w/index.php?title=File:Linda_Corbould_on_the_flight_deck_of_a_C-17_aircraft.jpg *License:* Public Domain *Contributors:* Michael Fletcher/U. S. Air Force 289
Figure 172 *Source:* https://en.wikipedia.org/w/index.php?title=File:Female_Australian_soldiers_Afghanistan.jpg *License:* Creative Commons Attribution 2.0 *Contributors:* ISAF Headquarters Public Affairs Office from Kabul, Afghanistan 290
Figure 173 *Source:* https://en.wikipedia.org/w/index.php?title=File:Sydney_Mardi_Gras_2013_-_8522985059.jpg *License:* Creative Commons Attribution 2.0 *Contributors:* Bidgee, 1 anonymous edits 294
Figure 174 *Source:* https://en.wikipedia.org/w/index.php?title=File:HMAS_Kuttabul,_2007_(03).JPG *Contributors:* User:Bahnfrend 300

333

License

Creative Commons Attribution-Share Alike 3.0
//creativecommons.org/licenses/by-sa/3.0/

Index

.338 Lapua Magnum, 152
.50 BMG, 152, 153

A-18, 268
A-18F Super Hornet, 261
A-18 Hornet, 7, 30, 92, 261, 272
AAI RQ-7 Shadow, 30, 151
Abbott Government, 8
ABCA Armies, 35
Ab Initio, 277
Able seaman (rank), 226
Accuracy International Arctic Warfare, 152
Aceh, 133
Acheron-class torpedo boat, 53, 165
Acting sub lieutenant, 225
Adelaide, 143, 304, 306
Adelaide class frigate, 229
Adelaide-class frigate, 29, 204, 206, 216, 233, 236
Adelaide, South Australia, 32, 230
Admiral, 12
Admiral (Australia), 225
Admiral of the Fleet (Australia), 225
Admiralty, 61, 165, 177, 180, 205, 213
Adrian dHagé, 295
Advanced Individual Combat Weapon, 157
Aegis combat system, 209, 222, 233
Aerial refueling, 273
Aermacchi MB-326, 85
Aerobatics, 279
Aeronautical Information Service RAAF, 277
Aerospace Operational Support Group RAAF, 15
AeroVironment Wasp III, 158
Afghanistan, 7, 270
Afghan National Army, 95
Afrikaner, 111
Afrikaners, 55
AGM-154, 275
AGM-158, 275
AHS Centaur, 76
AIM-120 AMRAAM, 275
AIM-9 Sidewinder, 275
AIM-9X, 275

Air Board (Australia), 263
Airborne early warning and control, 273
Airborne Early Warning & Control, 16
Airbus A330 MRTT, 9, 31, 100, 261, 270, 273, 281
Air chief marshal, 12
Air Combat Group RAAF, 15, 279
Air Commodore, 290
Aircraft carrier, 191
Aircraft Research and Development Unit RAAF, 277
Aircraft Stores Compatibility Engineering Squadron, 277
Aircraft Systems Engineering Squadron, 277
Airdrop, 99
Airfield Defence Guards, 16
Air force, 260
Air Force Band RAAF, 277
Air Force Headquarters RAAF, 279
Air Force Training Group RAAF, 15, 279
Air Mobility Control Centre RAAF, 279
Air Mobility Group RAAF, 15, 279
Air Movements Training and Development RAAF, 277
Air raids on Australia, 1942–43, 76
Air raids on Darwin, 19 February 1942, 255
Air System Development and Test Wing RAAF, 279
Air-to-air missile, 275
Air-to-air refuelling, 7
Air-to-surface missile, 275
Air traffic controllers, 127
Air Training Wing RAAF, 279
Air transports of heads of state and government, 273
Air Warfare Centre RAAF, 279
Albany, Western Australia, 64
Aleksandr Kolchak, 69
Alenia C-27J Spartan, 30, 148
Alexander Downer, 296
Alexandria, 177, 180
Al-Faw Peninsula, 201
Alfred Deakin, 61, 165
Alfredo Reinado, 95

Alice Springs, 36
Allied intervention in the Russian Civil War, 70
Allied invasion of Sicily, 182
Allies of World War II, 116
Al Minhad Air Base, 270
Al Muthanna, 127
Al Muthanna Task Group, 7, 98, 127

Álvaro de Bazán-class frigate, 209, 222

Amanda Rishworth, 297
Ambon Island, 117
American-British-Dutch-Australian Command, 183
American-led intervention in Iraq (2014–present), 260, 261
American Samoa, 171
Amiens, 68
Amphibious vehicle, 149
Amphibious warfare, 229
Andrew Cunningham, 1st Viscount Cunningham of Hyndhope, 177, 179
Andrew Hastie (politician), 297
Anglesea Barracks, 305, 307
Anglo-Celtic Australian, 26
Anglo-Iraqi War, 213
Anglo-Japanese Alliance, 166, 174
Angus Campbell (general), 1, 12, 130, 211
Antarctic Circle, 164
Anti-communist, 258, 269
Anti-materiel rifle, 152
Anti-personnel mine, 155
Anti-ship missile, 276
Anti-submarine auxiliaries, 176
Anti-submarine warfare, 218, 273, 276
Anti-tank, 155
Anti-tank guided missile, 155
Anti-tank warfare, 155
Anton Denikin, 69
Anzac class frigate, 229
Anzac-class frigate, 29, 201, 206, 207, 216, 234
Anzac Cove, 64
Anzac day, 22, 65, 113
ANZAC Force, 183
Anzac Mounted Division, 65
Anzac spirit, 44, 45
ANZUS, 35, 45, 192
AP-3C Orion, 95, 261, 280
Apia, 171, 172
Arabian Sea, 96
Armed forces, 2
Armed Forces of the Philippines, 10, 37
Armentières, 66
Armidale-class patrol boat, 29, 206, 207, 216, 229, 237

Armored car (military), 147
Armored Personnel Carrier, 146
Armored recovery vehicle, 138
Armor Piercing Ammunition, 152
Armoured fighting vehicle, 30, 147
Armoured Personnel Carrier, 139, 147
Arms industry, 299
Army Aboriginal Community Assistance Program, 34
Army Logistic Training Centre (Australia), 135
Army Recruit Training Centre, 23, 135
Army Recruit Training Centre (Australia), 304
Arthur Tange, 4, 90
Artillery, 139
Asian and Pacific theatre of World War I, 169
Asia Pacific, 206
ASLAV, 8, 30, 97, 98, 139, 144, 146
ASRAAM, 275
Assault rifle, 151
Atomic bombings of Hiroshima and Nagasaki, 257, 266
Attack-class patrol boat, 197
Attack on Sydney Harbour, 184
Attorney-Generals Department (Australia), 18
Auckland, 171
Austal Ships, 237, 247
Austeyr, 151, 156
Australia, 1, 2, 27, 130, 146, 147, 151, 155, 156, 223, 225, 260, 273, 303
Australia and the Empire Air Training Scheme, 263
Australia and weapons of mass destruction, 28
Australia–Papua New Guinea relations, 102
Australia in the War of 1939–1945, 105, 210, 302
Australian 10th Light Horse Regiment, 115
Australian 171st Aviation Squadron, 204
Australian 2nd Division, 113
Australian 34th Brigade, 120
Australian 3rd Division, 114
Australian 5th Division (World War I), 114
Australian Aboriginals, 44
Australian Air Corps, 251, 253, 263
Australian Air Warfare Destroyer, 209
Australian and New Zealand Army Corps (army corps), 64, 113
Australian Armoured Units of World War II, 118
Australian Army, 1–3, 57, 126, **130**, 146, 198, 204, 206, 251, 261, 263, 285, 294–296, 303, 314
Australian Army Aviation, 30
Australian Army enlisted rank insignia, 137
Australian Army Medical Womens Service, 287
Australian Army Nursing Service, 285

338

Australian Army officer rank insignia, 137
Australian Army Reserve, 21, 32, 34, 143, 252
Australian Army Training Team Iraq, 127
Australian Army Training Team Vietnam, 88, 123
Australian Bicentenary, 246
Australian Border Force, 29, 34, 217, 229, 237, 247, 248
Australian Business Number, 299
Australian Capital Territory, 135, 252
Australian Charities and Not-for-profits Commission, 298
Australian Citizens Military Forces, 61, 112
Australian Commonwealth Horse, 57, 111
Australian Commonwealth Naval Board, 166
Australian Constitution, 2
Australian contribution to the 1991 Gulf War, 5, 102, 201
Australian contribution to the 2003 invasion of Iraq, 7, 103, 148, 201
Australian contribution to the Allied Intervention in Russia 1918–1919, 101
Australian contribution to UNTAC in Cambodia 1992–1993, 5, 101
Australian contribution to UNTAG, 5
Australian Corps, 68, 115
Australian Customs and Border Protection Service, 247
Australian Cyber Security Centre, 18
Australian Defence College, 259
Australian Defence Force, **1**, 2, 90, 125, 130, 131, 211, 212, 260, 261, 285, 293, 294, 299, 303
Australian Defence Force Academy, 23, 225, 303
Australian Defence Force Basic Flying Training School, 276
Australian Defence Force ranks and insignia, 2
Australian Defence Industries, 203, 238
Australian Defence Organisation, 1, 11, 290
Australian Defence Satellite Communications Station, 36
Australian Dictionary of Biography, 323
Australian dollar, 1, 197, 280
Australian Federal Police, 18, 126
Australian First Tactical Air Force, 77, 257, 266
Australian Flying Corps, 3, 62, 251, 252, 261
Australian frontier wars, 44
Australian Geospatial-Intelligence Organisation, 18
Australian Government, 173
Australian Human Rights Commission, 291, 295
Australian Hydrographic Service, 218
Australian International Airshow, 269

Australian Labor Party, 8, 91
Australian Light Horse, 63, 112
Australian Maritime Safety Authority, 34
Australian Military Forces, 62, 314
Australian modifications, 234
Australian Mounted Division, 65
Australian National Maritime Museum, 247
Australian Naval and Military Expeditionary Force, 63, 112, 169, 252
Australian Navy Cadets, 223
Australian Patrol Boat Group, 207, 215, 237
Australian Public Service, 20
Australian Red Cross, 197
Australian Secret Intelligence Service, 10, 19
Australian Security Intelligence Organisation, 18
Australian Signals Directorate, 18
Australian Special Air Service Regiment, 15, 17, 123, 125, 143
Australian Squadron, 162
Australian Strategic Policy Institute, 28, 291, 300, 301
Australian submarine AE1, 63
Australian Submarine Corporation, 207, 230
Australian War Memorial, 45, 137, 210, 259, 319
Australian White Ensign, 212
Australian Womens Army Service, 287
Australian Womens Land Army, 287
Australias Federation Guard, 125, 151
Australia Squadron, 161
Australia Station, 47, 162, 177
Austria, 151
Automatic weapons, 126
Auxiliary Minesweepers, 176
Avro Lancaster, 254, 264
Avro Lincoln, 82, 267
Avro York, 266
AW .28Arctic Warfare.29, 152
AW50F, 138, 152
Axis naval activity in Australian waters, 76, 183, 185

B-24 Liberator, 256, 266
BAE Systems Australia, 231
BAE Systems Hawk, 273
Baghdad, 99
Balikpapan, 119
Balikpapan-class landing craft heavy, 208
Bandiana, Victoria, 305
Bandwagoning, 45
Baoding, 60
Bapaume, 67
Bardia, 72
Barracks, 52
Barracuda-class submarine, 230

Barrett M82, 138, 153
B.A. Santamaria, 71
Bathurst-class corvette, 182, 183
Bathurst Rebellion, 47
Battalion, 7, 96
Battle cruiser, 162
Battlegroup (army), 15, 96
Battle honours, 136, 137
Battle of Aidabasalala, 94
Battle of Ambon, 75
Battle of Amiens (1918), 68, 115
Battle of Arras (1917), 114
Battle of Babang, 86
Battle of Beersheba (1917), 66
Battle of Belmont (1899), 56
Battle of Binh Ba, 89
Battle of Bita Paka, 63
Battle of Broodseinde, 68
Battle of Bullecourt, 114
Battle of Buna–Gona, 76
Battle of Buna–Gona, 76, 118
Battle of Calabria, 177
Battle of Cape Matapan, 179
Battle of Cape Spada, 178
Battle of Chongju, 80
Battle of Chora, 97
Battle of Chuam-ni, 81
Battle of Cocos, 64, 169
Battle of Colenso, 56
Battle of Coral–Balmoral, 88
Battle of Crete, 72, 116
Battle of Dakar, 180, 213
Battle of Derapet, 97
Battle of Dernancourt, 68
Battle of Doan, 97
Battle of Elands River (1900), 58
Battle of Fromelles, 66, 114
Battle of Gang Toi, 88
Battle of Greece, 72, 116
Battle of Hamel, 68, 115
Battle of Hat Dich, 89
Battle of Inchon, 80
Battle of Java (1942), 75
Battle of Jerusalem (1917), 66
Battle of Jutland, 170
Battle of Kaiapit, 118
Battle of Kapyong, 82
Battle of Kindau, 86
Battle of Kujin, 80
Battle of Leyte Gulf, 187
Battle of Long Khanh, 89
Battle of Long Tan, 88, 123
Battle of Madagascar, 213
Battle of Maehwa-San, 81
Battle of Magdhaba, 170
Battle of Magersfontein, 56

Battle of Malaya, 75, 264, 265
Battle of Megiddo (1918), 66, 115
Battle of Menin Road, 68
Battle of Messines (1917), 67, 114
Battle of Milne Bay, 76, 118, 256, 265
Battle of Modder River, 57
Battle of Mont St Quentin, 69
Battle of Mouquet Farm, 66, 114
Battle of Mughar Ridge, 66
Battle of Okinawa, 188
Battle of Paardeberg, 57
Battle of Pakchon, 81
Battle of Passchendaele, 68
Battle of Pinjarra, 49
Battle of Poelcappelle, 68
Battle of Polygon Wood, 68
Battle of Pozières, 66, 114
Battle of Rabaul (1942), 75, 265
Battle of Romani, 65, 114
Battle of Rufiji Delta, 169
Battle of Same, 95
Battle of Savo Island, 186
Battle of Singapore, 75, 117, 264, 265
Battle of Spion Kop, 56
Battle of Stormberg, 56
Battle of St. Quentin Canal, 68
Battle of Sunda Strait, 184
Battle of Sungei Koemba, 86
Battle of Suoi Bong Trang, 88
Battle of Surigao Strait, 187
Battle of the Atlantic, 74, 185
Battle of the Bismarck Sea, 256, 266
Battle of the Coral Sea, 75, 184
Battle of the Espero Convoy, 177
Battle of the Java Sea, 184
Battle of the Lys (1918), 68
Battle of the Mediterranean, 177, 213
Battle of the Samichon River, 82
Battle of the Somme, 66
Battle of Tientsin, 60
Battle of Timor, 75
Battle of Timor (1942-43), 180, 184
Battle of Uijeongbu (1951), 81
Battle of Wau, 76
Battle of Yongju, 80
Battle rifle, 151
Bay-class landing ship, 217
Bay class landing ship dock, 240
Bay-class minehunter, 238
Bay-class patrol boat, 237, 247
Bayonet, 156
Beechcraft Super King Air, 31, 261, 273
Beersheba, 114
Beijing, China, 60
Beitang, Tanggu District, 60
Belgium, 151–153

Bell 206, 139
Bell 429 GlobalRanger, 29, 212
Bell OH-58 Kiowa, 30, 150
Bendigo, Victoria, 18
Benghazi, 72
Berbera, 181
Berber, Sudan, 55
Berlin Airlift, 79, 102, 260, 261, 266
Beyond-visual-range missile, 275
Bien Hoa, 88
Biological Weapons Convention, 28
Bipartisan, 8
B.J. Habibie, 93
Black Hornet Nano, 158
Black Sea, 69
Black War, 48, 49
Black Week, 56
Blaser R93 Tactical, 138, 152
Blitzkrieg, 116
Bloemfontein, 57
Blohm + Voss, 234
Bluebirds (Australian nurses), 286
Blue-water navy, 164, 166, 212
Board of Inquiry, 196
Bob Hawke, 200
Boeing 707, 95
Boeing 737, 31, 261, 273
Boeing 737 AEW&C, 9, 30, 100, 261, 270, 273
Boeing C-17 Globemaster III, 30, 99, 270, 273
Boeing CH-47 Chinook, 8, 30, 139, 147, 150
Boeing EA-18G Growler, 30, 261, 273
Boeing Insitu ScanEagle, 151
Boeing P-8 Poseidon, 30, 273, 280
Boeing ScanEagle, 139, 158
Bolshevik, 69
Bolt action, 152
Bombardier Challenger 600, 31, 261
Bombardier Challenger 600 series, 273
Bombing of Darwin, 74, 75
Bombing of Darwin (February 1942), 265
Bonegilla, Victoria, 305
Boom gate vessels, 176
Borneo, 85, 119, 193, 256, 266
Borneo Barracks, 304
Borneo Campaign (1945), 77, 266
Bougainville campaign (1944-45), 119
Bougainville Island, 77
Bougainville Province, 5, 93, 133
Boxer (armoured fighting vehicle), 146, 147
Boxer Rebellion, 54, 101, 111
Breaker Morant, 58, 111
Brewster Buffalo, 265
Brewster F2A Buffalo, 264
Brian Courtice, 295
Bridges Barracks, 305

Brigade, 9, 53, 63, 112
Brigantine rig, 246
Brisbane, 31, 50, 143, 183, 286, 304, 306
Bristol Beaufighter, 256, 266
Bristol Beaufort, 254, 263
British Army, 46, 109, 137
British Battalion, 71
British Commonwealth, 85
British Commonwealth Forces Korea, 80, 121, 190
British Commonwealth Occupation Force, 78, 102, 120, 189, 257, 266
British crown, 52
British Dominion, 192
British Eastern Fleet, 188
British Empire, 53, 251, 252, 262
British Expeditionary Force (World War II), 116
British Grand Fleet, 171
British India, 190
British Indian Army, 120, 252, 262
British Malaya, 75, 117
British Mediterranean Fleet, 72
British Power Boat Company Type Two 63 ft HSL, 176
British Solomon Islands Protectorate, 70
Broadmeadows, Victoria, 305
Brooke Marine, 246
Browning Hi-Power, 28, 138, 153
Bruce Kafer, 223
Brunei, 119
Buckingham Palace, 124, 126
Buckland Military Training Area, 305
Bullecourt Barracks, 304
Bullpup, 151
Bungendore, New South Wales, 13
Burma, 117
Burma Railway, 119
Burnie, 305
Burnie Army Reserve, 305
Bushmaster PMV, 30, 139
Bushmaster Protected Mobility Vehicle, 144, 147
Bushmens Contingents, 57
Bushranging, 47
Bushveldt Carbineers, 58, 111

C-130 Hercules, 85
C-130J, 273
C-130J Super Hercules, 261
C-17 Globemaster III, 261
C-27J, 273
C-27J Spartan, 261
C-47 Skytrain, 82
C-5 Galaxy, 124
Cabarlah, 304

Cable repair ships, 176
CAC Boomerang, 77, 255, 265
CAC Sabre, 83
Cairns, 32, 218, 244
Cairns, Queensland, 190
Campbell Barracks (Australia), 32, 143, 305
Campbell Park, Australia, 303
Camp Mirage, 96
Canada, 146, 155, 273
Canadian Army, 121
Canadian Corps, 115
Canberra, 31, 90, 211, 214, 260
Canberra-class landing helicopter dock, 29, 136, 209, 216, 221, 229
Canungra, 304
Canungra, Queensland, 123
Cape-class patrol boat, 29, 217, 229, 237
Cape Colony, 55
Cape Matapan, 177, 179
Cape Rachado, 193
Cape St. Vincent, 179
Cape Town, 111
Captain (naval), 225
Carbine, 151
Cargo aircraft, 15, 212, 261
Carl Gustav recoilless rifle, 155
Caroline Islands, 63, 169
Carrier battle group, 191
Casablanca, 180
Castle Hill convict rebellion, 46, 47
Casuarina, Northern Territory, 198
Category:History of Australia, 43
Cate McGregor, 297
C band (IEEE), 17
Central Flying School RAAF, 251, 252, 262, 276
Central Powers, 64, 113
Ceylon, 117
CH093, 231
CH-47, 96
CH-47 Chinook, 158
Chain of command, 2, 62
Changi, 119
Charles Bean, 103
Charles F. Adams-class destroyer, 84, 191
Charles George Gordon, 55
Charles Hercules Green, 81
CHC Helicopter, 16, 273
Chemical Weapons Convention, 28
Chester Herald, 271
Chief of Air Force (Australia), 13, 260
Chief of Army (Australia), 13, 130, 131
Chief of Joint Operations (Australia), 13
Chief of Navy (Australia), 13, 205, 211, 212, 214, 223

Chief of the Defence Force (Australia), 1, 11, 91, 130, 131, 211
Chief Petty Officer, 226
China Station, 166
Christopher Pyne, 12
Chronological items, 207
CIMIC, 127
CITEREFAir Power Development Centre2015, 310, 311
CITEREFAir Power Development Centre2016, 310
CITEREFAustralian Army2014, 310, 311
CITEREFAustralian Government2014, 310
CITEREFAustralian Government2016, 309, 311
CITEREFAustralian National Audit Office2001, 310
CITEREFAustralian National Audit Office2014, 311
CITEREFBallRobinsonTranter2016, 311
CITEREFBarnes2000, 323
CITEREFBeaumont2001, 310, 311
CITEREFBelkinMcNichol2000, 311
CITEREFBlaxland2014, 311
CITEREFBullard2017, 309
CITEREFChief of Navy2017, 309–311
CITEREFCouncil of Australian Governments2015, 311
CITEREFDavies2010, 310
CITEREFDaviesJenningsSchreer2014, 310
CITEREFDefence People Group2017, 310
CITEREFDennis et al2008, 309–311
CITEREFDepartment of Defence2009, 310
CITEREFDepartment of Defence2016, 310, 324
CITEREFDepartment of Defence2017, 310
CITEREFDepartment of Defence2017a, 310, 311
CITEREFDepartment of Defence2018, 324
CITEREFEdwards2016, 309
CITEREFFerguson2010, 324
CITEREFForeign Affairs, Defence and Trade Group2000, 310
CITEREFGrey2008, 309, 311, 318
CITEREFHenry2005, 309
CITEREFHoglin2016, 311
CITEREFHorner2001, 309, 310, 318
CITEREFHorner2007, 309
CITEREFInternational Institute for Strategic Studies2016, 311
CITEREFJennings2016, 309
CITEREFJobson2009, 318
CITEREFJoint Standing Committee on Foreign Affairs, Defence and Trade2015, 324
CITEREFJoint Standing Committee on Treaties2014, 311

CITEREFKhosa2010, 309–311
CITEREFKhosa2011, 309–311
CITEREFMcKeownJordan2010, 309
CITEREFOdgers1988, 318
CITEREFPeacockvon Rosenbach2011, 311
CITEREFPittaway2014, 310
CITEREFSmith2009, 324
CITEREFSmith2014, 310
CITEREFSmithBergin2006, 311
CITEREFSutton2017, 311
CITEREFTewesRaynerKavanaugh2004, 309
CITEREFThomson2005, 309–311
CITEREFThomson2005a, 310
CITEREFThomson2006, 309
CITEREFThomson2009, 310
CITEREFThomson2012, 309
CITEREFThomson2016, 309–311
CITEREFThomson2017, 309–311, 324
CITEREFWilsonPittaway2017, 310, 311
Citizens Military Force, 131
Civilian control of the military, 3
CK043, 231
CL-604, 273
Clearance Diving Team (RAN), 5, 92, 197, 201, 207, 220
Climate change, 11
Close air support, 255, 265
Cluster munition, 29
Coalition (Australia), 8
Coat of arms of Australia, 137
Cockatoo Island Dockyard, 243
Cocos (Keeling) Islands, 169
Cold War, 3, 44, 79, 214
Collective security, 46
Collins class submarine, 229
Collins-class submarine, 17, 206, 207, 215, 230
Collins-class submarine replacement project, 222, 230
Colonial forces of Australia, 131
Colonial navies of Australia, 53, 212
Colonial Office, 52
Colony of Natal, 55
Colt revolver, 49
Combat aircraft, 272
Combat knife, 156
Combat Support Coordination Centre RAAF, 279
Combat Support Group RAAF, 15, 16, 279
Combat Survival Training School RAAF, 277
Combined arms, 15, 29, 68
Combined Arms Training Centre (Australia), 135
Combined Maritime Forces, 10, 317
Combined Task Force 150, 317
Combined Task Force 151, 317
Combined Task Force 152, 317
Combined Task Force 158, 203
Commander Australian Fleet, 14, 211, 214, 223
Commander Forces Command (Australia), 130
Commander in chief, 3
Commander-in-chief, 117, 130, 211, 225, 260
Commando, 57
Commission (document), 224
Commodore (rank), 47, 214, 223, 225
Commodore (Royal Navy), 162
Commons:Category:Australian Army, 146
Commons:Category:Military history of Australia, 107
Commons:Category:Military of Australia, 41
Commons:Category:Royal Australian Air Force, 283
Commons:Category:Royal Australian Navy, 228
Commons:Category:Weapons of Australia, 159
Commons:Category:Women in the Australian military, 292
Commonwealth Aircraft Corporation, 257, 266
Commonwealth Naval Force, 60
Commonwealth Naval Forces, 165
Commonwealth of Australia, 112, 165
Commonwealth of Nations, 192, 251, 263
Communism, 87
Communist Party of Australia, 71
Company (military), 5
Company (military unit), 22
Conscription, 69, 116, 117
Conscription in Australia, 19, 79
Consolidated PBY Catalina, 266
Consolidated PBY Catalina in Royal Australian Air Force service, 266
Constitutional history of Australia, 43
Constitution of Australia, 60
Conventional variant, 230
Conventional weapon, 28
Core nations, 46
Coronation of King George VI and Queen Elizabeth, 116
Coronation of the British Monarch, 121
Coronet, 120
Corps of Royal Engineers, 52
Corvette, 182
Corvettes, 175
Cory Bernardi, 297
Counter-insurgency, 58
Counter-terrorism, 34
County-class cruiser, 176
County-class destroyer, 191
Court martial, 58, 111
Crete, 72, 177–179

CTOL, 280
Curtiss P-40 Warhawk, 265
Cyberwarfare, 18

Dakar, 180
Damascus, 115
Da Nang, 258
Dardanelles, 169
Dar-es-Salaam, 169
Darling Downs, 304
Darwin Mobile Force, 116
Darwin, Northern Territory, 32, 75, 143, 197, 304, 306
Dassault Mirage III, 85, 267
David Horner, 105, 145, 259
David Hurley, 296
David Johnston (admiral), 211, 223
Defence Abuse Response Taskforce, 25
Defence Establishment Myambat, 303
Defence Explosive Ordnance Training School, 277
Defence Housing Australia, 31
Defence industry of Australia, 2, **299**
Defence Intelligence and Security Group, 18
Defence Intelligence Organisation, 11, 18
Defence Material Organisation, 156
Defence Materiel Organisation, 16
Defence of Australia Policy, 4, 91
Defence of Pukekohe East 1863, 51
Defence Plaza, Melbourne, 303
Defence Plaza, Sydney, 303
Defence Science and Technology Group, 11
Defence Science and Technology Organisation, 156
Defending Australia in the Asia Pacific Century: Force 2030, 8
De Havilland Australia, 273
De Havilland Canada DHC-4 Caribou, 88, 257
De Havilland Vampire, 267
Demobilisation of the Australian military after World War II, 78, 120
Demographics of Australia, 11
Department of Air (Australia), 91
Department of Defence (Australia), 2, 4, 11, 60, 214, 299
Department of Supply, 91
Department of the Army (Australia), 91
Department of the Navy (Australia), 91
Deputy Chief of Air Force (Australia), 260
Deputy Chief of Army (Australia), 130
Deputy Chief of Navy (Australia), 211, 223
Derwent Barracks, 305
Des Ball, 39
Desert Air Force, 254, 261, 263
Desert - DPDU, 156
Designated marksman rifle, 138, 152

Destroyer, 84, 180, 191
Destroyers, 175
Devonport, Tasmania, 305
Dhi Qar, 127
Diamond Hill, 57
Diarchy, 11
Diego Garcia, 95
Diesel-electric transmission, 215
Digger (soldier), 46
Digital object identifier, 107
Dili, 94
Diplomatic history of Australia, 43
Direction Island, Cocos (Keeling) Islands, 169
Disruptive Pattern Combat Uniform, 156, 271
Division (military), 63, 112, 116
DMS Maritime, 215, 229
Donald Hardman, 267
Double Eagle (mine disposal vehicle), 238
Douglas C-47 Skytrain, 267
Douglas MacArthur, 75, 119
Dumbarton, 166
Duncan Kerr, 295
Dunkirk evacuation, 116
Dunsterforce, 69
Duntroon, Australian Capital Territory, 251, 252
Durance-class tanker, 217, 243
Dutch East Indies, 256

East African Campaign (World War I), 169
East African Campaign (World War II), 213
East Indies Station, 47, 162
East of Suez, 4, 91
East Timor, 44, 203, 258, 269, 290
East Timor Special Autonomy Referendum, 93
Economic depression, 110
Economic exclusion zone, 229
Economic history of Australia, 43
Edward Hutton (army), 61, 112
Edward Hutton (British Army officer), 53
Egalitarianism, 45
Eglo Engineering, 244
Egypt, 113, 177, 252, 262
Egyptian Revolution of 1919, 66
Eight-Nation Alliance, 59
Elbit Skylark, 139
Electronic signals intelligence, 273
Electronic warfare, 261
Electronic-warfare aircraft, 273
Elizabeth II of the United Kingdom, 121
Emile Dechaineux, 187
Empire Air Training Scheme, 71, 254
Empire of Japan, 116, 265
End of major combat operations (May 2003), 127
English Electric Canberra, 82, 257, 268

Enoggera Barracks, 134, 158
Enoggera, Queensland, 304
Epaulette, 271
Erwin Rommel, 119
Eureka Stockade, 47
Eurocopter AS350, 29
Eurocopter EC135, 29, 139, 150
Eurocopter Tiger, 30, 139, 144, 158
European Australian, 44
European land exploration of Australia, 43
European maritime exploration of Australia, 43
European Theatre of World War II, 254, 264
Everymans Welfare Service, 303
Evolutionary, 46
Exclusive economic zone, 198
Executive government, 3
Exmouth, Western Australia, 36
Expeditionary warfare, 45

F-117 Nighthawk, 268
F-15E Strike Eagle, 268
F1 fragmentation hand grenade, 155
F-35, 261
F-35 Lightning II, 280
F-4 Phantom, 196, 269
F88 Austeyr, 28, 138
F89 Minimi, 28, 138
Fairey Firefly, 191
Falklands War, 200
Fantome-class survey motor boat, 244
Far East Air Force (Royal Air Force), 82, 265
Far East Strategic Reserve, 83, 193
Far North Queensland Regiment, 26
Federation, 110
Federation of Australia, 3, 43, 54, 109, 110, 161, 164, 212
Federation of Malaya, 193
FFG Upgrade, 236
FGM-148 Javelin, 30, 155
Field or senior officers, 224
Fighter aircraft, 261
Fiji, 5, 171
Fiji Times, 321
Finisterre Range campaign, 76
Fire Support Base Coral, 123
First and Second Battles of Kakarak, 97
First Army (Australia), 117
First Australian Imperial Force, 63, 112, 131, 251, 263, 286
First Battle of Bullecourt (10–11 April 1917), 67
First Battle of El Alamein, 73
First Battle of Maryang San, 82
First Battle of Villers-Bretonneux, 68
First Keating Ministry, 295
First Taranaki War, 51, 165

First World War, 131
Five Power Defence Arrangements, 35, 91
Flag of Australia, 137
Flag officer, 224
Flag of Japan, 271
Fleet Air Arm (RAN), 14, 32, 150, 191, 195, 197, 204, 207, 208, 214
Fleet Base East, 31, 233, 235, 237, 240, 244
Fleet Base West, 31, 231, 235, 242
Fleet carrier, 78
Fleet Command (Australia), 14
Fleet Oilers, 176
Flintlock, 49
FN MAG, 28, 138, 153
FN Minimi, 153
Forced labour, 119
Force Element Group, 206, 214
Forces Command (Australia), 14, 133, 134
Force structure, 8
Foreign relations of Australia, 6, 93
Forward operating base, 127
Fragmentation grenade, 155
France, 150, 273
Francisco Franco, 71
Franklin D. Roosevelt, 186
Freedom of navigation, 92
Freetown, 180
Fremantle-class patrol boat, 207, 237
Fremantle, Western Australia, 172
French cruiser Gloire (1935), 180
French Navy, 243
French West Africa, 180
Frigate, 14, 204, 206, 207, 215
Frigates, 175
F Super Hornet, 9, 30, 100, 270, 272

Gaeta-class minehunter, 238
Gallipoli, 64, 113
Gallipoli Barracks, 32, 143, 304
Gallipoli Campaign, 45, 113
Gapyeong, 82
Garden Island, New South Wales, 306
Garden Island (Western Australia), 200
Garden Island, Western Australia, 307
Garrison, 109
Gary Wight, 223
Gavin Long, 105
Gaza City, 114
Gaza Ridge Barracks, 305
GBU-10 Paveway II, 276
GBU-15, 276
Gender dysphoria, 296, 297
Gender-neutral, 297
Gender transition, 293
General Atomics MQ-9 Reaper, 281
General (Australia), 1

General Dynamics F-111, 85
General Officer Commanding, 120
General-purpose bomb, 276
General purpose machine gun, 138, 153
General-purpose machine gun, 153
General (United States), 119
GEOINT, 18
George Edwin Patey, 167
George Odgers, 106, 259
George V, 213
George V of the United Kingdom, 166, 251, 253, 263
Geraldton, Western Australia, 36
German auxiliary cruiser Kormoran, 181
German East Africa, 169
German East Asia Squadron, 169, 213
German Empire, 60, 167
German High Seas Fleet, 170
German New Guinea, 63, 169, 262
German submarine U-127 (1941), 179
German submarine U-559, 179
Germany, 147, 148, 150–154
G for George, 74
Glenorchy, Tasmania, 305
Gloster Meteor, 257, 266
Gough Whitlam, 89, 197
Govan, 165
Government Aircraft Factories, 254, 263
Government minister, 62
Government of Australia, 2, 4, 90
Governor General of Australia, 225
Governor-General of Australia, 1, 2, 130, 167, 174, 211, 260
Grand Fleet, 170
Great Depression, 174, 213
Great White Fleet, 61, 165
Grenade launcher, 154
Ground Training Wing RAAF, 279
Grumman F4F Wildcat, 271
Guadalcanal, 186
Guam Doctrine, 4, 91
Guerrilla warfare, 57
Gulf of Aden, 96
Gulf of Chihli, 60
Gulf of Oman, 201
Gulfstream G550, 273
Gulf War, 44, 92, 125, 201, 205, 211
Gus McLachlan, 130
G-Wagon, 139

Hampstead Barracks, 304
Harbour Defence Motor Launch, 176
Harpoon missile, 231
Harpoon (missile), 234, 276
Harry S. Truman, 192
Hartbeesfontein, 58

Hawk 127, 273
Hawkei, 144, 147, 158
Hawker de Havilland, 150
Hawker-Siddeley Hawk, 31
Hawker Siddeley HS 748, 197
Headquarters Joint Operations Command (Australia), 13
Health Services Wing RAAF, 279
Heavy bomber, 256, 266
Heavy cruiser, 163
Heavy cruisers, 175
Heavy lift ship, 231
Heavy machine gun, 153
Heckler & Koch HK417, 152
Heckler & Koch MP5, 154
Heckler & Koch USP, 138, 153
Helicopter, 273
Helicopters, 139
Henry Forster, 1st Baron Forster, 174
Her Majestys Australian Ship, 215
Her Majestys Government, 61, 165, 186
Hindenburg Line, 67
Hiroshima Prefecture, 79, 120
His Majestys Australian Ship, 166
History of Adelaide, 44
History of Australia, 43, 45
History of Australia (1788–1850), 43
History of Australia (1851–1900), 43
History of Australia (1901–45), 43
History of Australia since 1945, 43
History of Brisbane, 44
History of Canberra, 44
History of Darwin, 44
History of Hobart, 44
History of Indigenous Australians, 43
History of Iraq (2003–2011), 98
History of Melbourne, 44
History of monarchy in Australia, 43
History of New South Wales, 44
History of Perth, Western Australia, 44
History of Queensland, 44
History of rail transport in Australia, 43
History of South Australia, 44
History of Sydney, 44
History of Tasmania, 44
History of the Australian Army, **109**
History of the Australian Capital Territory, 44
History of the Northern Territory, 44
History of the Royal Australian Air Force, **251**
History of the Royal Australian Navy, **161**
History of Victoria, 44
History of Western Australia, 44
HK416, 138, 151
HK417, 138
HMAS Adelaide (1918), 70, 176
HMAS Adelaide (FFG 01), 201, 203, 237

HMAS Adelaide (L01), 231–233
HMAS Advance (P 83), 197
HMAS AE1, 167
HMAS AE2, 167, 169
HMAS Albany (ACPB 86), 33, 237
HMAS Albatross (1928), 174
HMAS Albatross (air station), 32, 208, 218, 306
HMAS Anzac (D59), 193
HMAS Anzac (FFH 150), 98, 201, 203, 207, 235
HMAS Ararat (ACPB 89), 238
HMAS Armidale (ACPB 83), 237
HMAS Armidale (J240), 184
HMAS Arrow (P 88), 197
HMAS Arunta (FFH 151), 235
HMAS Arunta (I30), 79, 186, 187, 193
HMAS Assail (P 89), 197
HMAS Attack (P 90), 197
HMAS Australia (1911), 61, 62, 162, 167
HMAS Australia (D84), 79, 163, 174, 176, 184
HMAS Balikpapan (L 126), 197, 203
HMAS Ballarat (FFH 155), 235
HMAS Ballarat (J184), 189
HMAS Bataan (I91), 79, 192
HMAS Bathurst (ACPB 85), 237
HMAS Benalla (A 04), 245, 246
HMAS Betano (L 133), 197
HMAS Brisbane (1915), 167, 171
HMAS Brisbane (D 41), 85, 196, 198, 201
HMAS Broome (ACPB 90), 238, 239
HMAS Brunei (L 127), 198, 203
HMAS Bundaberg (ACPB 91), 237, 238, 247
HMAS Cairns (naval base), 32, 208, 215, 218, 229, 238, 244, 246–248, 307
HMAS Canberra (D33), 174, 176, 186
HMAS Canberra (FFG 02), 237
HMAS Canberra (L02), 221, 231, 233
HMAS Canberra (LHD 02), 29
HMAS Cerberus (naval base), 23, 307
HMAS Cessnock (J175), 189
HMAS Childers (ACPB 93), 238
HMAS Choules (L100), 29, 217, 229, 240, 241
HMAS Collins (SSG 73), 207, 230, 231
HMAS Commonwealth, 190
HMAS Coonawarra, 32, 197, 208, 215, 229, 237, 238, 307
HMAS Creswell, 23, 306
HMAS Culgoa (K408), 79
HMAS Darwin (FFG 04), 98, 201, 203, 236, 237
HMAS Dechaineux (SSG 76), 231
HMAS Derwent (DE 49), 193
HMAS Diamantina (M 86), 240
HMAS Duchess (D154), 193

HMAS Encounter (1902), 167, 172
HMAS Fantome, 171
HMAS Farncomb (SSG 74), 203, 231
HMAS Flinders, 198
HMAS Fremantle (FCPB 203), 204
HMAS Gascoyne (K354), 189
HMAS Gascoyne (M 85), 239, 240
HMAS Gawler (J188), 182
HMAS Glenelg (ACPB 96), 238
HMAS Harman, 306
HMAS Hawkesbury (M 83), 204, 240
HMAS Hawk (M 1139), 193
HMAS Hobart (D 39), 85, 195, 196, 198
HMAS Hobart (D63), 79, 175, 176, 181, 184, 187, 189
HMAS Hobart (DDG 39), 233, 234
HMAS Huon (M 82), 240
HMAS Ipswich (J186), 189
HMAS Jeparit, 197
HMAS Jervis Bay (AKR 45), 203
HMAS Kangaroo, 176
HMAS Kanimbla (C78), 79
HMAS Kanimbla (L 51), 97, 203, 204
HMAS Kuttabul (naval base), 200, 208, 215, 229, 306
HMAS Kuttabul (ship), 184
HMAS Labuan (L 128), 203, 204
HMAS Larrakia (ACPB 84), 237
HMAS Launceston (ACPB 94), 238
HMAS Leeuwin (A 245), 244, 245
HMAS Maitland (ACPB 88), 238
HMAS Manoora (1935), 177
HMAS Manoora (F48), 79
HMAS Manoora (L 52), 204
HMAS Maryborough (ACPB 95), 238
HMAS Maryborough (J195), 182
HMAS Melbourne (1912), 61, 167
HMAS Melbourne (FFG 05), 31, 203, 237
HMAS Melbourne (R21), 4, 85, 191, 193, 194, 196, 198, 214
HMAS Melville (A 246), 244
HMAS Mermaid (A 02), 246
HMAS Moreton, 307
HMAS Murchison (K442), 79
HMAS Napier (G97), 188, 189
HMAS Nepal (G25), 188
HMAS Nestor (G02), 179, 188
HMAS Newcastle (FFG 06), 31, 203, 204, 237, 300
HMAS Nizam (G38), 188, 189
HMAS Norman (G49), 188
HMAS Norman (M 84), 240
HMAS Paluma (A 01), 246
HMAS Parramatta (D55), 165
HMAS Parramatta (DE 46), 193
HMAS Parramatta (FFH 154), 235

HMAS Parramatta (U44), 176, 179
HMAS Penguin (naval base), 306
HMAS Perth (D29), 175, 176, 184
HMAS Perth (D 38), 84, 85, 196
HMAS Perth (FFH 157), 207, 235
HMAS Pioneer, 169
HMAS Pirie (ACPB 87), 237
HMAS Pirie (J189), 189
HMAS Protector (1884), 54, 59
HMAS Quadrant (G11), 79, 188, 193
HMAS Quality (G62), 188
HMAS Queenborough (G70), 188, 193, 195
HMAS Quiberon (G81), 79, 182, 188, 190, 193, 195
HMAS Quickmatch (G92), 188, 193, 195
HMAS Rankin (SSG 78), 231
HMAS Sheean (SSG 77), 231
HMAS Shepparton (A 03), 246
HMAS Shoalhaven (K535), 79, 190, 192
HMAS Sirius (O 266), 29, 208, 217, 229, 242
HMAS Stalwart (D 215), 198
HMAS Stirling, 200, 207, 208, 215, 229, 307
HMAS Stuart (D00), 177, 180
HMAS Stuart (DE 48), 198
HMAS Stuart (FFH 153), 235
HMAS Success (AOR 304), 217
HMAS Success (AOR-304), 125
HMAS Success (OR 304), 29, 201, 203, 204, 208, 229, 243, 244
HMAS Supply, 198
HMAS Swan (D61), 69
HMAS Swan (DE 50), 289
HMAS Swan (U74), 176
HMAS Sydney (1912), 61, 64, 167
HMAS Sydney (1934), 72
HMAS Sydney (D48), 175, 176, 181
HMAS Sydney (FFG 03), 92, 201, 203, 237
HMAS Sydney (R17), 80, 191, 192, 196, 214
HMAS Tarakan (L 129), 198, 203
HMAS Teal, 193
HMAS Tobruk (D37), 193
HMAS Tobruk (L 50), 203, 208, 240, 288
HMAS Toowoomba (FFH 156), 235
HMAS Vampire (D11), 193, 195
HMAS Vampire (D68), 177, 180
HMAS Vendetta (D08), 193, 194, 196, 198
HMAS Vendetta (D69), 180
HMAS Voyager (D04), 193, 194
HMAS Voyager (D31), 177, 180
HMAS Waller (SSG 75), 203, 231
HMAS Warramunga (FFH 152), 235
HMAS Warramunga (I44), 187, 189, 192
HMAS Warrego (D70), 167
HMAS Warrego (U73), 176
HMAS Warrnambool (J202), 190
HMAS Waterhen (D22), 180
HMAS Waterhen (naval base), 215, 229, 238, 240, 246, 306
HMAS Watson, 306
HMAS Westralia (F95), 79
HMAS Westralia (O 195), 125, 201, 203, 290
HMAS Wewak (L 130), 198, 204
HMAS Whyalla (FCPB 208), 204
HMAS Wollongong (ACPB 92), 238
HMAS Yarra (D79), 165, 213
HMAS Yarra (DE 45), 193
HMAS Yarra (M 87), 240
HMAS Yarra (U77), 176
HMQS Paluma, 164
HMS Cumberland (57), 180
HMS Dainty (H53), 177
HMS Decoy (H75), 177
HMS Defender (H07), 177
HMS Havock (H43), 178
HMS Ilex (D61), 177
HMS Invincible (R05), 200
HMS Nelson (1881), 54
HMS New Zealand (1911), 170
HMS Rover (N62), 180
HMS Shropshire, 79
HMS Shropshire (73), 186, 189
HMS Victoria (1855), 51, 165
HMVS Cerberus, 54, 165
Hobart-class destroyer, 29, 216, 222, 229
Hobart, Tasmania, 305
Hōfu, Yamaguchi, 79
Holsworthy Barracks, 32, 126, 143, 304
Holsworthy Barracks terror plot, 126
Holsworthy, New South Wales, 126
Honiara, 204
Honshū, 120
Hooge, Ypres, 67
Hopkins Barracks, 305
Horatio Kitchener, 1st Earl Kitchener of Khartoum, 61, 112
Hormone replacement therapy (transgender), 297
Howard Government, 296
Howitzer, 149
HQJOC, 303
HRH The Duke of Edinburgh, 224
H. Rider Haggard, 272
Hugh White (strategist), 12
HUMINT, 86
Hundred Days Offensive, 68
Hungnam, 192
Hunter-class frigate, 222
Huon-class minehunter, 29, 208, 216, 229
Huon Peninsula, 76
Huon Peninsula campaign, 76
Hydrographic survey, 244
Hyundai Mipo Dockyard, 241

IAI Heron, 281
I Anzac Corps, 66, 114
I Corps (Australia), 72, 116
II Anzac Corps, 67
III Corps (Australia), 117
Imjin River, 82
Immigration history of Australia, 43
Imperial Camel Corps Brigade, 114
Imperial Conference, 252, 262
Imperial General Headquarters, 75
Imperial Japanese Army, 117
Imperial Japanese Navy, 75, 183, 184, 190
Indian Ocean Raid, 180, 188
Indigenous Australian, 34
Indigenous Australians, 26
Indigenous peoples of the Americas, 49
Indonesia, 133
Indonesia–Malaysia confrontation, 130, 260, 261
Indonesia-Malaysia confrontation, 44, 85, 131
Indonesian Confrontation, 192, 211
Industrial action, 33
Infantry, 131
Infantry fighting vehicle, 139
Information Warfare Directorate RAAF, 279
Infrared homing, 275
Insitu Aerosonde, 139
Intelligence analysis, 17
INTERFET, 203, 214
Intermarine SpA, 238
International Brigades, 71
International Day Against Homophobia, Transphobia and Biphobia, 297
International Force East Timor, 94
International Force for East Timor, 6, 93, 130, 133
International relations theory, 46
International Standard Book Number, 37–39, 103–107, 128, 129, 145, 209, 210, 227, 249, 258, 259, 282, 283, 291, 298, 301, 302
International Standard Serial Number, 39, 40, 103, 105–107, 128, 210, 282, 301
Invasion of Lingayen Gulf, 188
Ipswich, Queensland, 32
Iraq, 9, 131, 201, 252, 262, 290
Iraqi Coastal Defense Force, 203
Iraq sanctions, 6, 92
Iraq War, 44, 130, 211, 260, 261
Irian Jaya, 102
Irwin Barracks, 143, 305
Islamic State of Iraq and the Levant, 9, 100, 270
Islamist, 95
ISTAR, 15
Italian Campaign (World War II), 73

Italian conquest of British Somaliland, 181
Italian cruiser Bartolomeo Colleoni, 178
Italian cruiser Giovanni dalle Bande Nere, 178
Italian destroyer Espero (1927), 177
Italian Navy, 238
Italian submarine Console Generale Liuzzi, 177
Italian submarine Uebi Scebeli, 177
Italy, 273
Iwakuni, Yamaguchi, 79
IX Corps (United Kingdom), 170

Jake Ellwood, 130
James Bevan Edwards, 53
Janes Fighting Ships, 249
Japanese battleship Yamashiro, 188
Japanese Instrument of Surrender, 189
Japanese submarine I-124, 185
Japanese submarine RO-33, 186
Java Sea, 184
JDAM, 276
Jeffrey Grey, 104, 128, 145, 227, 282
Jerusalem, 114
Jervis Bay, 225
Jervis Bay (Australia), 175, 194
Jervis Bay Territory, 200, 306
Jindalee Operational Radar Network, 17, 32
Joan Beaumont, 38, 103
Joel Fitzgibbon, 290
Johannesburg, 57
John Augustine Collins, 187
John Charles Hoad, 56
John Coates (general), 104
John Curtin, 117
John French, 1st Earl of Ypres, 57
John Gorton, 197
John Howard, 6, 93, 127
John Jellicoe, 1st Earl Jellicoe, 173
John Monash, 68, 115
Joint Electronic Warfare Operational Support Unit, 277
Joint Logistics Command, 16
Joint Space Operations Center, 17
Joint Standoff Weapon, 275
Joint Terminal Attack Controller, 16
Joint warfare, 3, 90
Jonathan Mead, 211
Jordan Valley (Middle East), 115
Joseph Cook, 63
Joseph Goebbels, 72, 180
Judaeo-Christian, 46
Judge Advocate General (Australia), 20
Julia Gillard, 8
Julie Hammer, 290
Junior officer, 224

Kaichu type submarine, 186

Kalimantan, 86
Kamikaze, 187
Kandahar, 96
Kandahar Airfield, 270
Kanimbla-class landing platform amphibious, 208, 240
Karl von Müller, 169
Karrakatta, Western Australia, 143, 305
Katherine, Northern Territory, 32, 306
KC-135 Stratotanker, 268
Keating Government, 293
Kedah, 122
Keswick Barracks, 143, 304
Kevin Rudd, 99
Kilindi, 188
Kimberley region, 50
Kingdom of Italy (1861–1946), 177, 181
Kings Guard, 116
Knights Armament Company SR-25, 152
Kockums, 230
Ko-hyoteki-class submarine, 184, 185
Kokoda Barracks, 304
Kokoda Barracks, Tasmania, 305
Kokoda Track campaign, 76, 118, 256
Koos de la Rey, 58
Korean War, 44, 79, 121, 130, 137, 161, 192, 211, 257, 260, 261, 266, 288
Korea War, 131
Kure, Hiroshima, 120, 190
Kuwait, 148, 201
Kwaio, 70

L118, 139
L119, 139
L16 81mm mortar, 155
L1A1 Self-Loading Rifle, 151
Labis, 86
Labor strike, 110
Labour force, 290
Labour market, 11
Ladysmith, KwaZulu-Natal, 56
Lae, 76
Lagnicourt-Marcel, 67
Lancer Barracks, 304
Land 17 artillery replacement, 149
Landing at Suvla Bay, 170
Landing Craft Mechanized, 149
Landing helicopter dock, 231
Landing ship infantry, 176
Land mine, 29
Land Rover, 139
Land Rover Perentie, 147, 148
LARC-V, 149
Largest naval battle in history, 187
Larrakeyah Barracks, 304
Larrikinism, 45

Laser-guided bomb, 98, 276
Latchford Barracks, 305
Latin language, 260
Launceston, Tasmania, 305
Lavarack Barracks, 32, 143, 304
Law enforcement in Australia, 34
LCM-1E, 13, 232
LCM-8, 30, 149, 240
LCU Mark 10, 240
LCVP (Australia), 240
Leading Seaman, 226
Leander-class cruiser (1931), 184
Lebanon, 116
Leeuwin Barracks(Australia), 305
Leeuwin-class survey vessel, 29, 208, 216, 229
Leo Davies, 260
Leopard 1, 146
Leyte (island), 187
LGBTI, 293
Liberal international relations theory, 46
Liberal Party of Australia, 6, 93
Lieutenant Commander, 225
Lieutenant general (Australia), 130
Lieutenant (navy), 225
Light cruisers, 175
Light machine gun, 153
Light Utility Vehicle, 139
Lincoln Battalion, 71
Linda Corbould, 289
List of active Royal Australian Navy ships, **229**
List of Australian intelligence agencies, 18
List of Australian military bases, **303**
List of countries by number of military and paramilitary personnel, 20
List of Defence Maritime Services vessels, 215
List of diplomatic missions of Australia, 35
List of equipment of the Australian Army, **146**
List of intelligence gathering disciplines, 17
List of recent Australian warship deployments to the Middle East, 6, 93, 201
List of Royal Australian Air Force aircraft squadrons, 16
List of Royal Australian Navy bases, 231, 233, 235, 237, 240, 242, 244, 246, 248
Lockheed AP-3C Orion, 17, 30, 269, 270, 273
Lockheed Hudson, 265
Lockheed Martin, 280
Lockheed Martin C-130J Super Hercules, 30, 99, 270
Lockheed Martin F-16, 268
Lockheed Martin F-35 Lightning II, 10, 30, 273
Lone Pine Barracks, 143, 304
Long Range Patrol Vehicle, 148
Luftwaffe, 254, 263
Lürssen, 220

M113, 139
M113 APC, 144
M113 armored personnel carrier, 30
M113 armoured personnel carrier, 147
M18A1 Claymore Antipersonnel Mine, 155
M198 howitzer, 139
M1A1 Abrams, 30, 138
M1 Abrams, 141, 146
M203 grenade launcher, 154
M242 Bushmaster, 233, 237
M2 Browning machine gun, 28, 153
M4 carbine, 138, 151, 156
M60 machine gun, 153
M72 LAW, 155
M777 howitzer, 30, 139, 149
M88 Hercules, 146
M9 Bayonet, 156
Mafeking, 57
Mahdi, 54
Mahdist War, 54
Main battle tank, 138, 146
Majestic-class aircraft carrier, 191
Malaita, 70
Malaita massacre, 70
Malayan Campaign, 117
Malayan Communist Party, 82
Malayan Emergency, 44, 82, 102, 130, 131, 137, 193, 211, 260, 261, 267
Malayan Races Liberation Army, 193
Malay Peninsula, 85
Malaysia, 35, 102, 193
Malcolm Fraser, 207
Malta, 177, 188, 267
Malta garrison, 102
Manas Air Base, 95
Mandatory retirement, 19
Man-portable air-defense system, 144, 149
Māori people, 49, 51
Maori Wars, 109
Marawi crisis, 270
Marine Rotational Force – Darwin, 37
Marise Payne, 1, 12, 297
Maritime Border Command (Australia), 14, 34
Maritime patrol aircraft, 273
Mark 32 Surface Vessel Torpedo Tubes, 233, 234, 236
Mark 41 Vertical Launching System, 234, 236
Mark 41 Vertical Launch System, 233
Mark 46 torpedo, 276
Mark 48 torpedo, 231
Mark Hammond (admiral), 211, 223
Marsa Matruh, 180
Martini-Henry rifle, 49
Mateship, 45
Maygar Barracks, 305
Medical evacuation, 258, 269

Medicare (Australia), 297
Mediterranean, 254, 261, 263
Mediterranean Fleet (Royal Navy), 177
Mediterranean Sea, 177, 181
MEKO, 234
Melbourne, 143, 306
Melbourne-Evans collision, 196
Melville Island (Northern Territory), 197
Mercedes-Benz G-Class, 148
Meritorious Unit Commendation, 196
Mesopotamian Half Flight, 66, 252, 262
Mexeflote, 240
MH-60R Seahawk, 233
Michael Duffy (Australian politician), 295
Michael Hudson (admiral), 205
Michael McCormack (Australian politician), 12
Michael Noonan (admiral), 211, 223
Middelburg, Mpumalanga, 58
Middle East, 102
Middle power, 46
Midshipman, 225
Mikoyan-Gurevich MiG-15, 257, 266
Military aid to the civil power, 33
Military aircraft, 15
Military attaché, 35
Military bases, 303
Military doctrine, 3, 90
Military history of Australia, 2, 43, **43**
Military history of Australia during the Indonesia-Malaysia Confrontation, 102
Military history of Australia during the Korean War, 102
Military history of Australia during the Second Boer War, 101
Military history of Australia during the Vietnam War, 4, 102
Military history of Australia during World War I, 3, 101
Military history of Australia during World War II, 3, 101
Military intelligence, 17
Military intervention against ISIL, 9
Military logistics, 16
Military reserve force, 2
Military service, 44
Military transport aircraft, 273
Military vehicle, 148
Militia, 109
Milne Bay, 76
Minehunter, 208, 238
Minelayers, 176
Minesweeper (ship), 193
Mine Warfare, Hydrographic and Patrol Boat Force, 215
Minister for Defence (Australia), 1, 3, 11, 12
Minister for Defence Industry, 12

Minister for Defence Personnel, 12
Minister of Defence (Australia), 131
Ministry of Defence (United Kingdom), 205
Miscellaneous vessels, 176
Mk 13 missile launcher, 236
Mk 14 Enhanced Battle Rifle, 138, 153
Mk 19 grenade launcher, 154
Mk 47 Striker, 154, 158
Mk48, 138
Mk 48 machine gun, 138
Modified Leander group, 176
Morotai, 120
Mortar (weapon), 155
Motaain, 94
Motorised infantry, 139, 147
Motor launch, 208
Motor Launches, 176
Mounted infantry, 56, 111
Mounted police, 48
MP5, 138
MRAP (armored vehicle), 147
Muhammad Ahmad, 54
MultiCam, 156
Multinational Force and Observers, 44, 100, 131, 133
Multirole combat aircraft, 272
Musket, 49
Myall Creek massacre, 49

Namibia, 124
NASAMS 2, 150
National interest, 46
National Security Committee of Cabinet (Australia), 3
National Service, 61
National Service Act (1964), 84
NATO, 20
Natural disaster, 21
Nauru, 37, 169, 171, 177
Naval auxiliary patrol vessels, 176
Naval brigade, 53, 111
Naval Communication Station Harold E. Holt, 17
Naval Group, 230
Naval mine, 203
Naval operations in the Dardanelles Campaign, 169
Naval squadron, 47
Navantia, 231
Navy, 14, 211, 212
Navy Strategic Command, 14, 214
Navy Unit Commendation, 196
Nazi Germany, 175, 177
N-class destroyer, 188
Netherlands, 147
Netherlands East Indies, 76, 264, 265

Netherlands East Indies campaign, 183
New Britain, 77, 169
New Caledonia, 75
Newcastle, New South Wales, 32, 238, 305
New Guinea, 75, 112, 118, 169, 252, 255, 256, 262, 265
New Guinea campaign, 75
New Guinea Force, 117
New Iraqi Army, 98
New South Wales, 46, 110, 117, 162, 200, 219, 225, 286
New South Wales Contingent, 55
New South Wales Corps, 46
New South Wales Marine Corps, 46
New Zealand, 120, 234
New Zealand and Australian Division, 113
New Zealand Wars, 1861–1864, 101
Ngo Dinh Diem, 88
NHIndustries NH90, 29, 150, 212
NHI NH90, 140, 158
NHQ South Australia (naval base), 307
NHQ Tasmania (naval base), 307
Nightcliff, Northern Territory, 198
No. 10 Squadron RAAF, 254, 276
No. 114 Mobile Control and Reporting Unit RAAF, 270, 277
No. 11 Squadron RAAF, 271, 276
No. 12 Squadron RAAF, 255
No. 13 Squadron RAAF, 255, 277
No. 1 Combat Communications Squadron RAAF, 277
No. 1 Expeditionary Health Squadron RAAF, 277
No. 1 Flying Training School RAAF, 253, 263
No. 1 Radar Surveillance Unit RAAF, 277
No. 1 Recruit Training Unit RAAF, 277
No. 1 Security Forces Squadron RAAF, 277
No. 1 Squadron RAAF, 82, 252, 263, 267, 276
No. 20 Squadron RAAF, 277
No. 21 Squadron RAAF, 255, 265, 277
No. 22 Squadron RAAF, 277
No. 23 Squadron RAAF, 277
No. 24 Squadron RAAF, 265, 277
No. 25 Squadron RAAF, 277
No. 26 Squadron RAAF, 277
No. 278 Squadron RAAF, 277
No. 27 Squadron RAAF, 277
No. 285 Squadron RAAF, 276
No. 28 Squadron RAAF, 277
No. 292 Squadron RAAF, 276
No. 29 Squadron RAAF, 277
No. 2 Expeditionary Health Squadron RAAF, 277
No. 2 Flying Training School RAAF, 276
No. 2 Operational Conversion Unit RAAF, 277
No. 2 Security Forces Squadron RAAF, 277

No. 2 Squadron RAAF, 82, 252, 257, 263, 268, 276
No. 30 Squadron RAAF, 277
No. 31 Squadron RAAF, 277
No. 322 Expeditionary Combat Support Squadron RAAF, 277
No. 324 Combat Support Squadron RAAF, 277
No. 32 Squadron RAAF, 276
No. 33 Squadron RAAF, 276
No. 34 Squadron RAAF, 276
No. 35 Squadron RAAF, 257, 268, 276
No. 36 Squadron RAAF, 276
No. 37 Squadron RAAF, 276
No. 381 Expeditionary Combat Support Squadron RAAF, 277
No. 382 Expeditionary Combat Support Squadron RAAF, 277
No. 38 Squadron RAAF, 82, 268, 276
No. 395 Expeditionary Combat Support Wing RAAF, 279
No. 3 Airfield Defence Squadron RAAF, 277
No. 3 Control and Reporting Unit RAAF, 277
No. 3 Expeditionary Health Squadron RAAF, 277
No. 3 Squadron RAAF, 85, 252, 263, 276
No. 41 Wing RAAF, 278
No. 42 Wing RAAF, 278
No. 44 Wing RAAF, 278
No. 452 Squadron RAAF, 255, 277
No. 453 Squadron RAAF, 255, 265, 277
No. 455 Squadron RAAF, 254
No. 460 Squadron RAAF, 74, 254, 264, 277
No. 462 Squadron RAAF, 255, 277
No. 4 Expeditionary Health Squadron RAAF, 277
No. 4 Squadron RAAF, 252, 263, 276
No. 5 Squadron RAAF, 252, 263
No. 65 Squadron RAAF, 277
No. 6 Squadron RAAF, 252, 263, 276
No. 75 Squadron RAAF, 85, 255, 258, 269, 276, 286
No. 76 Squadron RAAF, 79, 255, 276
No. 77 Squadron RAAF, 79, 255, 257, 266, 276
No. 78 Wing RAAF, 79, 83, 267, 278
No. 79 Squadron RAAF, 276
No. 7 Squadron RAAF, 252, 263
No. 81 Wing RAAF, 79, 278
No. 82 Squadron RAAF, 79
No. 82 Wing RAAF, 278
No. 84 Wing RAAF, 278
No. 86 Wing RAAF, 278
No. 87 Squadron RAAF, 17, 277
No. 8 Squadron RAAF, 252, 263
No. 92 Wing RAAF, 17, 279

No. 96 Wing RAAF, 279
No. 9 Squadron RAAF, 88, 195, 257, 268
Non-Commissioned Officer, 137
Norfolk Island, 46
NORFORCE, 26
North African Campaign, 116
North American P-51 Mustang, 266
Northern Command (Australia), 14, 91
Northern Hemisphere, 177, 255, 265
Northern Iraq offensive (June 2014), 99
Northern Territory, 50
Northern Territory Force, 117
Northern Territory National Emergency Response, 34
North Keeling Island, 169
North Korea, 190, 193, 257
North Queensland, 190
Northrop Grumman MQ-4C Triton, 273
North Russian Expeditionary Force, 69
North Russia Relief Force, 69
North Vietnam, 88
North Vietnamese Army, 88
North Western Area Campaign, 76, 256
North West Shelf Venture, 237
Norway, 150
Nowra, New South Wales, 32, 218
No. 9 Operational Group RAAF, 256
NQEA Australia, 244
Nuclear Non-Proliferation Treaty, 29
Nui Dat, 88
Nuku'alofa, 172

Oakey, 304
Oakey Army Aviation Centre, 32, 35, 135, 143, 304
Oakey, Queensland, 32, 143
Oakleigh Barracks, 305
Oakleigh South, Victoria, 305
Oberon-class submarine, 85, 191, 207
OBG(W), 127
Occupied Japan, 120
OCLC, 37, 103–106, 128, 129, 209, 210, 249, 259, 282
Oerlikon 20 mm cannon, 184
Officer (armed forces), 137
Officers Training School RAAF, 23
Officer Training School RAAF, 277
Official History of Australia in the War of 1914–1918, 103, 210
Okayama prefecture, 120
Oliver Hazard Perry-class frigate, 207, 236
Olive Zakharov, 295
One-star rank, 290
Onverwacht, Gauteng, 58
Operational Conversion Unit, 16
Operation Anaconda, 97

Operation Astute, 7, 95, 130, 203, 260, 261
Operation Bel Isi, 102
Operation Bribie, 88
Operation Cartwheel, 76
Operation Claret, 86
Operation Coburg, 88
Operation Commando (1951), 82
Operation Compass, 72
Operation Crimp, 88
Operation Demon, 180
Operation Downfall, 257, 266
Operation Enduring Freedom, 208
Operation Falconer, 127, 258, 269
Operation Gateway, 92
Operation Highroad, 9
Operation Kruger, 99
Operation Morris Dance, 5, 91
Operation Navy Help Darwin, 197
Operation Okra, 9
Operation Perth, 97
Operation Provide Comfort, 125
Operation Quickstep, 103, 204
Operation Resolute, 10, 34
Operation Sea Dragon (Vietnam War), 196
Operation Slipper, 7, 102, 126, 139, 214, 222
Operation Solace, 5, 93, 102, 126
Operation Sumatra Assist, 7, 133
Operation Torch, 182
Operation Vigorous, 188

Ōrākau, 51

Orange Free State, 55
OTO Melara DP gun, 236
Ottoman Empire, 64, 113, 213
Overwatch Battle Group (West), 7, 98, 127
Owen Stanley Range, 256
Owen Stanley Ranges, 76
Oxford University Press, 258

P-3 Orion, 85
P-40, 255
P-51 Mustang, 79, 257, 266
P8-A Poseidon, 261
Pacific class patrol boat, 37
Pacific-class patrol boat, 199
Pacific Rim, 212
Pacific War, 45, 73, 213, 255, 265
Paid off, 212
Palestine (region), 66, 251, 262
Paluma-class motor launch, 208
Paluma-class survey motor launch, 29, 217, 229
Panavia Tornado, 268
Papua New Guinea, 294
Papua New Guinea Defence Force, 37, 198

Parker Hale M82, 152
Parliament of Australia, 3, 174
Paterson Barracks, 305
Patrol aircraft, 261
Patrol boat, 14, 145, 197, 199, 207
Paul Ham, 105
Pauline Hanson, 297
Paul Keating, 295
Paul Kruger, 55
Peaceful Penetration, 68
Peacekeeping, 44
Pennant number, 231, 233, 235, 237, 240, 242, 244, 246, 248
Pentropic organisation, 122
Peoples Volunteer Army, 81
Perak, 122
Per Ardua ad Astra, 260, 272
Periphery nations, 46
Persian Gulf, 5, 7, 98, 201
Perth, 143, 306
Perth-class destroyer, 191, 233, 236
Perth, Western Australia, 31
Peter Cosgrove, 1, 94, 130, 211, 260
Peter Handcock, 58
Petty Officer, 226, 297
Phalanx CIWS, 233, 236
Philippines, 119, 256
Phuoc Tuy Province, 88, 123
Piet Cronjé, 57
Pilatus PC-21, 31, 273, 281
Pilatus PC-9, 31, 261, 273, 279
Pine Gap, 36
Plan Beersheba, 136
Plane guard, 194
Pneumonia, 171
Point Cook, Victoria, 251, 252, 262
Pontian, Johor, 86
Port Adelaide, South Australia, 244
Portal:Australia, 44
Portal:Feminism, 285
Port Moresby, 75, 169, 184, 186
Port Phillip, 166
Portuguese Timor, 184
Prehistory of Australia, 43
Pretoria, 57
Prime Minister of Australia, 117
Prime Minister of the United Kingdom, 117
Prince Philip, Duke of Edinburgh, 138
Prisoners of war, 181
Private military company, 17, 99
Private sector, 17
Professionalisation, 44
Proposed Japanese invasion of Australia during World War II, 75
Puckapunyal, 135, 143
Puckapunyal, Victoria, 305

Punitive expedition, 70
Pusan, 80, 192
Pyongyang, 80

Q and R-class destroyer, 84, 194
Q-class destroyer, 188
Queens Guard, 121, 124, 126
Queensland, 32, 50, 117, 158

RAAF, 148
RAAF Air Command, 15, 32, 260, 279
RAAF Bare Bases, 32, 306
RAAF Base, 274
RAAF Base Amberley, 32, 277, 306
RAAF Base Butterworth, 83
RAAF Base Curtin, 306
RAAF Base Darwin, 32, 277, 306
RAAF Base East Sale, 32, 277, 279, 306
RAAF Base Edinburgh, 32, 277, 304, 306
RAAF Base Fairbairn, 305
RAAF Base Glenbrook, 32, 305
RAAF Base Learmonth, 306
RAAF Base Pearce, 32, 263, 277, 306
RAAF Base Rathmines, 263
RAAF Base Richmond, 32, 263, 277, 305
RAAF Base Scherger, 306
RAAF Base Tindal, 32, 277, 306
RAAF Base Townsville, 32, 277, 306
RAAF Base Wagga, 23, 277, 305
RAAF Base Williams, 306
RAAF Base Williamtown, 32, 277, 305
RAAF Base Woomera, 306
RAAF Home Command, 267
RAAF Institute of Aviation Medicine, 277
RAAF Maintenance Command, 267
RAAF Museum, 104, 258, 277, 282
RAAF Operational Command, 267
RAAF Squadron Berlin Air Lift, 266
RAAF Station Laverton, 263
RAAF Support Command, 267
RAAF Training Command, 267
RAAF Williams, 277
RAAF Woomera, 277
RAAF Woomera Range Complex, 306
Rabaul, 112, 117, 169
Radar, 139
Radar jamming and deception, 273
RAF, 268
RAF Bomber Command, 73, 254, 264
RAF Far East Air Force, 268
Raffles Lighthouse, 193
RAF Foulsham, 255
RAF Leuchars, 254
Rainbow flag (LGBT movement), 296
RAMSI, 101, 103, 214
Randwick Barracks, 304

Rapid Creek, Northern Territory, 198
Rapier (missile), 144
Raufoss Mk211, 152
RBS 70, 19, 144, 149
RBS-70, 30, 139
Realism in international relations, 46
Real versus nominal value (economics), 7, 95
Rear admiral, 162
Rear admiral (Australia), 214, 223, 225
Rear Admiral Commanding HM Australian Fleet, 167
Recoilless rifle, 155
Red kangaroo, 271
Red Sea, 181, 201
Referendum, 116
Referendums in Australia, 69
Regimental Sergeant Major of the Army, 227
Regimental Sergeant Major of the Army (Australia), 137
Regional Assistance Mission to Solomon Islands, 130
Regional Assistance Mission to the Solomon Islands, 7, 204
Regional Force Surveillance Units, 17
Regular army, 78, 121
Remington 870, 154
Repair ships, 176
Republic of Singapore Air Force, 35
Responsible government, 52
Returned and Services League of Australia, 71, 295
Revolutionary, 46
RGM-84 Harpoon, 233
Rheinmetall MAN Military Vehicles (RMMV) HX range of tactical trucks, 148
Rhodesia, 254
Richmond, Tasmania, 305
Rick Burr, 130
Rifle Company Butterworth, 92
Rigid-hulled inflatable boat, 237, 247
RIMPAC, 220
Ringwood Barracks, 305
Ringwood East, Victoria, 305
Rising Sun (badge), 137, 296
River boat, 149
River-class destroyer escort, 85, 191
River-class torpedo-boat destroyer, 62, 165
RMAF Base Butterworth, 31
RMAF Butterworth, 277
Ro-100 class submarine, 188
Robert Menzies, 84, 192, 195
Robert Ray (Australian politician), 295
Robertson Barracks, 32, 143, 304
Royal Air Force, 99, 251, 257, 263, 267, 271
Royal Air Force March Past, 260

Royal Australian Air Force, 1–3, 62, 125, 131, 137, 251, **260**, 285, 303
Royal Australian Air Force College RAAF, 279
Royal Australian Air Force Ensign, 261
Royal Australian Air Force Reserve, 21
Royal Australian Air Force VIP aircraft, 31
Royal Australian Engineers, 34
Royal Australian Naval College, 175, 225
Royal Australian Naval Nursing Service, 206
Royal Australian Naval Reserve, 21, 223
Royal Australian Navy, 1–3, 47, 125, 131, 139, 140, 161, 166, 189, 201, 204, 205, **211**, 229, 261, 285, 303
Royal Australian Navy Bridging Train, 170
Royal Australian Navy Hydrographic Service, 207, 215
Royal Australian Navy minesweeping after World War II, 102, 190
Royal Australian Navy (music), 211
Royal Australian Navy Submarine Service, 14, 207, 215, 229
Royal Australian Regiment, 79, 120
Royal Canadian Navy, 318
Royal commission, 25, 195
Royal Fleet Auxiliary, 240
Royal Italian Army during World War II, 116
Royal Malay Regiment, 122
Royal Marines, 201
Royal Military College, Duntroon, 23, 61, 112, 135, 252, 304
Royal Navy, 47, 161, 170, 178, 180, 205, 212, 213, 222
Royal Netherlands East Indies Army, 184
Royal New Zealand Navy, 208, 216, 235
RQ-7 Shadow, 158
Rudd Government (2007–10), 7, 127, 293
Rum Rebellion, 46
Russell Offices, 12, 90, 91, 211, 303
Russian Civil War, 69
Rwanda, 44, 290

S-2 Tracker, 199
Sabah, 119
Saigon, 195
Sail Training, 246
Salamaua-Lae campaign, 76
Sale, Victoria, 32, 306
Samoa, 171
Sandakan, 119
Sarawak, 86, 119
SC Group, 139, 148
School of Administrative and Logistics Training RAAF, 277
School of Air Traffic Control RAAF, 277
School of Air Warfare RAAF, 277
School of Post Graduate Studies RAAF, 277

School of Technical Training RAAF, 277
Scorched earth, 58
Scott-class destroyer, 180
Scrap Iron Flotilla, 72, 175, 177, 180
Scylla, 231
Sealift, 240
Sea Lines of Communication, 199
Seaman, 226
Search and rescue, 34, 273
Search for HMAS Sydney and German auxiliary cruiser Kormoran, 181
Sea Slug missile, 191
SEATO, 102
Seattle, Washington, 236
Sebatik Island, 194
SECDET Iraq, 99
Second Army (Australia), 117
Second Australian Imperial Force, 71, 116, 131
Second Battle of Bullecourt (3–17 May 1917), 67
Second Battle of El Alamein, 73, 119
Second Battle of the Somme (1918), 69
Second Boer War, 55, 110, 130, 131, 137, 286, 294
Second Spanish Republic, 71
Second Turnbull Ministry, 12
Second World War, 131, 261
Section 51(vi) of the Constitution of Australia, 2
Section (military unit), 153
Security and Fire School RAAF, 277
Security Detachment Iraq (Australia), 7, 127
Security dilemma, 44, 46
Self-governing colonies, 109
Self-propelled gun, 149
Semi-automatic pistol, 153
Semi-automatic rifle, 152
Senussi Campaign, 65
Seoul, 80
September 11 attacks, 7
Service pistol, 138
Service rifle, 138
Services reconnaissance, 176
Sex-change surgery, 297
Sex discrimination, 297
Sex reassignment surgery (male-to-female), 297
Sexual harassment, 289
Sexual orientation, 293
Sexual orientation and gender identity in the Australian military, **293**
Shah Wali Kot Offensive, 97, 132
Shikoku, 120
Shimane prefecture, 120
Ship commissioning, 14, 229, 231, 233, 235, 237, 240, 242, 244, 246

Ship decommissioning, 236
Ship prefix, 247
Shoalwater Bay, 36
Short Range Air Defense, 149
Short Sunderland, 254
SHORT-TAS, 231
Shotgun, 154
Siberia, 69
Side-scan sonar, 246
Siege of Kimberley, 56
Siege of Tobruk, 72, 73, 116, 180
Siege of Toma, 63
Sierra Leone, 180
Signals intelligence, 18, 86, 273
Sikorsky MH-60R, 212
Sikorsky S-70, 30, 140, 142, 204
Sikorsky S-76, 273
Sikorsky SH-60 Seahawk, 29, 234, 236
Sikorsky UH-60 Black Hawk, 135
Simpson Barracks, 305
Sinai and Palestine Campaign, 65, 114
Singapore Armed Forces, 36
Singapore Strait, 87, 193
Singapore strategy, 74
Singleton, New South Wales, 143
Sir William Deane, 137
Skills Australia, 299
Sloops, 175
Small arms, 28, 138
SMS Emden (1906), 64, 169
SMS Königsberg (1905), 169
Snider-Enfield, 49
Sniper rifle, 138, 152
Solomon Islands, 7, 133, 204, 256, 265
Somalia, 44
Sopwith 1½ Strutter, 162
Sortie, 257, 268
Sorties, 192
South Africa, 110
South African Army, 125
South African Republic, 55
South Australia, 50, 111
South China Sea, 196
South East Asia, 161
Southeast Asia Treaty Organization, 193
South Vietnam, 88, 197
South West Africa, 124
Southwest Asia, 156
South West Pacific Area, 261
South West Pacific Area (command), 183
Sovereign state, 46
Soviet Air Forces, 257
Soviet Navy, 199
Spain under Franco, 71
Spanish Civil War, 71
Spanish Flu, 171

Spanish ship Juan Carlos I (L61), 231
Special Air Service Regiment, 87, 148, 204
Special forces, 7, 134, 135, 138
Special Operations Command (Australia), 14, 135, 151, 153, 154
Special Operations Engineer Regiment (Australia), 15
Spherion B, 234
Spring Offensive, 68, 114
SPS-49, 234, 236
SPS-55, 236
SPY-1, 233
SQS-56, 236
Squad automatic weapon, 138
Squadron (army), 19
SR-25, 138
SR-98, 138
SS Talune, 171
Staging post, 120
Starboard, 194
States and territories of Australia, 31
States of Australia, 303
Steele Barracks (Moorebank), 143, 304
Stephen Loosley, 295
Stockholm International Peace Research Institute, 28, 300
Stokes Hill Wharf, 197
STOL, 257, 268
Stonefish (mine), 231
Store ships, 176
Strategic airlift, 273
Strategic Defence and Security Review 2010, 240
STS Young Endeavour, 29, 217, 229, 246
Suai, East Timor, 94
Suakin, 55
Suakin Expedition, 54
Sub Lieutenant, 225
Submachine gun, 154
Submarine, 14, 85, 191, 206, 207
Sudan, 110
Sudan, 1885, 101
Suez Canal, 64, 114, 192
Suharto, 87
Supermarine Walrus, 180
Surface-to-air missile, 150, 258, 268
Surveillance aircraft, 212
Surveillance and Control Training Unit RAAF, 277
Surveillance and Response Group RAAF, 15, 279
Survey ships, 176
Survey vessel, 208
Suva, 172
Swanbourne, Western Australia, 143, 305
Swan Hunter, 240

Swan Island (Victoria), 303
Sweden, 149, 155
Switzerland, 273
Sydney, 305
Sydney Airport, 262
Sydney Cove, 46
Sydney Gay and Lesbian Mardi Gras, 294, 296
Sydney Harbour, 167, 184
Sydney Heads, 62, 161, 174
Sydney Mardi Gras, 27
Sydney, New South Wales, 238
Syria, 9, 116
Syria-Lebanon Campaign, 73

Tactical airlift, 273
Tactical Assault Group (Australia), 34
Tahiti, 162
Taliban, 95
Tamai, 55
Tan Son Nhut Airport, 123
Tarakan Island, 119
Taranaki Region, 51
Tarinkot, 96
Tarin Kowt, 96
Tartar missile, 191
Task Force 44, 184
Tasmania, 49, 111
Teddy Sheean, 184
Ted Grace, 295
Template:History of Australia, 44
Template talk:History of Australia, 44
Template talk:Women in society sidebar, 285
Template:Women in society sidebar, 285
Tenix, 198, 234, 236
Terendak Camp, 86
Territories of Australia, 303
Territory of New Guinea, 256
Terry Aulich, 295
Tet Offensive, 88
Thailand, 102
Thales Australia, 155
The Battle of Te Ranga, 51
The Official History of Australias Involvement in Southeast Asian Conflicts 1948–1975, 106, 282
The People of the Mist, 272
Third Battle of Gaza, 114
Third Battle of Ypres, 67, 114
Thomas Blamey, 116, 138
Tianjin, 60
Tiger ARH, 150
Tiger Force (air), 257, 266
Tim Barrett (admiral), 212
Timeline of Australian history, 43
Timor, 117
Timor Barracks, 304

Timor Leste Defence Force, 7, 37, 95
Tjilatjap, 184
Tobruk, 72, 179, 180
Tobruk Barracks, 305
Todd Pacific Shipyards, 236
Tokyo Bay, 189
Tom Frame (bishop), 104, 209, 227
Ton-class minesweeper, 193
Tonga, 171
Torpedo-boat destroyer, 165
Torpedo bomber, 254, 263
Tottori prefecture, 120
Town-class cruiser (1910), 176
Townsville, 32, 143, 304, 306
TPQ-36 Firefinder radar, 139
TPS-77, 270
Trade magazine, 301
Trainer (aircraft), 212, 261, 273
Transgender, 27, 293
Transgender issues, 297
Trench warfare, 82
Tribal-class destroyer (1936), 193
Trincomalee, 188
Tropical Cyclone Tracy, 197
TSS Kanowna, 169
Tuggeranong, 303
Tugs, 176
Tulagi, 70
Tunisia Campaign, 73
Type 1007, 231
Type 12 frigate, 191
Type 26 frigate, 222
Typhoon Weapons System, 233

UH-1 Iroquois, 86, 88, 150, 257, 268
UH-60, 94
UH-60 Black Hawk, 150
UKUSA Agreement, 35
Umm Qasr, 203
Unauthorised arrival, 237
UNC-Rear, 10
Unified Task Force, 130
Unimog, 139
United Arab Emirates, 270
United Kingdom, 147–149, 151, 152, 155, 273, 275
United Kingdom of Great Britain and Ireland, 116
United Nations, 44
United Nations Assistance Mission for Iraq, 99
United Nations Assistance Mission for Rwanda, 5, 101, 130
United Nations Command, 10
United Nations Convention on the Law of the Sea, 198

United Nations Military Observer Group in India and Pakistan, 102
United Nations Mission for the Referendum in Western Sahara, 102
United Nations Mission in East Timor, 93
United Nations Security Council, 80, 192
United Nations Transitional Administration in East Timor, 94
United States, 146, 147, 149–155, 272, 273, 275, 276
United States Air Force, 36
United States Army, 75, 195
United States Army Air Forces, 75, 257
United States Marine Corps, 36, 271
United States Military, 36
United States Navy, 205, 213
United States Pacific Fleet, 201
United States Seventh Fleet, 183, 187
Unmanned aerial vehicle, 158, 273
Unmanned Aerial Vehicles, 139
Urozgan Province, 7
Uruzgan, 96
USAF, 268
USS Canberra (CA-70), 186
USS Chicago (CA-29), 184
USS Frank E. Evans (DD-754), 196
USS Houston (CA-30), 184

Van Diemens Land, 46, 48
V and W-class destroyer, 175, 176, 180
Vanuatu, 187
Variants, 154, 272, 273
Varints, 273
VE day, 318
Vice admiral, 165, 214
Vice admiral (Australia), 211, 223, 225
Vice Chief of the Defence Force (Australia), 13, 211, 223
Vichy France, 73, 180
Vichy French, 116
Victoria (Australia), 50, 111
Victoria, Australia, 175
Victoria Barracks, Brisbane, 304
Victoria Barracks, Melbourne, 303
Victoria Barracks, Sydney, 32, 59, 111, 143, 304
Victoria Cross, 59, 111
Victoria Cross for Australia, 97
Victorian Mounted Rifles, 58
Vietnam, 195
Vietnamization, 89
Vietnam War, 44, 87, 130, 131, 137, 161, 192, 205, 211, 257, 260, 261, 268
Vigilare, 17
VMFA-212, 271
Volunteer military, 19

Vung Tau, 88, 196

Wadsworth Barracks, 305
Wagga Wagga, 305
Waikato, 51
War crime, 58, 111
War crimes trials, 77
War in Afghanistan (2001–present), 44, 130, 131, 211, 222, 260, 261
War Office, 46
Warradale Barracks, 304
Warrane Baracks, 305
Warrane, Tasmania, 305
Warrant Officer, 137, 226
Warrant Officer of the Air Force, 227, 260
Warrant Officer of the Navy, 223, 226, 227
Washington, D.C., 95
Washington Naval Treaty, 174
Waterloo Creek massacre, 50
Watsonia, Victoria, 305
Weapons of mass destruction, 28
Wedge-tailed eagle, 272
Wehrmacht, 116
Wellington, 171
Western Australia, 49, 111, 113, 117, 181, 200, 203, 207
Western Front (World War I), 64, 114, 252, 262
Western Front (World War II), 74
Western Sahara, 290
Westland Sea King, 204
Westland Wessex, 85
Westphalian sovereignty, 46
West Timor, 94
White Australia Policy, 174
White Movement, 69
White paper, 209
Whole-life cost, 281
Wideband Global SATCOM, 36
Wikipedia:Citation needed, 125, 139, 151, 155, 157, 161, 214, 225–227, 253, 254, 256, 258
Wikt:blue water, 61
Wilfrid Malleson, 69
William Birdwood, 64, 113
William Holmes (Australian general), 63
William Rooke Creswell, 59, 165
Williamstown, Victoria, 208, 234, 236
William Throsby Bridges, 63, 112
Winchester rifle, 49
Wing (air force unit), 15
Winston Churchill, 117
Women in combat, 285
Women in the Australian military, **285**
Womens Australian Army Corps, 288
Womens Australian National Services, 286

359

Womens Auxiliary Australian Air Force, 287
Womens Emergency Signalling Corps, 286
Womens Flying Club, 286
Womens National Emergency Legion, 286
Womens Royal Australian Air Force, 288
Womens Royal Australian Naval Service, 206, 287
Womens Transport Corps, 286
Wonsan, 192
Woodside Barracks, 32, 143, 304
Woodside, South Australia, 304
Woomera Test Facility, 277
World War I, 62, 112, 130, 137, 161, 173, 180, 211, 213, 251, 260
World War II, 116, 130, 131, 137, 161, 164, 167, 174, 206, 211, 213, 253, 260, 294
WP:NOTRS, 227

X Corps (United States), 192

Yamaguchi prefecture, 120
Yap, 169
Yokosuka, Kanagawa, 189
Youngtown Barracks, 305
Ypres Salient, 67

www.ingramcontent.com/pod-product-compliance
Lightning Source LLC
Chambersburg PA
CBHW030518230426
43665CB00010B/674